**Is this girl a devil in disguise...
or a misunderstood a**

A Devil and Her Love Song

Story and Art by Miyoshi Tomori

Meet Maria Kawai—she's gorgeous and whip-smart, a girl who seems to have it all. But when she unleashes her sharp tongue, it's no wonder some consider her to be the very devil! Maria's difficult ways even get her kicked out of an elite school, but this particular fall may actually turn out to be her saving grace...

A Devil and Her Love Song
1
Miyoshi Tomori
A Devil and Her Love Song
2
Miyoshi Tomori
A Devil and Her Love Song
3
Miyoshi Tomori
A Devil and Her Love Song
4

Only **$9.99 US / $12.99 CAN** each!

Vol. 1 ISBN: 978-1-4215-4164-8
Vol. 2 ISBN: 978-1-4215-4165-5
Vol. 3 ISBN: 978-1-4215-4166-2
Vol. 4 ISBN: 978-1-4215-4167-9

Check your local manga retailer for availability!

ratings.viz.com

Shojo Beat

VIZ MEDIA

www.viz.com

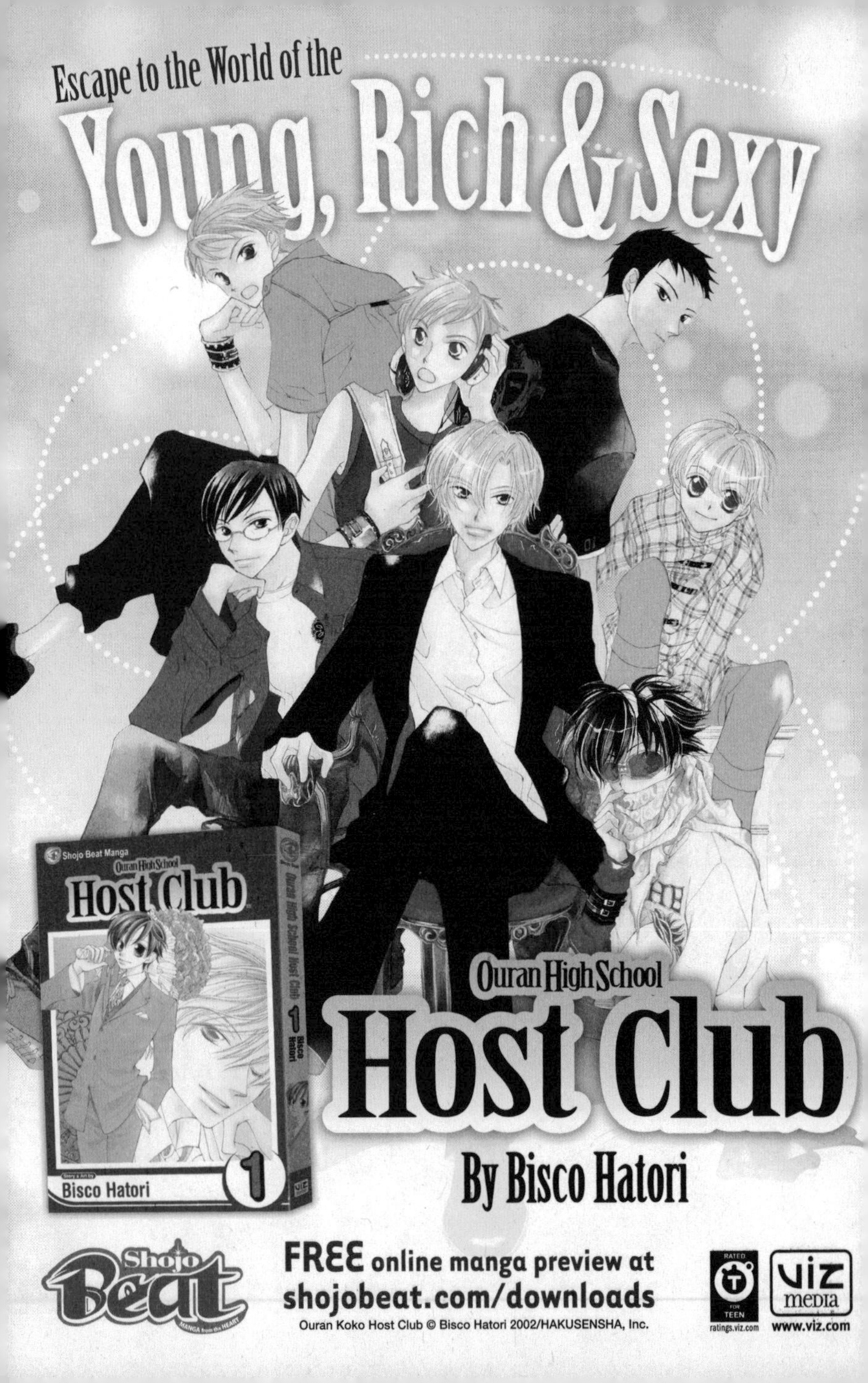

Hana-Kimi
Story & Art by HISAYA NAKAJO
VOLUMES 1·2·3
Hana-Kimi
Story & Art by HISAYA NAKAJO
VOLUMES 4·5·6
Hana-Kimi
Story & Art by HISAYA NAKAJO
VOLUMES 7·8·9

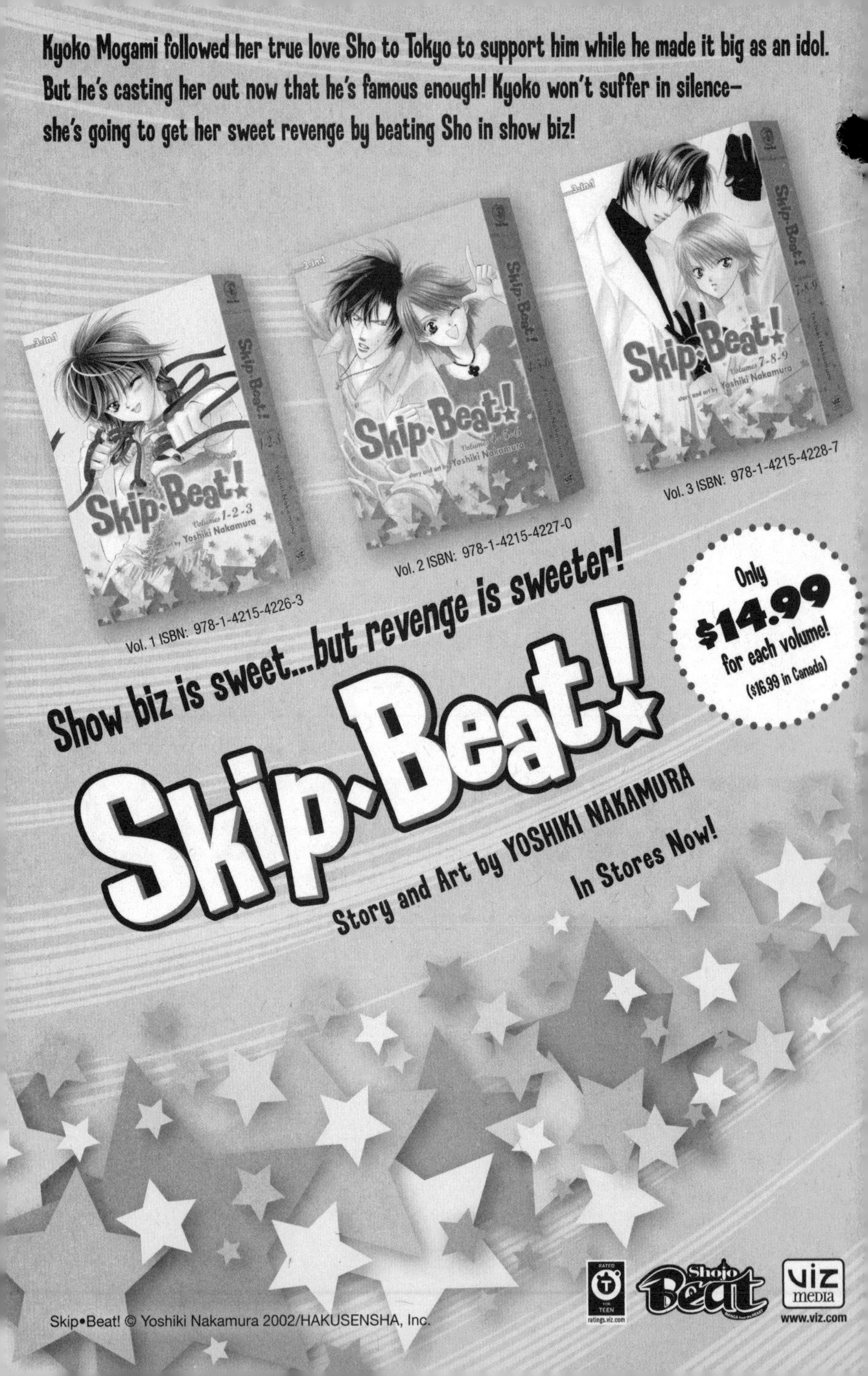
Kyoko Mogami followed her true love Sho to Tokyo to support him while he made it big as an idol. But he's casting her out now that he's famous enough! Kyoko won't suffer in silence–she's going to get her sweet revenge by beating Sho in show biz!
Vol. 1 ISBN: 978-1-4215-4226-3
Vol. 2 ISBN: 978-1-4215-4227-0
Vol. 3 ISBN: 978-1-4215-4228-7
Only $14.99 for each volume! ($16.99 in Canada)
Show biz is sweet...but revenge is sweeter!
Skip·Beat!
Story and Art by YOSHIKI NAKAMURA
In Stores Now!
Skip•Beat! © Yoshiki Nakamura 2002/HAKUSENSHA, Inc.
RATED T FOR TEEN
ratings.viz.com
Shojo Beat
viz media
www.viz.com

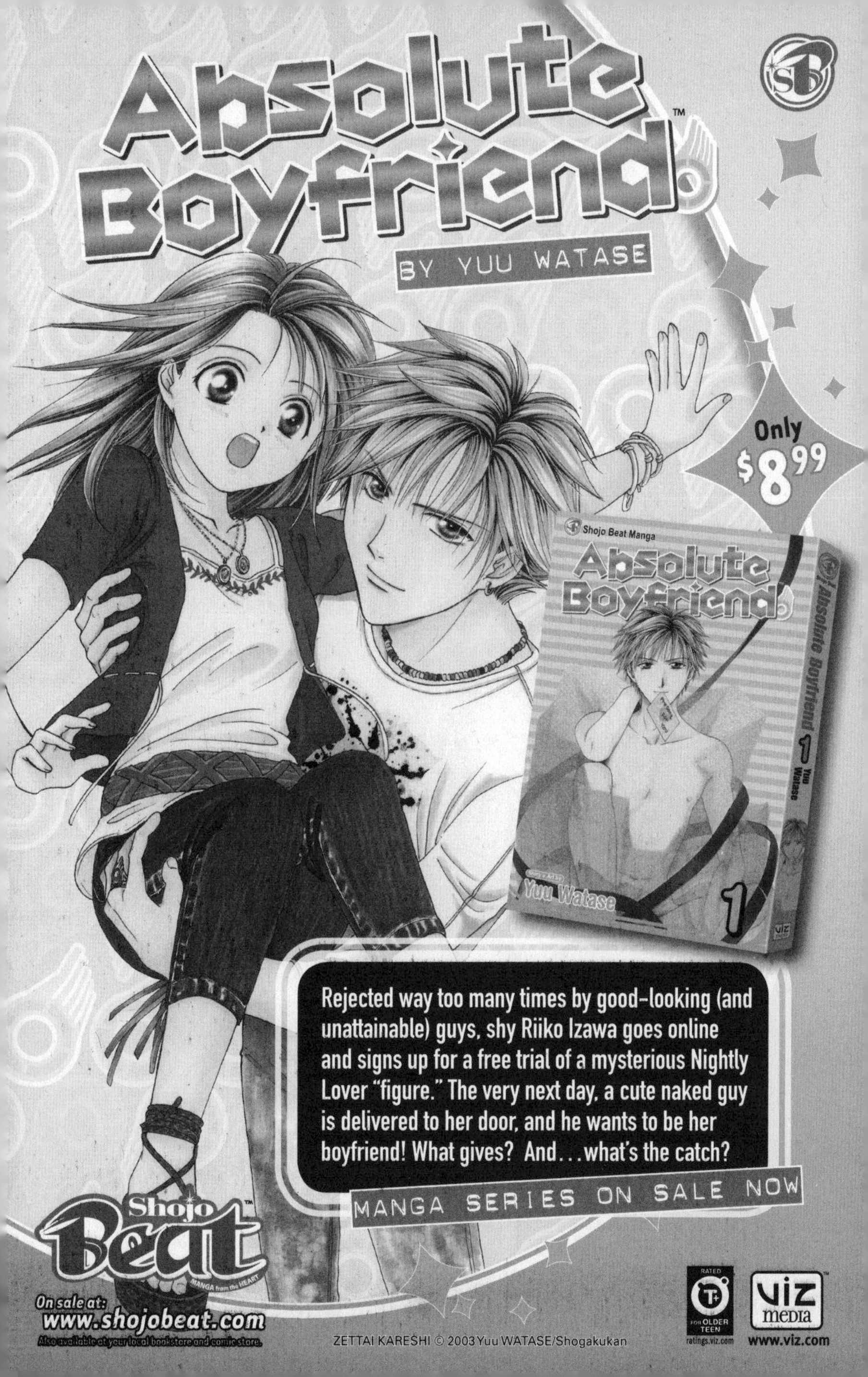
Absolute Boyfriend™
BY YUU WATASE
Only $8.99
Shojo Beat Manga
Absolute Boyfriend
Absolute Boyfriend 1 Yuu Watase
Yuu Watase
1
Rejected way too many times by good-looking (and unattainable) guys, shy Riiko Izawa goes online and signs up for a free trial of a mysterious Nightly Lover "figure." The very next day, a cute naked guy is delivered to her door, and he wants to be her boyfriend! What gives? And...what's the catch?
MANGA SERIES ON SALE NOW
Shojo Beat™
MANGA from the HEART
On sale at:
www.shojobeat.com
Also available at your local bookstore and comic store.
ZETTAI KARESHI © 2003 Yuu WATASE/Shogakukan
RATED T+ FOR OLDER TEEN
ratings.viz.com
viz media
www.viz.com

The VIZ Manga App has some new friends...

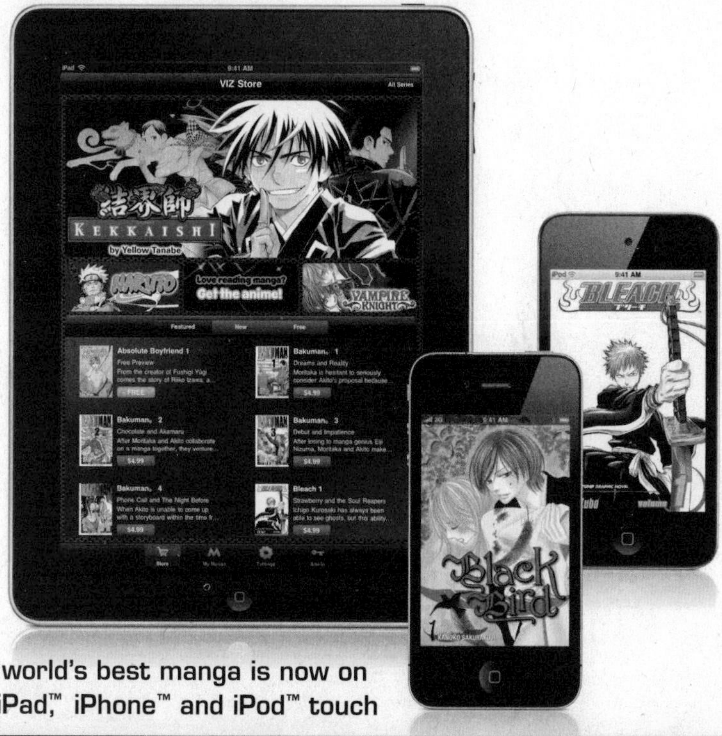

VIZ Store
All Series
KEKKAISHI
by Yellow Tanabe
Love reading manga?
Get the anime!
Featured
New
Free
Absolute Boyfriend 1
Bakuman。 1
Bakuman。 2
Bakuman。 3
Bakuman。 4
Bleach 1
BLEACH
Black Bird

The world's best manga is now on the iPad,™ iPhone™ and iPod™ touch

To learn more, visit viz.com

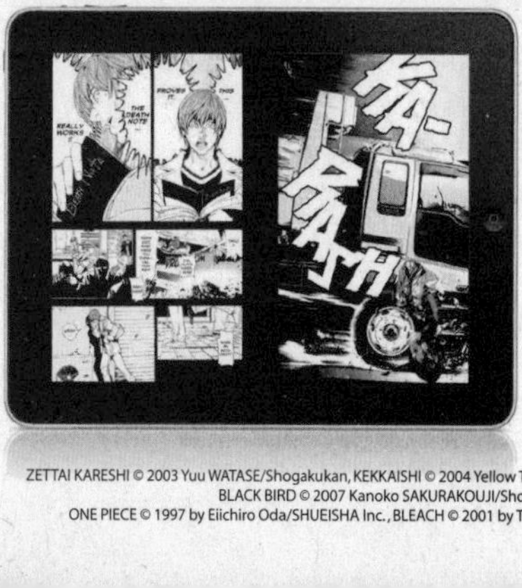

From legendary manga like *Death Note* to *Absolute Boyfriend*, the best manga in the world is now available on multiple devices through the official VIZ Manga app.

- Hundreds of volumes available
- Free App
- New content weekly
- Free chapter 1 previews

Ai Ore!

Volume 5
Shojo Beat Edition

STORY AND ART BY
MAYU SHINJO

Translation/Tetsuichiro Miyaki
Touch-up Art & Lettering/Inori Fukuda Trant
Design/Yukiko Whitley
Editor/Nancy Thistlethwaite

Ai Ore! ~Danshikou no Hime to Joshikou no Ouji~
Volume 2
© Mayu SHINJO 2008
First published in Japan in 2008 by KADOKAWA
SHOTEN Co., Ltd., Tokyo.
English translation rights arranged with
KADOKAWA SHOTEN Co., Ltd., Tokyo.

Printed in the U.S.A.

Published by VIZ Media, LLC
P.O. Box 77010
San Francisco, CA 94107

10 9 8 7 6 5 4 3 2 1
First printing, May 2012

www.viz.com

www.shojobeat.com

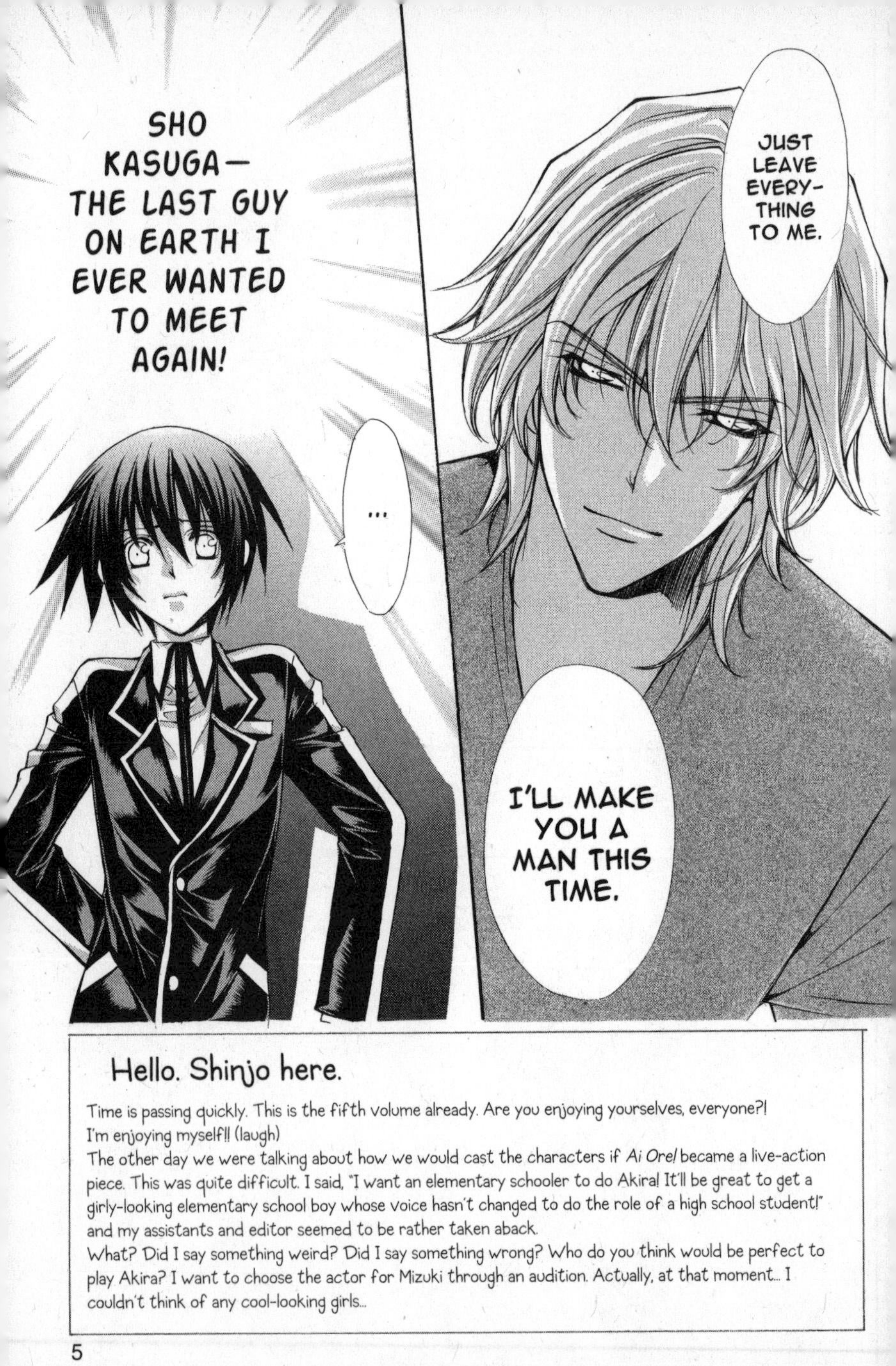
JUST LEAVE EVERY-THING TO ME.
I'LL MAKE YOU A MAN THIS TIME.
SHO KASUGA—THE LAST GUY ON EARTH I EVER WANTED TO MEET AGAIN!
...

Hello. Shinjo here.

Time is passing quickly. This is the fifth volume already. Are you enjoying yourselves, everyone?! I'm enjoying myself!! (laugh)
The other day we were talking about how we would cast the characters if *Ai Ore!* became a live-action piece. This was quite difficult. I said, "I want an elementary schooler to do Akira! It'll be great to get a girly-looking elementary school boy whose voice hasn't changed to do the role of a high school student!" and my assistants and editor seemed to be rather taken aback.
What? Did I say something weird? Did I say something wrong? Who do you think would be perfect to play Akira? I want to choose the actor for Mizuki through an audition. Actually, at that moment... I couldn't think of any cool-looking girls...

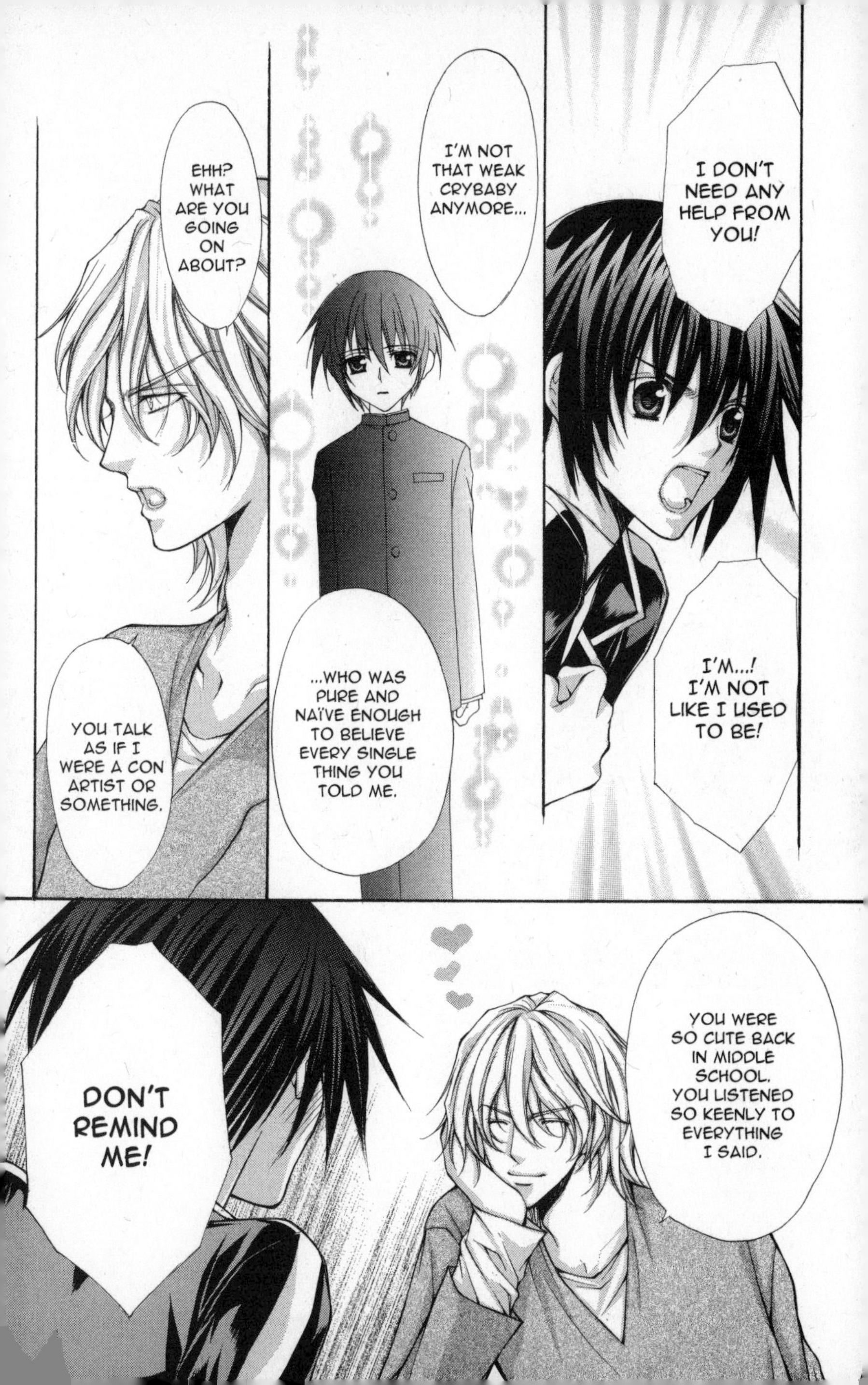
I DON'T NEED ANY HELP FROM YOU!
I'M...! I'M NOT LIKE I USED TO BE!
I'M NOT THAT WEAK CRYBABY ANYMORE...
...WHO WAS PURE AND NAÏVE ENOUGH TO BELIEVE EVERY SINGLE THING YOU TOLD ME.
EHH? WHAT ARE YOU GOING ON ABOUT?
YOU TALK AS IF I WERE A CON ARTIST OR SOMETHING.
YOU WERE SO CUTE BACK IN MIDDLE SCHOOL. YOU LISTENED SO KEENLY TO EVERYTHING I SAID.
DON'T REMIND ME!

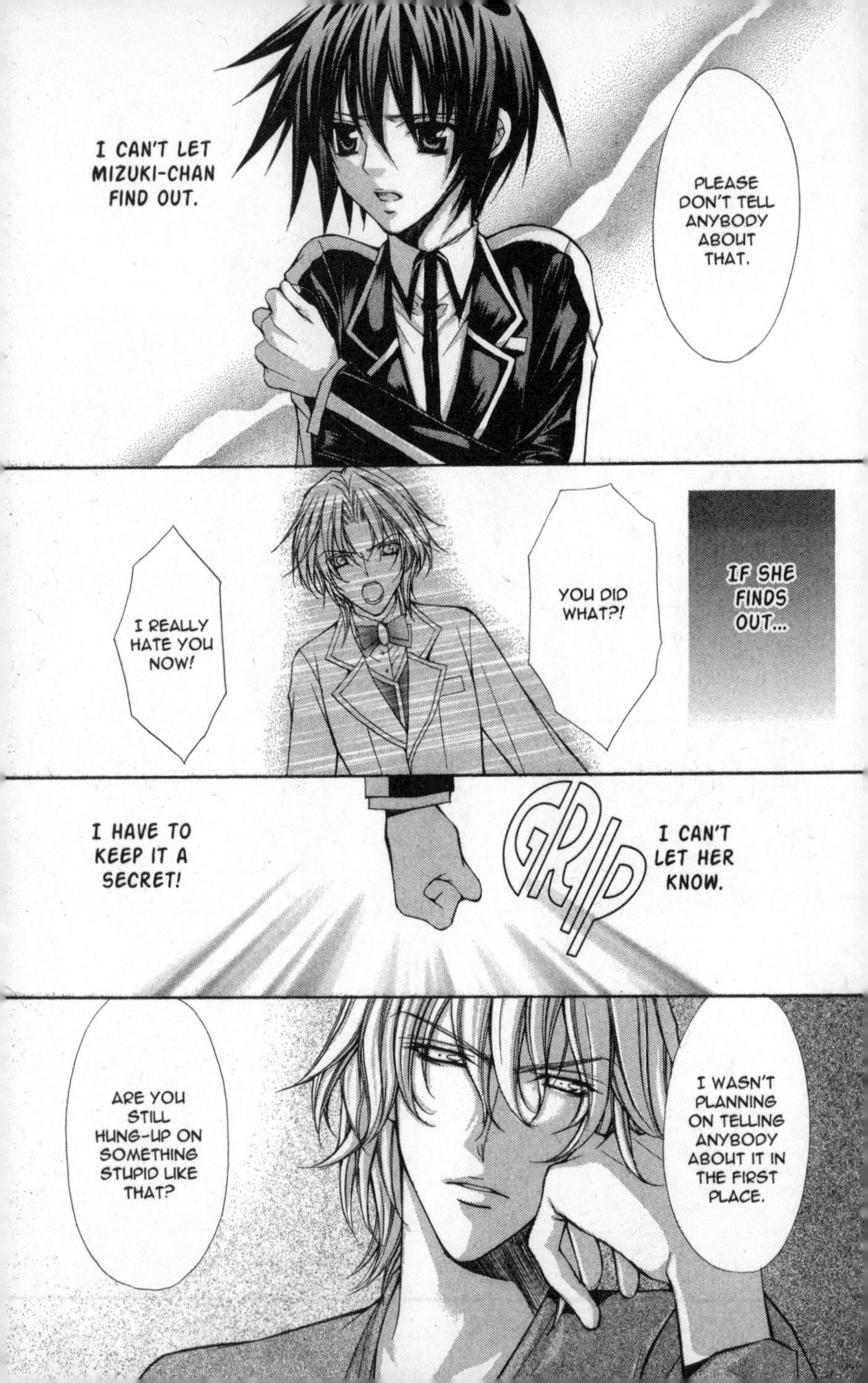

PLEASE DON'T TELL ANYBODY ABOUT THAT.
I CAN'T LET MIZUKI-CHAN FIND OUT.
IF SHE FINDS OUT...
YOU DID WHAT?!
I REALLY HATE YOU NOW!
I CAN'T LET HER KNOW.
GRIP
I HAVE TO KEEP IT A SECRET!
I WASN'T PLANNING ON TELLING ANYBODY ABOUT IT IN THE FIRST PLACE.
ARE YOU STILL HUNG-UP ON SOMETHING STUPID LIKE THAT?

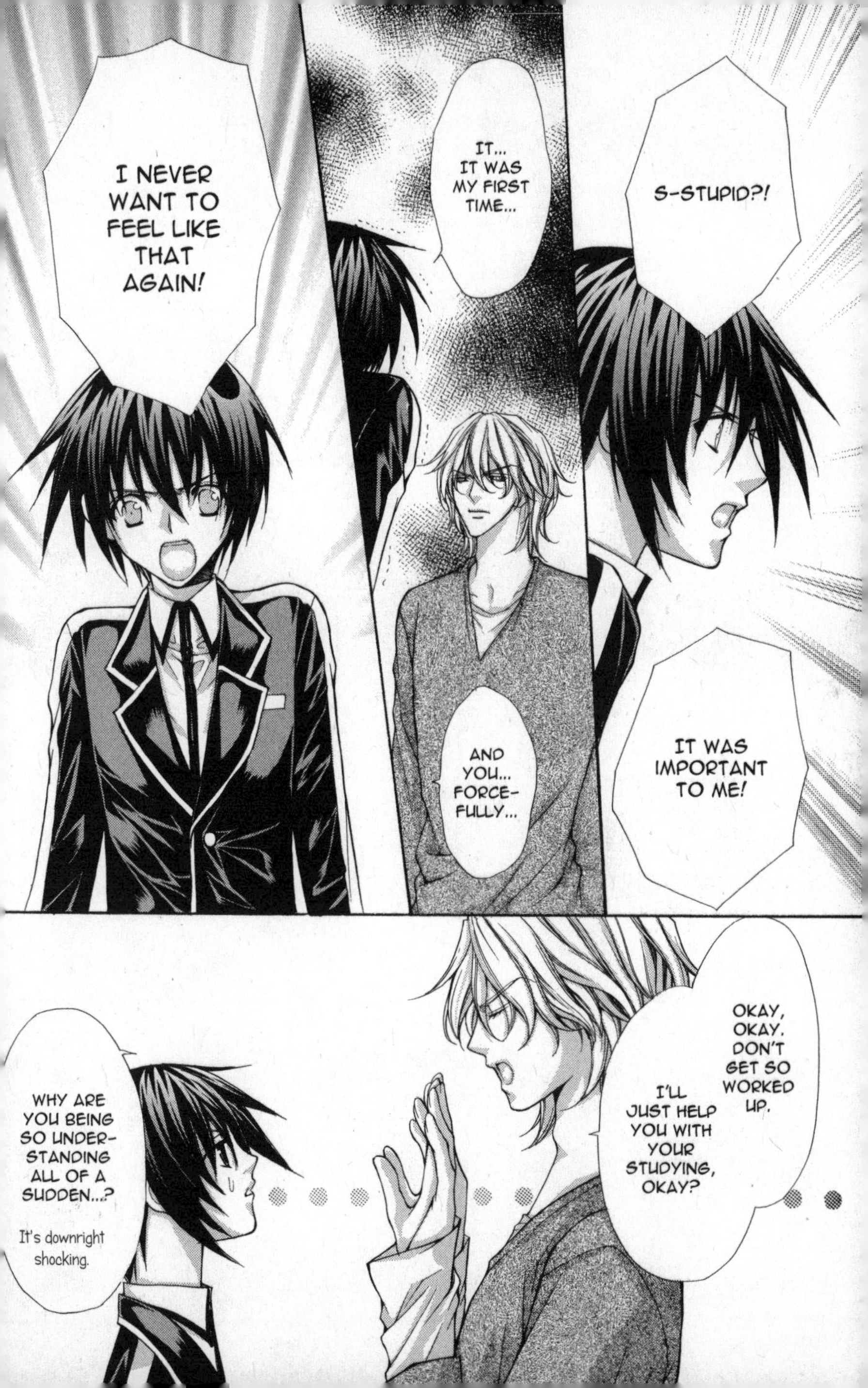
S-STUPID?!
IT WAS IMPORTANT TO ME!
IT... IT WAS MY FIRST TIME...
AND YOU... FORCE-FULLY...
I NEVER WANT TO FEEL LIKE THAT AGAIN!
OKAY, OKAY. DON'T GET SO WORKED UP.
I'LL JUST HELP YOU WITH YOUR STUDYING, OKAY?
WHY ARE YOU BEING SO UNDER-STANDING ALL OF A SUDDEN...?
It's downright shocking.

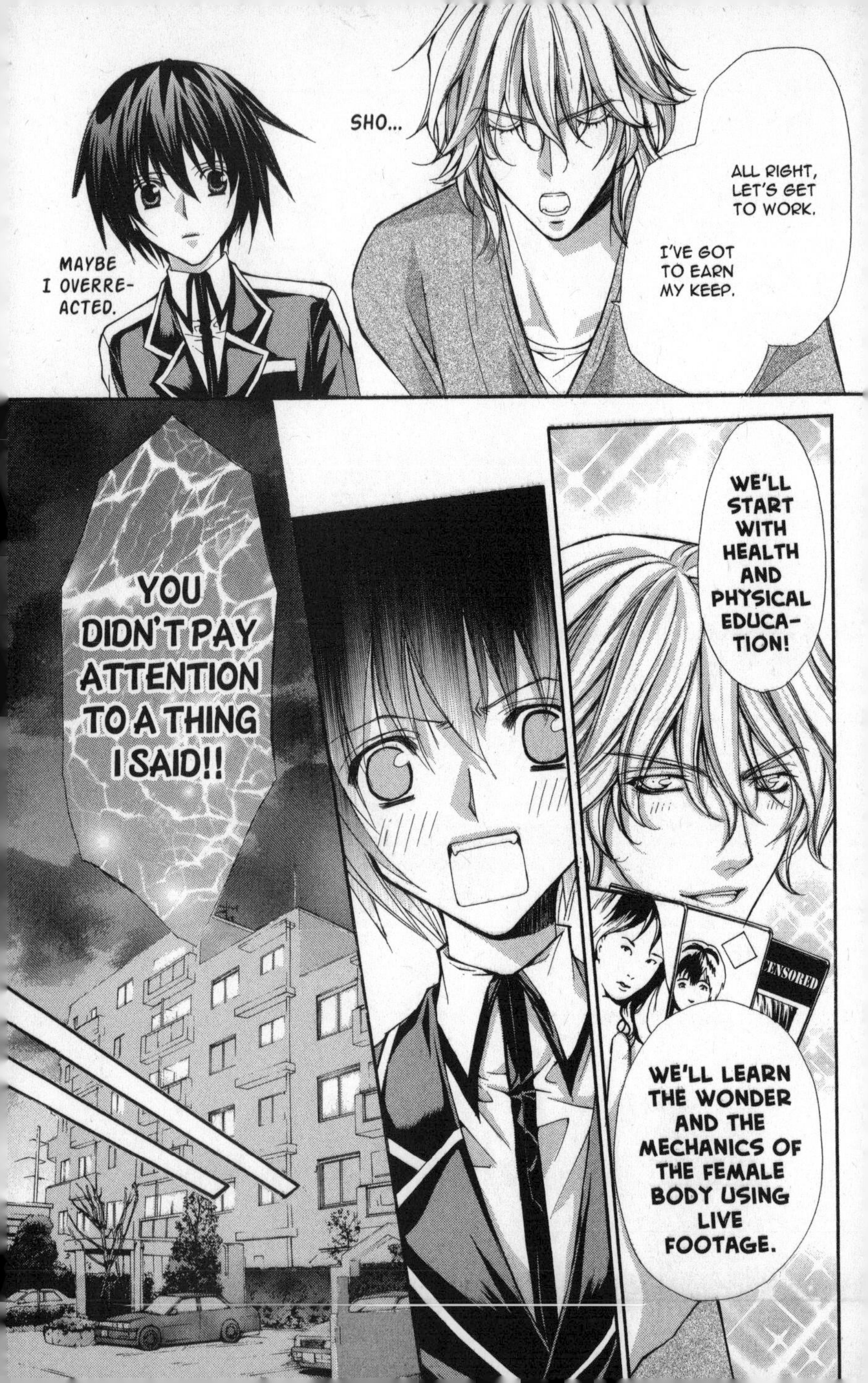
ALL RIGHT, LET'S GET TO WORK.
I'VE GOT TO EARN MY KEEP.
SHO...
MAYBE I OVERRE-ACTED.
WE'LL START WITH HEALTH AND PHYSICAL EDUCA-TION!
CENSORED
WE'LL LEARN THE WONDER AND THE MECHANICS OF THE FEMALE BODY USING LIVE FOOTAGE.
YOU DIDN'T PAY ATTENTION TO A THING I SAID!!

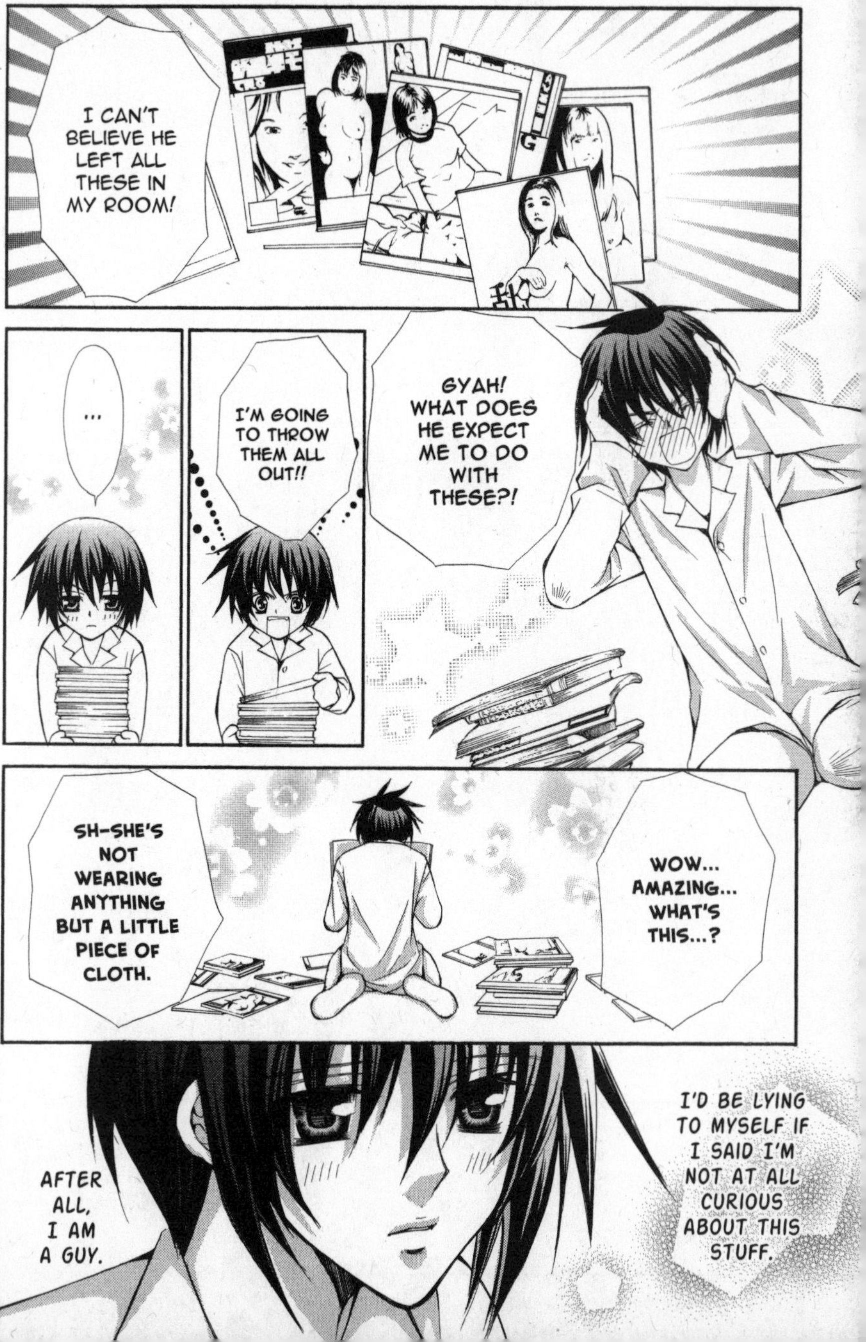
I CAN'T BELIEVE HE LEFT ALL THESE IN MY ROOM!
GYAH! WHAT DOES HE EXPECT ME TO DO WITH THESE?!
I'M GOING TO THROW THEM ALL OUT!!
...
WOW... AMAZING... WHAT'S THIS...?
SH-SHE'S NOT WEARING ANYTHING BUT A LITTLE PIECE OF CLOTH.
I'D BE LYING TO MYSELF IF I SAID I'M NOT AT ALL CURIOUS ABOUT THIS STUFF.
AFTER ALL, I AM A GUY.

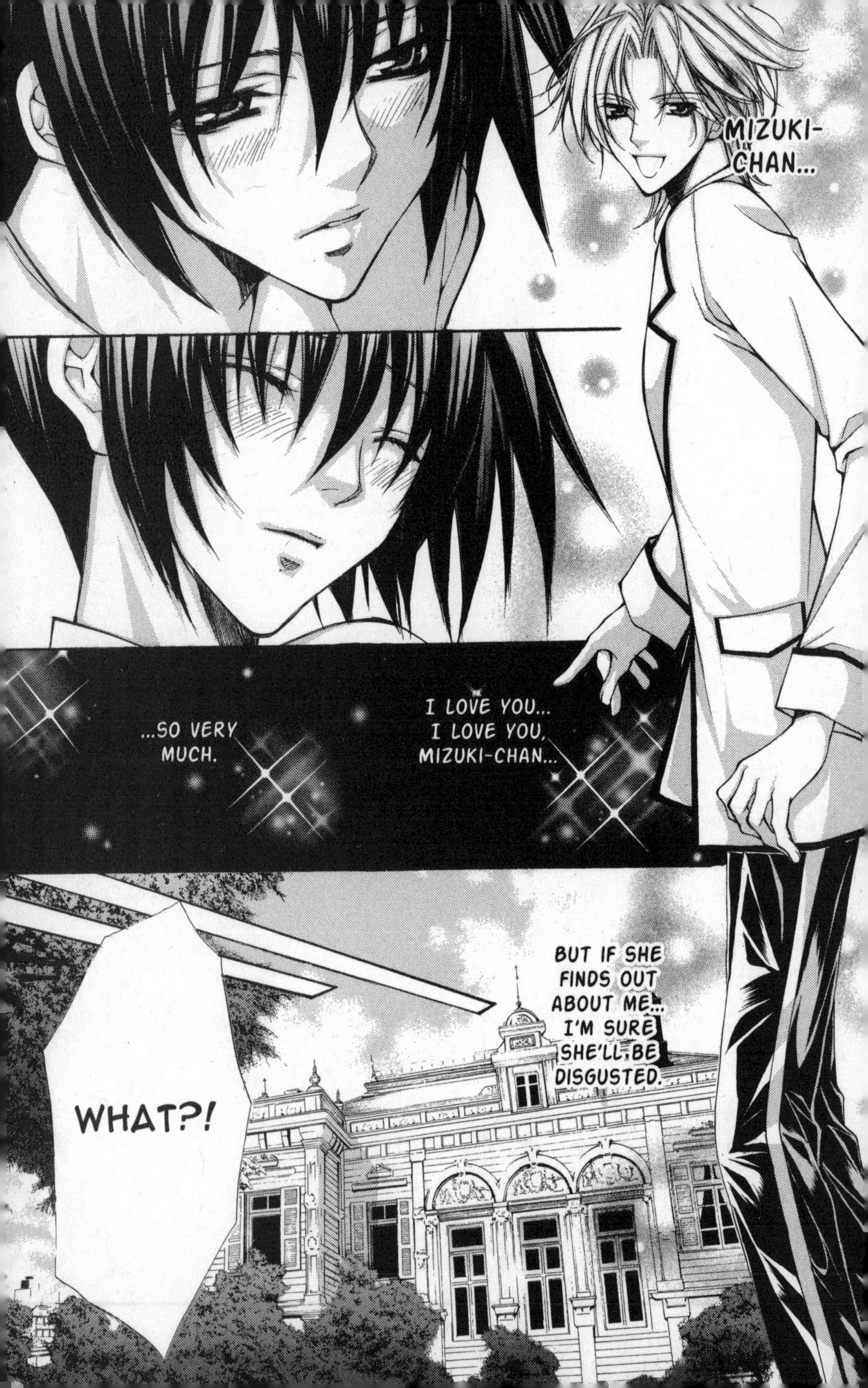
MIZUKI-CHAN...
I LOVE YOU... I LOVE YOU, MIZUKI-CHAN...
...SO VERY MUCH.
BUT IF SHE FINDS OUT ABOUT ME... I'M SURE SHE'LL BE DISGUSTED.
WHAT?!

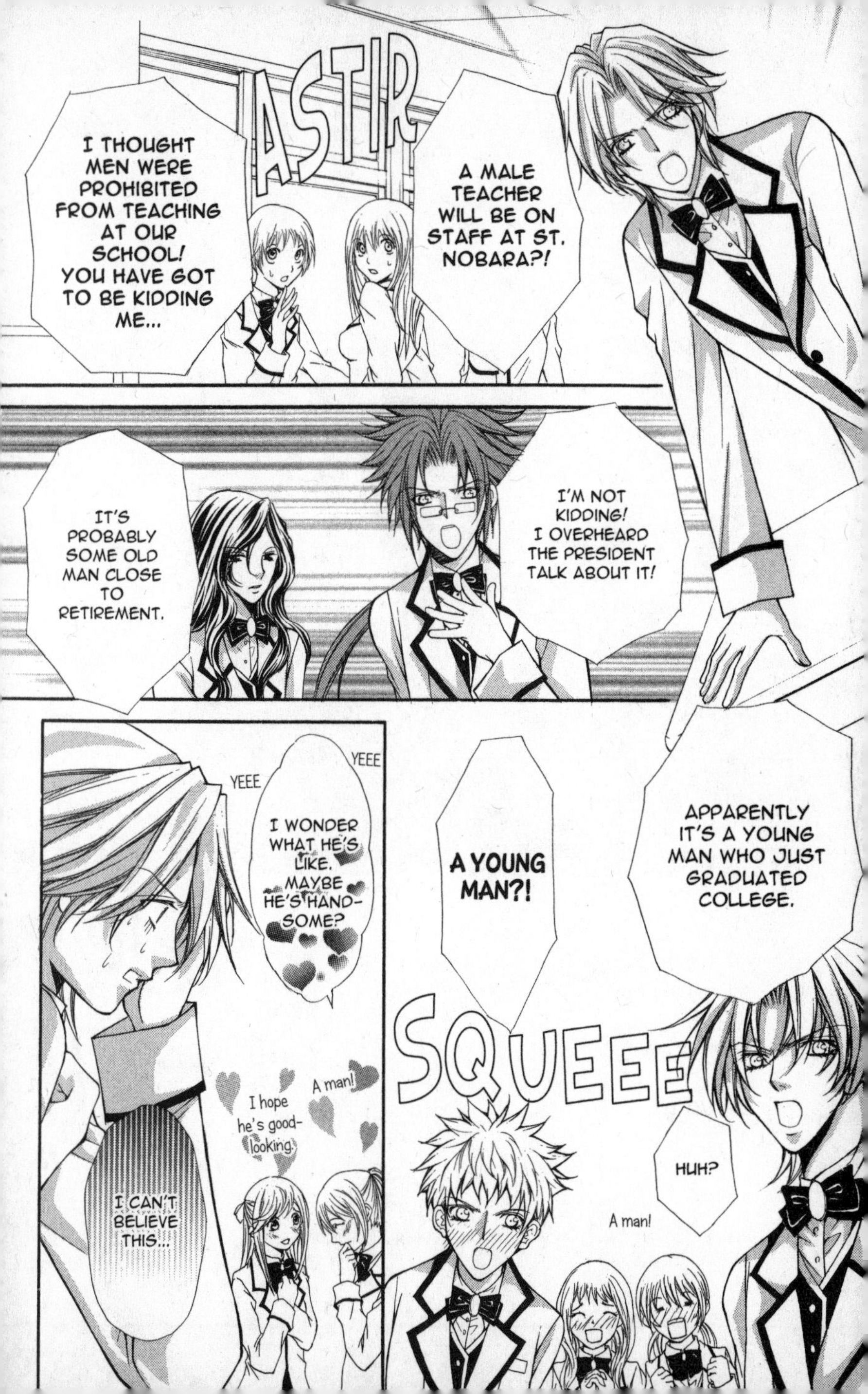
A MALE TEACHER WILL BE ON STAFF AT ST. NOBARA?!
ASTIR
I THOUGHT MEN WERE PROHIBITED FROM TEACHING AT OUR SCHOOL! YOU HAVE GOT TO BE KIDDING ME...
I'M NOT KIDDING! I OVERHEARD THE PRESIDENT TALK ABOUT IT!
IT'S PROBABLY SOME OLD MAN CLOSE TO RETIREMENT.
APPARENTLY IT'S A YOUNG MAN WHO JUST GRADUATED COLLEGE.
A YOUNG MAN?!
SQUEEE
HUH?
A man!
YEEE
YEEE
I WONDER WHAT HE'S LIKE. MAYBE HE'S HANDSOME?
A man!
I hope he's good-looking.
I CAN'T BELIEVE THIS...

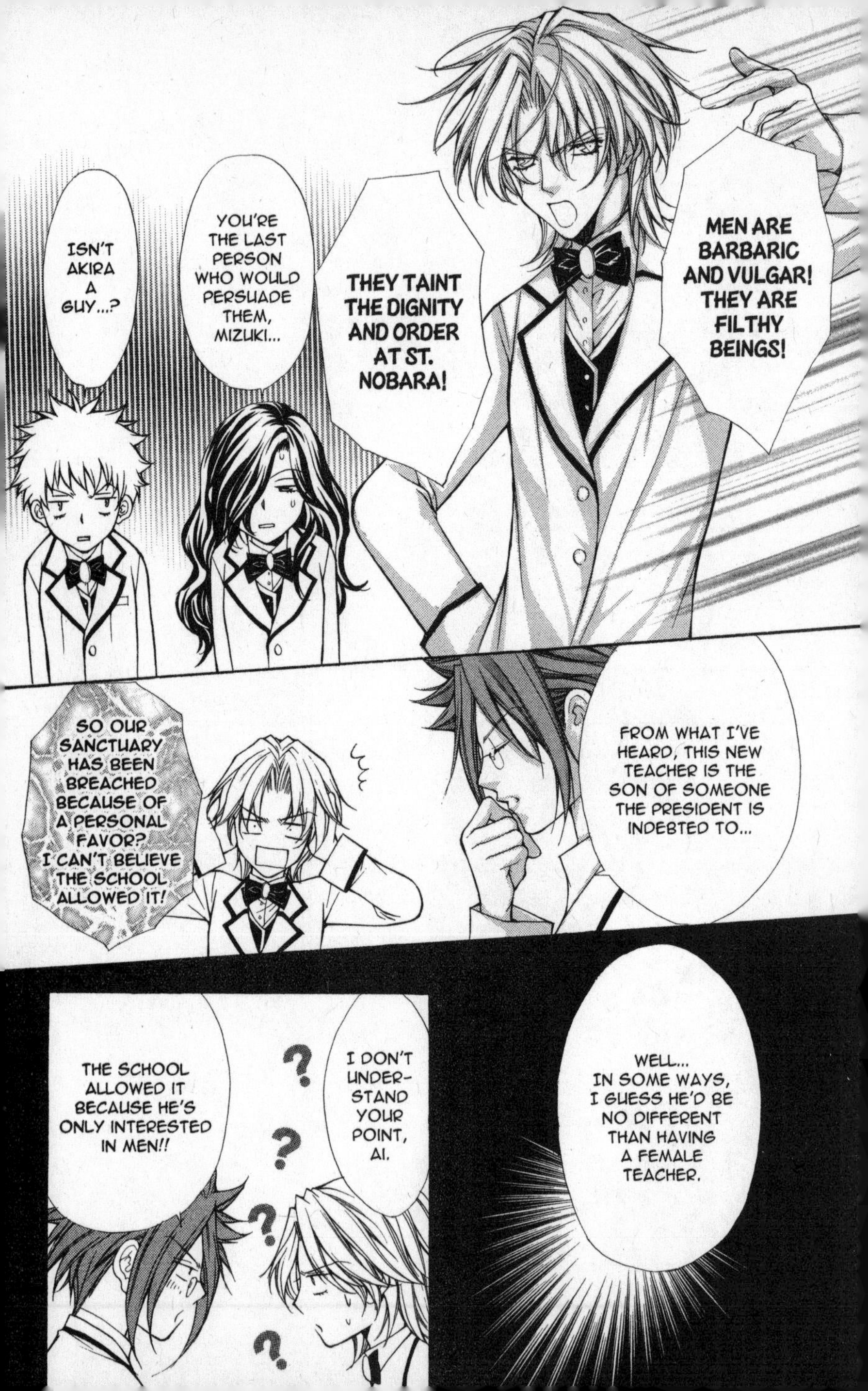
MEN ARE BARBARIC AND VULGAR! THEY ARE FILTHY BEINGS!
THEY TAINT THE DIGNITY AND ORDER AT ST. NOBARA!
YOU'RE THE LAST PERSON WHO WOULD PERSUADE THEM, MIZUKI...
ISN'T AKIRA A GUY...?
FROM WHAT I'VE HEARD, THIS NEW TEACHER IS THE SON OF SOMEONE THE PRESIDENT IS INDEBTED TO...
SO OUR SANCTUARY HAS BEEN BREACHED BECAUSE OF A PERSONAL FAVOR? I CAN'T BELIEVE THE SCHOOL ALLOWED IT!
WELL... IN SOME WAYS, I GUESS HE'D BE NO DIFFERENT THAN HAVING A FEMALE TEACHER.
I DON'T UNDER-STAND YOUR POINT, AI.
THE SCHOOL ALLOWED IT BECAUSE HE'S ONLY INTERESTED IN MEN!!

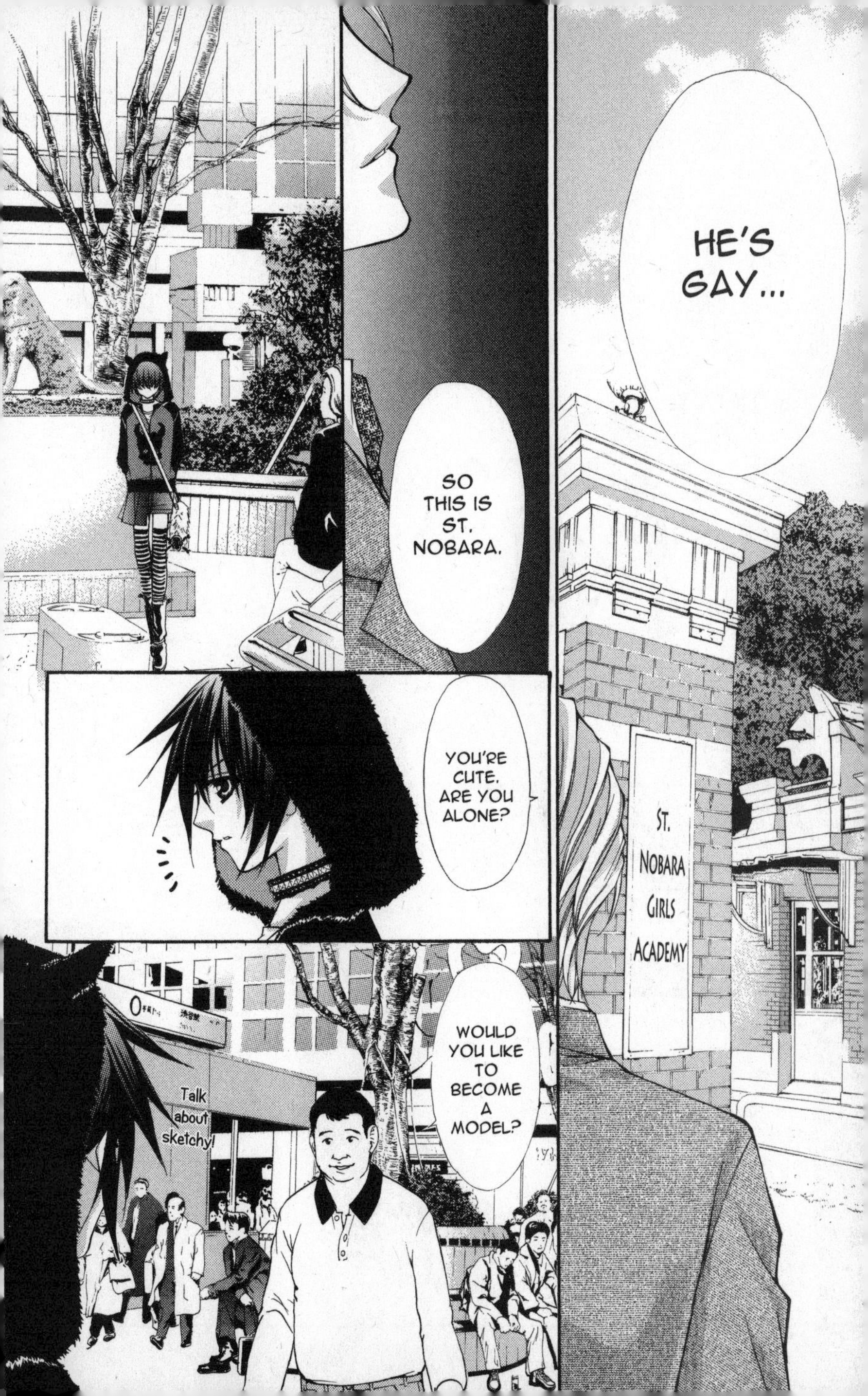
HE'S GAY...
ST. NOBARA GIRLS ACADEMY
SO THIS IS ST. NOBARA.
YOU'RE CUTE. ARE YOU ALONE?
WOULD YOU LIKE TO BECOME A MODEL?
Talk about sketchy!

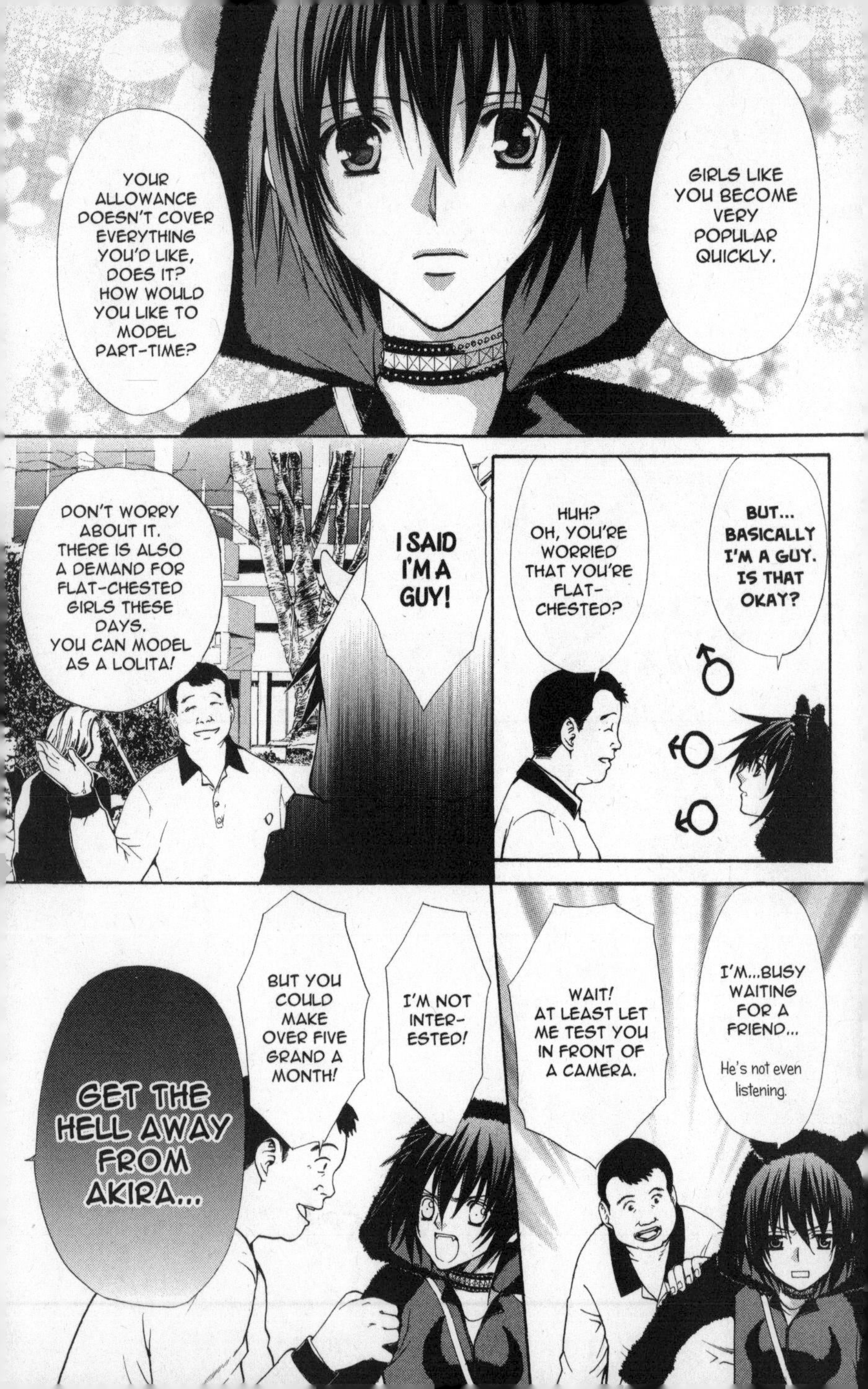
GIRLS LIKE YOU BECOME VERY POPULAR QUICKLY.
YOUR ALLOWANCE DOESN'T COVER EVERYTHING YOU'D LIKE, DOES IT? HOW WOULD YOU LIKE TO MODEL PART-TIME?
BUT... BASICALLY I'M A GUY. IS THAT OKAY?
HUH? OH, YOU'RE WORRIED THAT YOU'RE FLAT-CHESTED?
I SAID I'M A GUY!
DON'T WORRY ABOUT IT. THERE IS ALSO A DEMAND FOR FLAT-CHESTED GIRLS THESE DAYS. YOU CAN MODEL AS A LOLITA!
I'M...BUSY WAITING FOR A FRIEND...
He's not even listening.
WAIT! AT LEAST LET ME TEST YOU IN FRONT OF A CAMERA.
I'M NOT INTER-ESTED!
BUT YOU COULD MAKE OVER FIVE GRAND A MONTH!
GET THE HELL AWAY FROM AKIRA...

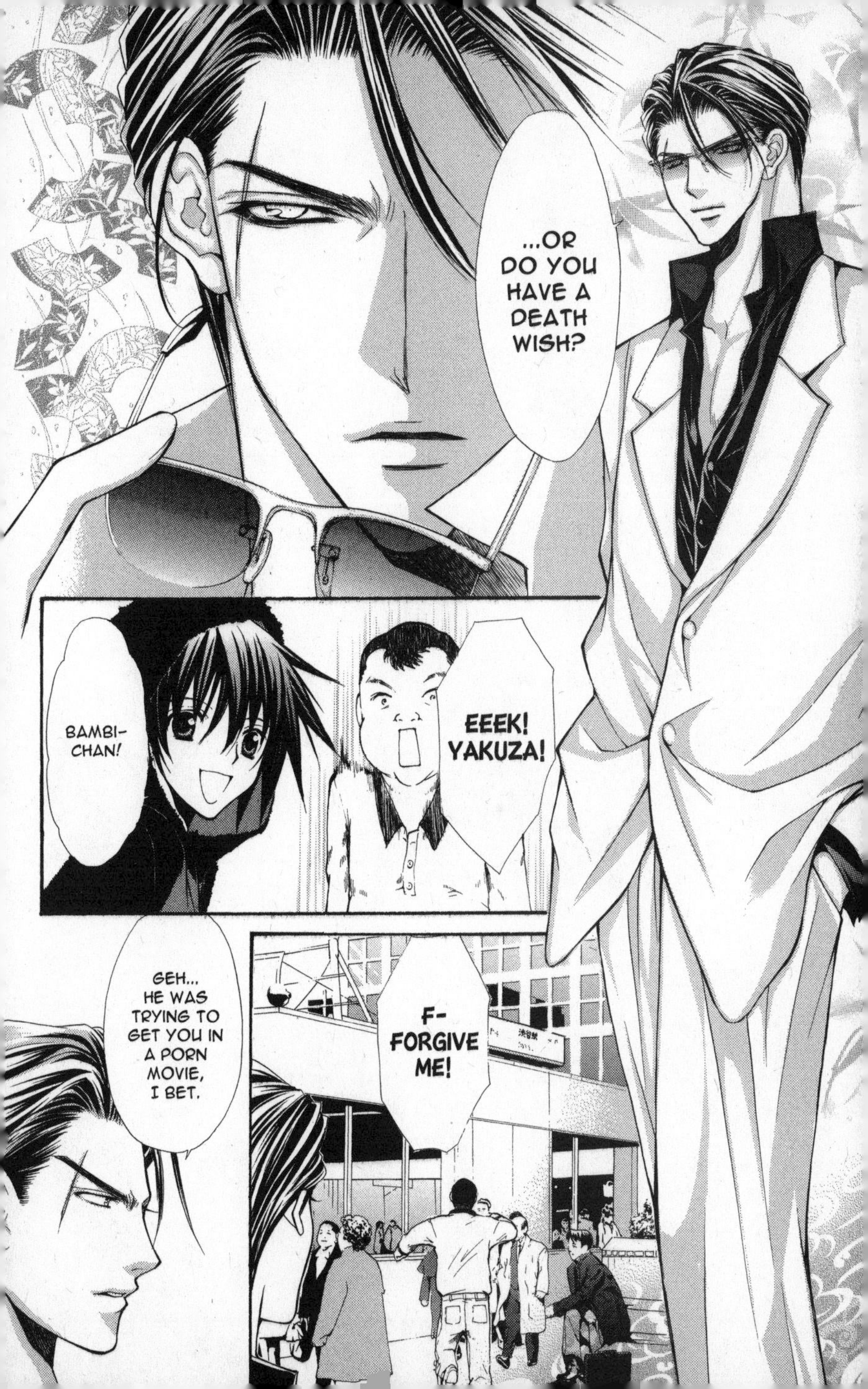
...OR DO YOU HAVE A DEATH WISH?
EEEK! YAKUZA!
BAMBI-CHAN!
F-FORGIVE ME!
GEH... HE WAS TRYING TO GET YOU IN A PORN MOVIE, I BET.

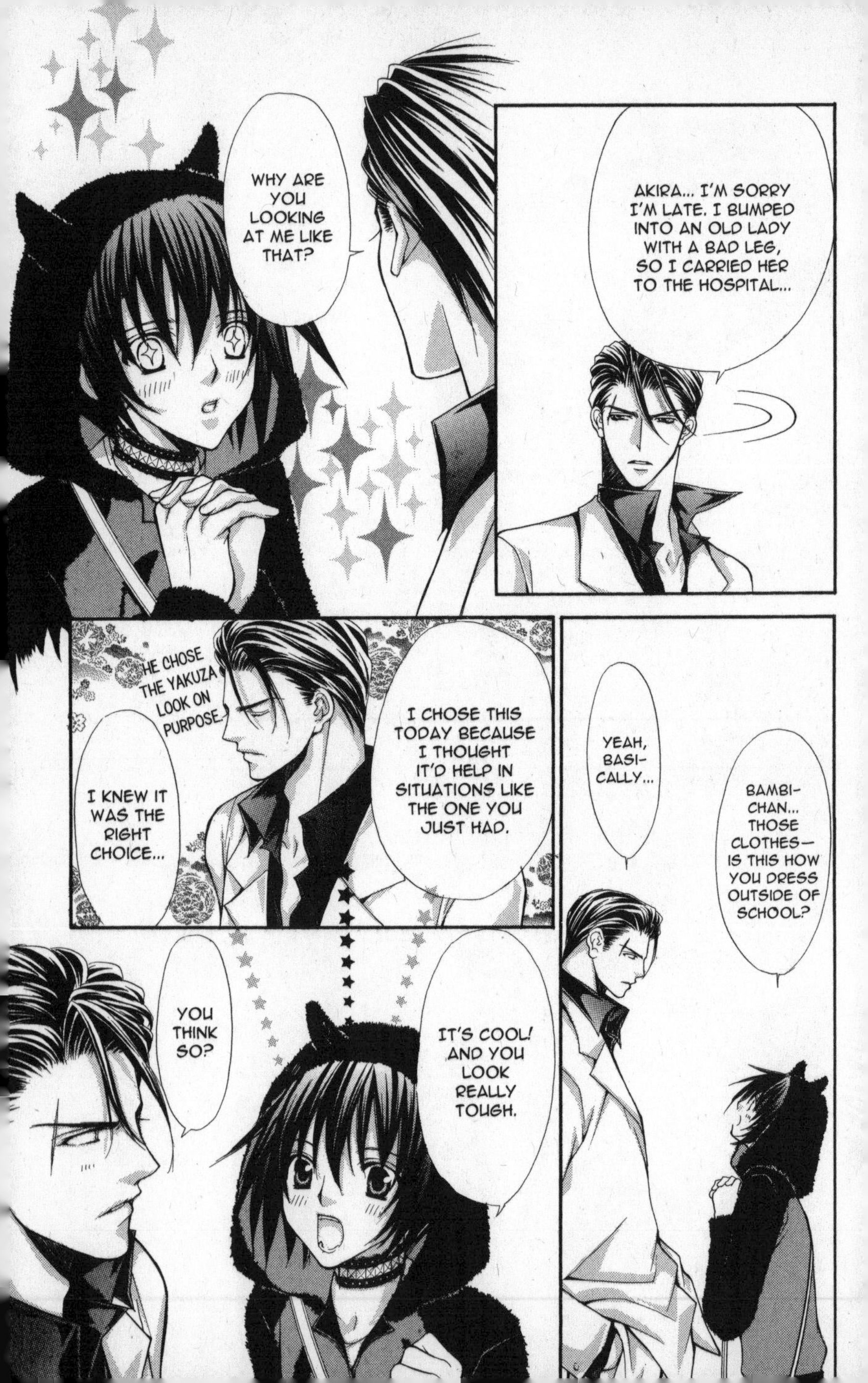
AKIRA... I'M SORRY I'M LATE. I BUMPED INTO AN OLD LADY WITH A BAD LEG, SO I CARRIED HER TO THE HOSPITAL...
WHY ARE YOU LOOKING AT ME LIKE THAT?
BAMBI-CHAN... THOSE CLOTHES— IS THIS HOW YOU DRESS OUTSIDE OF SCHOOL?
YEAH, BASI-CALLY...
I CHOSE THIS TODAY BECAUSE I THOUGHT IT'D HELP IN SITUATIONS LIKE THE ONE YOU JUST HAD.
HE CHOSE THE YAKUZA LOOK ON PURPOSE.
I KNEW IT WAS THE RIGHT CHOICE...
IT'S COOL! AND YOU LOOK REALLY TOUGH.
YOU THINK SO?

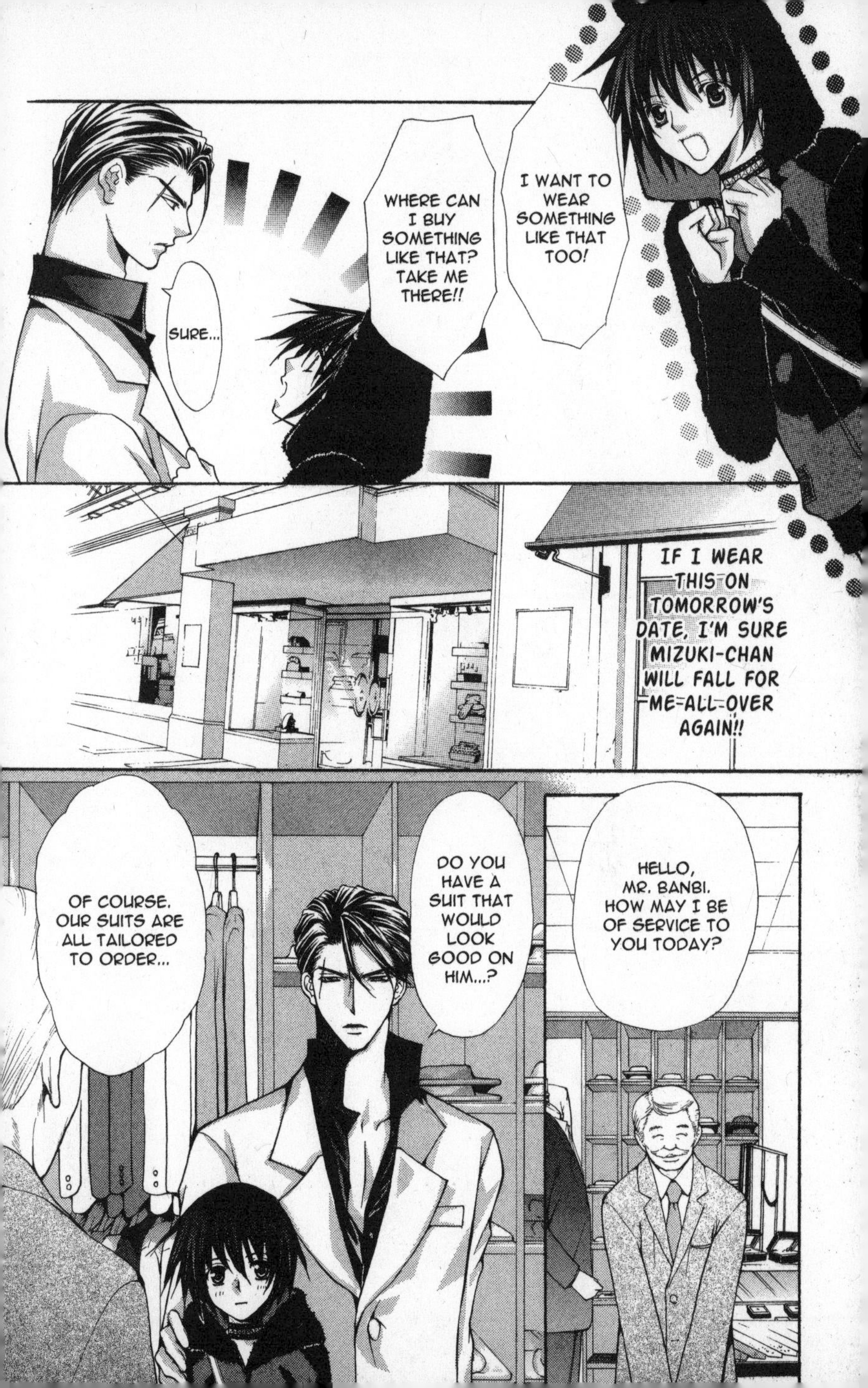
I WANT TO WEAR SOMETHING LIKE THAT TOO!
WHERE CAN I BUY SOMETHING LIKE THAT? TAKE ME THERE!!
SURE...
IF I WEAR THIS ON TOMORROW'S DATE, I'M SURE MIZUKI-CHAN WILL FALL FOR ME ALL OVER AGAIN!!
HELLO, MR. BANBI. HOW MAY I BE OF SERVICE TO YOU TODAY?
DO YOU HAVE A SUIT THAT WOULD LOOK GOOD ON HIM...?
OF COURSE. OUR SUITS ARE ALL TAILORED TO ORDER...

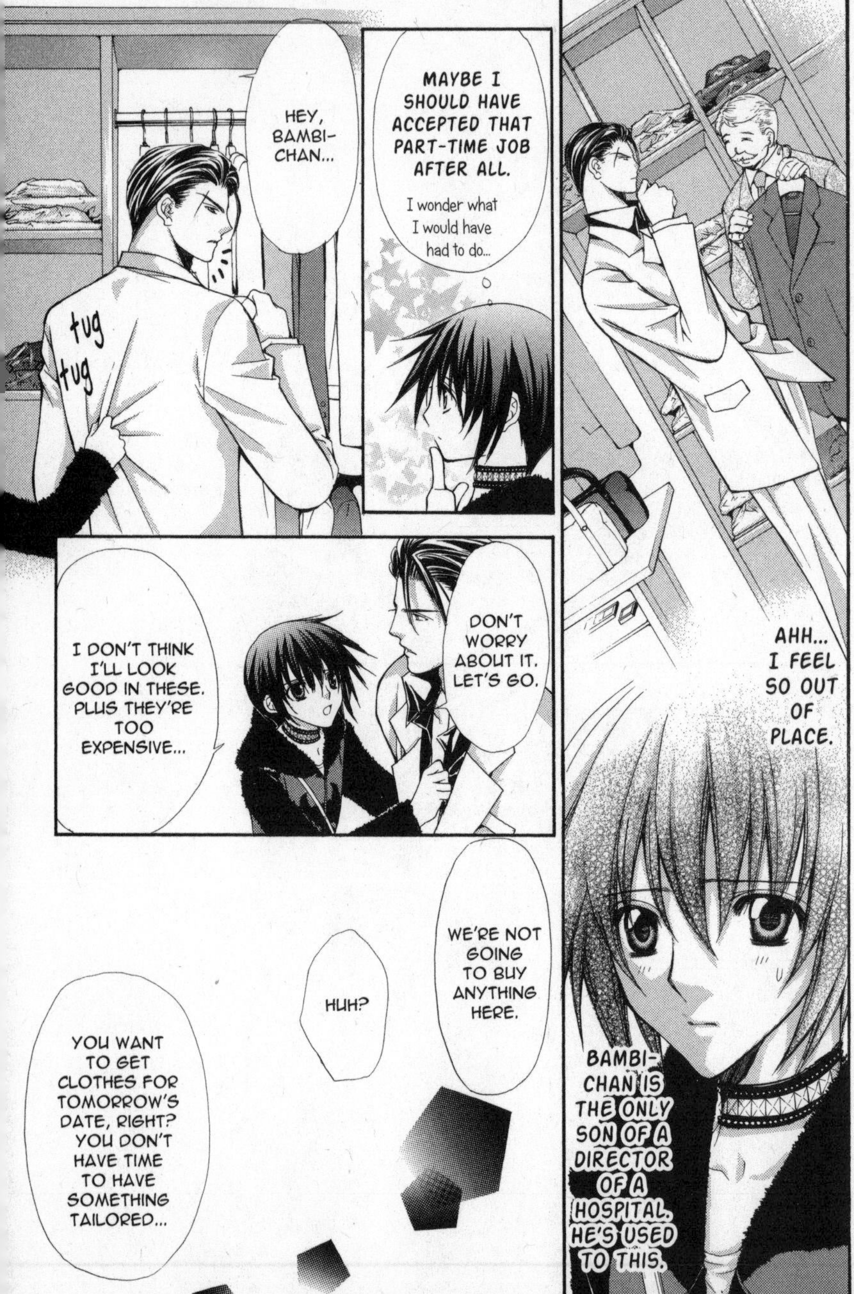
AHH... I FEEL SO OUT OF PLACE.
BAMBI-CHAN IS THE ONLY SON OF A DIRECTOR OF A HOSPITAL. HE'S USED TO THIS.
MAYBE I SHOULD HAVE ACCEPTED THAT PART-TIME JOB AFTER ALL.
I wonder what I would have had to do...
HEY, BAMBI-CHAN...
tug tug
DON'T WORRY ABOUT IT. LET'S GO.
I DON'T THINK I'LL LOOK GOOD IN THESE. PLUS THEY'RE TOO EXPENSIVE...
WE'RE NOT GOING TO BUY ANYTHING HERE.
HUH?
YOU WANT TO GET CLOTHES FOR TOMORROW'S DATE, RIGHT? YOU DON'T HAVE TIME TO HAVE SOMETHING TAILORED...

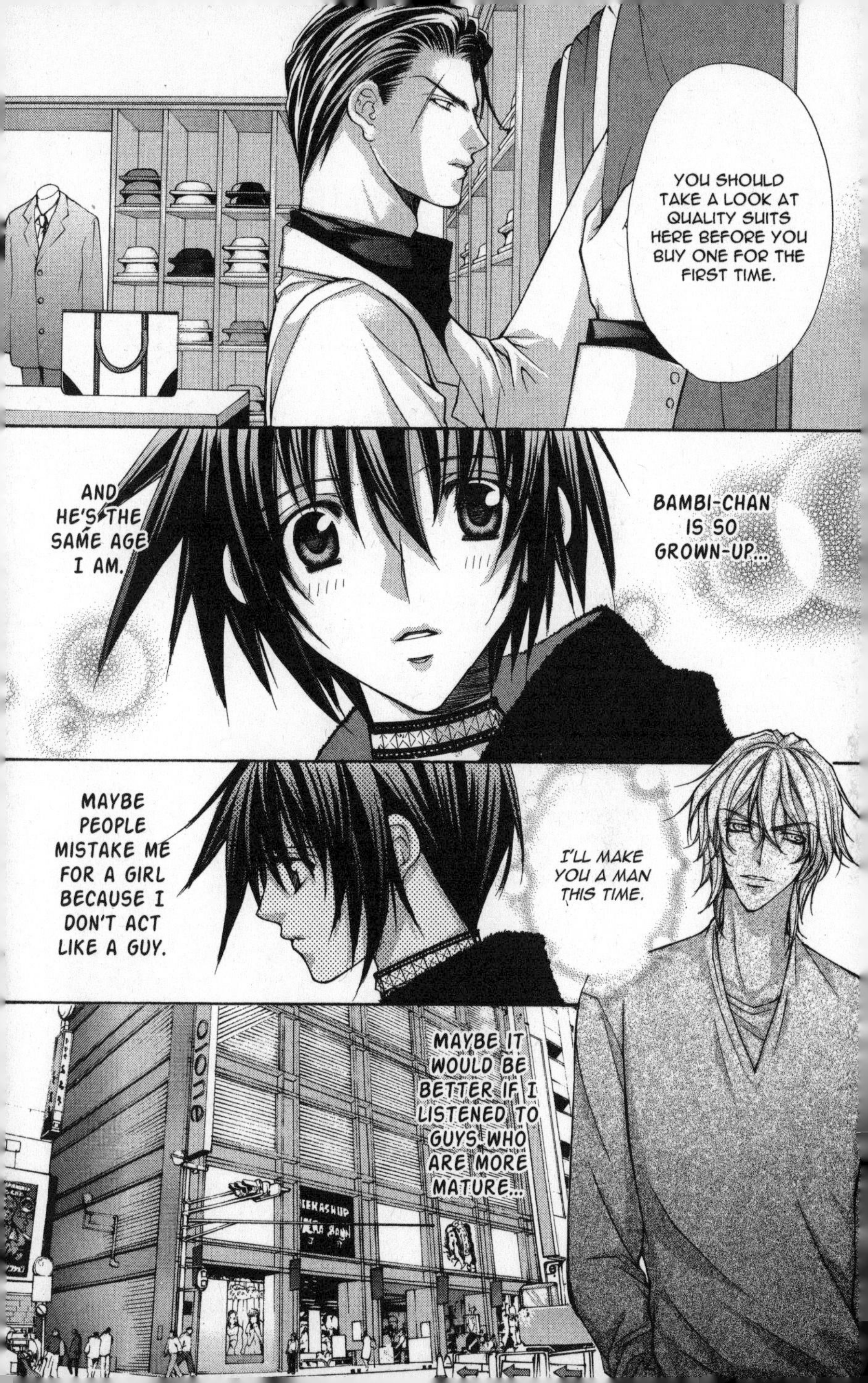
YOU SHOULD TAKE A LOOK AT QUALITY SUITS HERE BEFORE YOU BUY ONE FOR THE FIRST TIME.
BAMBI-CHAN IS SO GROWN-UP...
AND HE'S THE SAME AGE I AM.
I'LL MAKE YOU A MAN THIS TIME.
MAYBE PEOPLE MISTAKE ME FOR A GIRL BECAUSE I DON'T ACT LIKE A GUY.
MAYBE IT WOULD BE BETTER IF I LISTENED TO GUYS WHO ARE MORE MATURE...

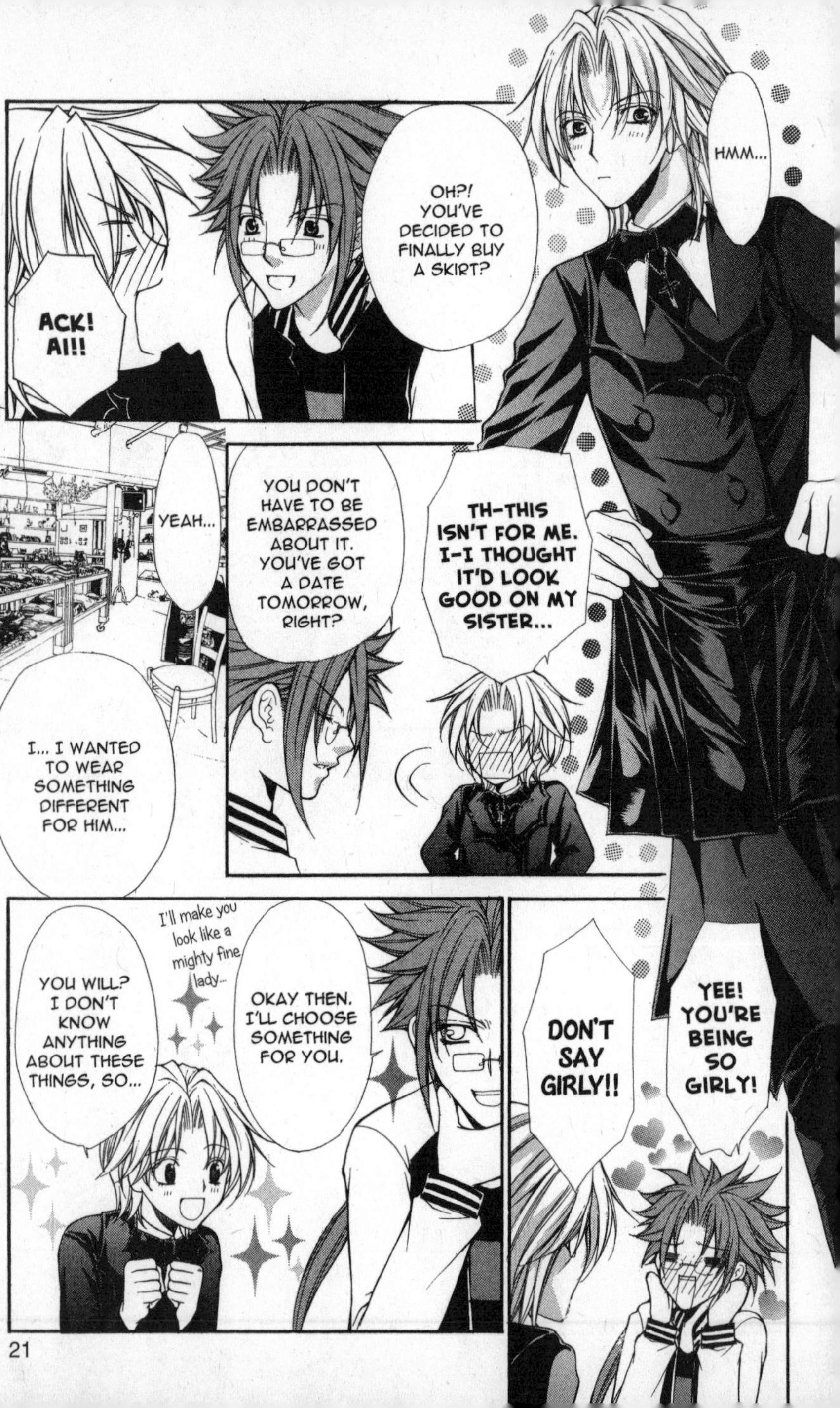
HMM...
OH?! YOU'VE DECIDED TO FINALLY BUY A SKIRT?
ACK! AI!!
TH-THIS ISN'T FOR ME. I-I THOUGHT IT'D LOOK GOOD ON MY SISTER...
YOU DON'T HAVE TO BE EMBARRASSED ABOUT IT. YOU'VE GOT A DATE TOMORROW, RIGHT?
YEAH...
I... I WANTED TO WEAR SOMETHING DIFFERENT FOR HIM...
YEE! YOU'RE BEING SO GIRLY!
DON'T SAY GIRLY!!
OKAY THEN. I'LL CHOOSE SOMETHING FOR YOU.
I'll make you look like a mighty fine lady...
YOU WILL? I DON'T KNOW ANYTHING ABOUT THESE THINGS, SO...

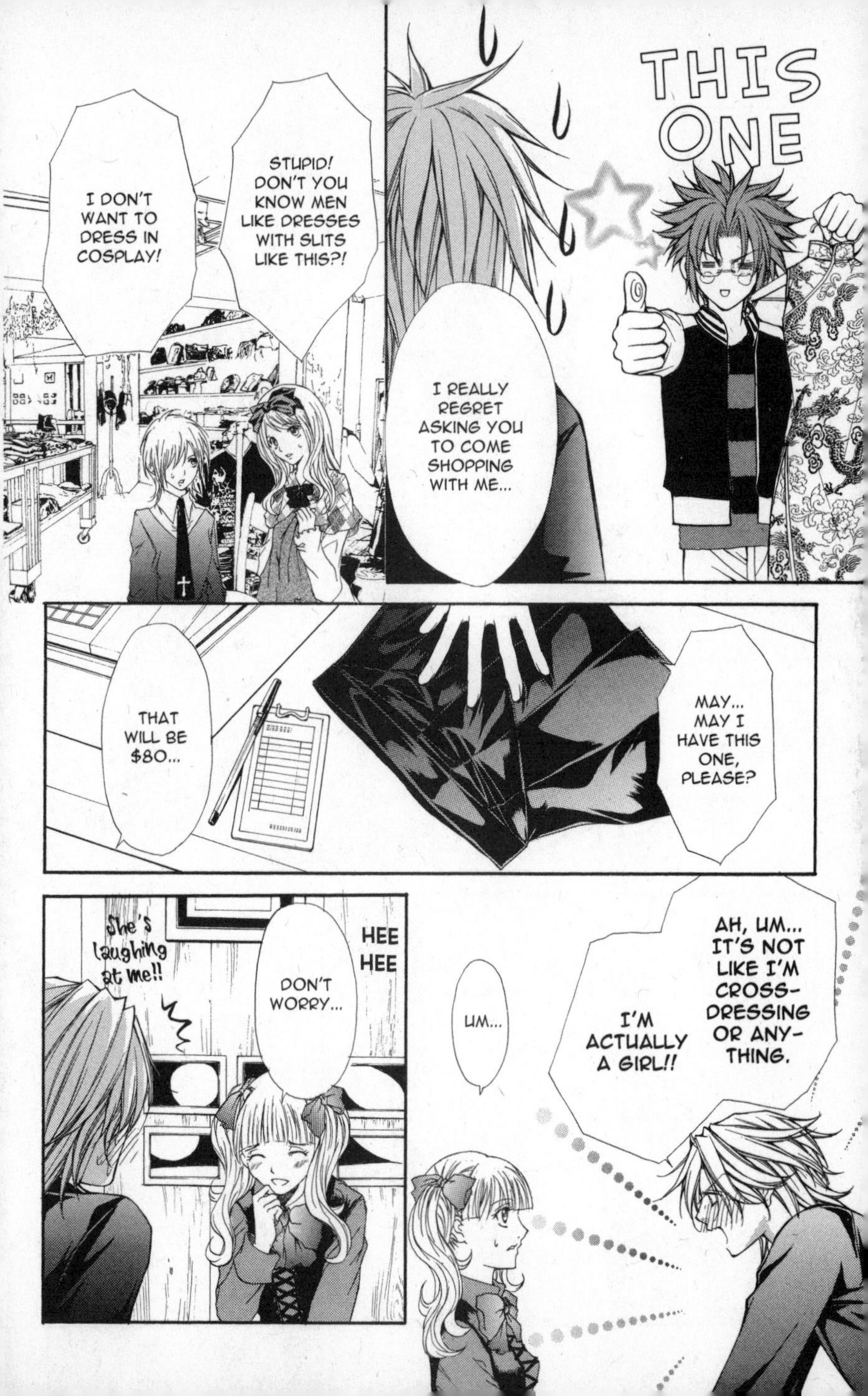
THIS ONE
I REALLY REGRET ASKING YOU TO COME SHOPPING WITH ME...
STUPID! DON'T YOU KNOW MEN LIKE DRESSES WITH SLITS LIKE THIS?!
I DON'T WANT TO DRESS IN COSPLAY!
MAY... MAY I HAVE THIS ONE, PLEASE?
THAT WILL BE $80...
AH, UM... IT'S NOT LIKE I'M CROSS-DRESSING OR ANY-THING.
I'M ACTUALLY A GIRL!!
UM...
HEE HEE
DON'T WORRY...
She's laughing at me!!

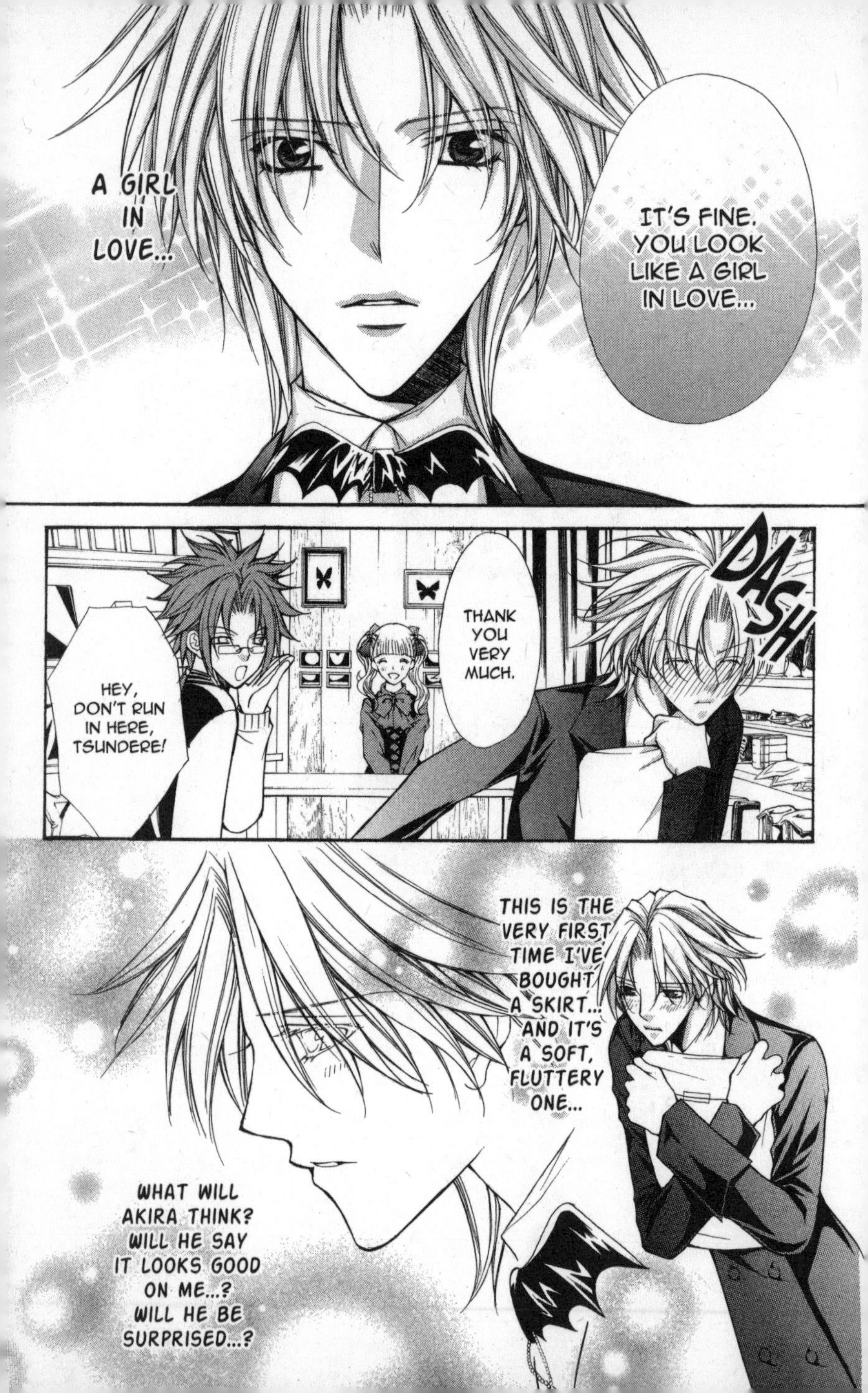
IT'S FINE. YOU LOOK LIKE A GIRL IN LOVE...
A GIRL IN LOVE...
DASH
THANK YOU VERY MUCH.
HEY, DON'T RUN IN HERE, TSUNDERE!
THIS IS THE VERY FIRST TIME I'VE BOUGHT A SKIRT... AND IT'S A SOFT, FLUTTERY ONE...
WHAT WILL AKIRA THINK? WILL HE SAY IT LOOKS GOOD ON ME...? WILL HE BE SURPRISED...?

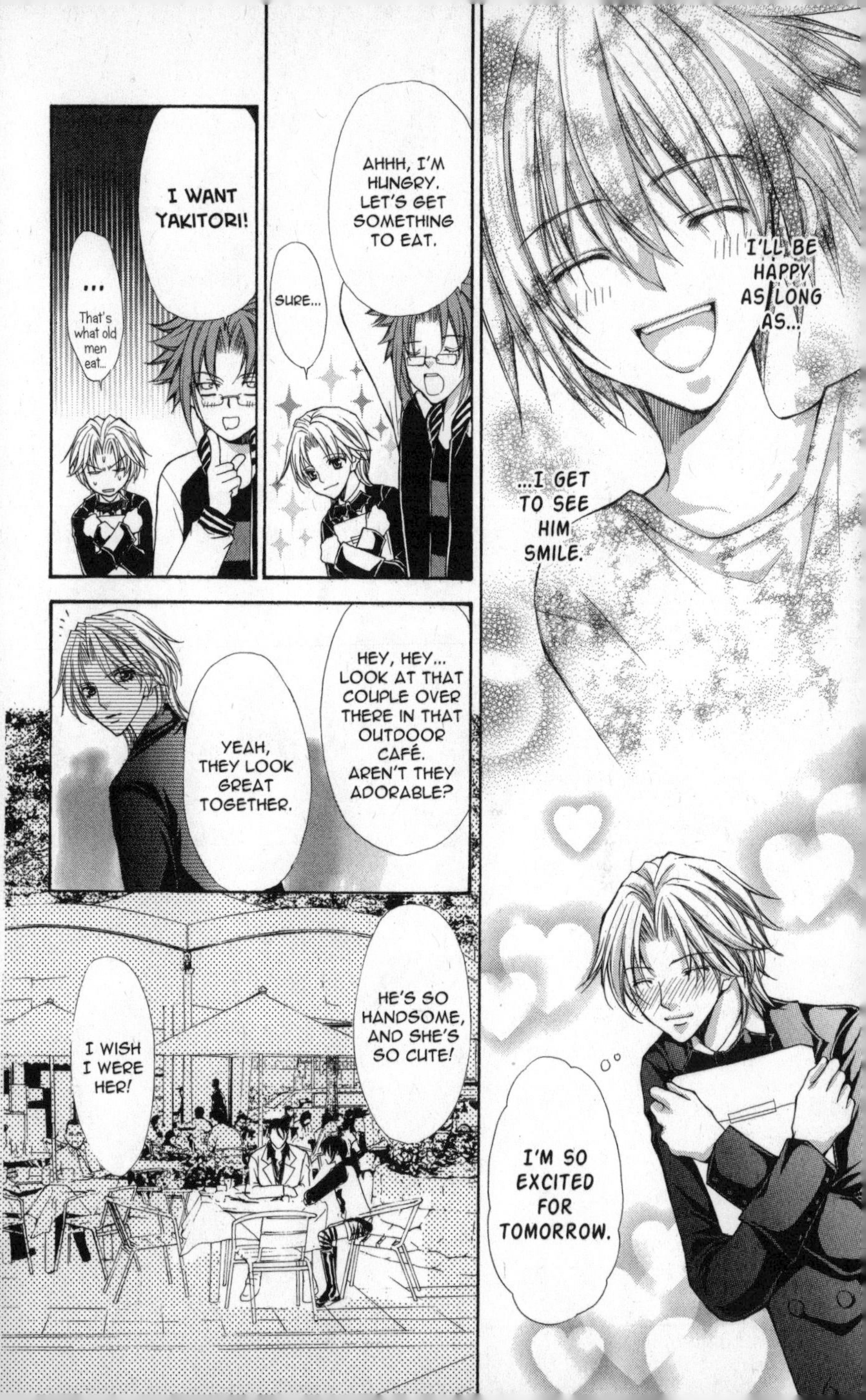
I'LL BE HAPPY AS LONG AS...
...I GET TO SEE HIM SMILE.
I'M SO EXCITED FOR TOMORROW.
AHHH, I'M HUNGRY. LET'S GET SOMETHING TO EAT.
SURE...
I WANT YAKITORI!
...
That's what old men eat...
HEY, HEY... LOOK AT THAT COUPLE OVER THERE IN THAT OUTDOOR CAFÉ. AREN'T THEY ADORABLE?
YEAH, THEY LOOK GREAT TOGETHER.
HE'S SO HANDSOME, AND SHE'S SO CUTE!
I WISH I WERE HER!

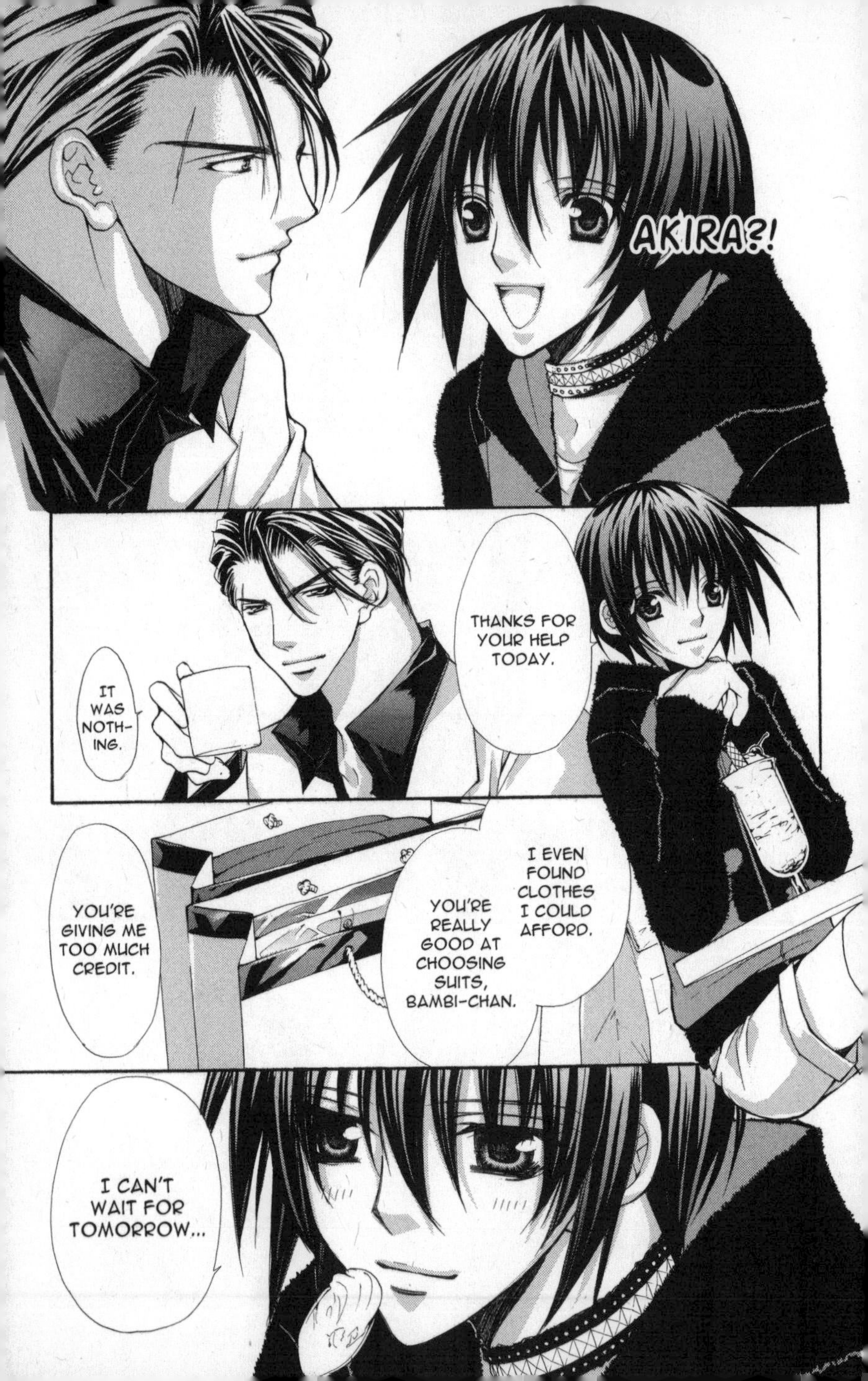
AKIRA?!
THANKS FOR YOUR HELP TODAY.
IT WAS NOTH-ING.
I EVEN FOUND CLOTHES I COULD AFFORD. YOU'RE REALLY GOOD AT CHOOSING SUITS, BAMBI-CHAN.
YOU'RE GIVING ME TOO MUCH CREDIT.
I CAN'T WAIT FOR TOMORROW...

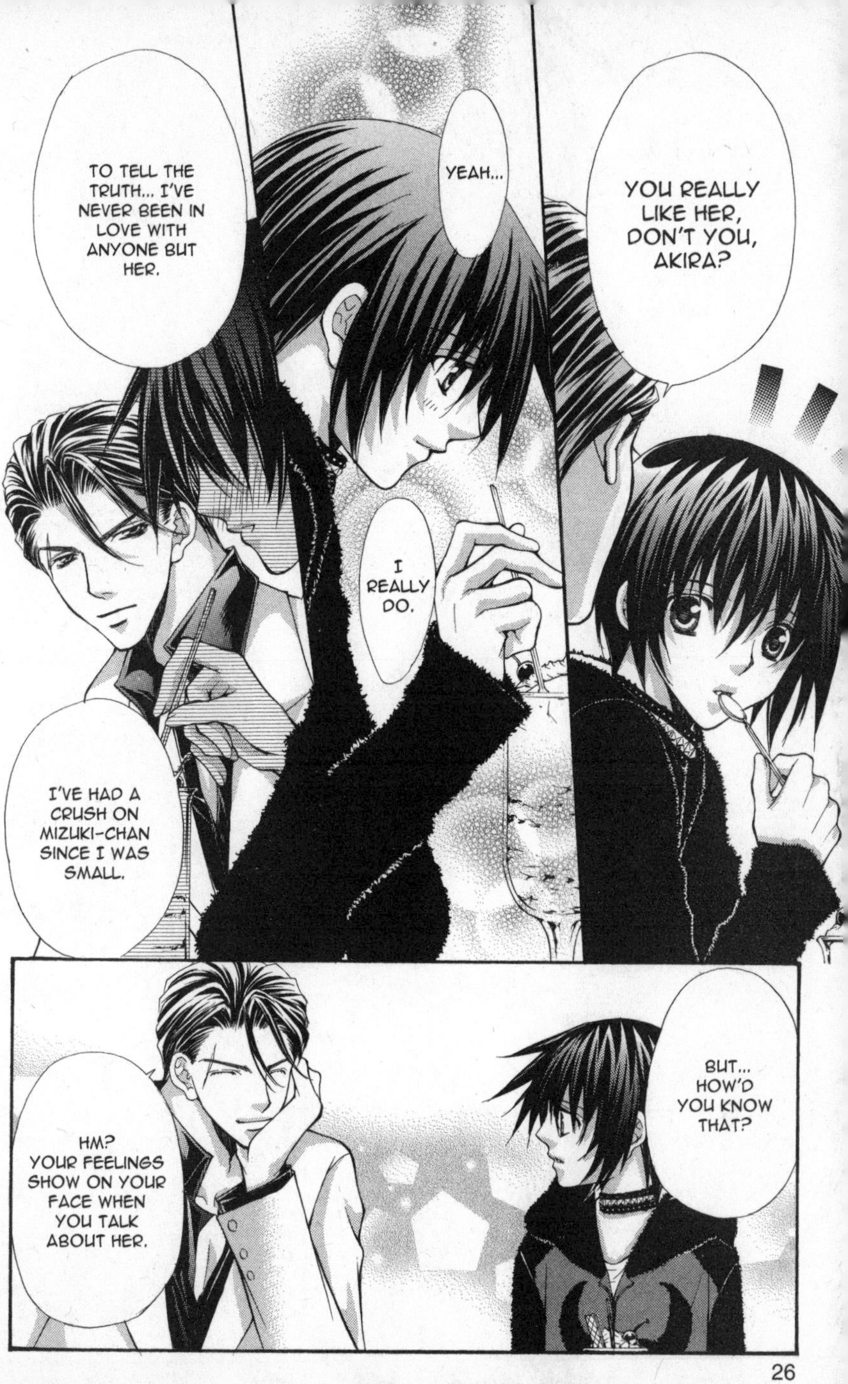
YOU REALLY LIKE HER, DON'T YOU, AKIRA?
YEAH...
I REALLY DO.
TO TELL THE TRUTH... I'VE NEVER BEEN IN LOVE WITH ANYONE BUT HER.
I'VE HAD A CRUSH ON MIZUKI-CHAN SINCE I WAS SMALL.
BUT... HOW'D YOU KNOW THAT?
HM? YOUR FEELINGS SHOW ON YOUR FACE WHEN YOU TALK ABOUT HER.

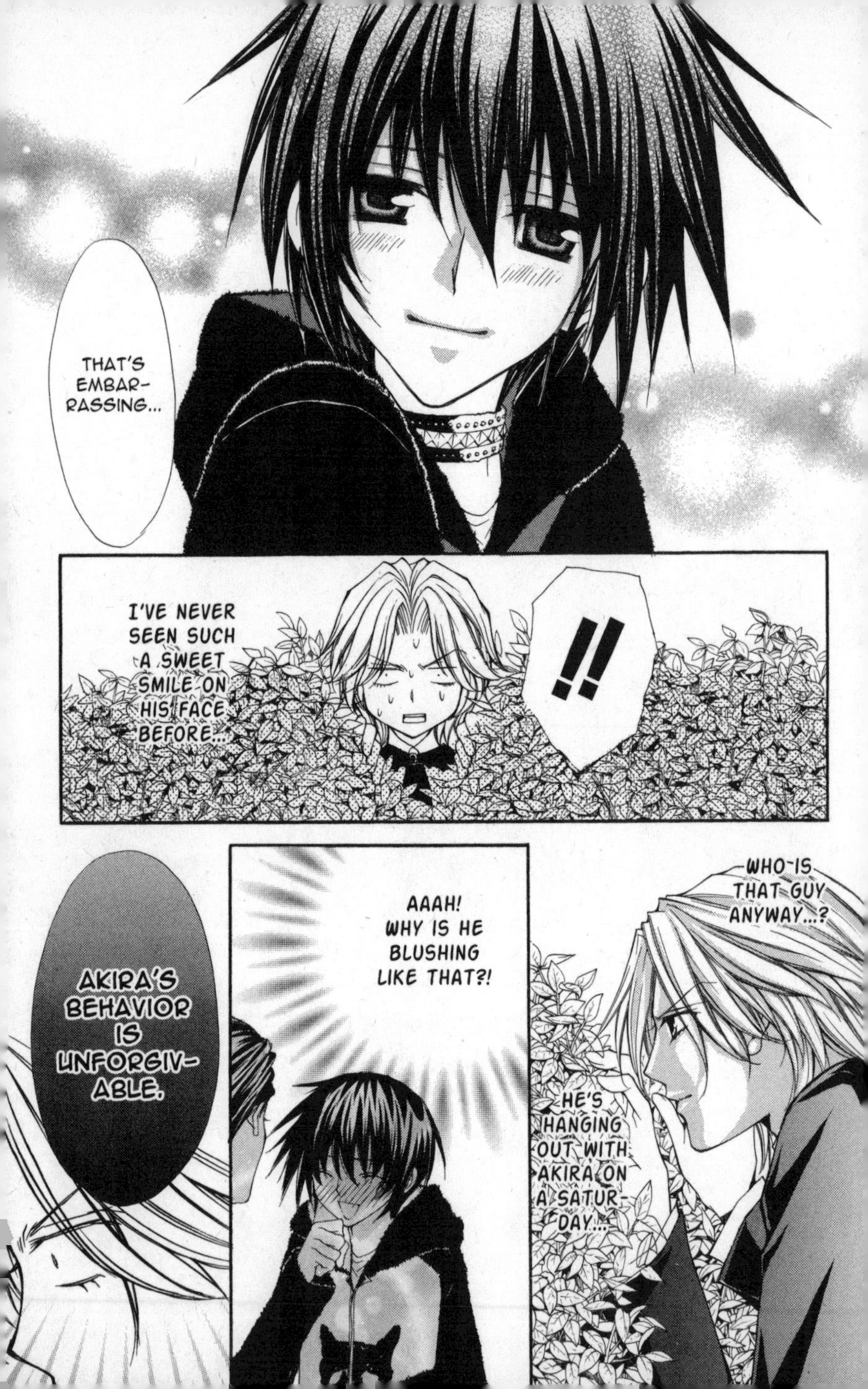
THAT'S EMBAR-RASSING...
!!
I'VE NEVER SEEN SUCH A SWEET SMILE ON HIS FACE BEFORE...
WHO IS THAT GUY ANYWAY...?
HE'S HANGING OUT WITH AKIRA ON A SATUR-DAY...
AAAH! WHY IS HE BLUSHING LIKE THAT?!
AKIRA'S BEHAVIOR IS UNFORGIV-ABLE.

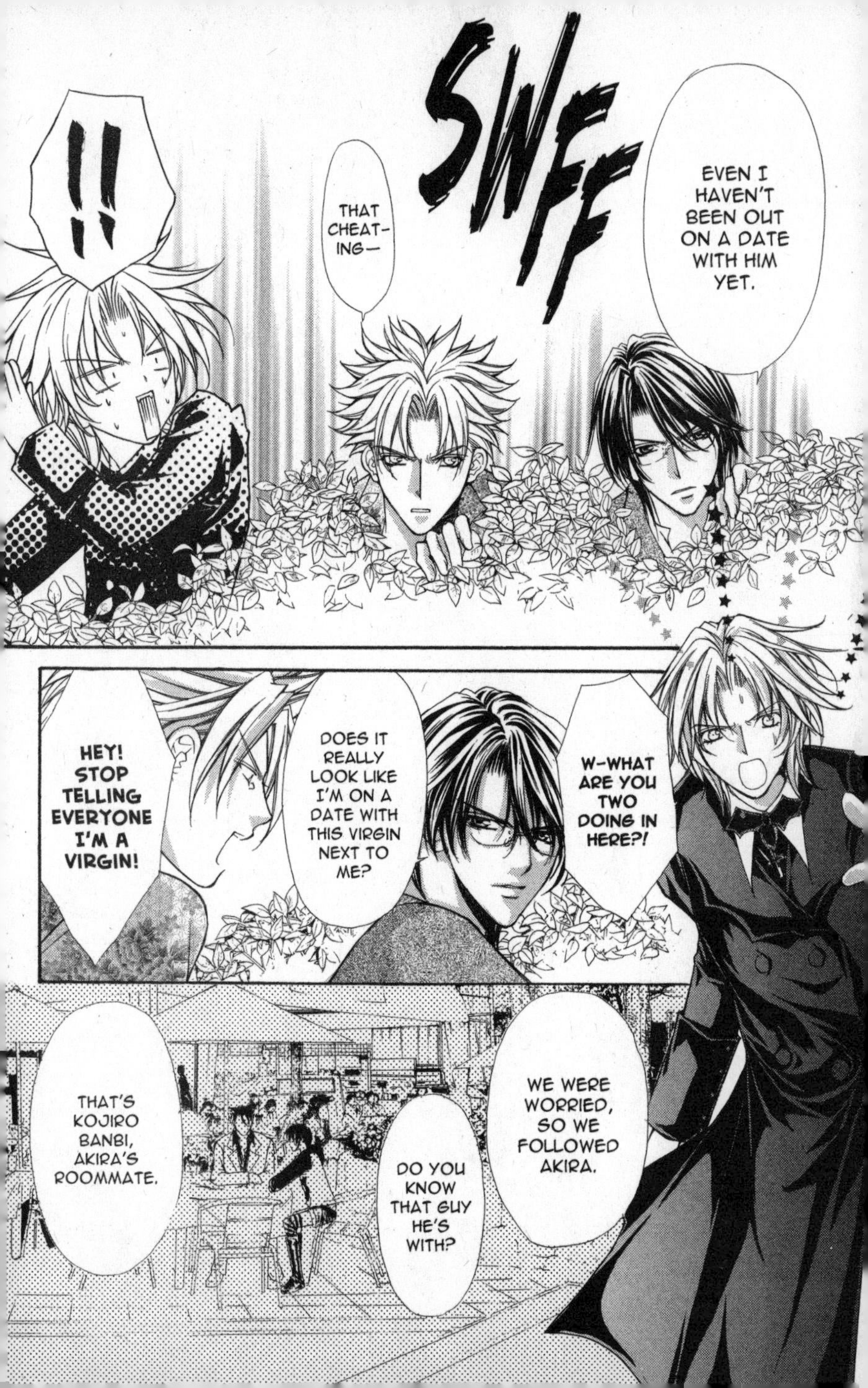
EVEN I HAVEN'T BEEN OUT ON A DATE WITH HIM YET.
SWFF
THAT CHEAT-ING—
!!
W-WHAT ARE YOU TWO DOING IN HERE?!
DOES IT REALLY LOOK LIKE I'M ON A DATE WITH THIS VIRGIN NEXT TO ME?
HEY! STOP TELLING EVERYONE I'M A VIRGIN!
WE WERE WORRIED, SO WE FOLLOWED AKIRA.
DO YOU KNOW THAT GUY HE'S WITH?
THAT'S KOJIRO BANBI, AKIRA'S ROOMMATE.

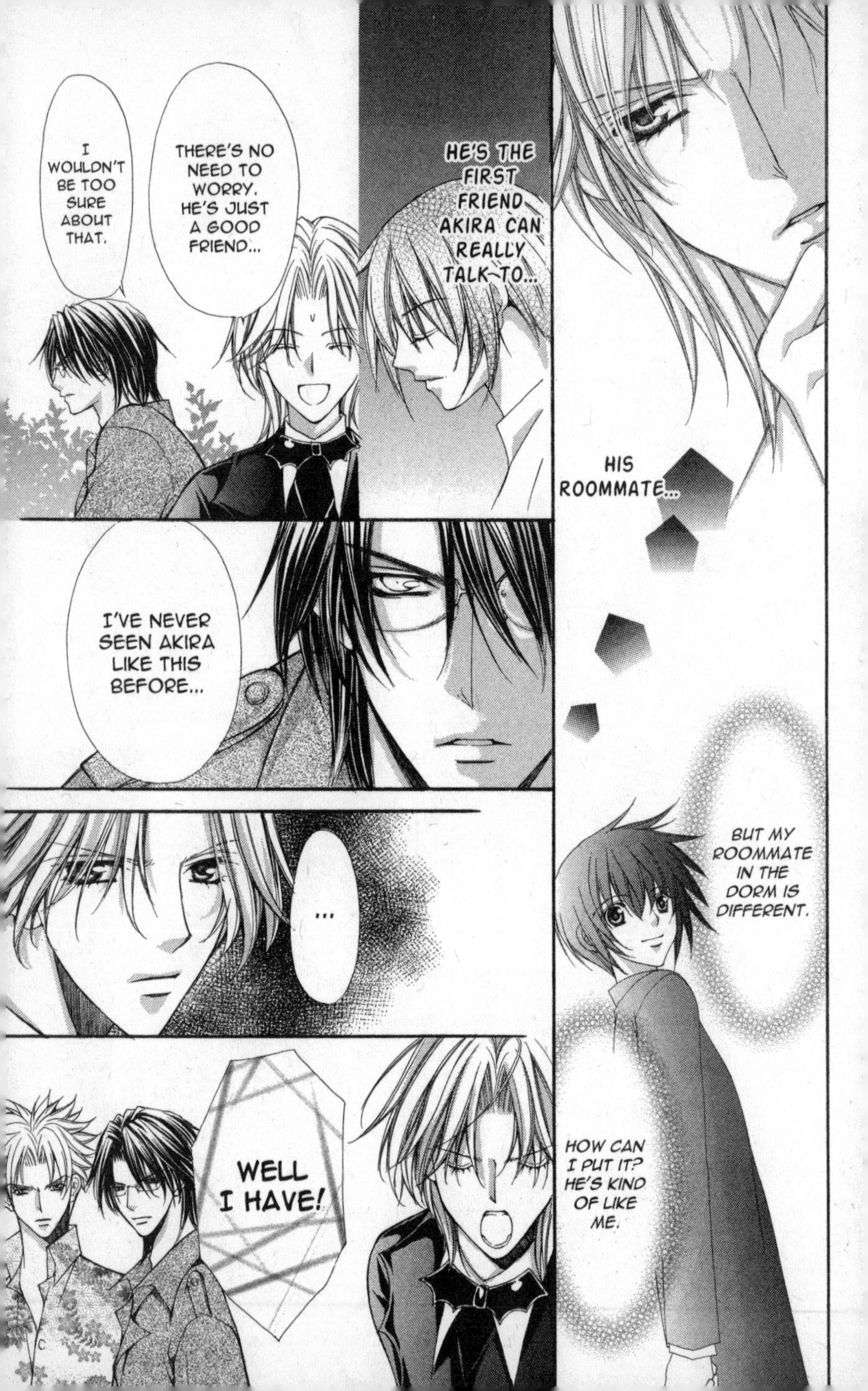
HIS ROOMMATE...
BUT MY ROOMMATE IN THE DORM IS DIFFERENT.
HOW CAN I PUT IT? HE'S KIND OF LIKE ME.
HE'S THE FIRST FRIEND AKIRA CAN REALLY TALK TO...
THERE'S NO NEED TO WORRY. HE'S JUST A GOOD FRIEND...
I WOULDN'T BE TOO SURE ABOUT THAT.
I'VE NEVER SEEN AKIRA LIKE THIS BEFORE...
...
WELL I HAVE!

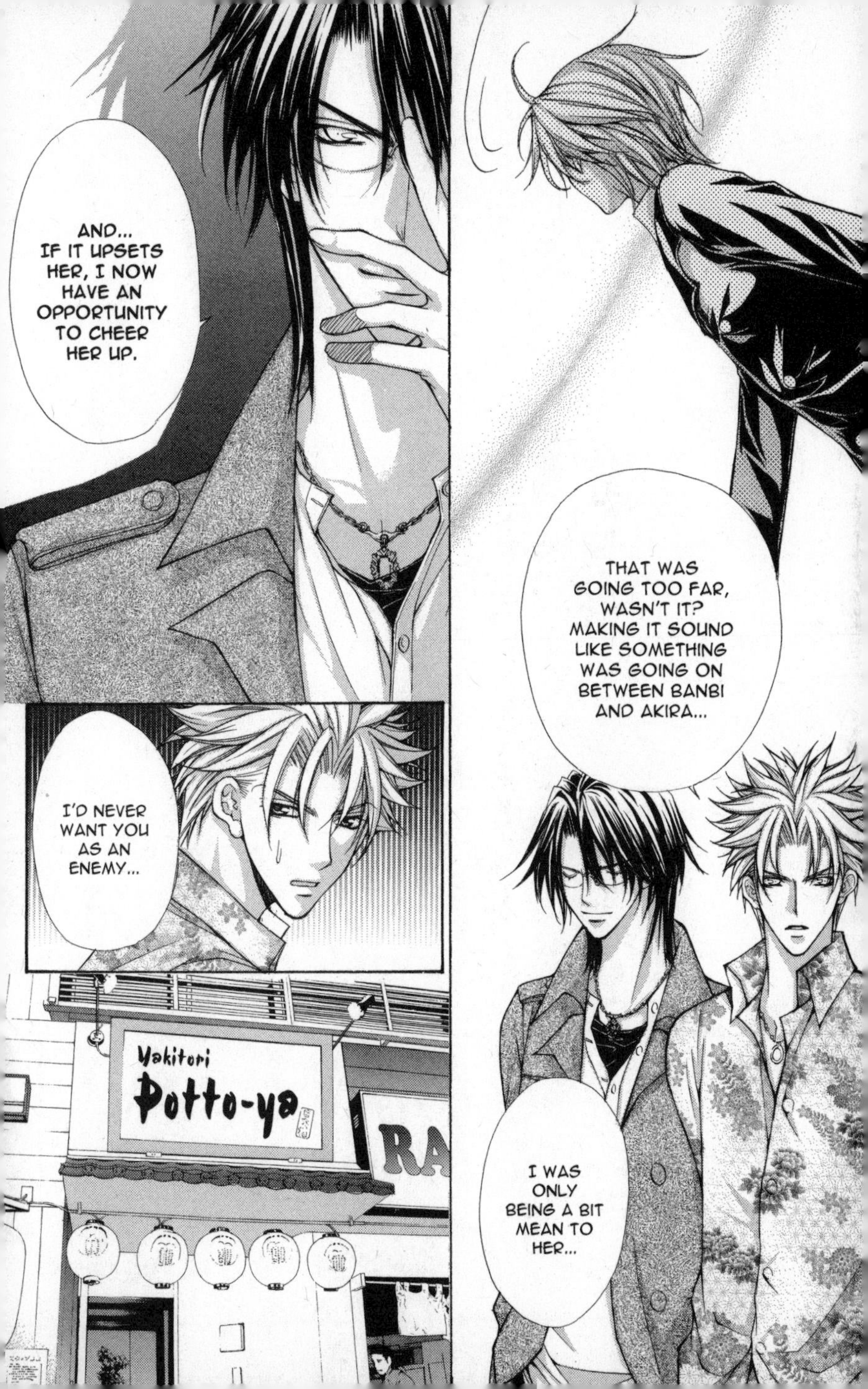
THAT WAS GOING TOO FAR, WASN'T IT? MAKING IT SOUND LIKE SOMETHING WAS GOING ON BETWEEN BANBI AND AKIRA...
I WAS ONLY BEING A BIT MEAN TO HER...
AND... IF IT UPSETS HER, I NOW HAVE AN OPPORTUNITY TO CHEER HER UP.
I'D NEVER WANT YOU AS AN ENEMY...
Yakitori Dotto-ya

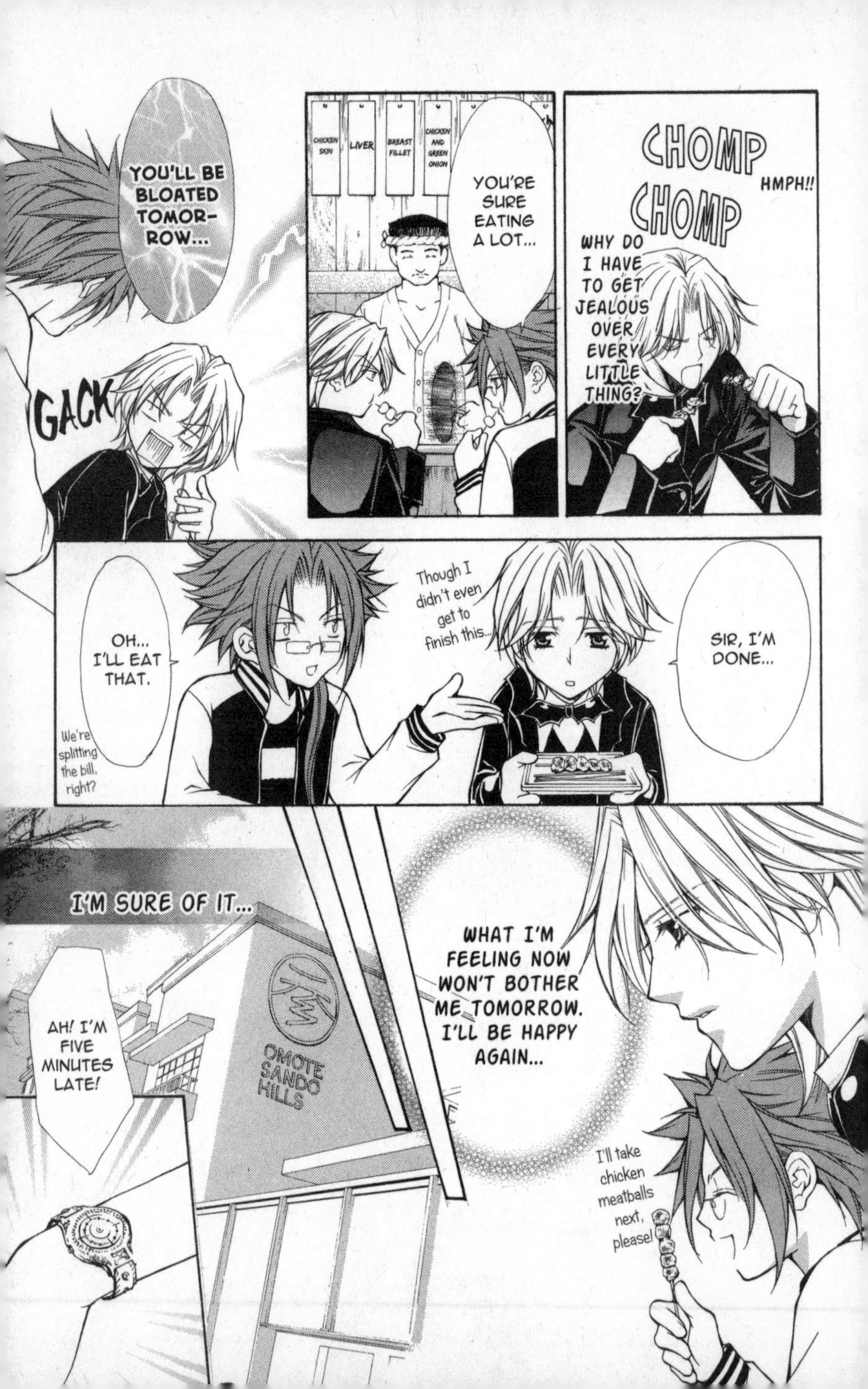
CHOMP CHOMP
HMPH!!
WHY DO I HAVE TO GET JEALOUS OVER EVERY LITTLE THING?
CHICKEN SKIN
LIVER
BREAST FILLET
CHICKEN AND GREEN ONION
YOU'RE SURE EATING A LOT...
YOU'LL BE BLOATED TOMOR-ROW...
GACK
SIR, I'M DONE...
Though I didn't even get to finish this...
OH... I'LL EAT THAT.
We're splitting the bill, right?
WHAT I'M FEELING NOW WON'T BOTHER ME TOMORROW. I'LL BE HAPPY AGAIN...
I'll take chicken meatballs next, please!
I'M SURE OF IT...
OMOTE SANDO HILLS
AH! I'M FIVE MINUTES LATE!

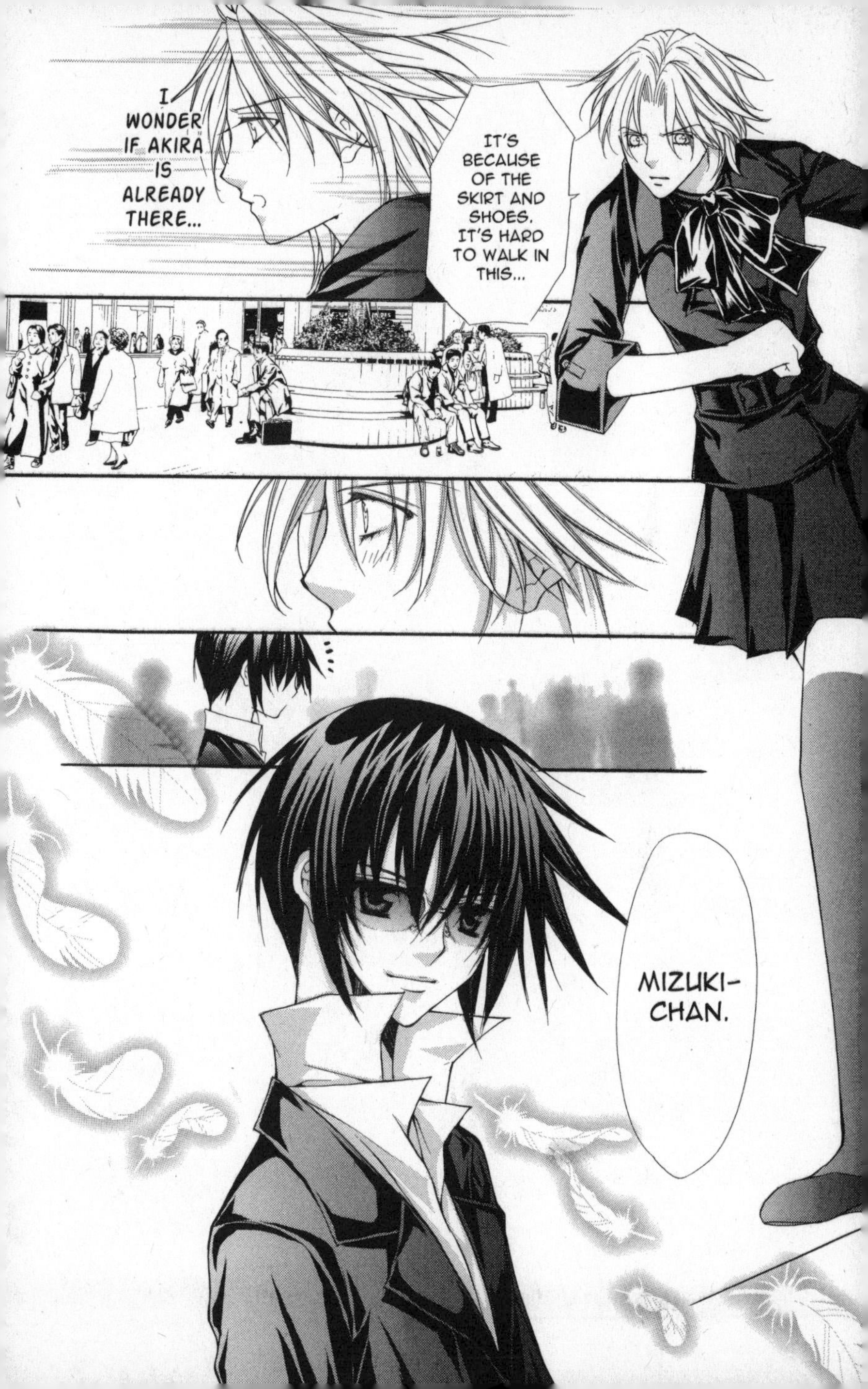
IT'S BECAUSE OF THE SKIRT AND SHOES. IT'S HARD TO WALK IN THIS...
I WONDER IF AKIRA IS ALREADY THERE...
MIZUKI-CHAN.

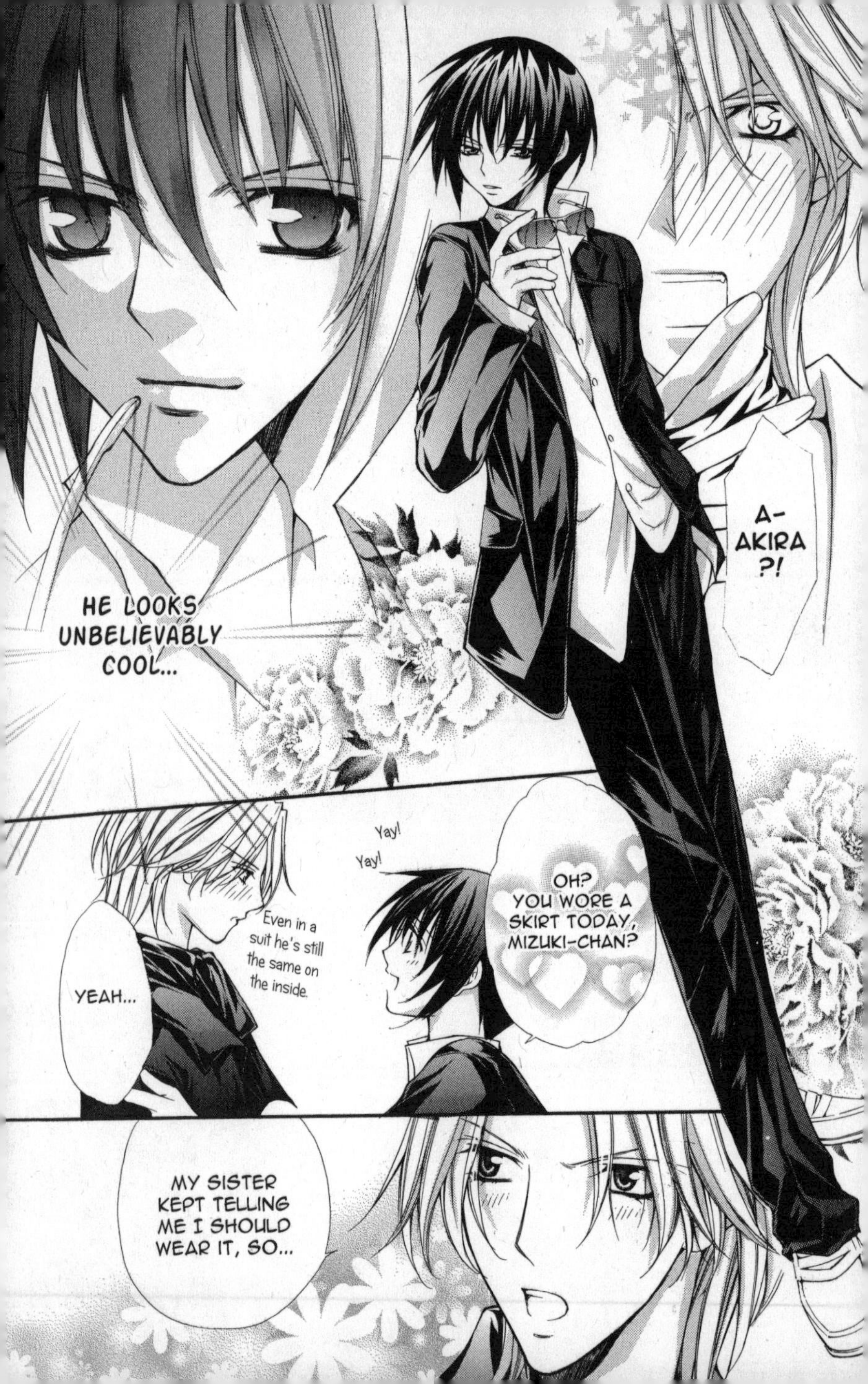
A-AKIRA?!
HE LOOKS UNBELIEVABLY COOL...
OH? YOU WORE A SKIRT TODAY, MIZUKI-CHAN?
Yay!
Yay!
Even in a suit he's still the same on the inside.
YEAH...
MY SISTER KEPT TELLING ME I SHOULD WEAR IT, SO...

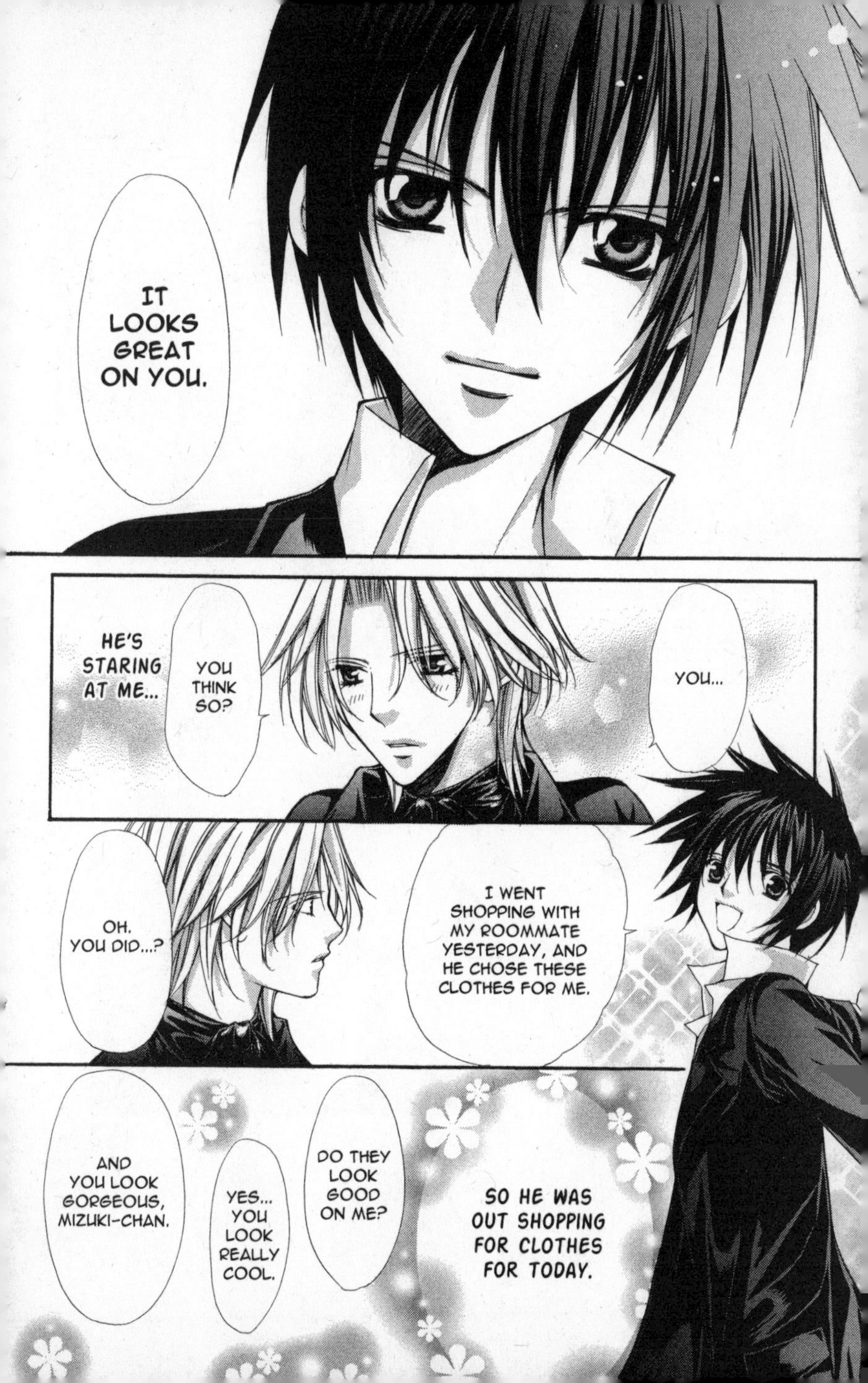
IT LOOKS GREAT ON YOU.
YOU...
YOU THINK SO?
HE'S STARING AT ME...
I WENT SHOPPING WITH MY ROOMMATE YESTERDAY, AND HE CHOSE THESE CLOTHES FOR ME.
OH. YOU DID...?
SO HE WAS OUT SHOPPING FOR CLOTHES FOR TODAY.
DO THEY LOOK GOOD ON ME?
YES... YOU LOOK REALLY COOL.
AND YOU LOOK GORGEOUS, MIZUKI-CHAN.

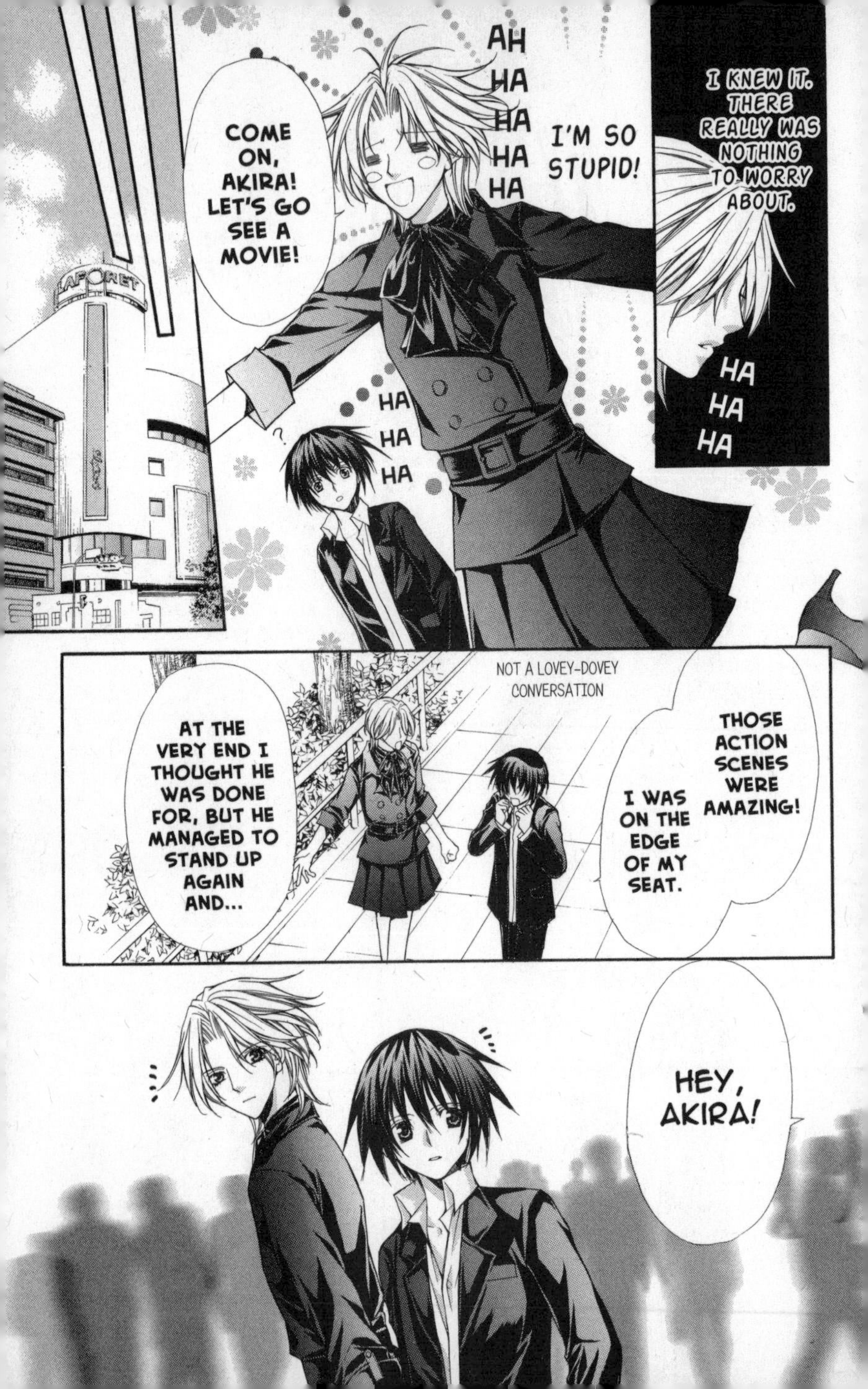
I KNEW IT. THERE REALLY WAS NOTHING TO WORRY ABOUT.
HA HA HA
AH HA HA HA HA
I'M SO STUPID!
COME ON, AKIRA! LET'S GO SEE A MOVIE!
HA HA HA
LAFORET
NOT A LOVEY-DOVEY CONVERSATION
THOSE ACTION SCENES WERE AMAZING!
I WAS ON THE EDGE OF MY SEAT.
AT THE VERY END I THOUGHT HE WAS DONE FOR, BUT HE MANAGED TO STAND UP AGAIN AND...
HEY, AKIRA!

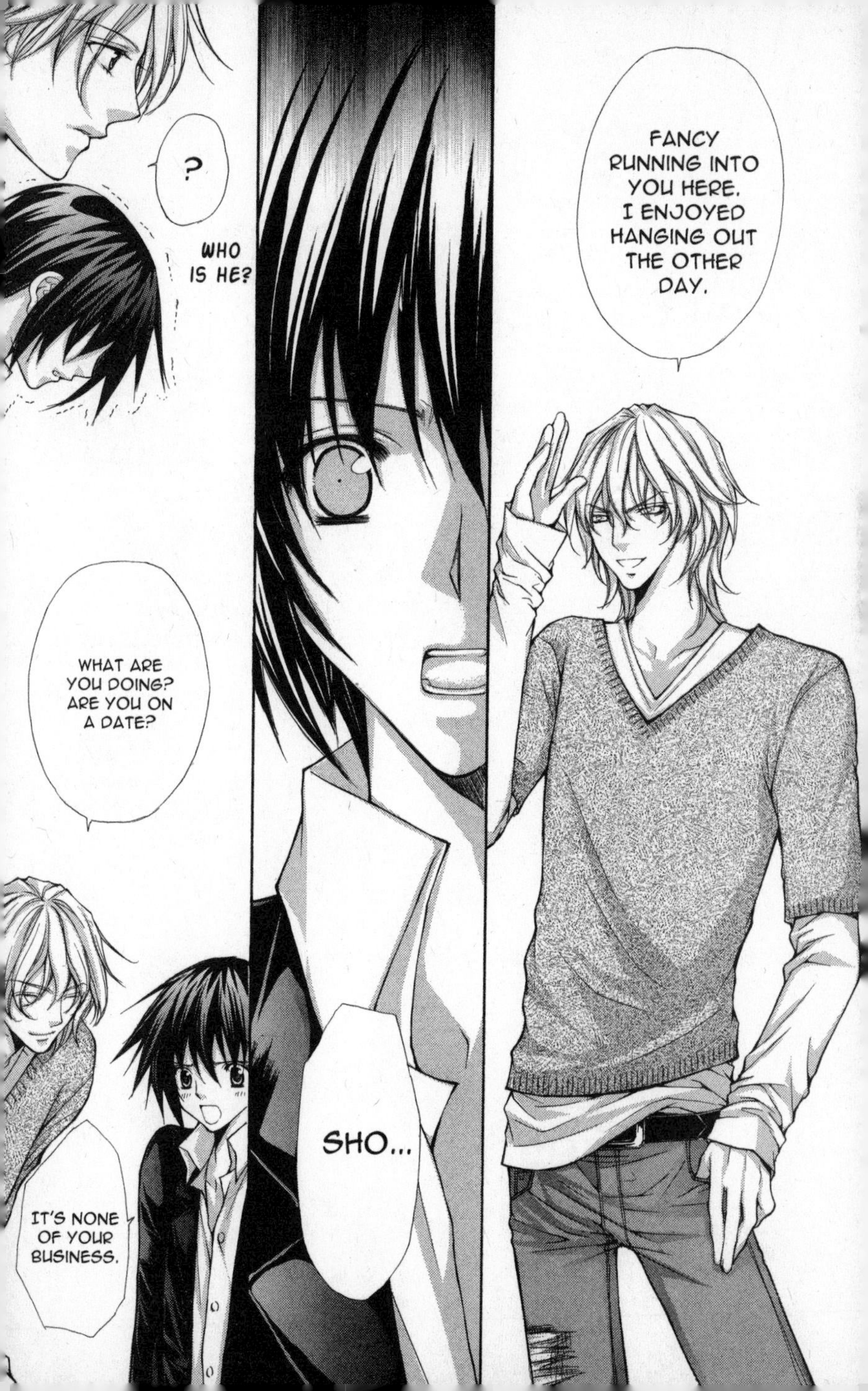
FANCY RUNNING INTO YOU HERE. I ENJOYED HANGING OUT THE OTHER DAY.
SHO...
?
WHO IS HE?
WHAT ARE YOU DOING? ARE YOU ON A DATE?
IT'S NONE OF YOUR BUSINESS.

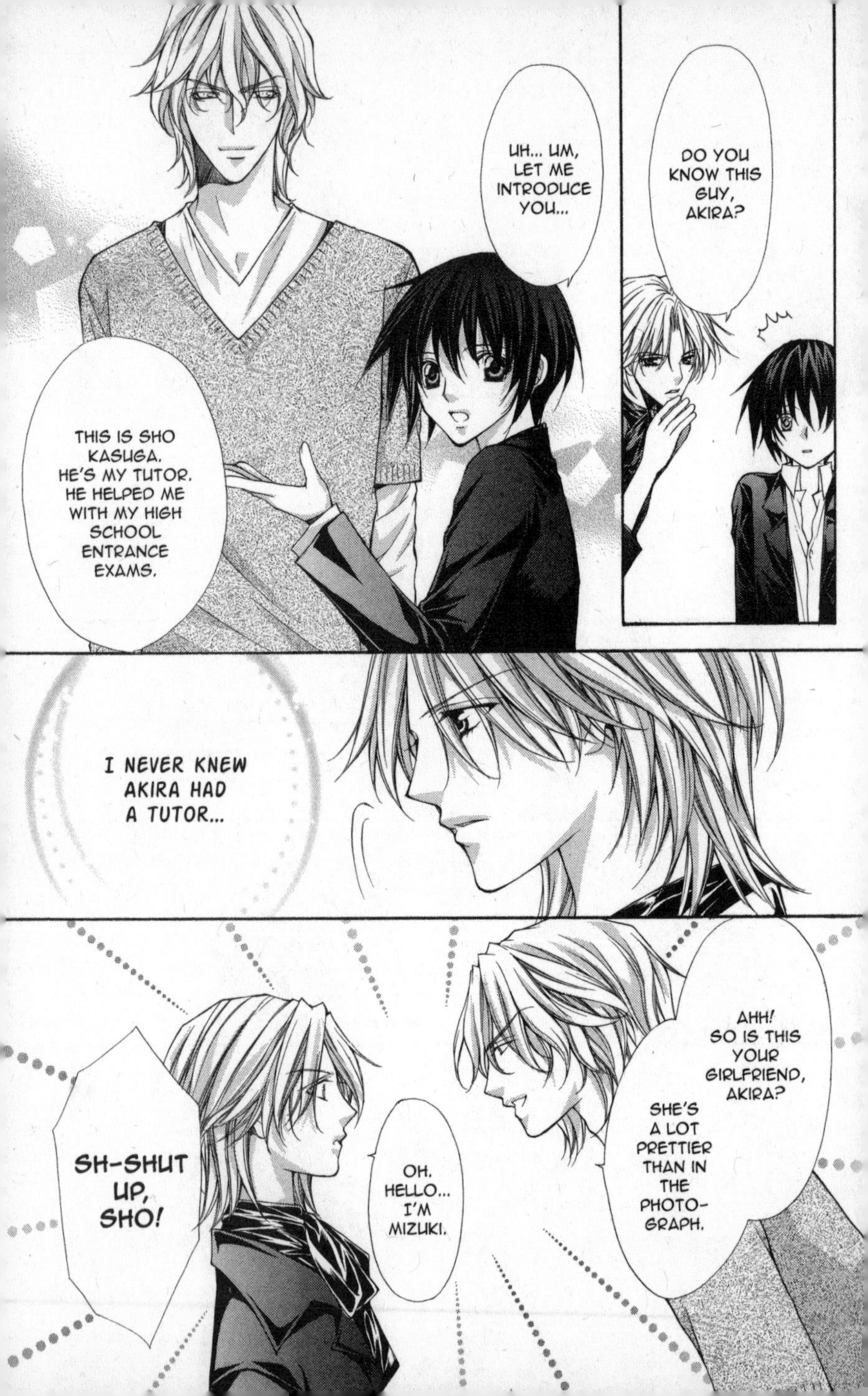
DO YOU KNOW THIS GUY, AKIRA?
UH... UM, LET ME INTRODUCE YOU...
THIS IS SHO KASUGA. HE'S MY TUTOR. HE HELPED ME WITH MY HIGH SCHOOL ENTRANCE EXAMS.
I NEVER KNEW AKIRA HAD A TUTOR...
AHH! SO IS THIS YOUR GIRLFRIEND, AKIRA?
SHE'S A LOT PRETTIER THAN IN THE PHOTOGRAPH.
OH. HELLO... I'M MIZUKI.
SH-SHUT UP, SHO!

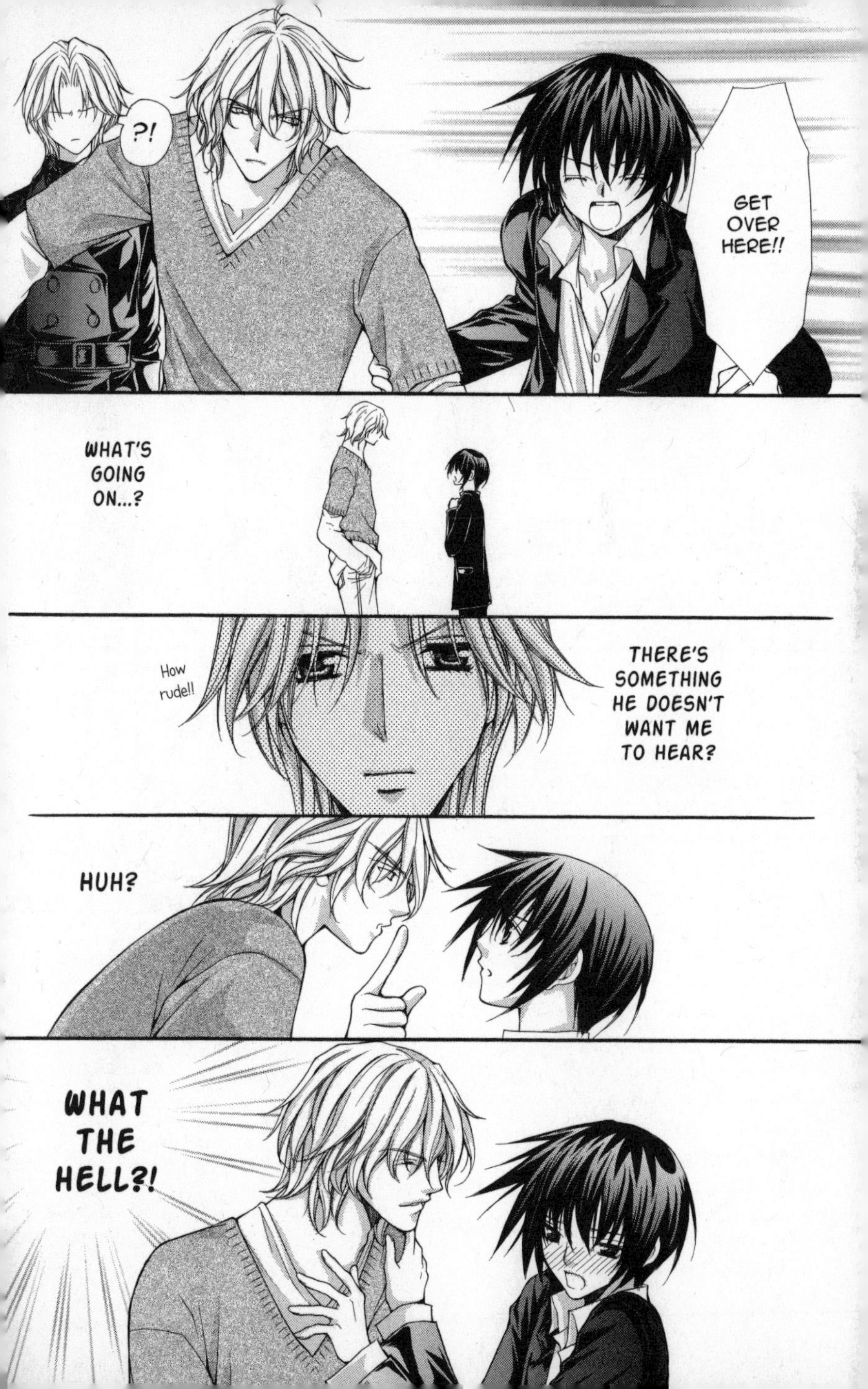
GET OVER HERE!!
?!
WHAT'S GOING ON...?
THERE'S SOMETHING HE DOESN'T WANT ME TO HEAR?
How rude!!
HUH?
WHAT THE HELL?!

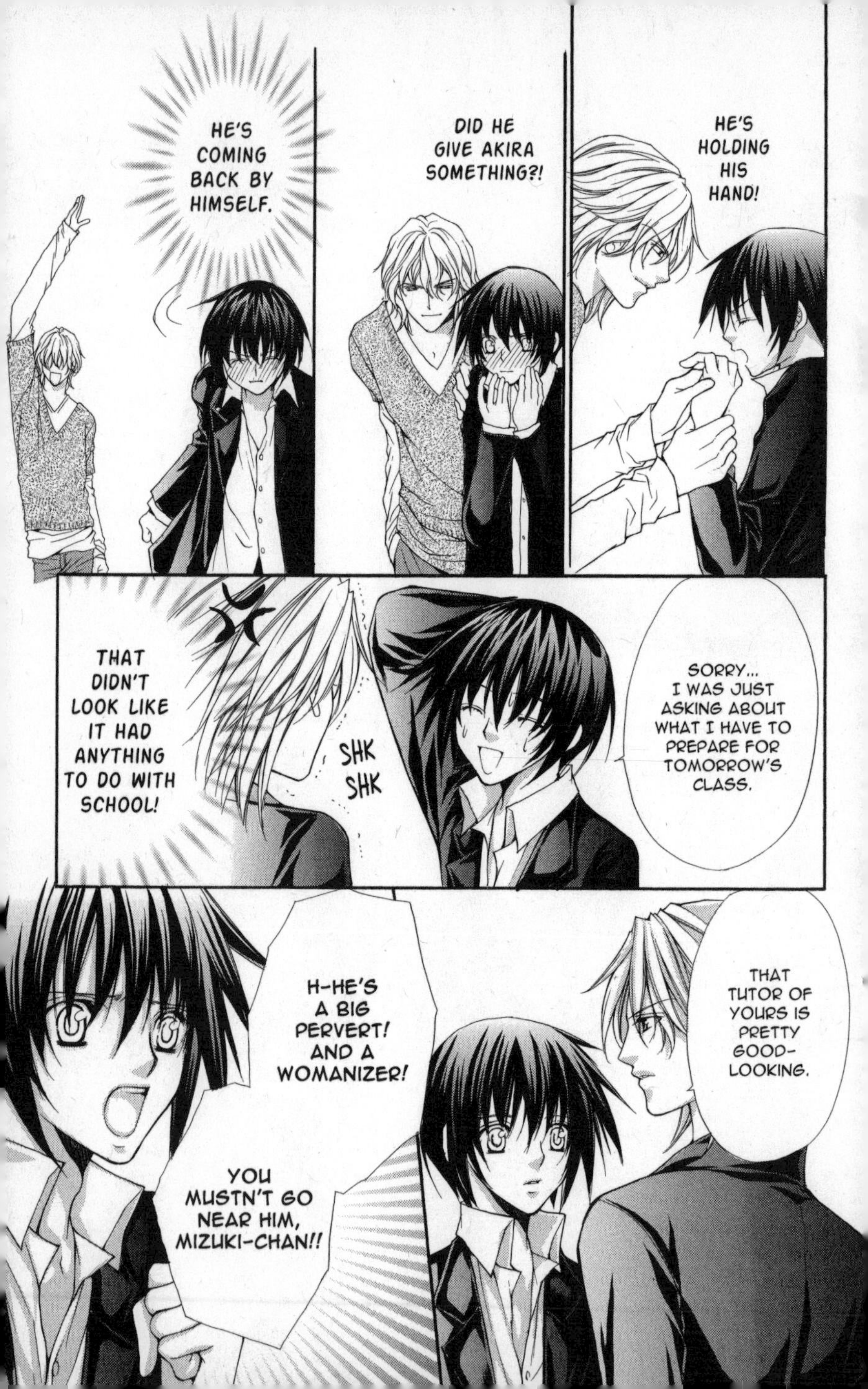
HE'S HOLDING HIS HAND!
DID HE GIVE AKIRA SOMETHING?!
HE'S COMING BACK BY HIMSELF.
SORRY... I WAS JUST ASKING ABOUT WHAT I HAVE TO PREPARE FOR TOMORROW'S CLASS.
SHK SHK
THAT DIDN'T LOOK LIKE IT HAD ANYTHING TO DO WITH SCHOOL!
THAT TUTOR OF YOURS IS PRETTY GOOD-LOOKING.
H-HE'S A BIG PERVERT! AND A WOMANIZER!
YOU MUSTN'T GO NEAR HIM, MIZUKI-CHAN!!

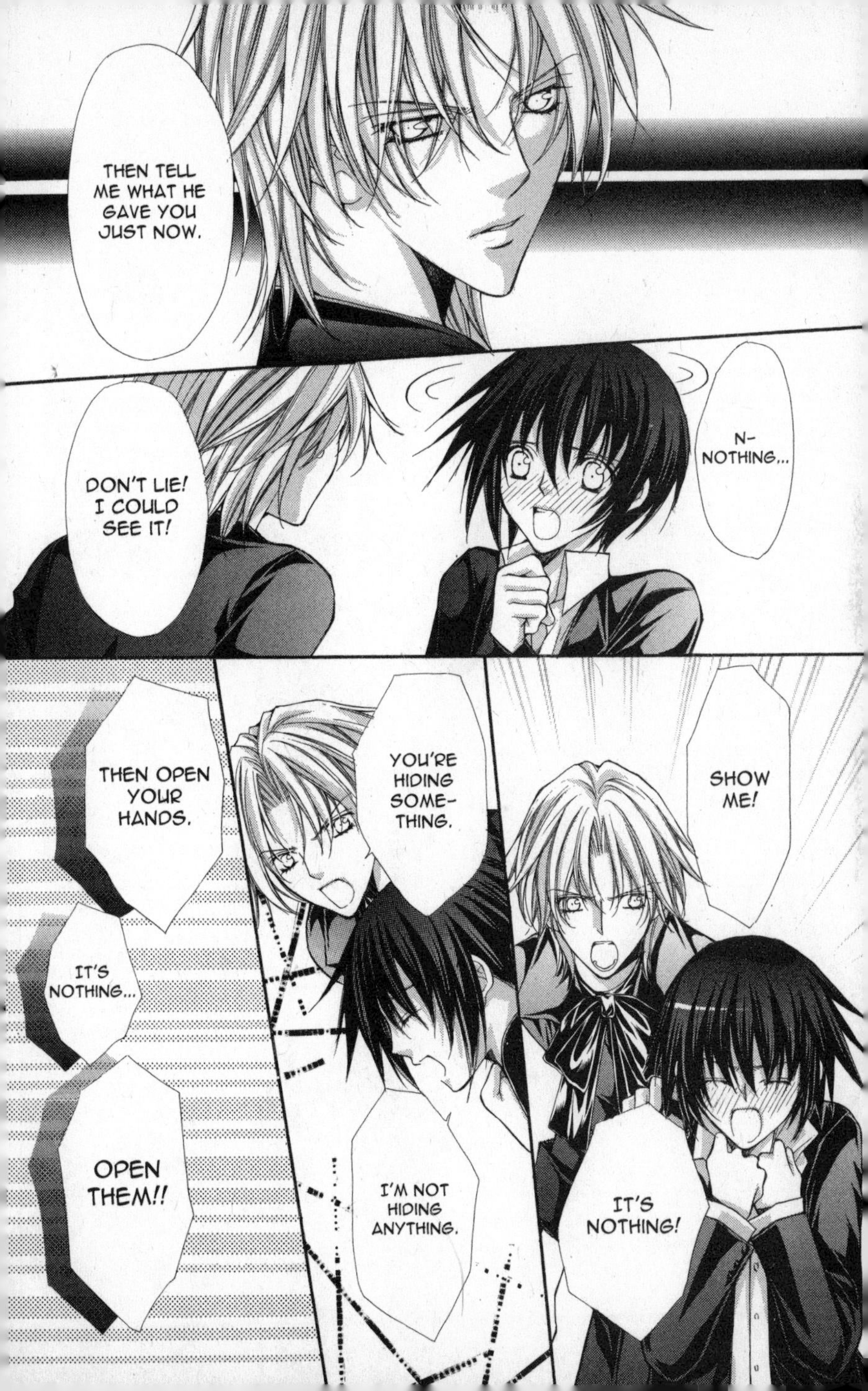
THEN TELL ME WHAT HE GAVE YOU JUST NOW.
N-NOTHING...
DON'T LIE! I COULD SEE IT!
SHOW ME!
IT'S NOTHING!
YOU'RE HIDING SOME-THING.
I'M NOT HIDING ANYTHING.
THEN OPEN YOUR HANDS.
IT'S NOTHING...
OPEN THEM!!

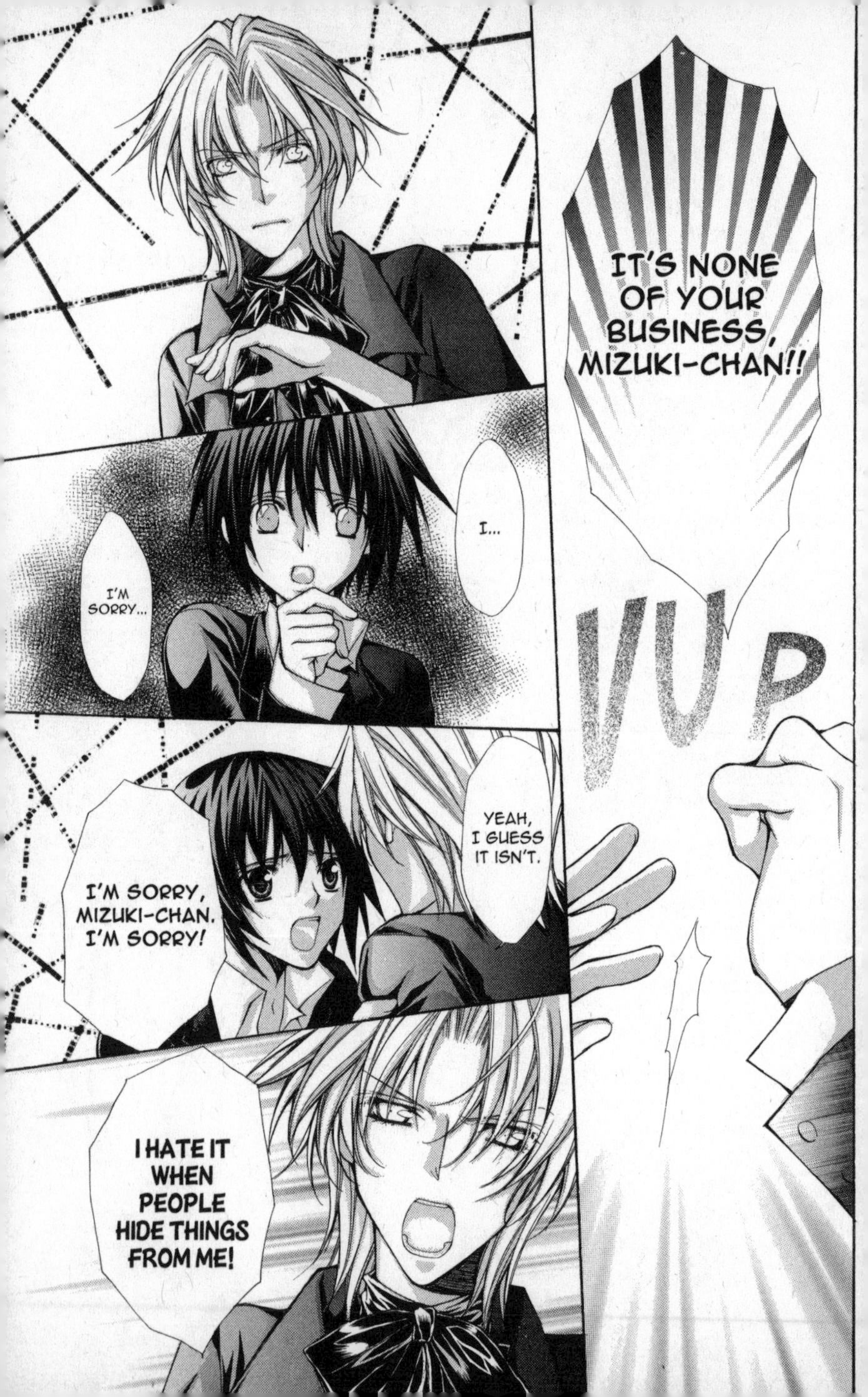
IT'S NONE OF YOUR BUSINESS, MIZUKI-CHAN!!
VUP
I...
I'M SORRY...
YEAH, I GUESS IT ISN'T.
I'M SORRY, MIZUKI-CHAN. I'M SORRY!
I HATE IT WHEN PEOPLE HIDE THINGS FROM ME!

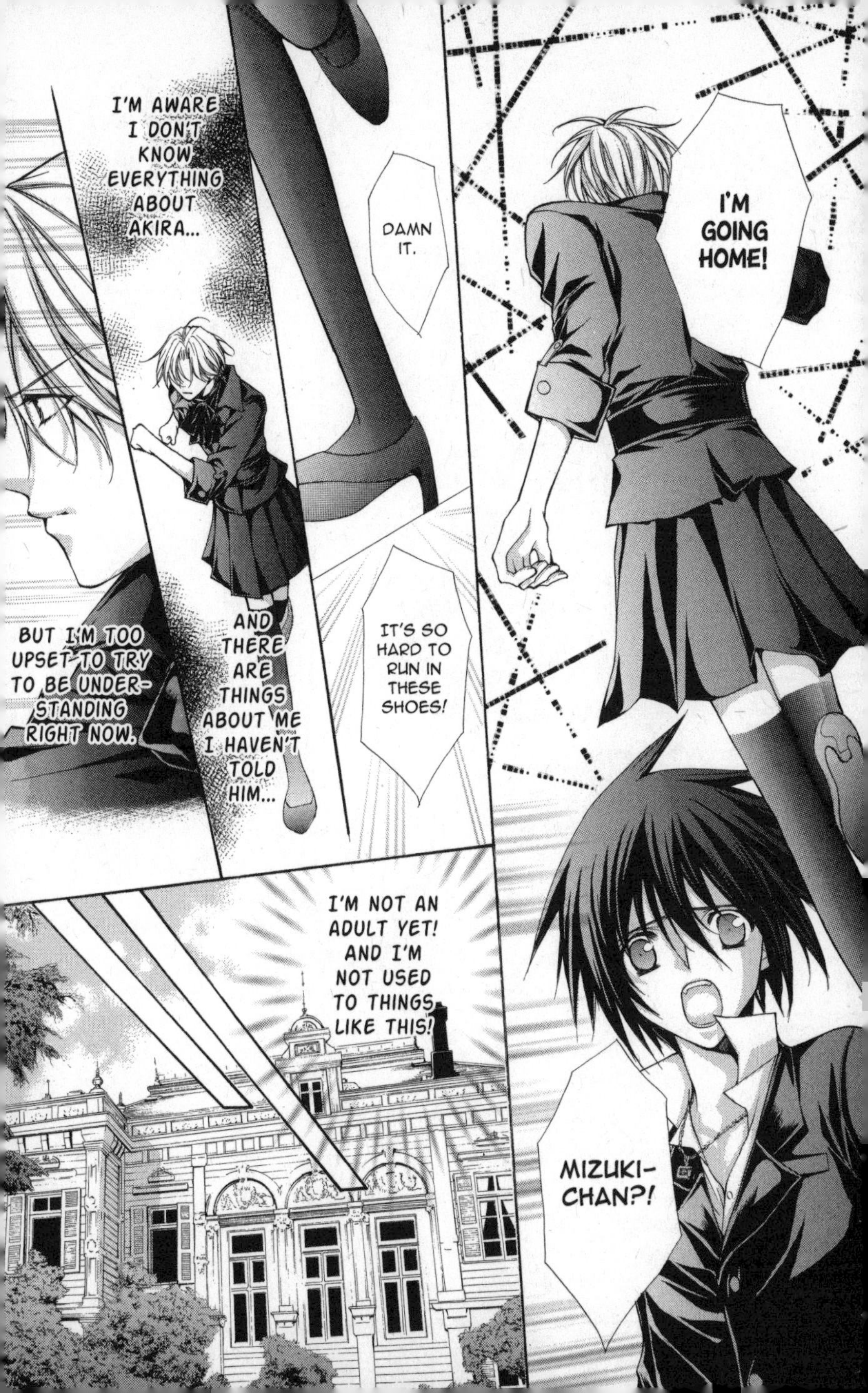
I'M GOING HOME!
DAMN IT.
IT'S SO HARD TO RUN IN THESE SHOES!
I'M AWARE I DON'T KNOW EVERYTHING ABOUT AKIRA...
AND THERE ARE THINGS ABOUT ME I HAVEN'T TOLD HIM...
BUT I'M TOO UPSET TO TRY TO BE UNDER-STANDING RIGHT NOW.
MIZUKI-CHAN?!
I'M NOT AN ADULT YET! AND I'M NOT USED TO THINGS LIKE THIS!

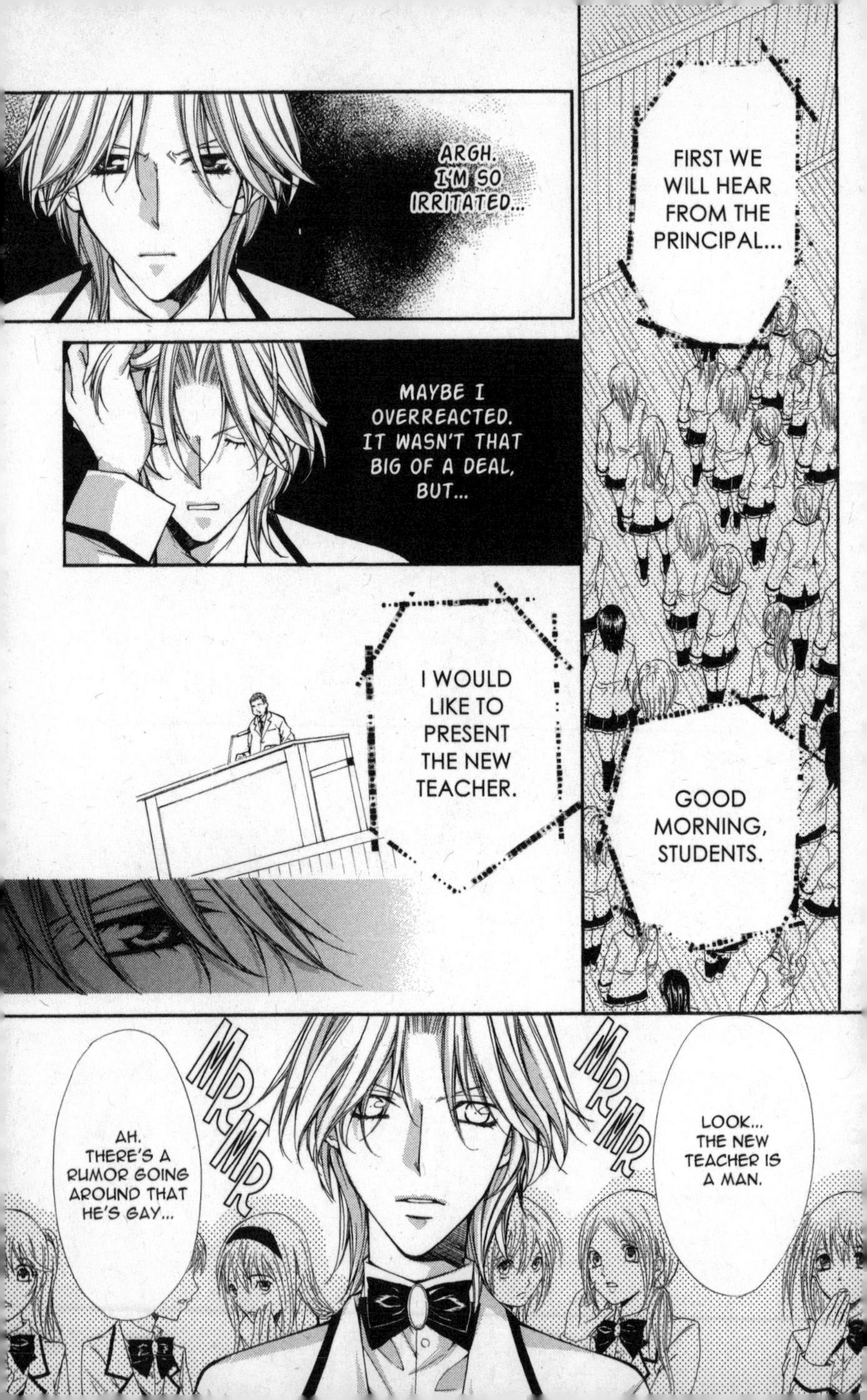

FIRST WE WILL HEAR FROM THE PRINCIPAL...
GOOD MORNING, STUDENTS.
ARGH. I'M SO IRRITATED...
MAYBE I OVERREACTED. IT WASN'T THAT BIG OF A DEAL, BUT...
I WOULD LIKE TO PRESENT THE NEW TEACHER.
LOOK... THE NEW TEACHER IS A MAN.
MRMR
AH. THERE'S A RUMOR GOING AROUND THAT HE'S GAY...
MRMR

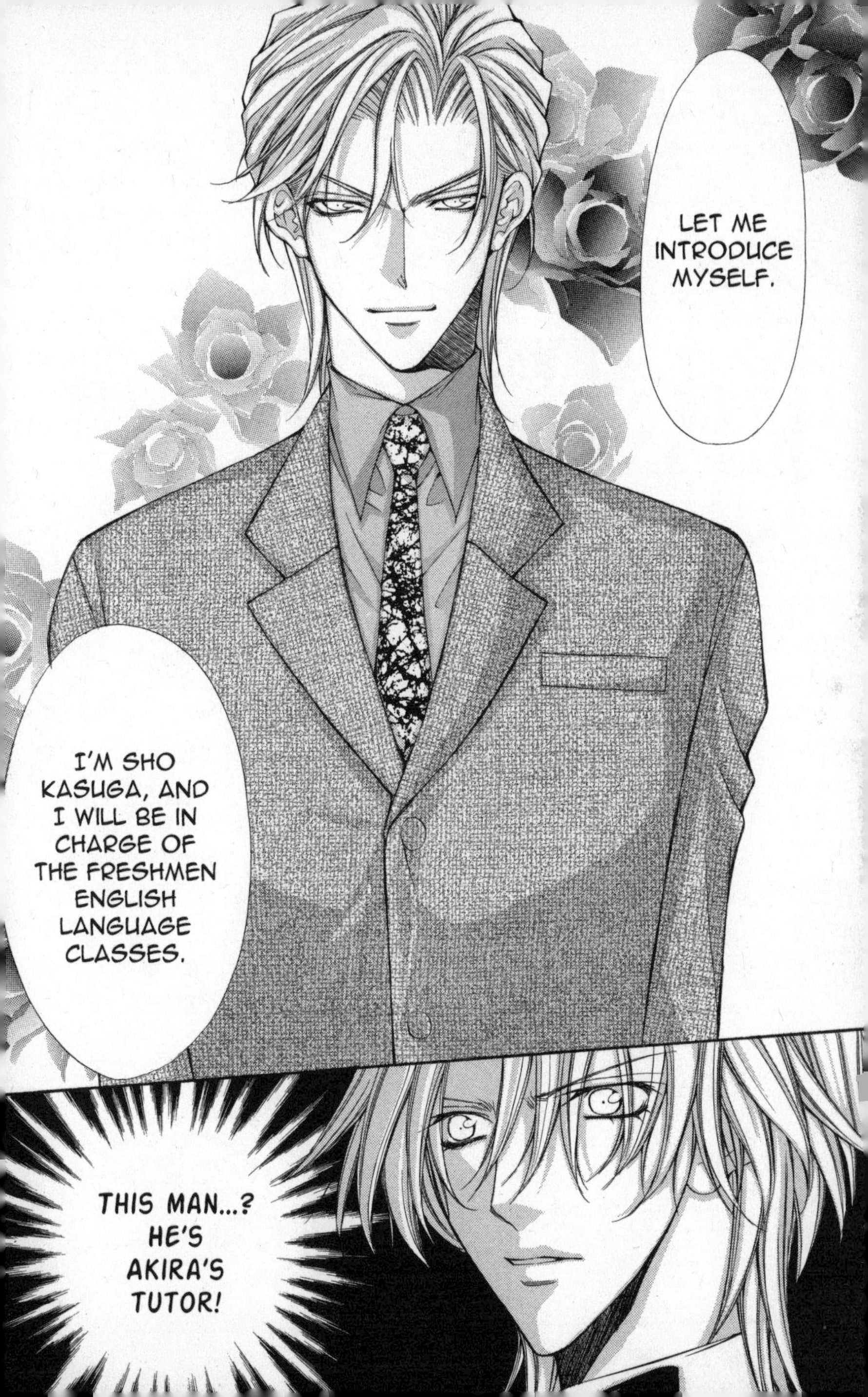
LET ME INTRODUCE MYSELF.
I'M SHO KASUGA, AND I WILL BE IN CHARGE OF THE FRESHMEN ENGLISH LANGUAGE CLASSES.
THIS MAN...? HE'S AKIRA'S TUTOR!

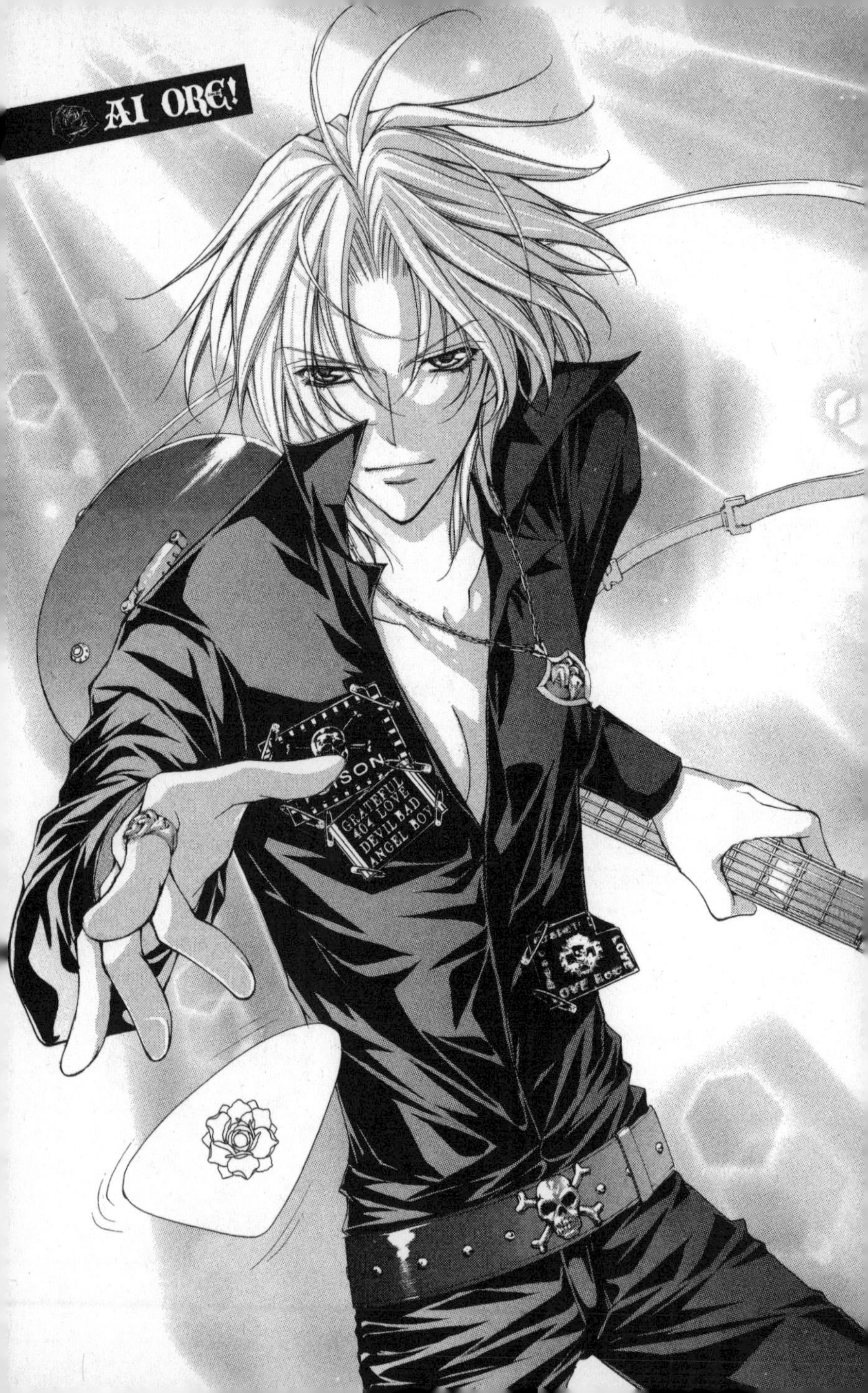
AI ORE!
GRATEFUL
404 LOVE
DEVIL BAD
ANGEL BOY
LOVE

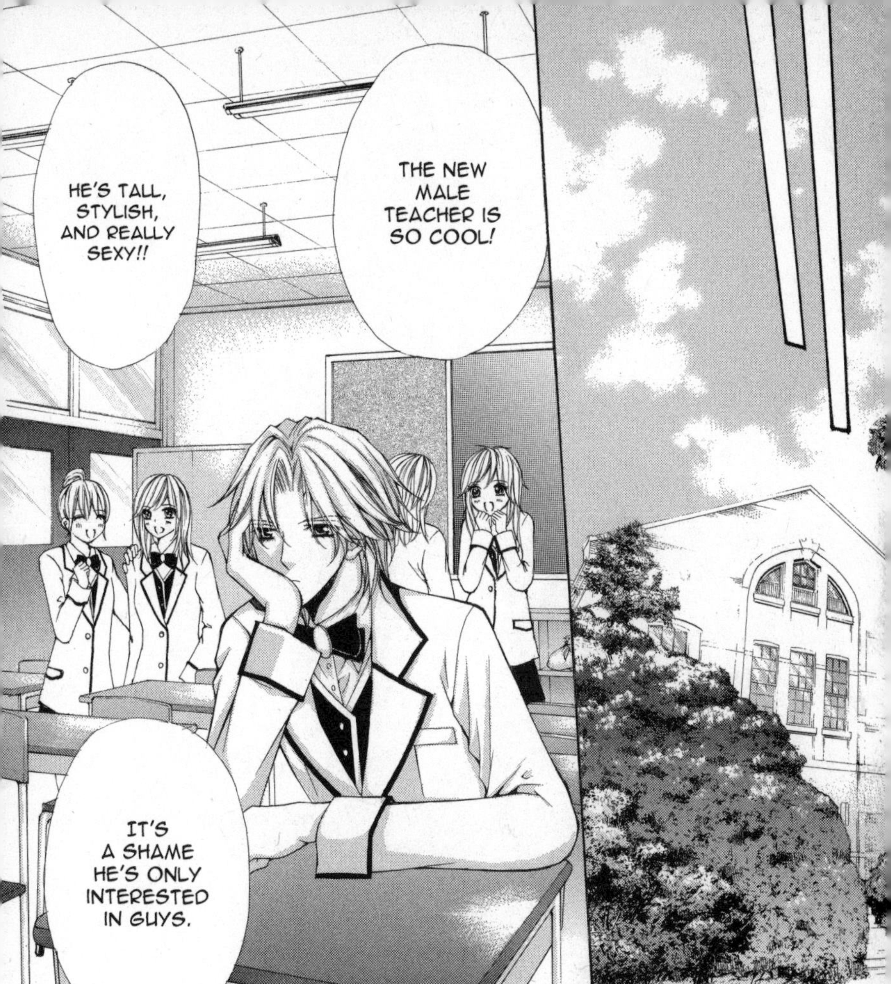
THE NEW MALE TEACHER IS SO COOL!
HE'S TALL, STYLISH, AND REALLY SEXY!!
IT'S A SHAME HE'S ONLY INTERESTED IN GUYS.

About Bambi

We all love Bambi-chan!! (laugh) I created this character from the name first. I just had to name him "Banbi," so I made his first name "Kojiro" to make it sound manly in comparison to "Banbi." I have a feeling that Bambi-chan is probably going to become a mother figure to Akira. (laugh) I really want to draw a chapter about Bambi-chan being extremely angry one day. But it probably wouldn't happen unless Akira went through something very serious, so it's difficult...

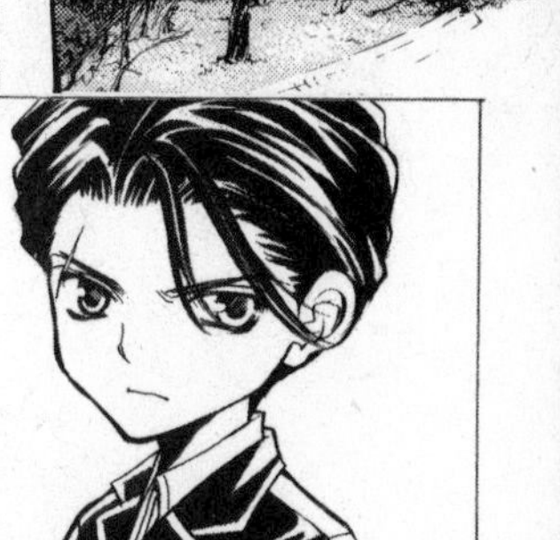

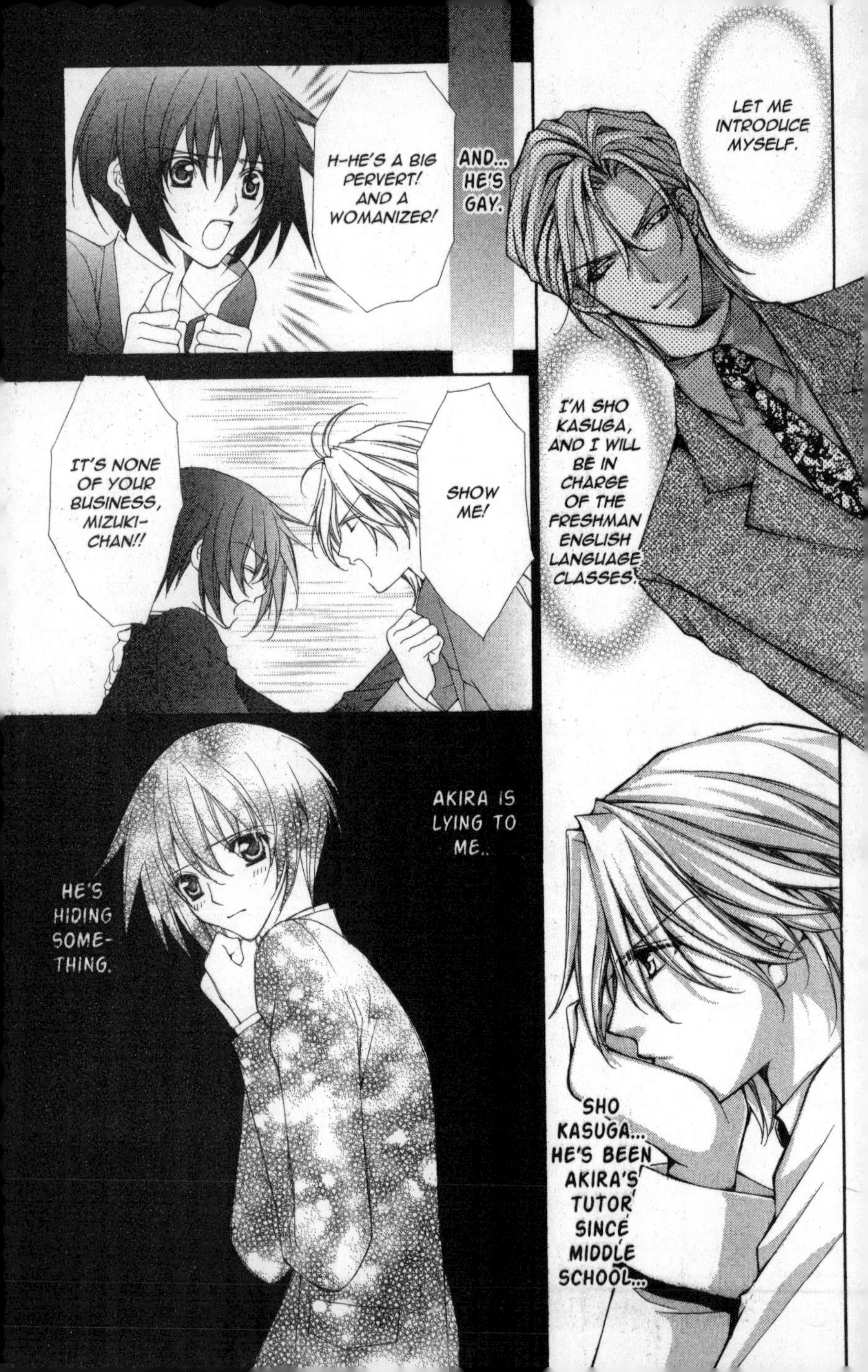
LET ME INTRODUCE MYSELF.
I'M SHO KASUGA, AND I WILL BE IN CHARGE OF THE FRESHMAN ENGLISH LANGUAGE CLASSES.
H-HE'S A BIG PERVERT! AND A WOMANIZER!
AND... HE'S GAY.
SHOW ME!
IT'S NONE OF YOUR BUSINESS, MIZUKI-CHAN!!
SHO KASUGA... HE'S BEEN AKIRA'S TUTOR SINCE MIDDLE SCHOOL...
AKIRA IS LYING TO ME..
HE'S HIDING SOME-THING.

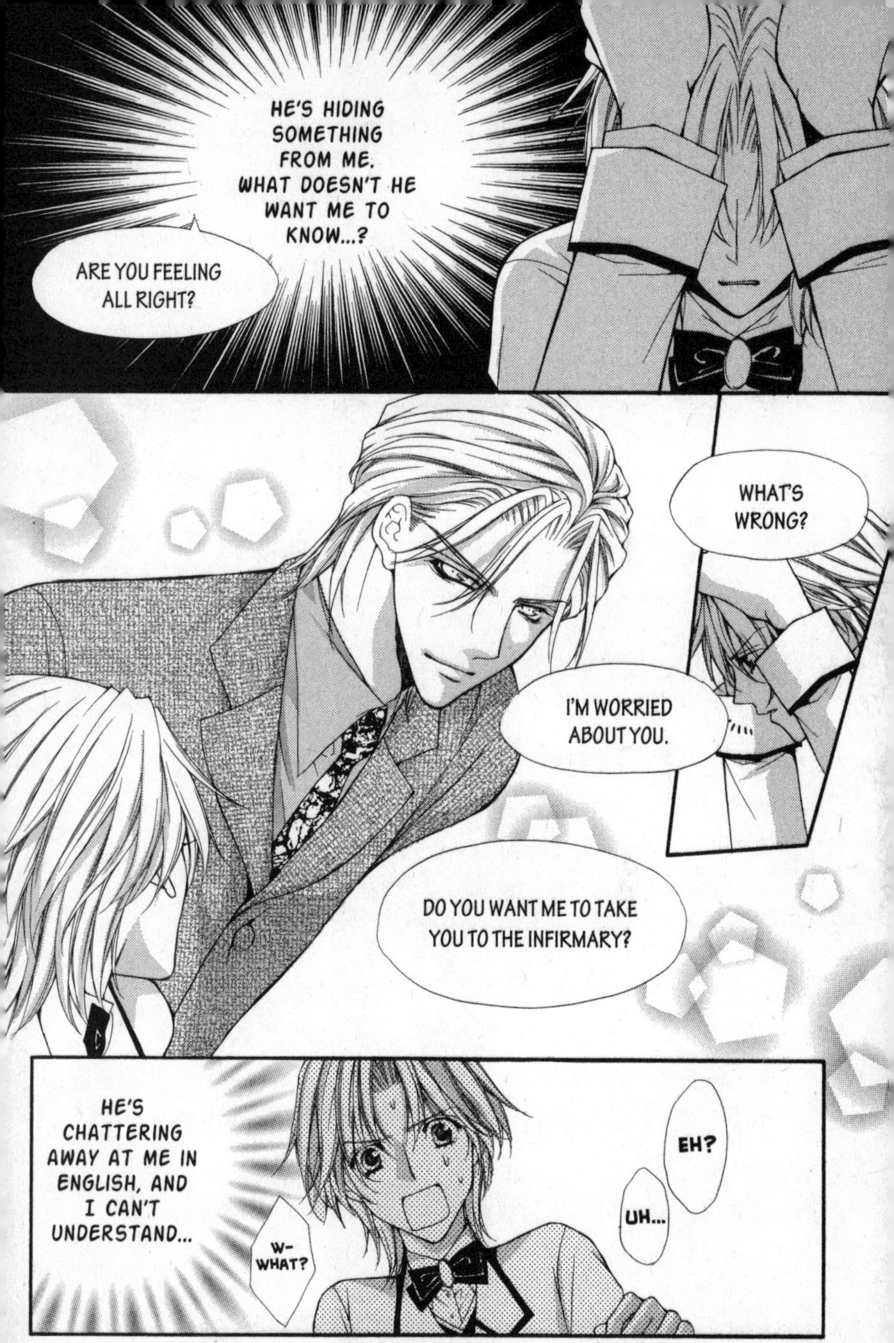
HE'S HIDING SOMETHING FROM ME. WHAT DOESN'T HE WANT ME TO KNOW...?
ARE YOU FEELING ALL RIGHT?
WHAT'S WRONG?
I'M WORRIED ABOUT YOU.
DO YOU WANT ME TO TAKE YOU TO THE INFIRMARY?
EH?
UH...
W-WHAT?
HE'S CHATTERING AWAY AT ME IN ENGLISH, AND I CAN'T UNDERSTAND...

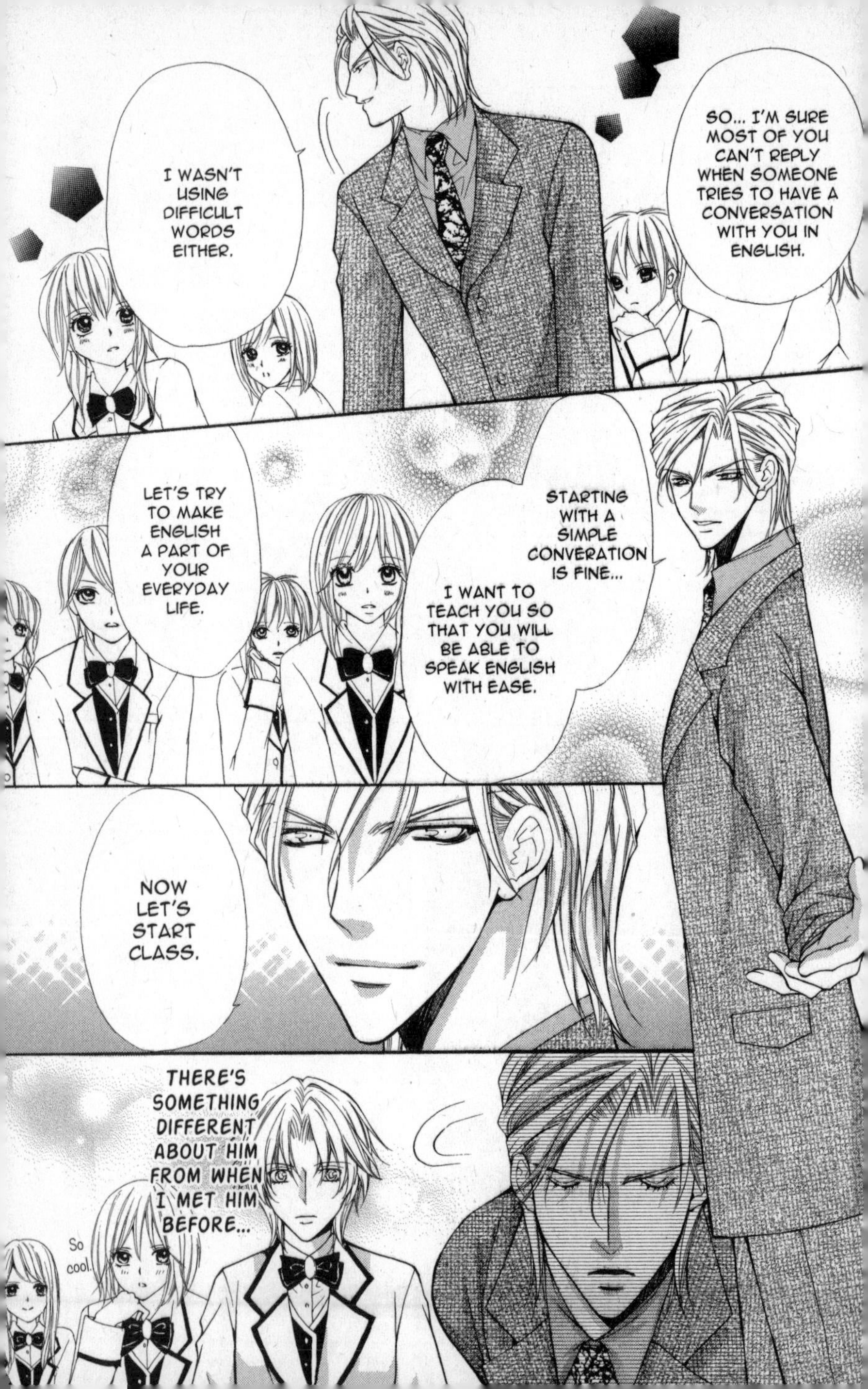
SO... I'M SURE MOST OF YOU CAN'T REPLY WHEN SOMEONE TRIES TO HAVE A CONVERSATION WITH YOU IN ENGLISH.
I WASN'T USING DIFFICULT WORDS EITHER.
STARTING WITH A SIMPLE CONVERATION IS FINE...
I WANT TO TEACH YOU SO THAT YOU WILL BE ABLE TO SPEAK ENGLISH WITH EASE.
LET'S TRY TO MAKE ENGLISH A PART OF YOUR EVERYDAY LIFE.
NOW LET'S START CLASS.
THERE'S SOMETHING DIFFERENT ABOUT HIM FROM WHEN I MET HIM BEFORE...
So cool.

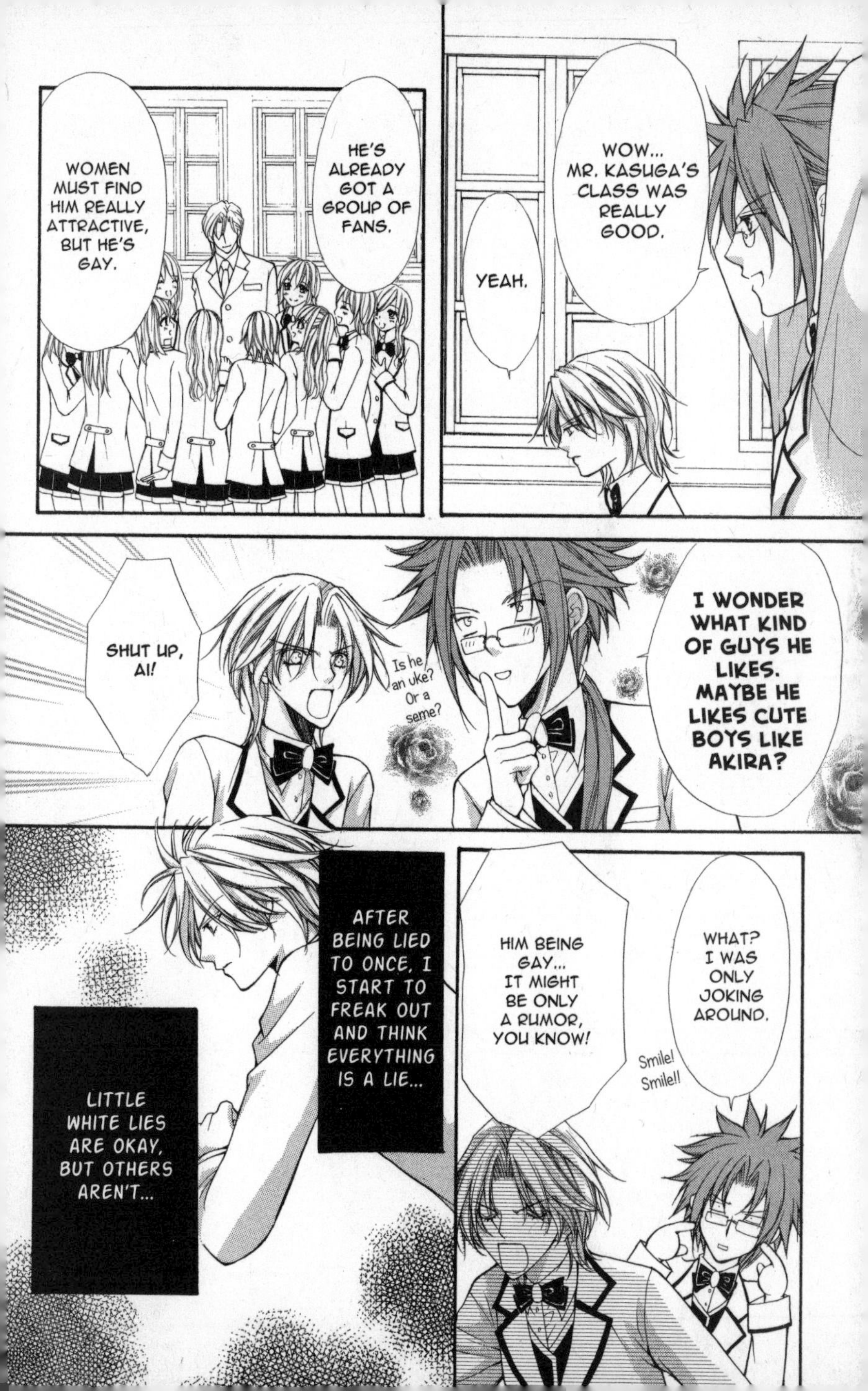
WOW... MR. KASUGA'S CLASS WAS REALLY GOOD.
YEAH.
HE'S ALREADY GOT A GROUP OF FANS.
WOMEN MUST FIND HIM REALLY ATTRACTIVE, BUT HE'S GAY.
I WONDER WHAT KIND OF GUYS HE LIKES. MAYBE HE LIKES CUTE BOYS LIKE AKIRA?
Is he an uke? Or a seme?
SHUT UP, AI!
WHAT? I WAS ONLY JOKING AROUND.
Smile! Smile!!
HIM BEING GAY... IT MIGHT BE ONLY A RUMOR, YOU KNOW!
AFTER BEING LIED TO ONCE, I START TO FREAK OUT AND THINK EVERYTHING IS A LIE...
LITTLE WHITE LIES ARE OKAY, BUT OTHERS AREN'T...

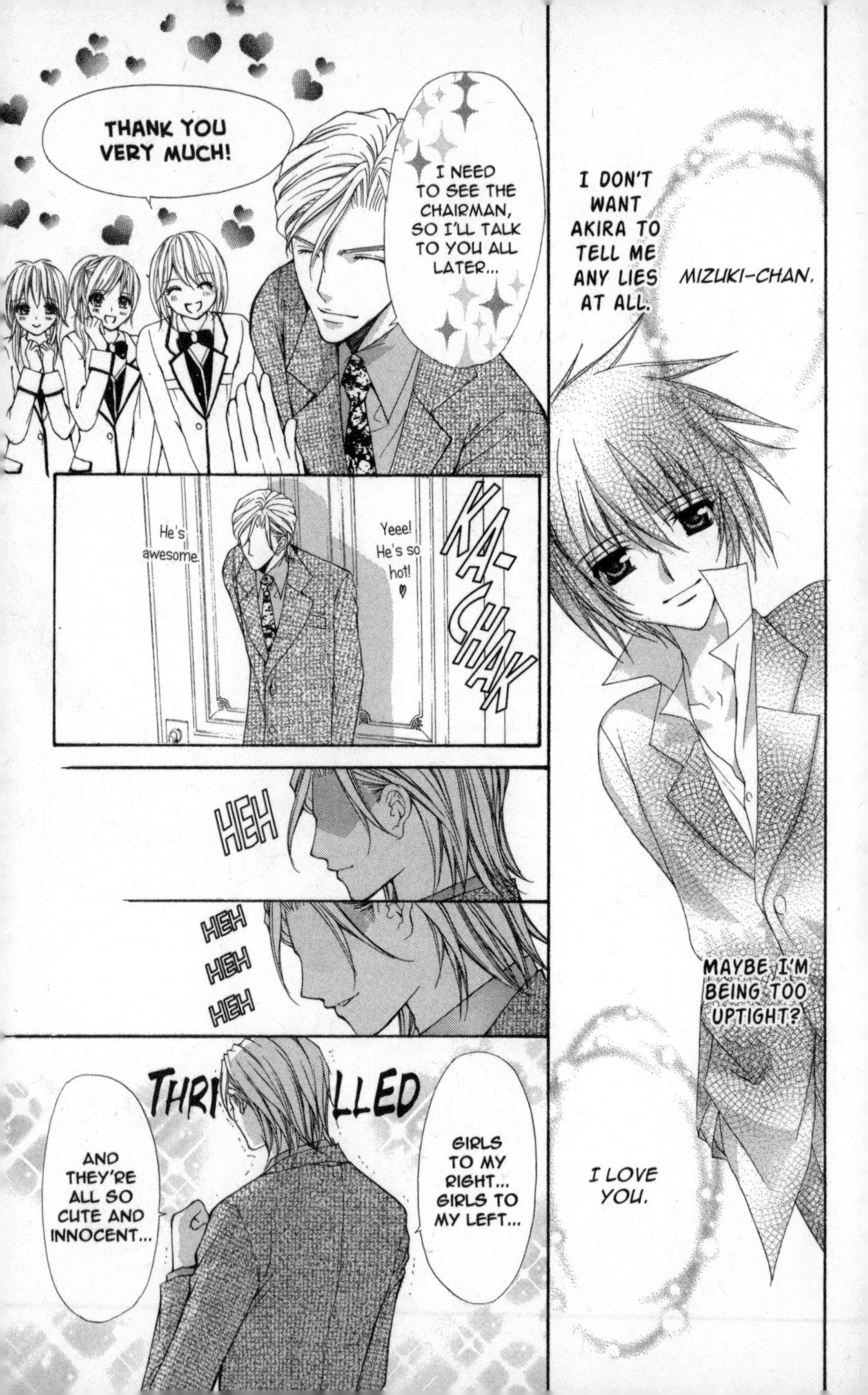
MIZUKI-CHAN.
I DON'T WANT AKIRA TO TELL ME ANY LIES AT ALL.
MAYBE I'M BEING TOO UPTIGHT?
I LOVE YOU.
I NEED TO SEE THE CHAIRMAN, SO I'LL TALK TO YOU ALL LATER...
THANK YOU VERY MUCH!
KA-CHAK
Yeee! He's so hot! ♡
He's awesome.
HEH
HEH HEH HEH
THRILLED
GIRLS TO MY RIGHT... GIRLS TO MY LEFT...
AND THEY'RE ALL SO CUTE AND INNOCENT...

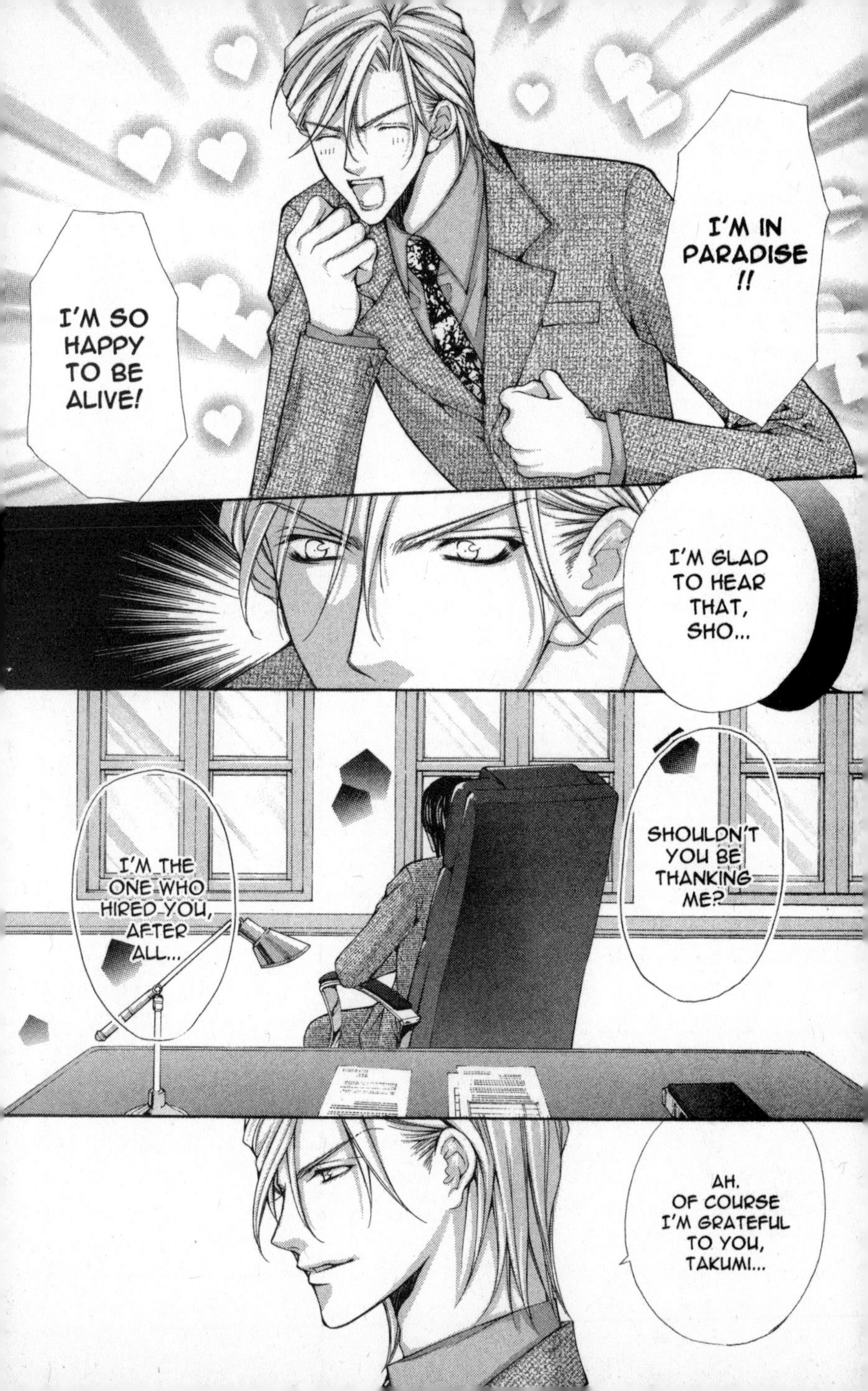
I'M IN PARADISE !!
I'M SO HAPPY TO BE ALIVE!
I'M GLAD TO HEAR THAT, SHO...
SHOULDN'T YOU BE THANKING ME?
I'M THE ONE WHO HIRED YOU, AFTER ALL...
AH. OF COURSE I'M GRATEFUL TO YOU, TAKUMI...

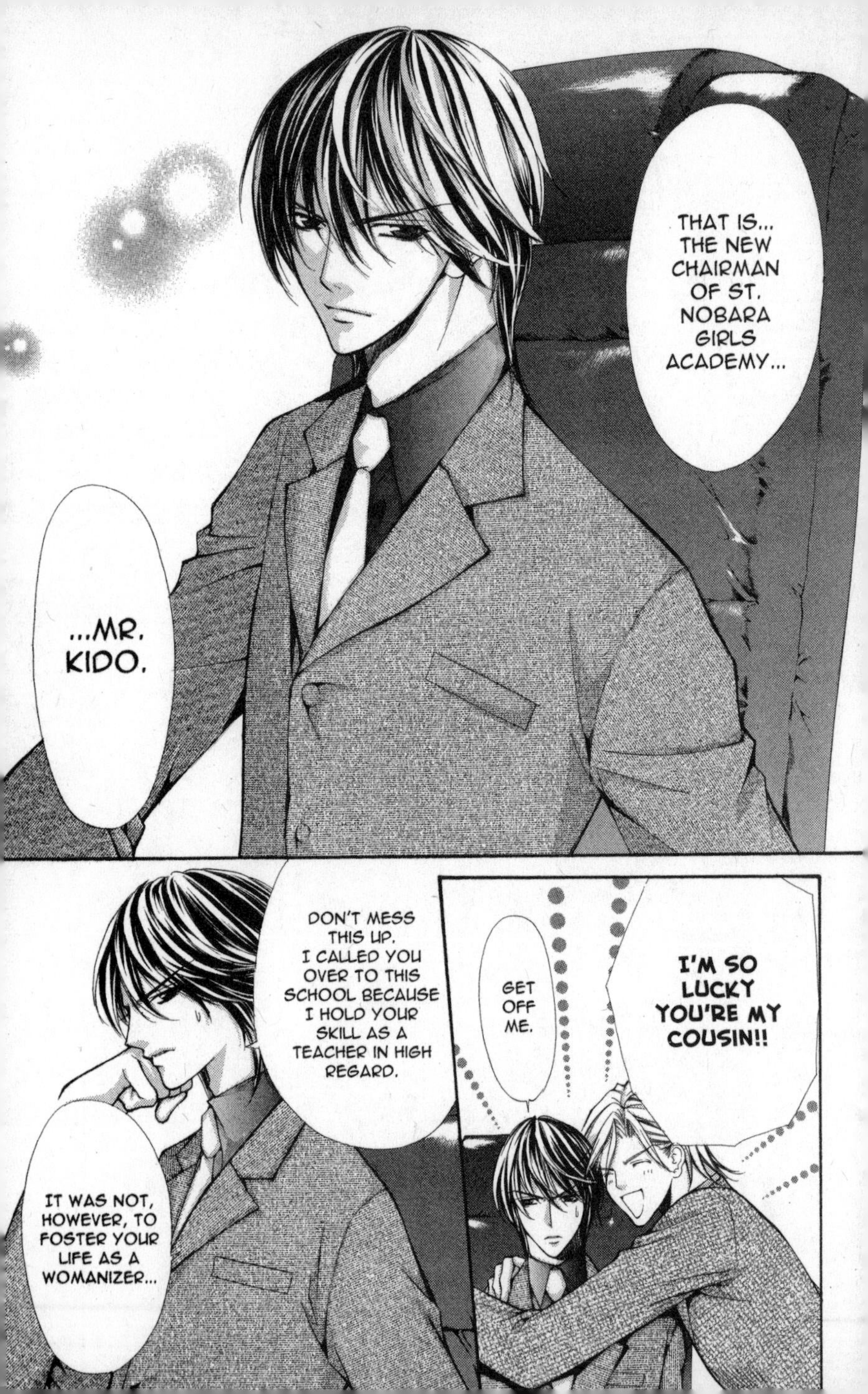
THAT IS... THE NEW CHAIRMAN OF ST. NOBARA GIRLS ACADEMY...
...MR. KIDO.
I'M SO LUCKY YOU'RE MY COUSIN!!
GET OFF ME.
DON'T MESS THIS UP. I CALLED YOU OVER TO THIS SCHOOL BECAUSE I HOLD YOUR SKILL AS A TEACHER IN HIGH REGARD.
IT WAS NOT, HOWEVER, TO FOSTER YOUR LIFE AS A WOMANIZER...

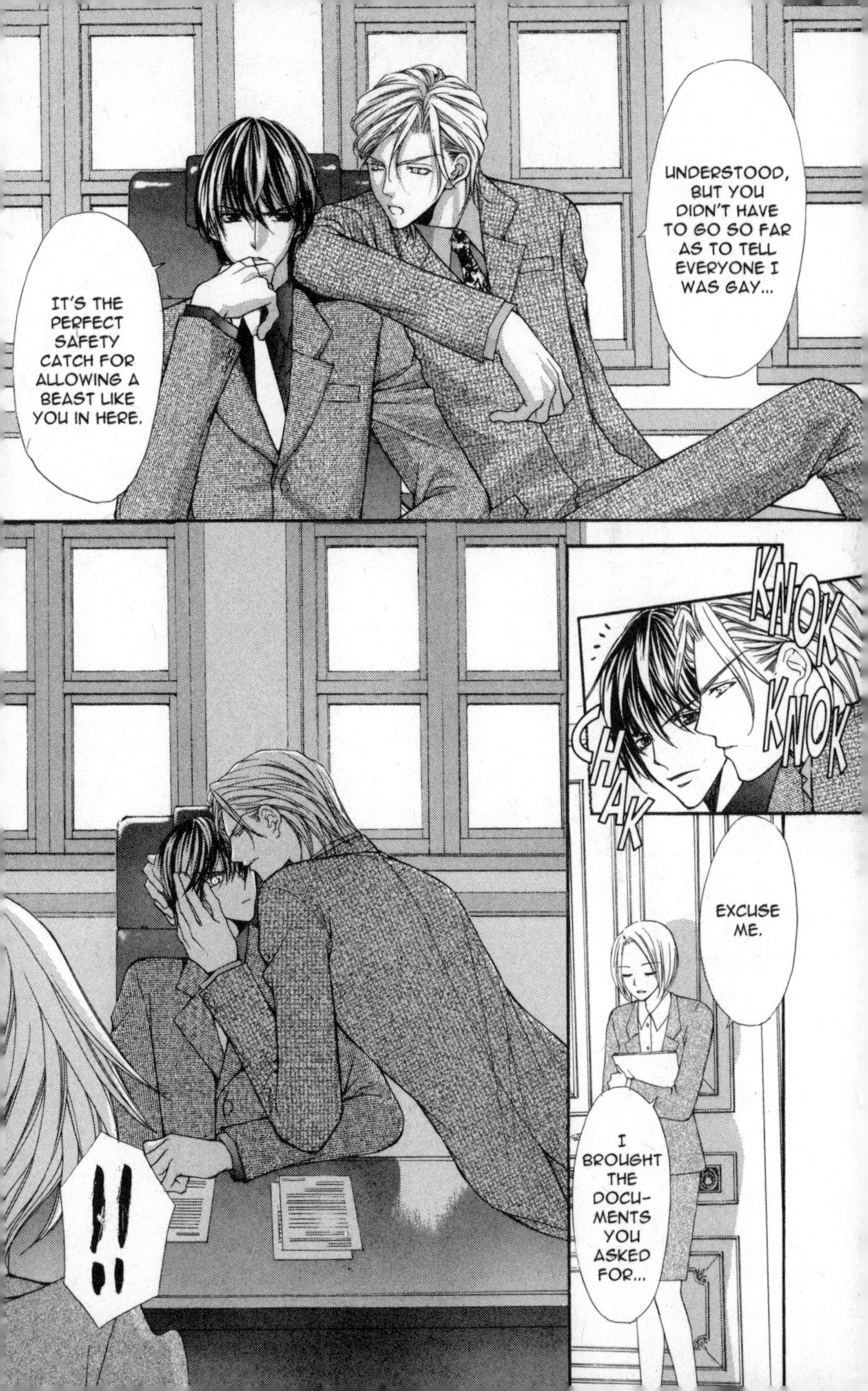
UNDERSTOOD, BUT YOU DIDN'T HAVE TO GO SO FAR AS TO TELL EVERYONE I WAS GAY...
IT'S THE PERFECT SAFETY CATCH FOR ALLOWING A BEAST LIKE YOU IN HERE.
KNOK KNOK
CHAK
EXCUSE ME.
I BROUGHT THE DOCU-MENTS YOU ASKED FOR...
!!

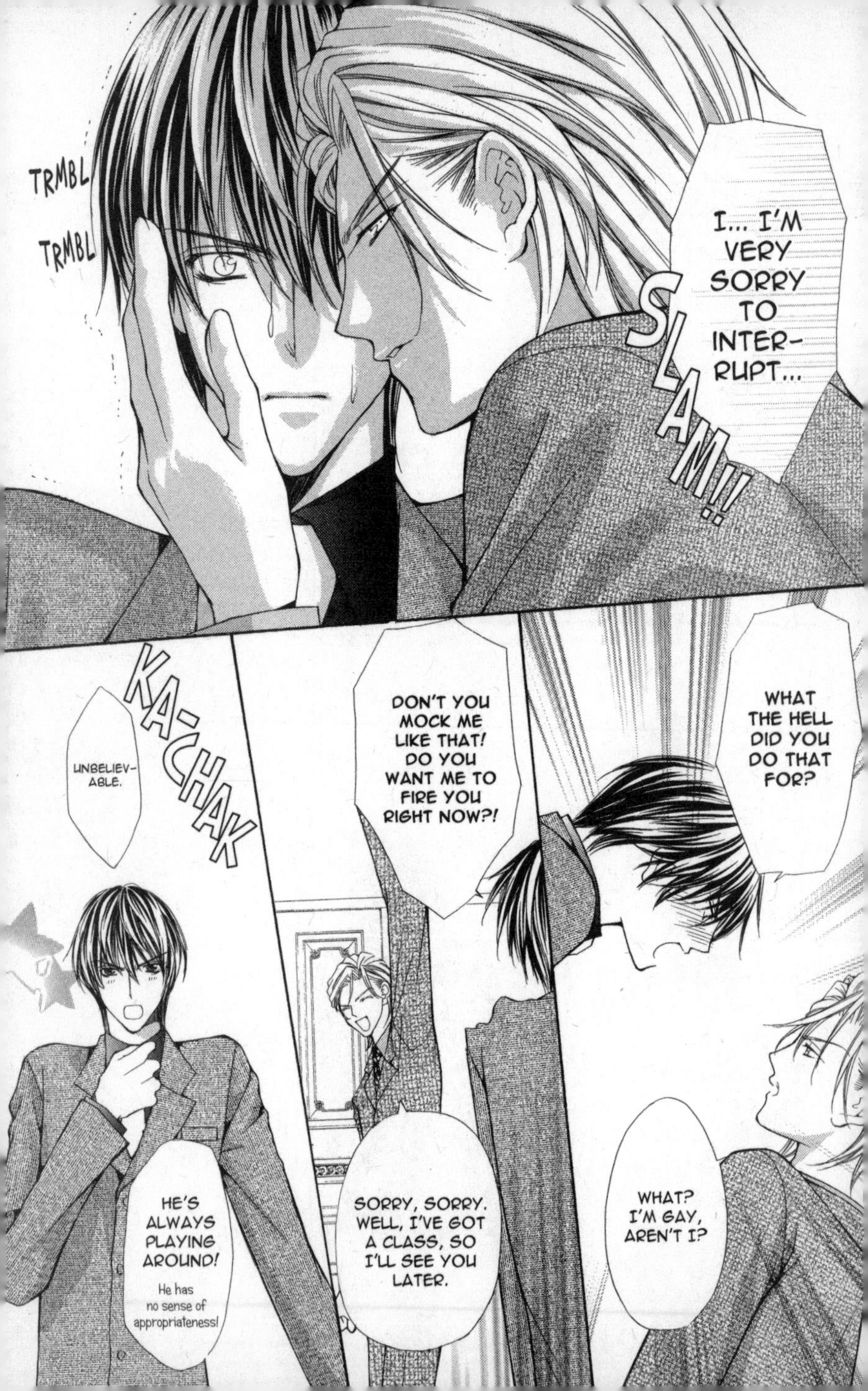
I... I'M VERY SORRY TO INTERRUPT...
SLAM!!
TRMBL
TRMBL
WHAT THE HELL DID YOU DO THAT FOR?
WHAT? I'M GAY, AREN'T I?
DON'T YOU MOCK ME LIKE THAT! DO YOU WANT ME TO FIRE YOU RIGHT NOW?!
SORRY, SORRY. WELL, I'VE GOT A CLASS, SO I'LL SEE YOU LATER.
KA-CHAK
UNBELIEVABLE.
HE'S ALWAYS PLAYING AROUND!
He has no sense of appropriateness!

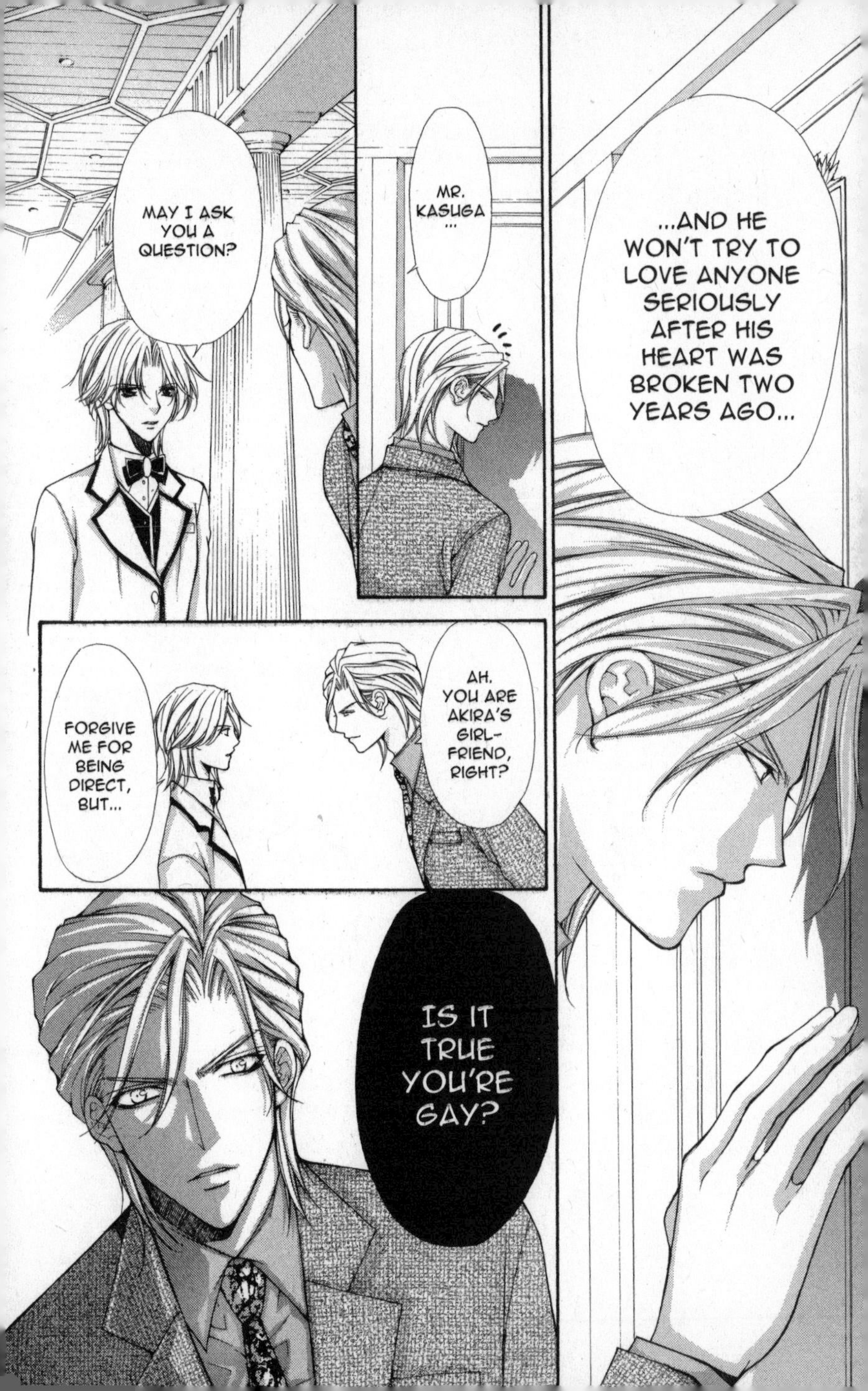
...AND HE WON'T TRY TO LOVE ANYONE SERIOUSLY AFTER HIS HEART WAS BROKEN TWO YEARS AGO...
MR. KASUGA...
MAY I ASK YOU A QUESTION?
AH. YOU ARE AKIRA'S GIRL-FRIEND, RIGHT?
FORGIVE ME FOR BEING DIRECT, BUT...
IS IT TRUE YOU'RE GAY?

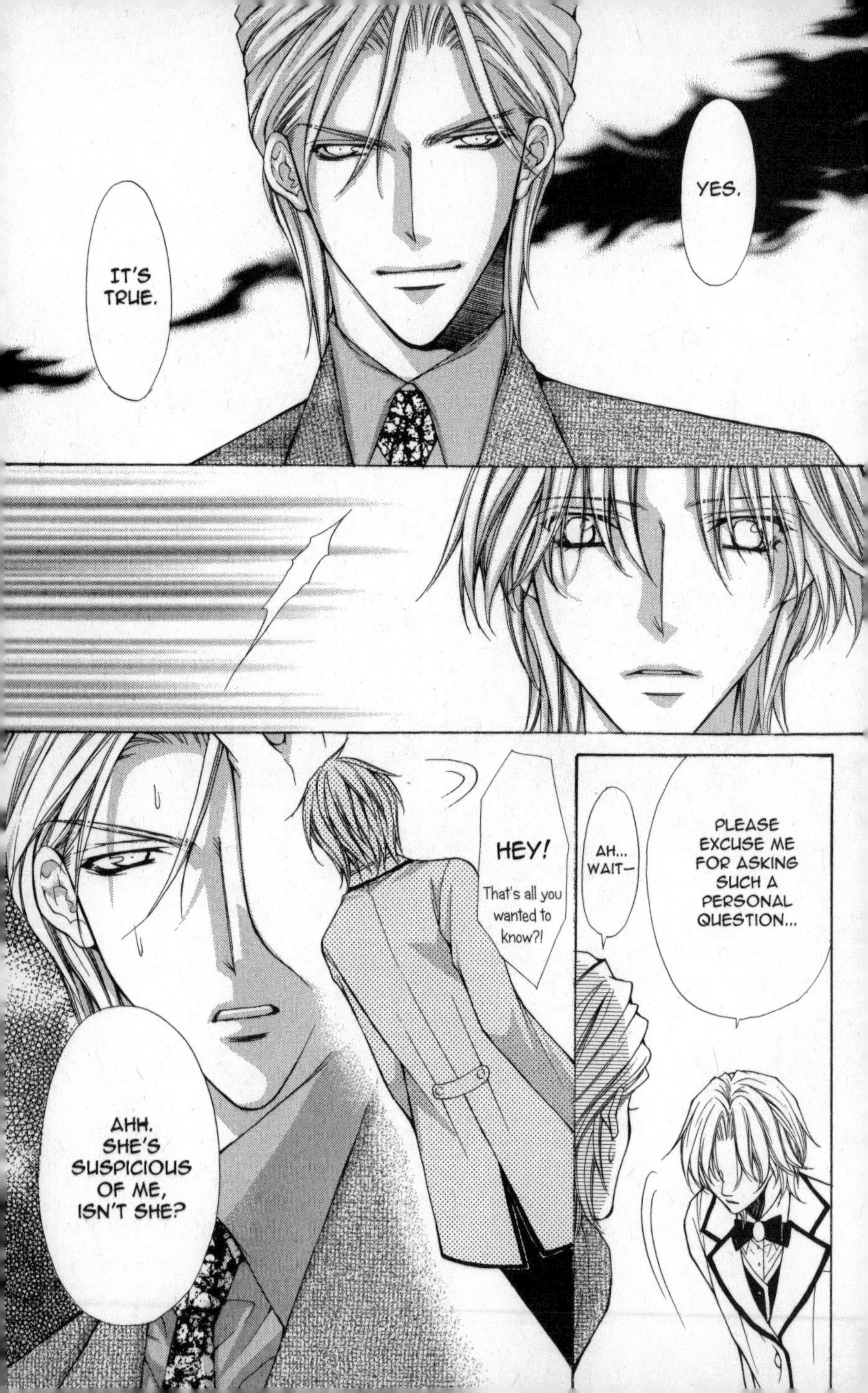
YES.
IT'S TRUE.
PLEASE EXCUSE ME FOR ASKING SUCH A PERSONAL QUESTION...
AH... WAIT—
HEY!
That's all you wanted to know?!
AHH. SHE'S SUSPICIOUS OF ME, ISN'T SHE?

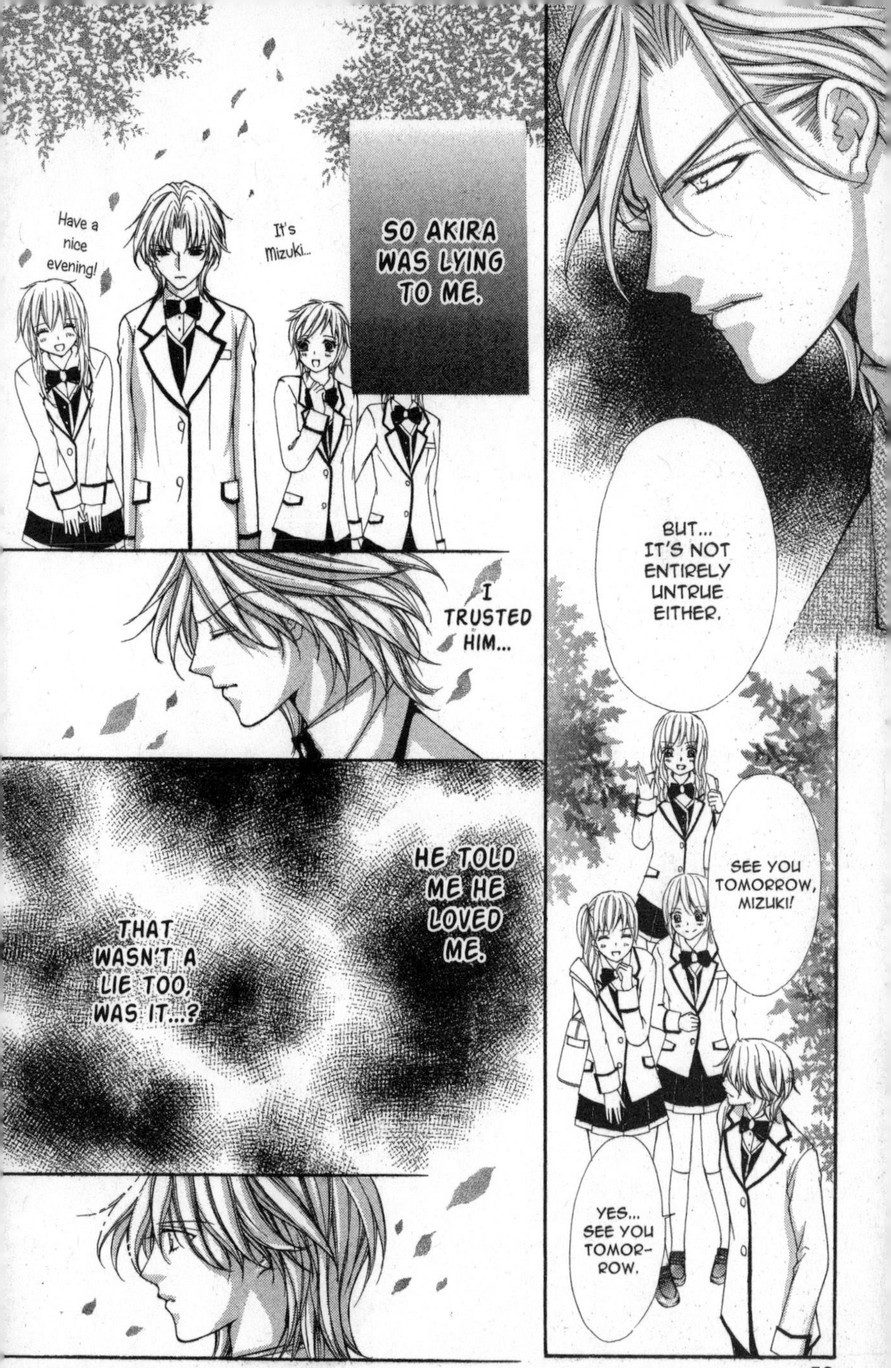
BUT... IT'S NOT ENTIRELY UNTRUE EITHER.
SEE YOU TOMORROW, MIZUKI!
YES... SEE YOU TOMOR-ROW.
SO AKIRA WAS LYING TO ME.
It's Mizuki...
Have a nice evening!
I TRUSTED HIM...
HE TOLD ME HE LOVED ME.
THAT WASN'T A LIE TOO, WAS IT...?

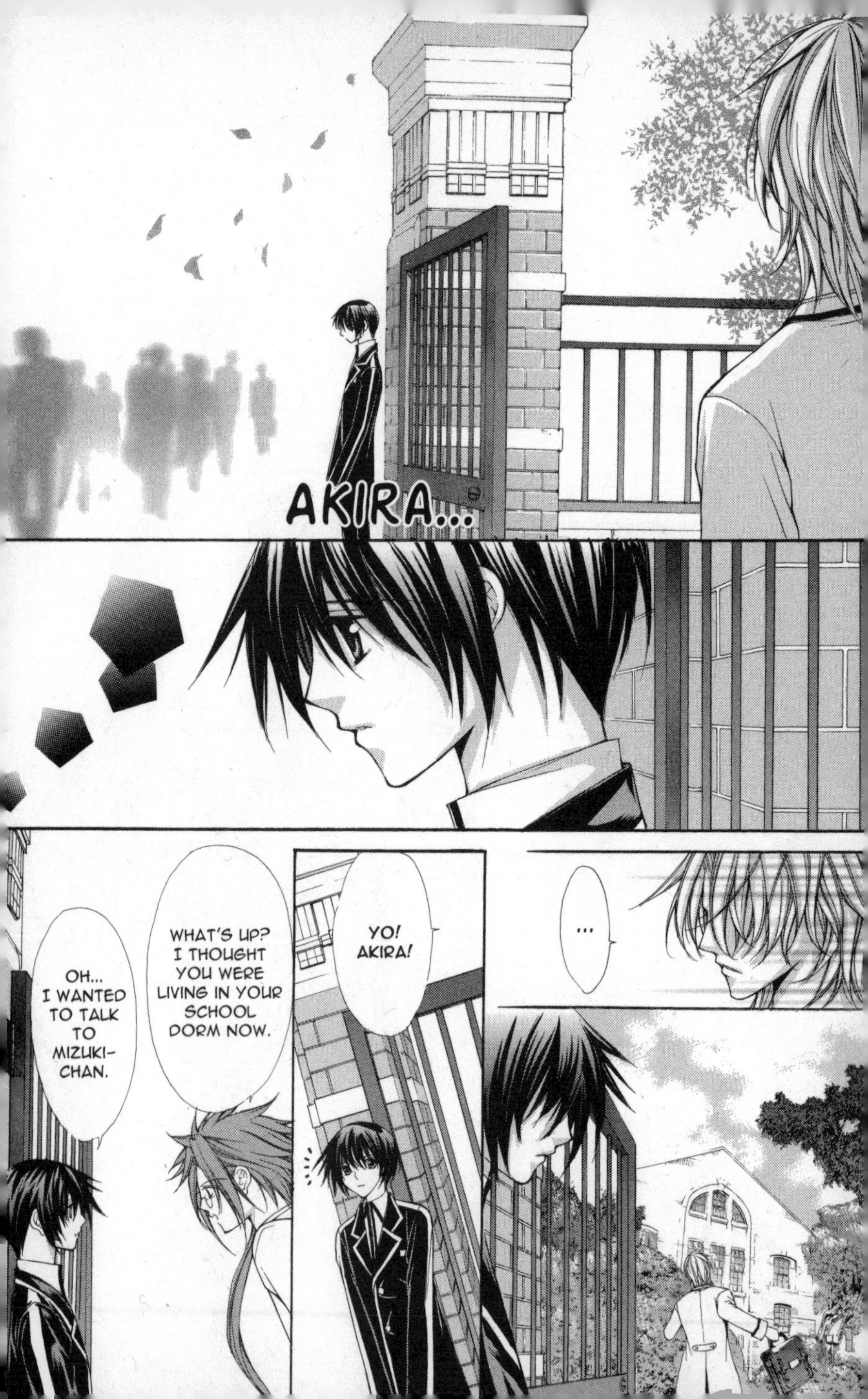
AKIRA...
...
YO! AKIRA!
WHAT'S UP? I THOUGHT YOU WERE LIVING IN YOUR SCHOOL DORM NOW.
OH... I WANTED TO TALK TO MIZUKI-CHAN.

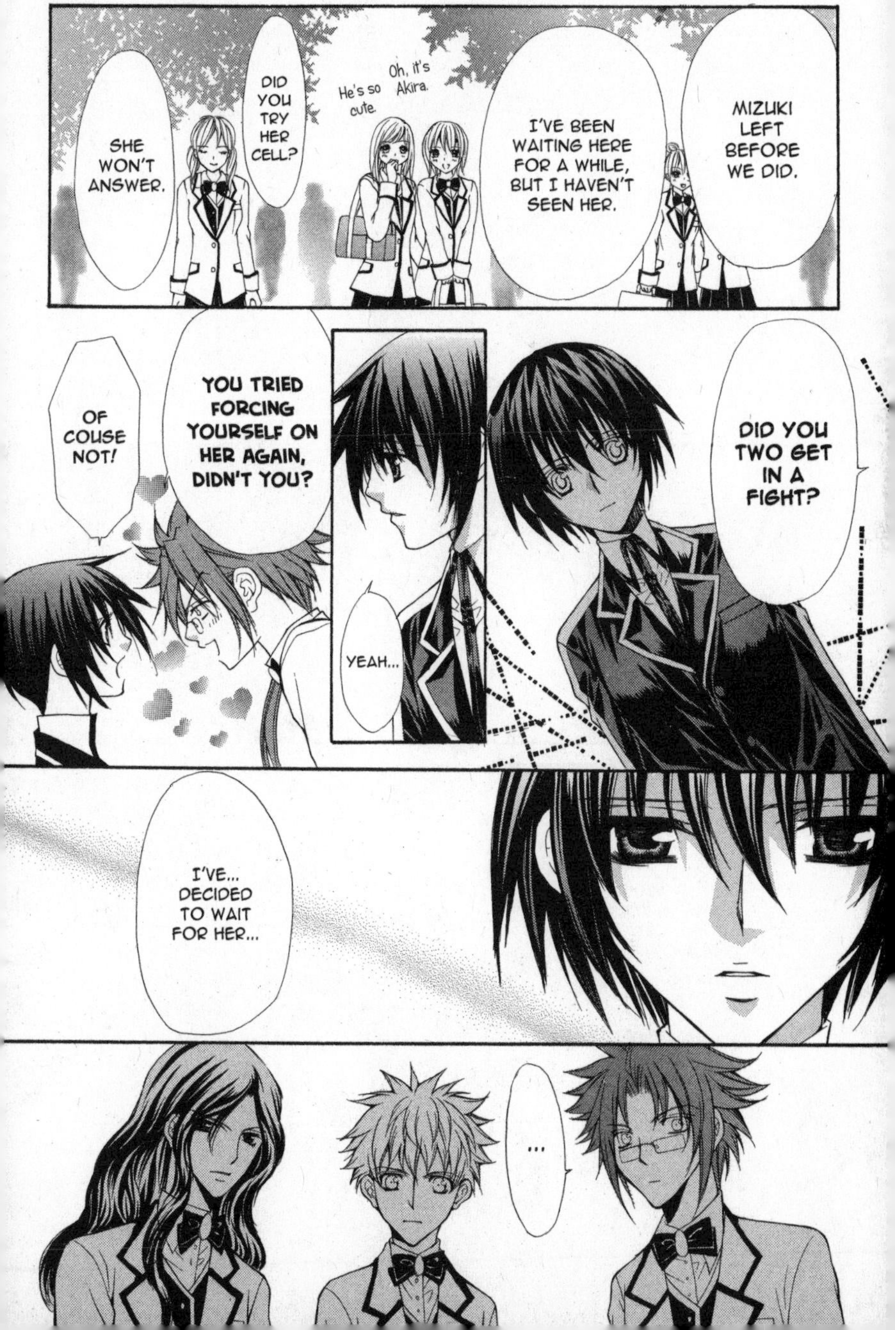
MIZUKI LEFT BEFORE WE DID.
I'VE BEEN WAITING HERE FOR A WHILE, BUT I HAVEN'T SEEN HER.
Oh, it's Akira.
He's so cute.
DID YOU TRY HER CELL?
SHE WON'T ANSWER.
DID YOU TWO GET IN A FIGHT?
YEAH...
YOU TRIED FORCING YOURSELF ON HER AGAIN, DIDN'T YOU?
OF COUSE NOT!
I'VE... DECIDED TO WAIT FOR HER...
...

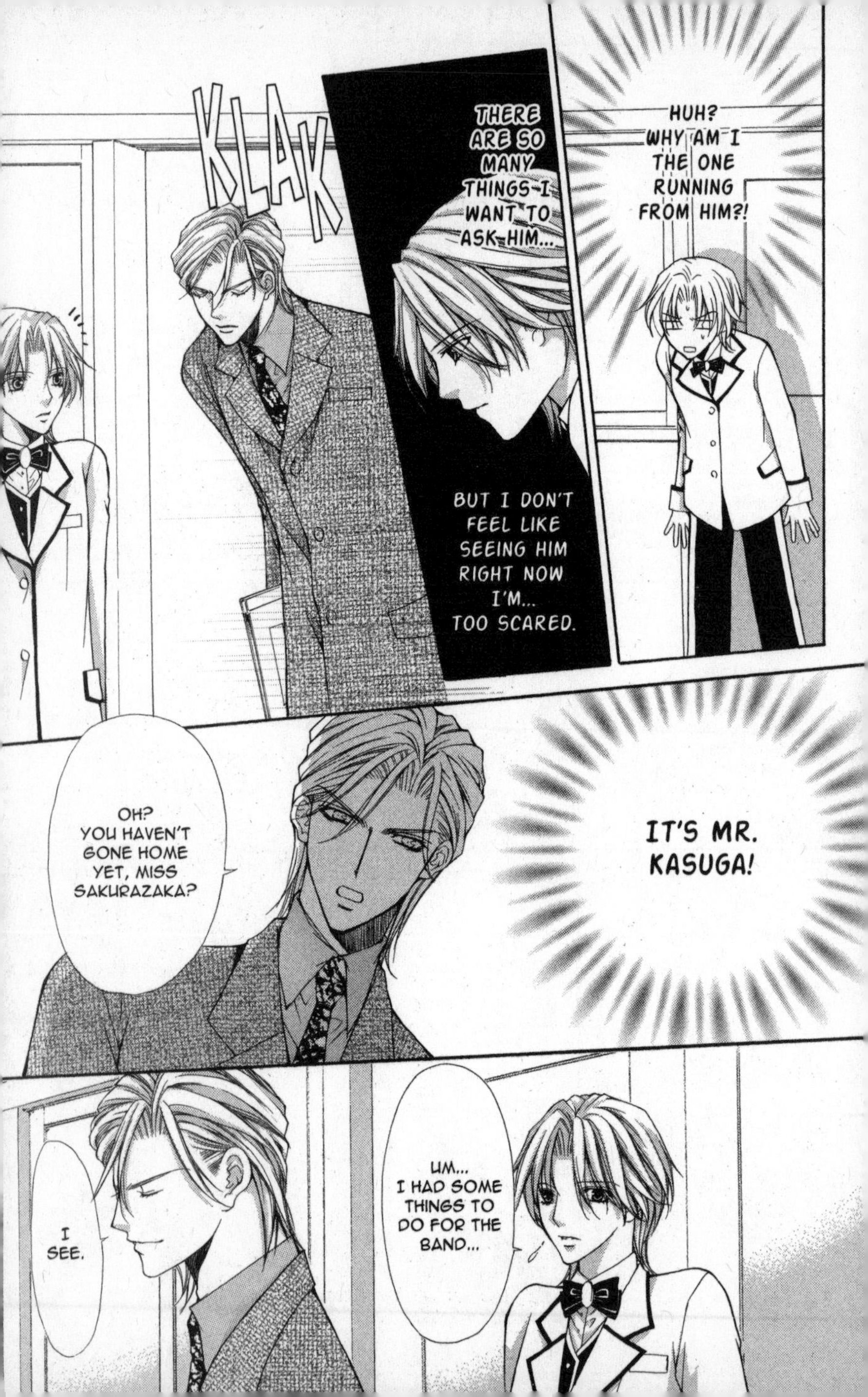
HUH? WHY AM I THE ONE RUNNING FROM HIM?!
THERE ARE SO MANY THINGS I WANT TO ASK HIM...
BUT I DON'T FEEL LIKE SEEING HIM RIGHT NOW I'M... TOO SCARED.
KLAK
IT'S MR. KASUGA!
OH? YOU HAVEN'T GONE HOME YET, MISS SAKURAZAKA?
UM... I HAD SOME THINGS TO DO FOR THE BAND...
I SEE.

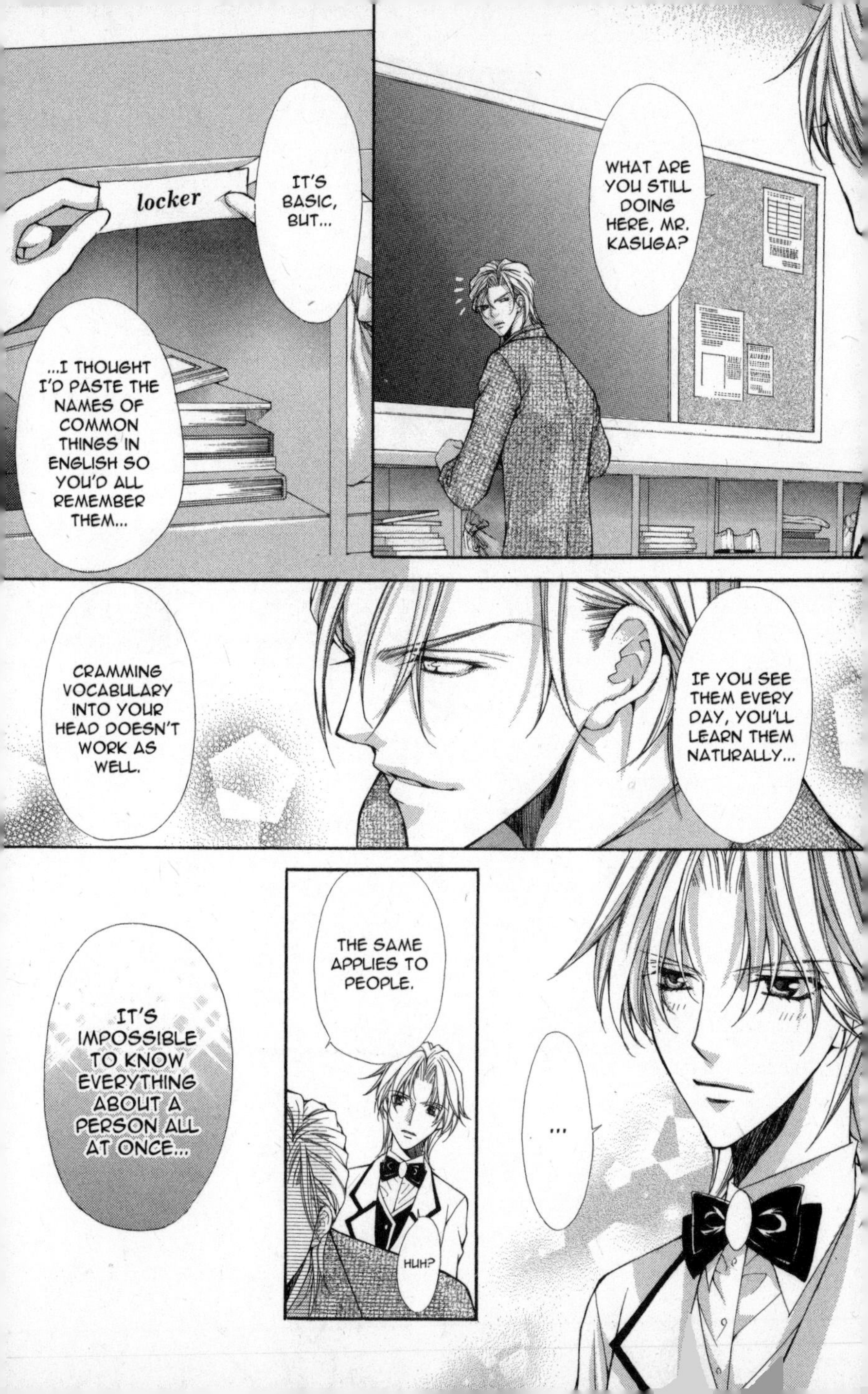
WHAT ARE YOU STILL DOING HERE, MR. KASUGA?
locker
IT'S BASIC, BUT...
...I THOUGHT I'D PASTE THE NAMES OF COMMON THINGS IN ENGLISH SO YOU'D ALL REMEMBER THEM...
IF YOU SEE THEM EVERY DAY, YOU'LL LEARN THEM NATURALLY...
CRAMMING VOCABULARY INTO YOUR HEAD DOESN'T WORK AS WELL.
...
THE SAME APPLIES TO PEOPLE.
HUH?
IT'S IMPOSSIBLE TO KNOW EVERYTHING ABOUT A PERSON ALL AT ONCE...

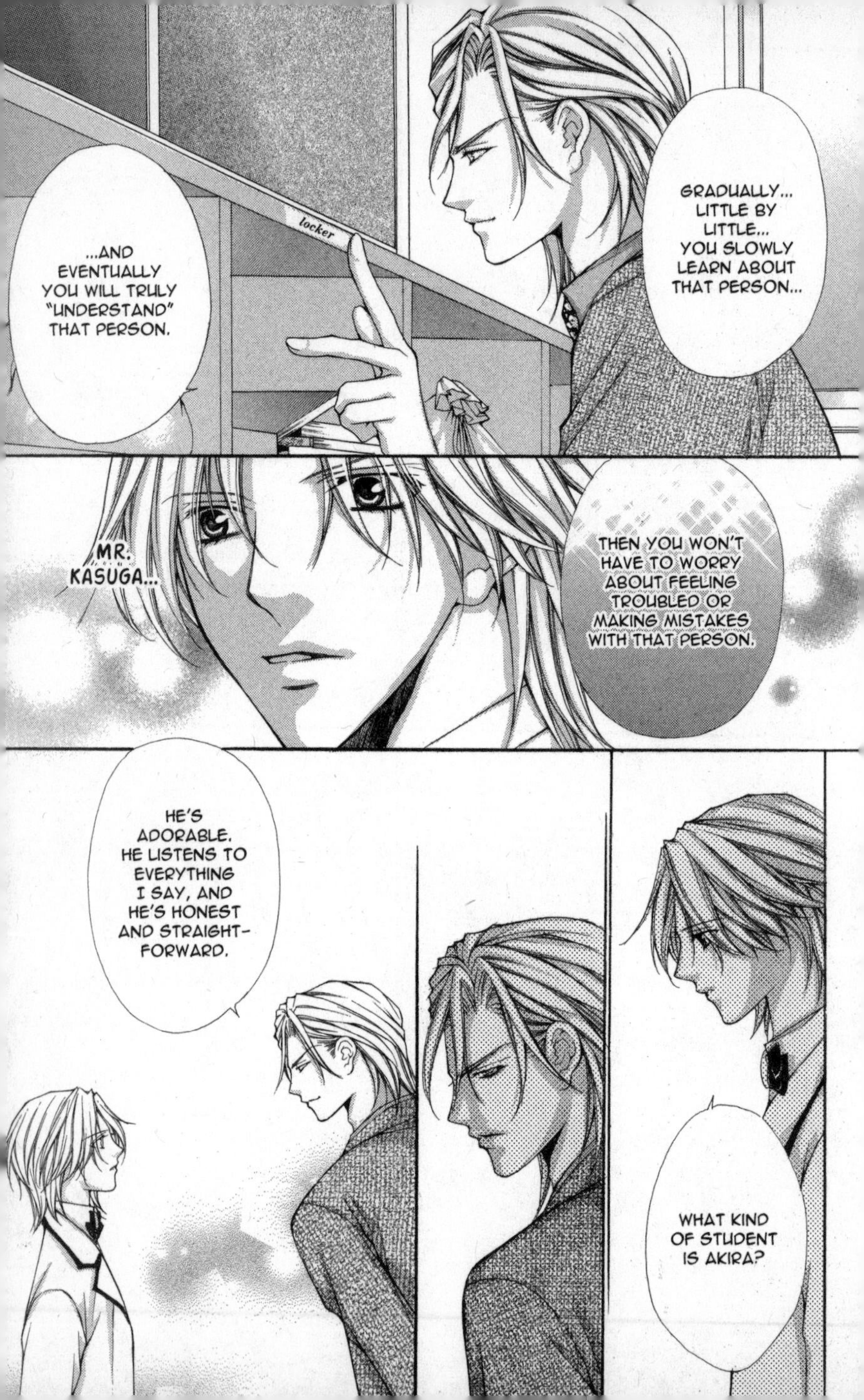
GRADUALLY... LITTLE BY LITTLE... YOU SLOWLY LEARN ABOUT THAT PERSON...
locker
...AND EVENTUALLY YOU WILL TRULY "UNDERSTAND" THAT PERSON.
THEN YOU WON'T HAVE TO WORRY ABOUT FEELING TROUBLED OR MAKING MISTAKES WITH THAT PERSON.
MR. KASUGA...
WHAT KIND OF STUDENT IS AKIRA?
HE'S ADORABLE. HE LISTENS TO EVERYTHING I SAY, AND HE'S HONEST AND STRAIGHT-FORWARD.

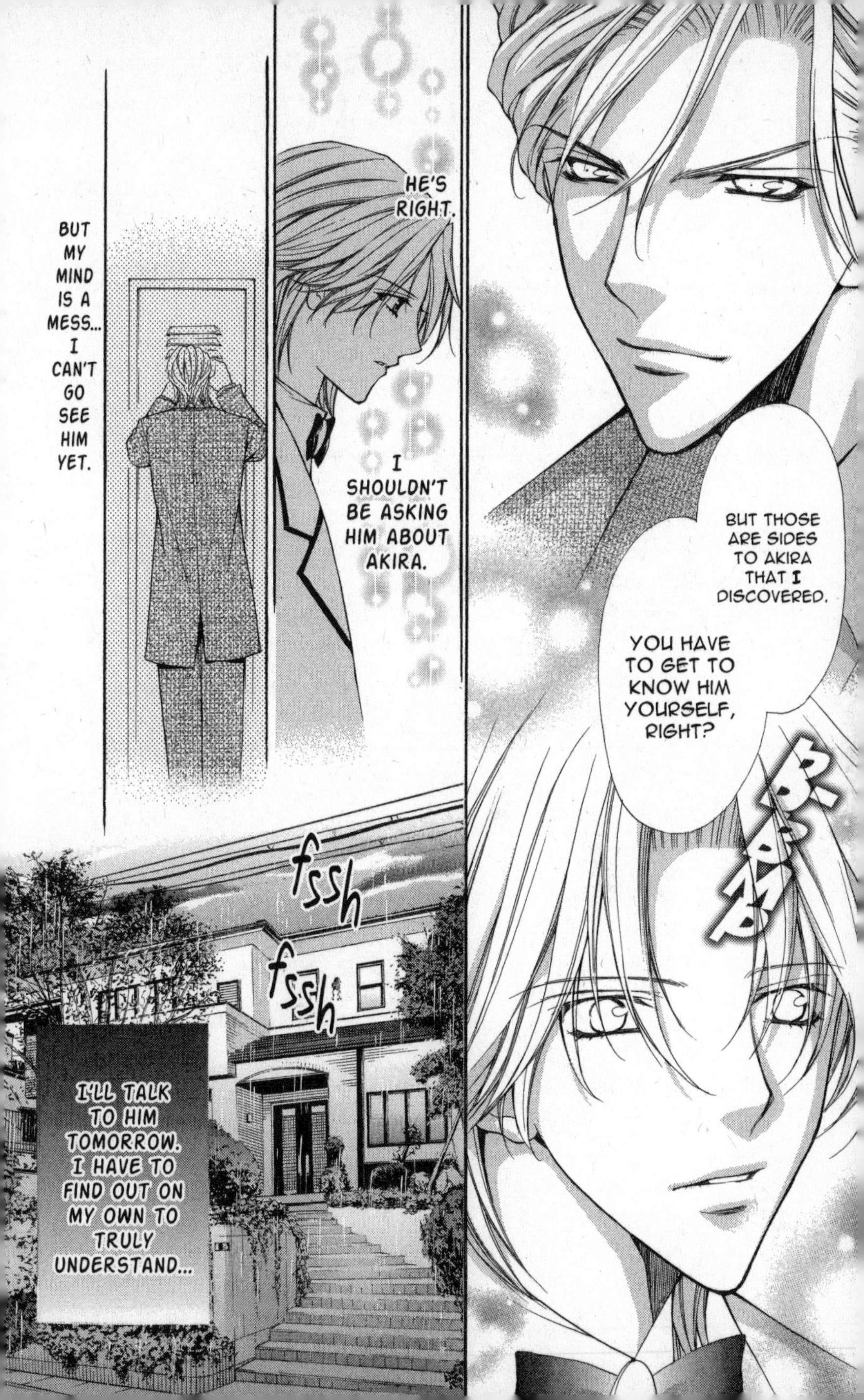
BUT THOSE ARE SIDES TO AKIRA THAT I DISCOVERED.
YOU HAVE TO GET TO KNOW HIM YOURSELF, RIGHT?
BA-BUMP
HE'S RIGHT.
I SHOULDN'T BE ASKING HIM ABOUT AKIRA.
BUT MY MIND IS A MESS... I CAN'T GO SEE HIM YET.
fssh
fssh
I'LL TALK TO HIM TOMORROW. I HAVE TO FIND OUT ON MY OWN TO TRULY UNDERSTAND...

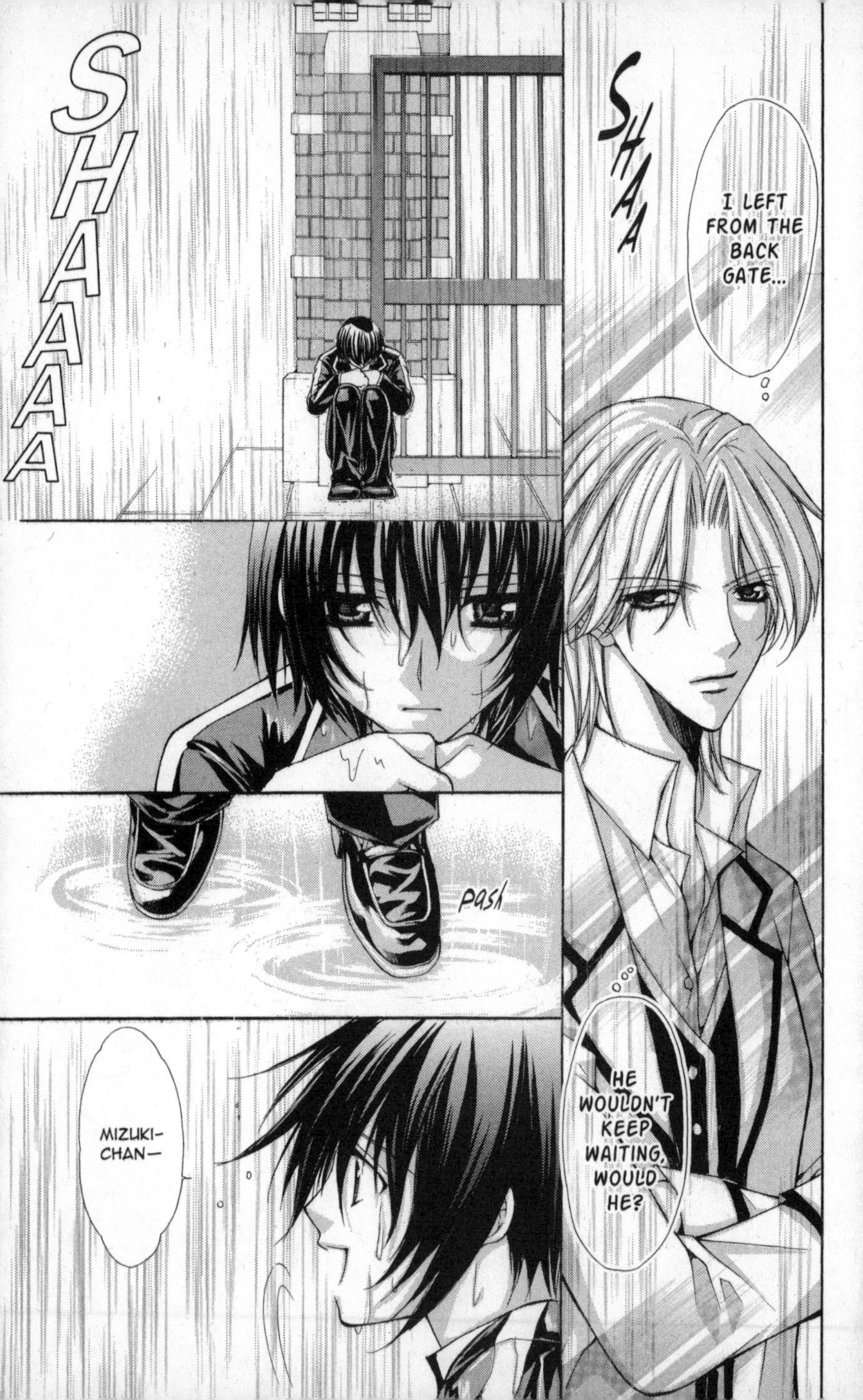
SHAA
I LEFT FROM THE BACK GATE...
HE WOULDN'T KEEP WAITING, WOULD HE?
SHAAAAA
pash
MIZUKI-CHAN—

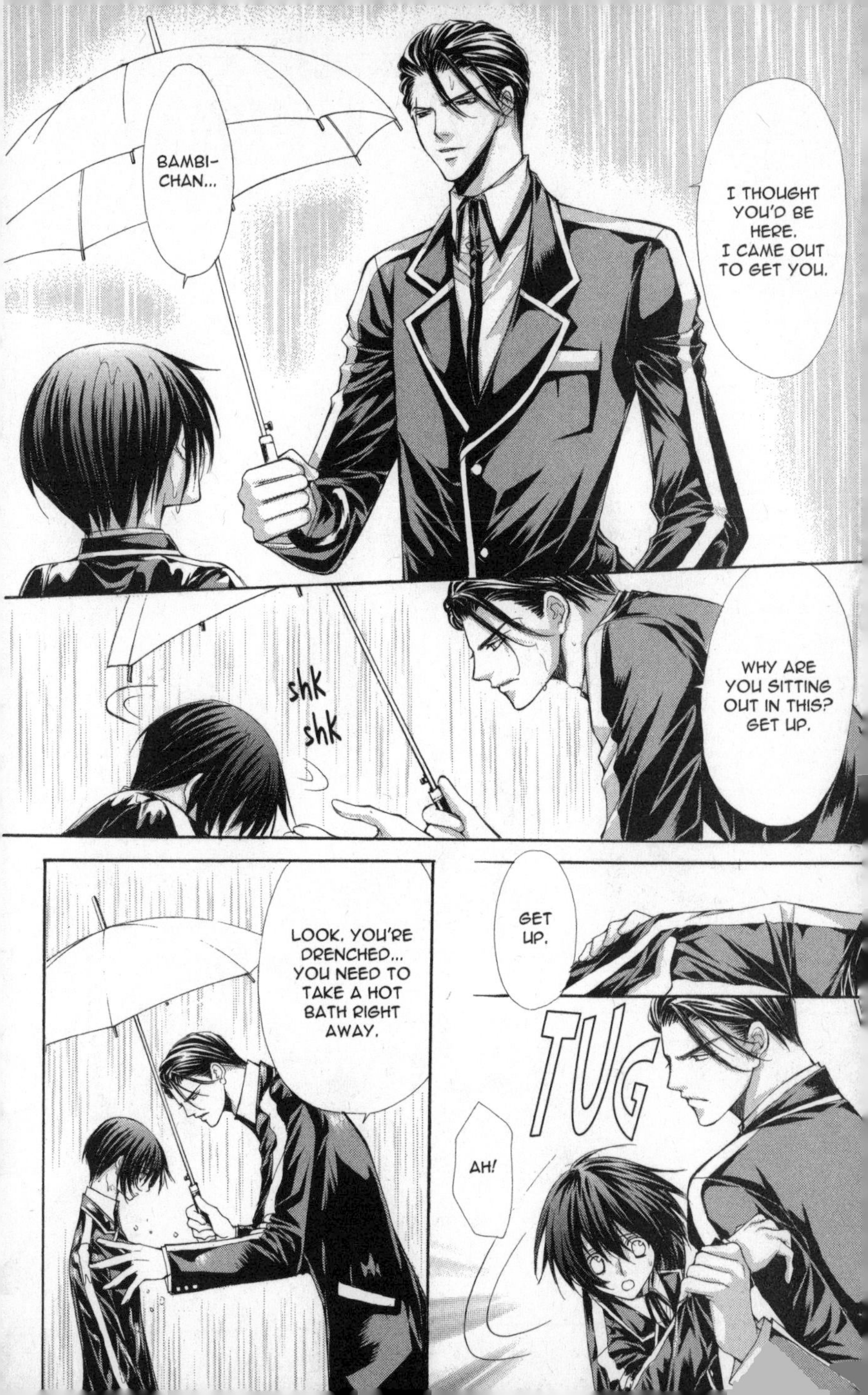
I THOUGHT YOU'D BE HERE. I CAME OUT TO GET YOU.
BAMBI-CHAN...
WHY ARE YOU SITTING OUT IN THIS? GET UP.
shk shk
GET UP.
TUG
AH!
LOOK. YOU'RE DRENCHED... YOU NEED TO TAKE A HOT BATH RIGHT AWAY.

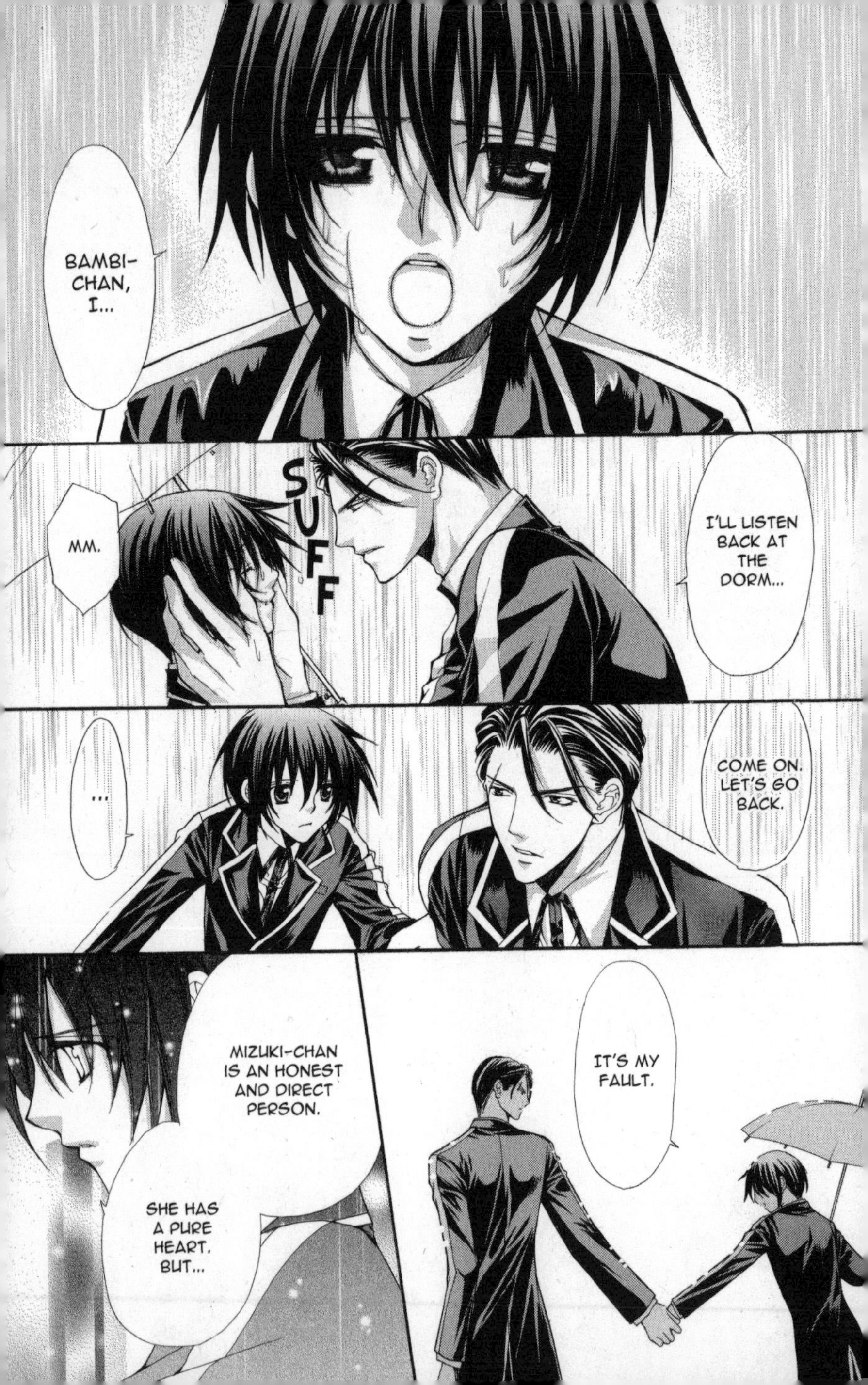
BAMBI-CHAN, I...
I'LL LISTEN BACK AT THE DORM...
SUFF
MM.
COME ON. LET'S GO BACK.
...
IT'S MY FAULT.
MIZUKI-CHAN IS AN HONEST AND DIRECT PERSON.
SHE HAS A PURE HEART. BUT...

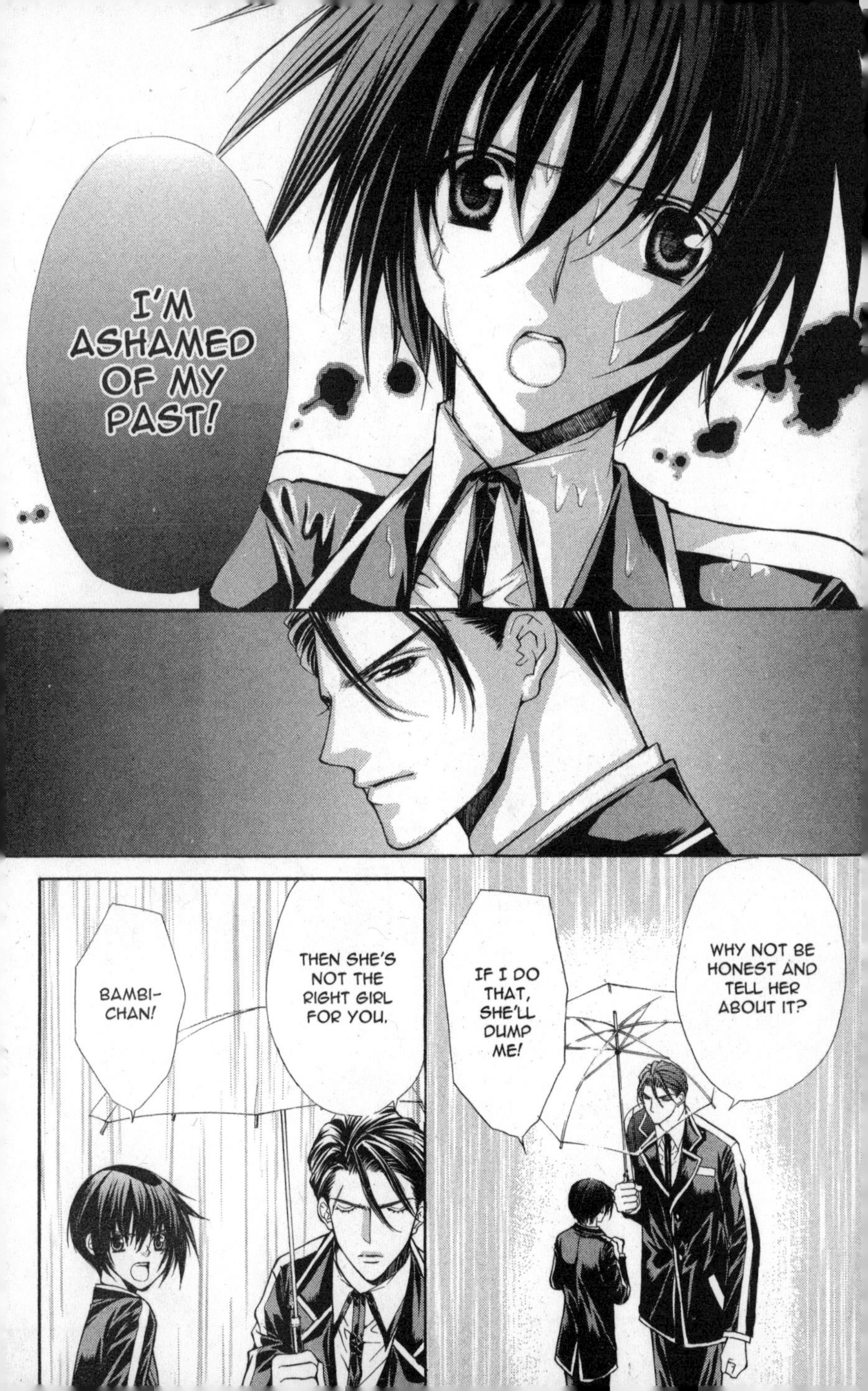
I'M ASHAMED OF MY PAST!
WHY NOT BE HONEST AND TELL HER ABOUT IT?
IF I DO THAT, SHE'LL DUMP ME!
THEN SHE'S NOT THE RIGHT GIRL FOR YOU.
BAMBI-CHAN!

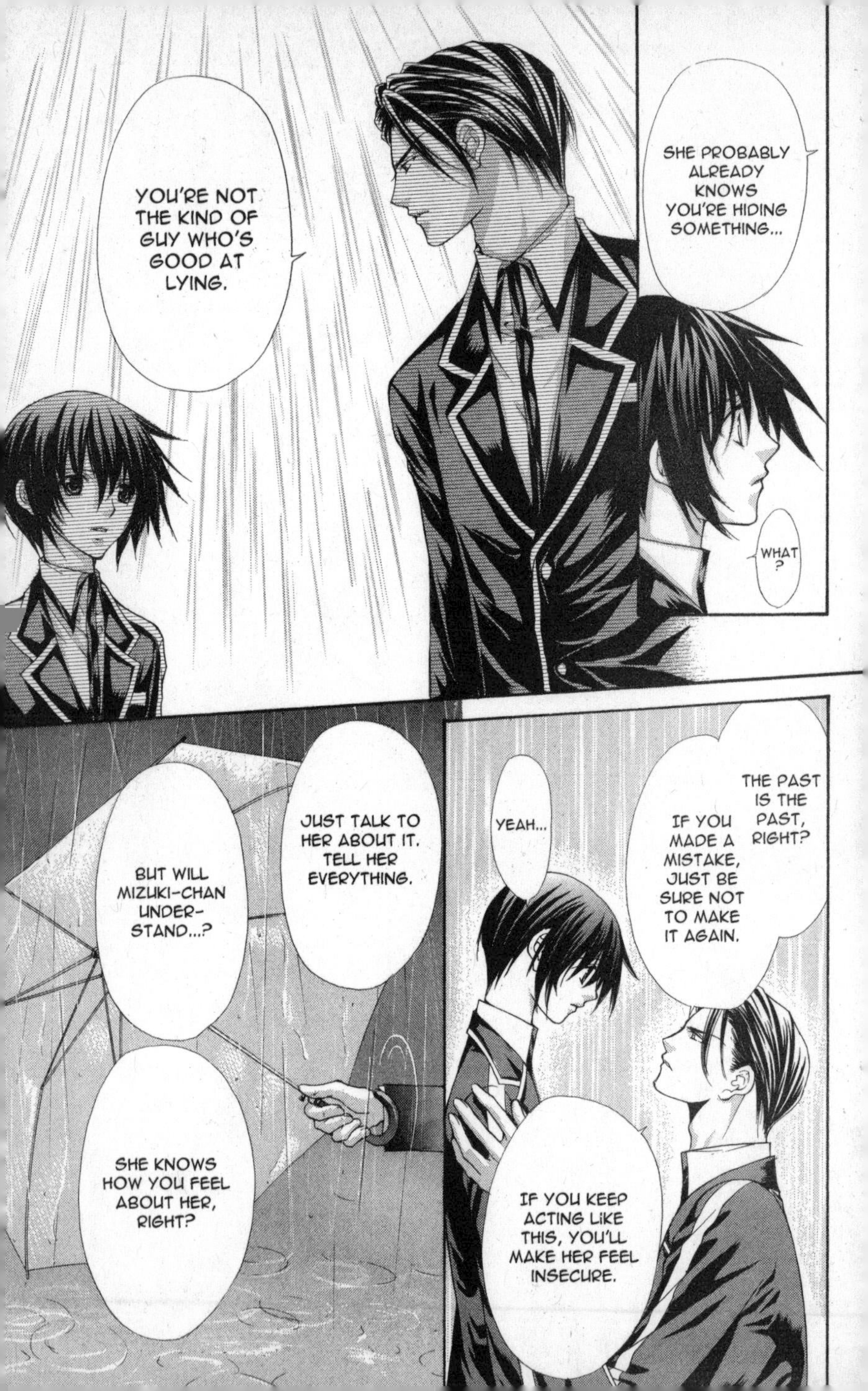
SHE PROBABLY ALREADY KNOWS YOU'RE HIDING SOMETHING...
WHAT?
YOU'RE NOT THE KIND OF GUY WHO'S GOOD AT LYING.
THE PAST IS THE PAST, RIGHT?
IF YOU MADE A MISTAKE, JUST BE SURE NOT TO MAKE IT AGAIN.
YEAH...
IF YOU KEEP ACTING LIKE THIS, YOU'LL MAKE HER FEEL INSECURE.
JUST TALK TO HER ABOUT IT. TELL HER EVERYTHING.
BUT WILL MIZUKI-CHAN UNDER-STAND...?
SHE KNOWS HOW YOU FEEL ABOUT HER, RIGHT?

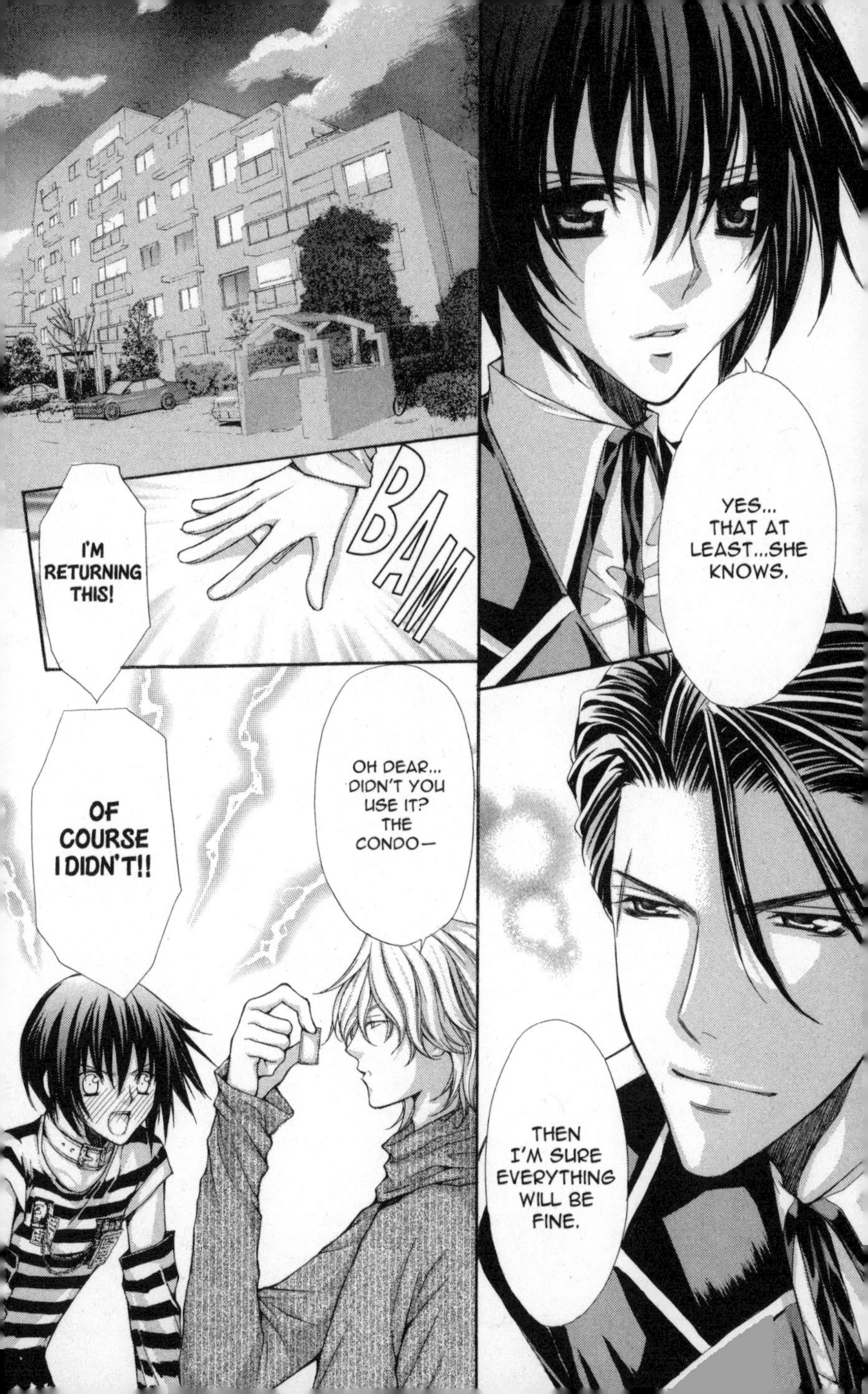
YES... THAT AT LEAST...SHE KNOWS.
THEN I'M SURE EVERYTHING WILL BE FINE.
BAM
I'M RETURNING THIS!
OH DEAR... DIDN'T YOU USE IT? THE CONDO—
OF COURSE I DIDN'T!!

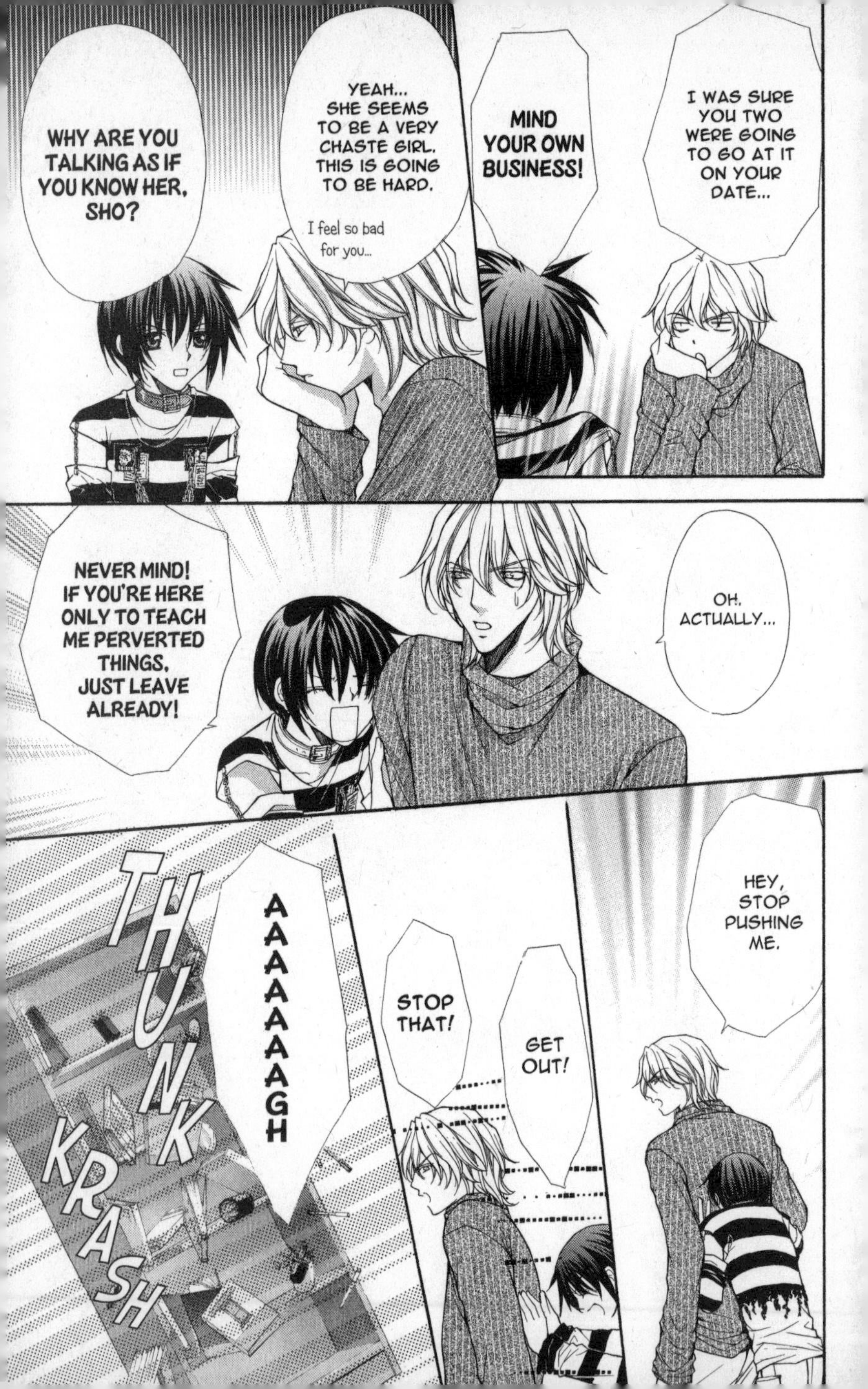
I WAS SURE YOU TWO WERE GOING TO GO AT IT ON YOUR DATE...
MIND YOUR OWN BUSINESS!
YEAH... SHE SEEMS TO BE A VERY CHASTE GIRL. THIS IS GOING TO BE HARD.
I feel so bad for you...
WHY ARE YOU TALKING AS IF YOU KNOW HER, SHO?
OH. ACTUALLY...
NEVER MIND! IF YOU'RE HERE ONLY TO TEACH ME PERVERTED THINGS, JUST LEAVE ALREADY!
HEY, STOP PUSHING ME.
GET OUT!
STOP THAT!
AAAAAAAAGH
THUNK
KRASH

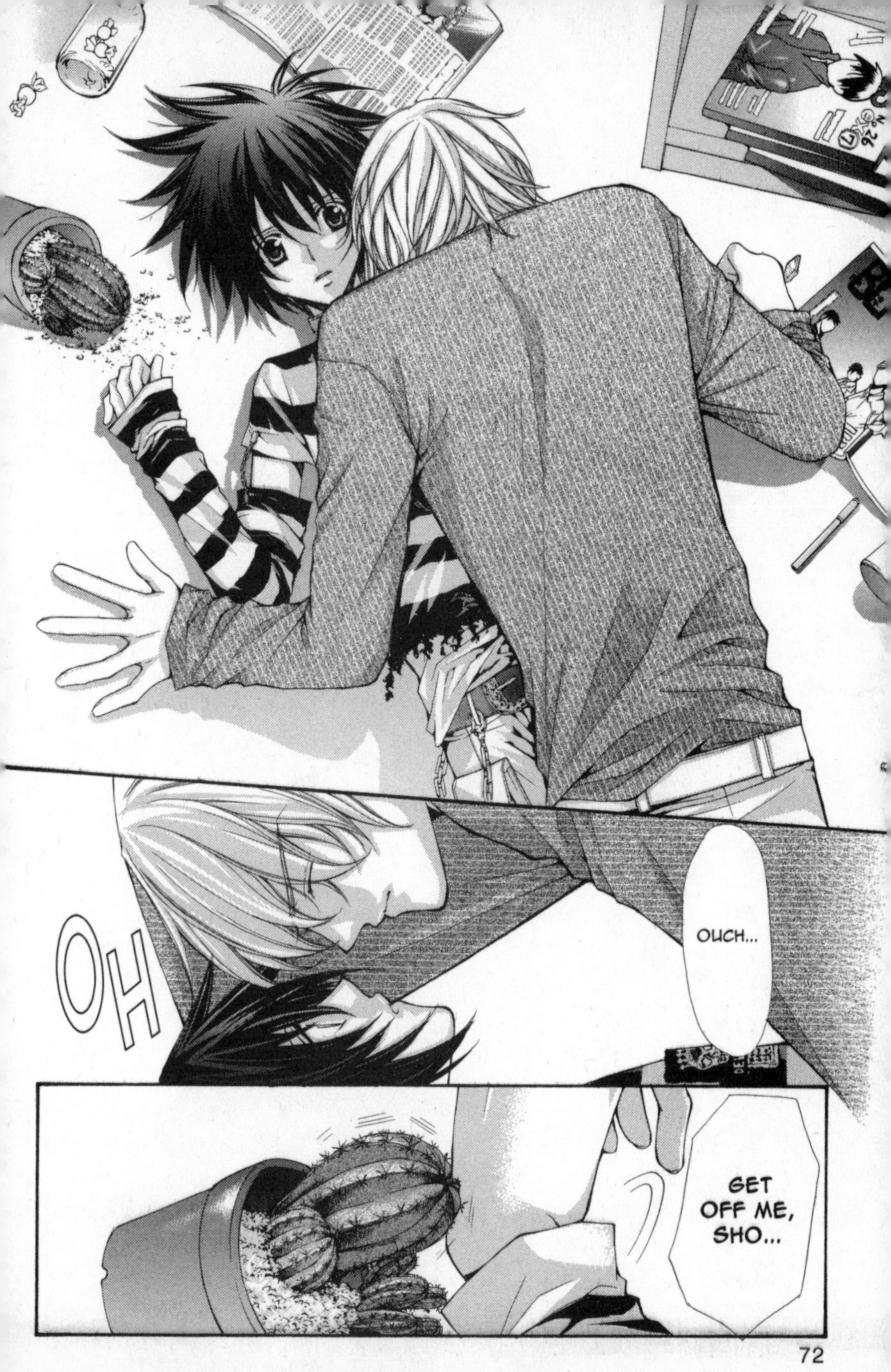
OUCH...
OH
GET OFF ME, SHO...

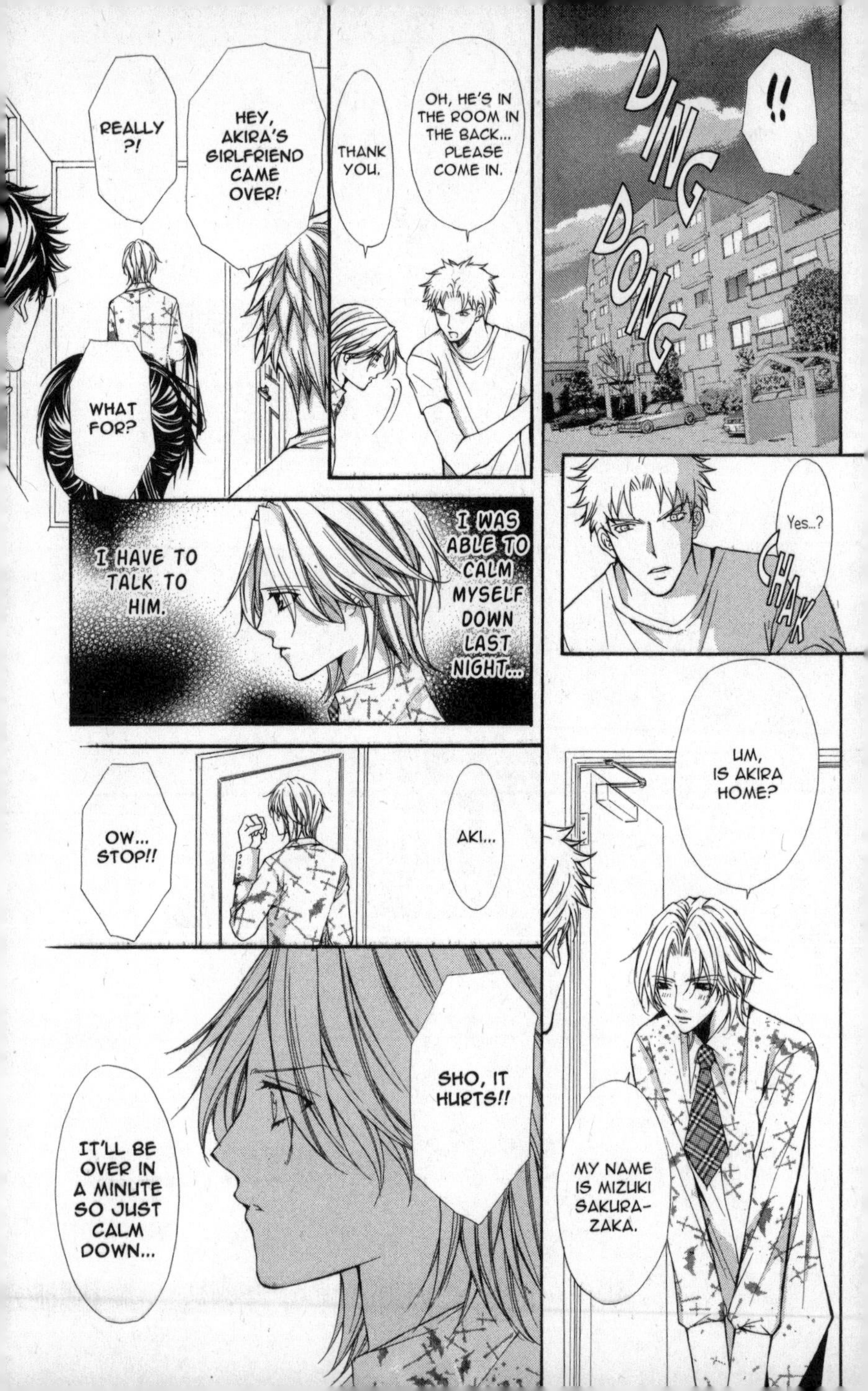
!!
DING DONG
Yes...?
CHAK
UM, IS AKIRA HOME?
MY NAME IS MIZUKI SAKURA-ZAKA.
OH, HE'S IN THE ROOM IN THE BACK... PLEASE COME IN.
THANK YOU.
HEY, AKIRA'S GIRLFRIEND CAME OVER!
REALLY ?!
WHAT FOR?
I WAS ABLE TO CALM MYSELF DOWN LAST NIGHT...
I HAVE TO TALK TO HIM.
AKI...
OW... STOP!!
SHO, IT HURTS!!
IT'LL BE OVER IN A MINUTE SO JUST CALM DOWN...

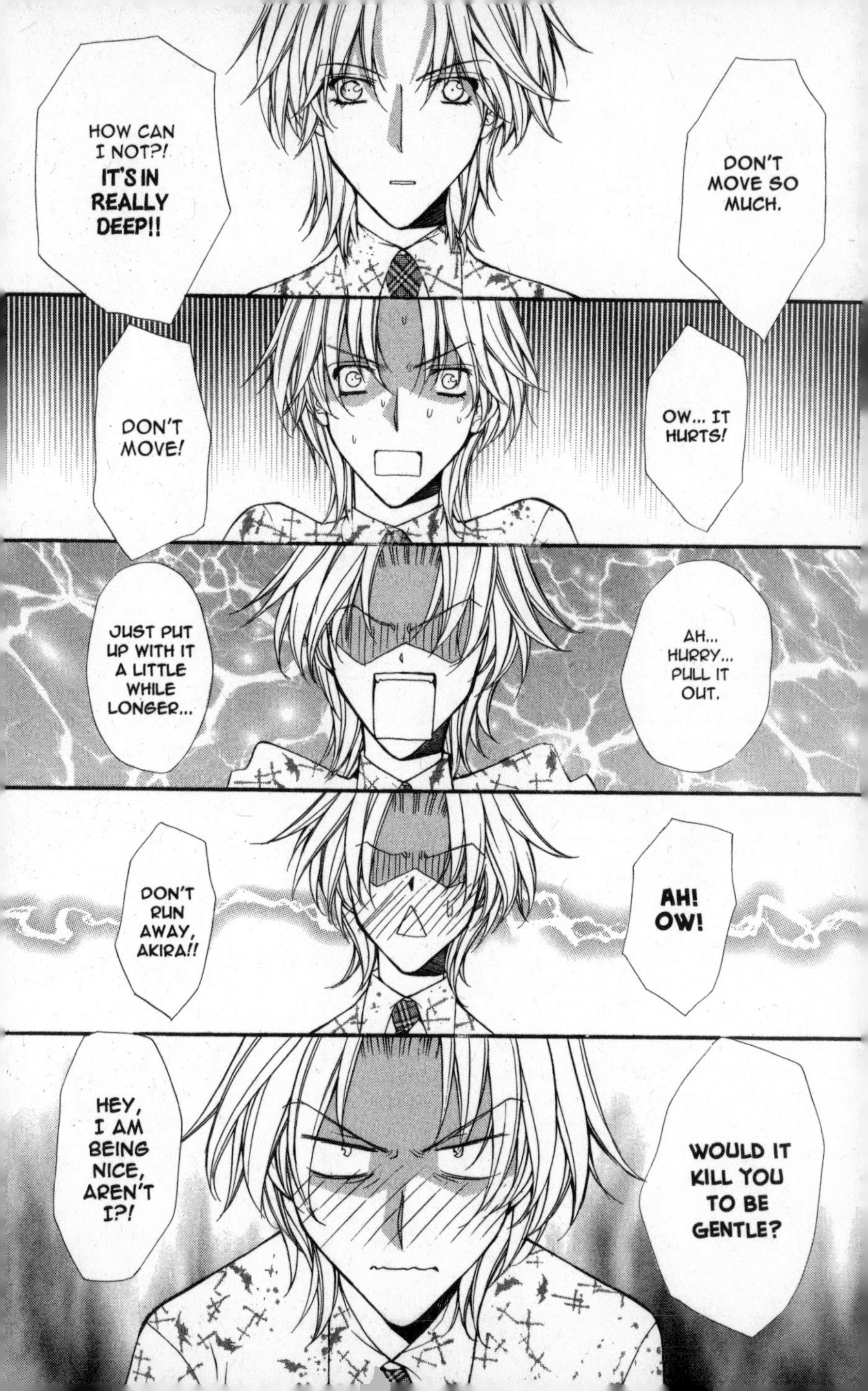
DON'T MOVE SO MUCH.
HOW CAN I NOT?! IT'S IN REALLY DEEP!!
OW... IT HURTS!
DON'T MOVE!
AH... HURRY... PULL IT OUT.
JUST PUT UP WITH IT A LITTLE WHILE LONGER...
AH! OW!
DON'T RUN AWAY, AKIRA!!
WOULD IT KILL YOU TO BE GENTLE?
HEY, I AM BEING NICE, AREN'T I?!

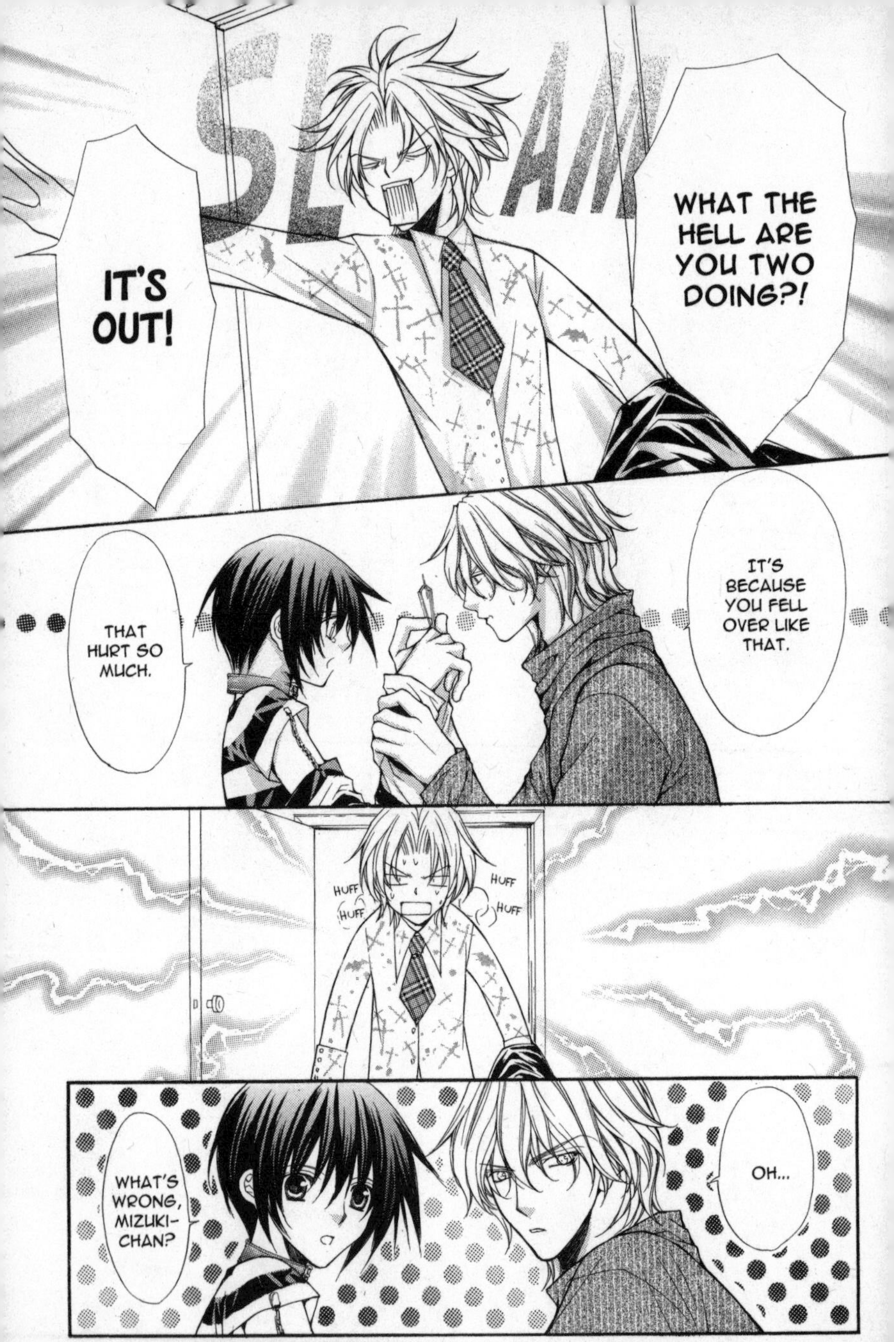
SLAM
WHAT THE HELL ARE YOU TWO DOING?!
IT'S OUT!
IT'S BECAUSE YOU FELL OVER LIKE THAT.
...
THAT HURT SO MUCH.
HUFF
HUFF
HUFF
HUFF
OH...
WHAT'S WRONG, MIZUKI-CHAN?

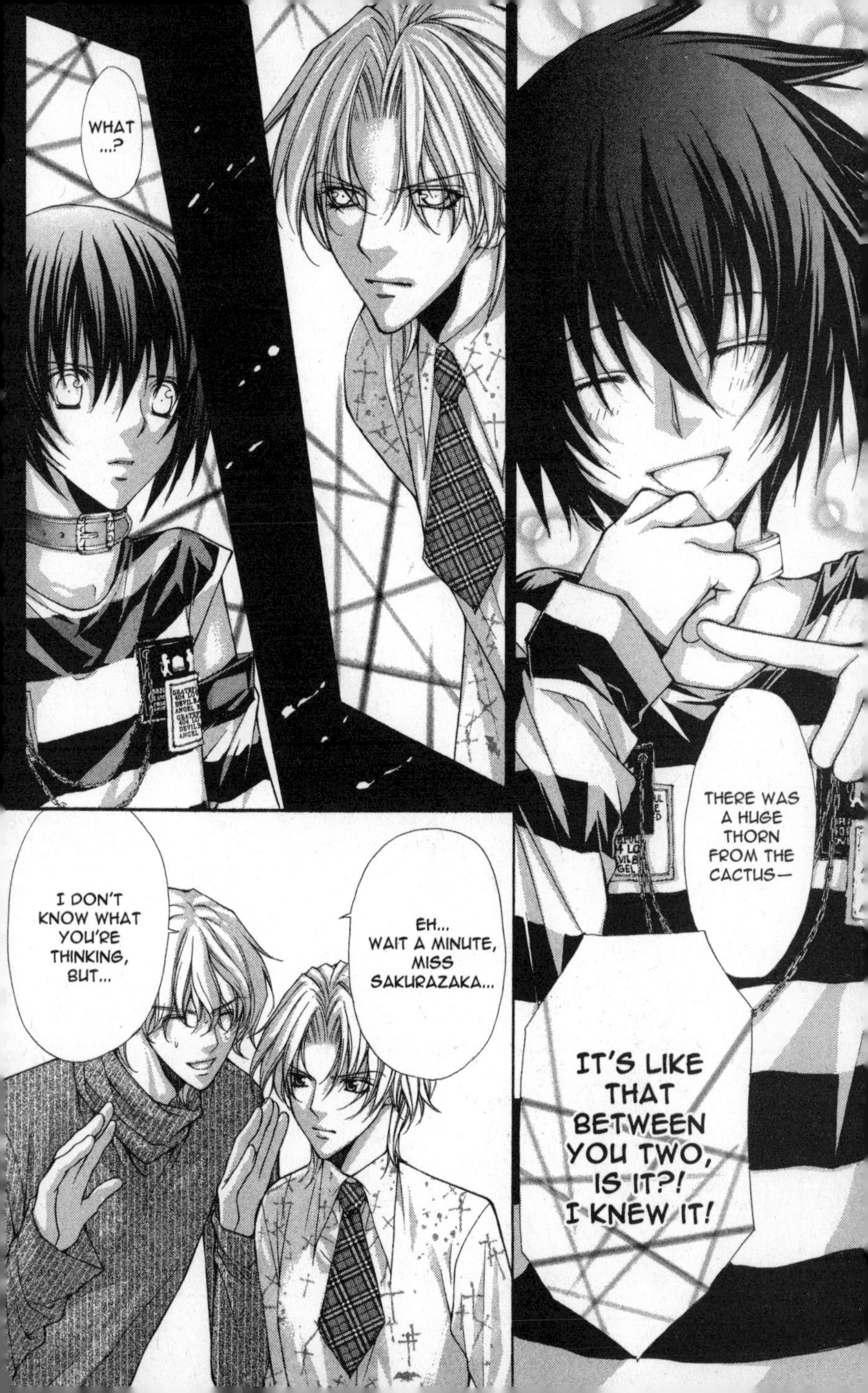
THERE WAS A HUGE THORN FROM THE CACTUS—
IT'S LIKE THAT BETWEEN YOU TWO, IS IT?! I KNEW IT!
WHAT ...?
EH... WAIT A MINUTE, MISS SAKURAZAKA...
I DON'T KNOW WHAT YOU'RE THINKING, BUT...

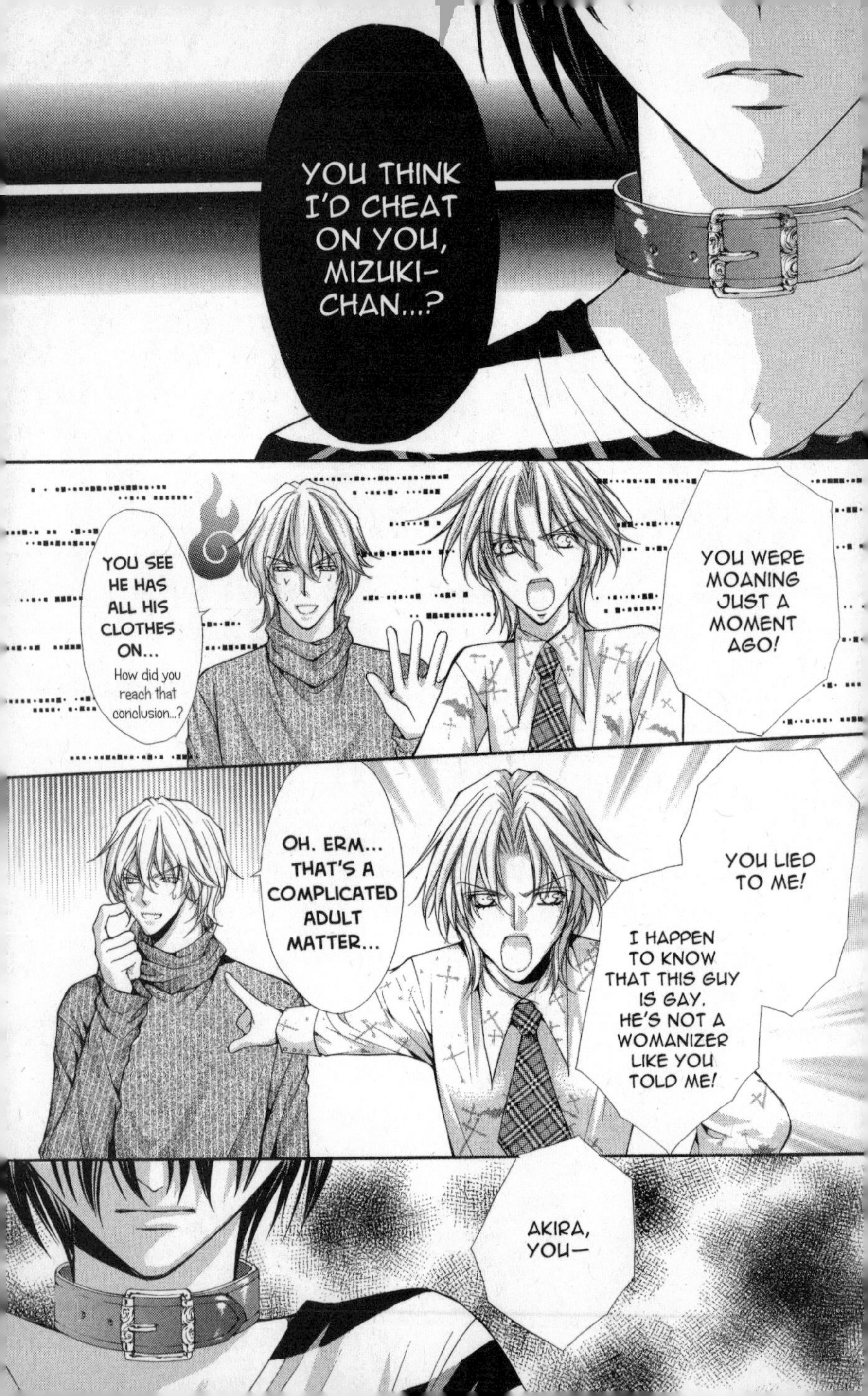
YOU THINK I'D CHEAT ON YOU, MIZUKI-CHAN...?
YOU WERE MOANING JUST A MOMENT AGO!
YOU SEE HE HAS ALL HIS CLOTHES ON...
How did you reach that conclusion...?
YOU LIED TO ME!
I HAPPEN TO KNOW THAT THIS GUY IS GAY. HE'S NOT A WOMANIZER LIKE YOU TOLD ME!
OH. ERM... THAT'S A COMPLICATED ADULT MATTER...
AKIRA, YOU—

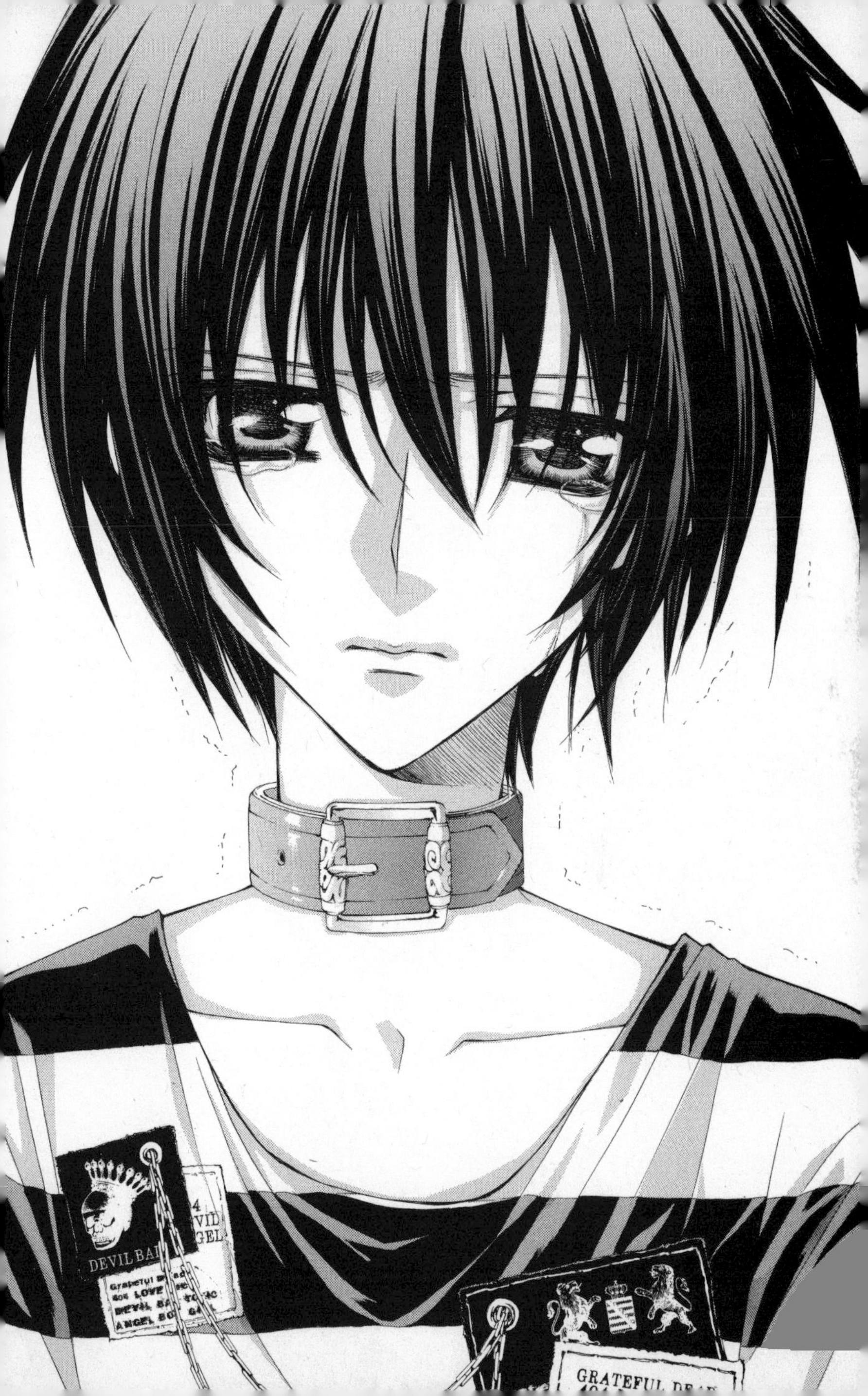

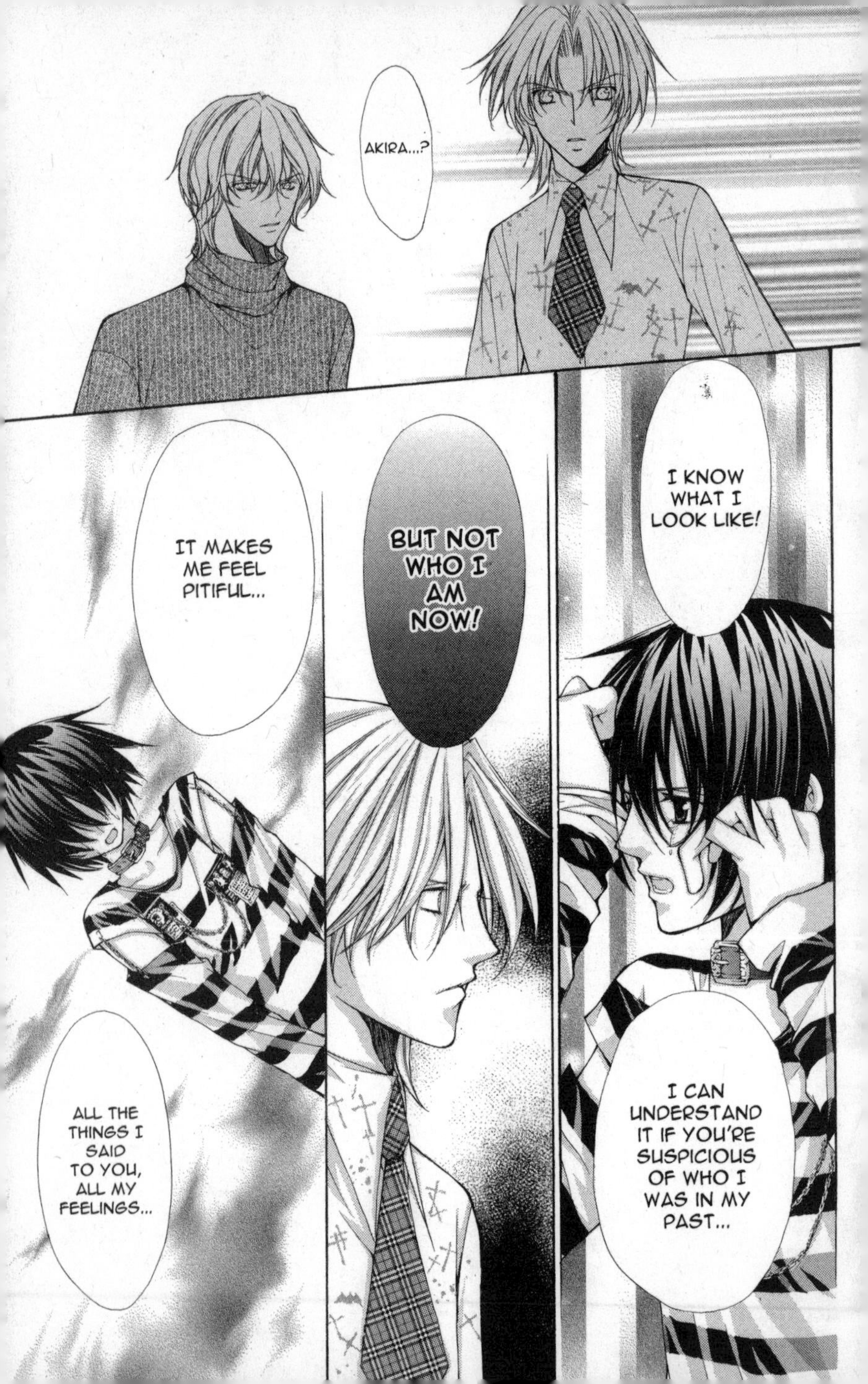
AKIRA...?
I KNOW WHAT I LOOK LIKE!
I CAN UNDERSTAND IT IF YOU'RE SUSPICIOUS OF WHO I WAS IN MY PAST...
BUT NOT WHO I AM NOW!
IT MAKES ME FEEL PITIFUL...
ALL THE THINGS I SAID TO YOU, ALL MY FEELINGS...

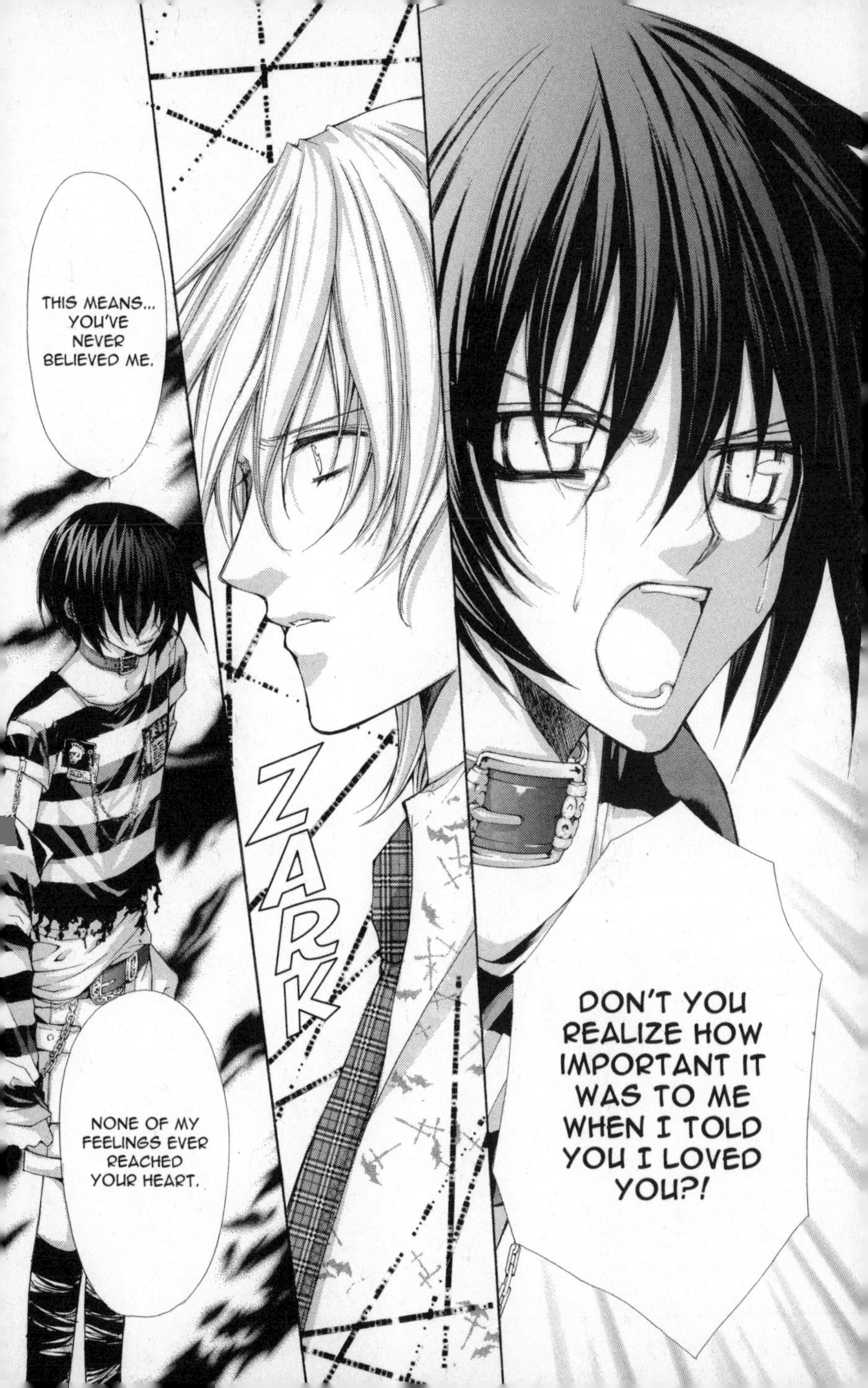
DON'T YOU REALIZE HOW IMPORTANT IT WAS TO ME WHEN I TOLD YOU I LOVED YOU?!
ZARK
THIS MEANS... YOU'VE NEVER BELIEVED ME.
NONE OF MY FEELINGS EVER REACHED YOUR HEART.

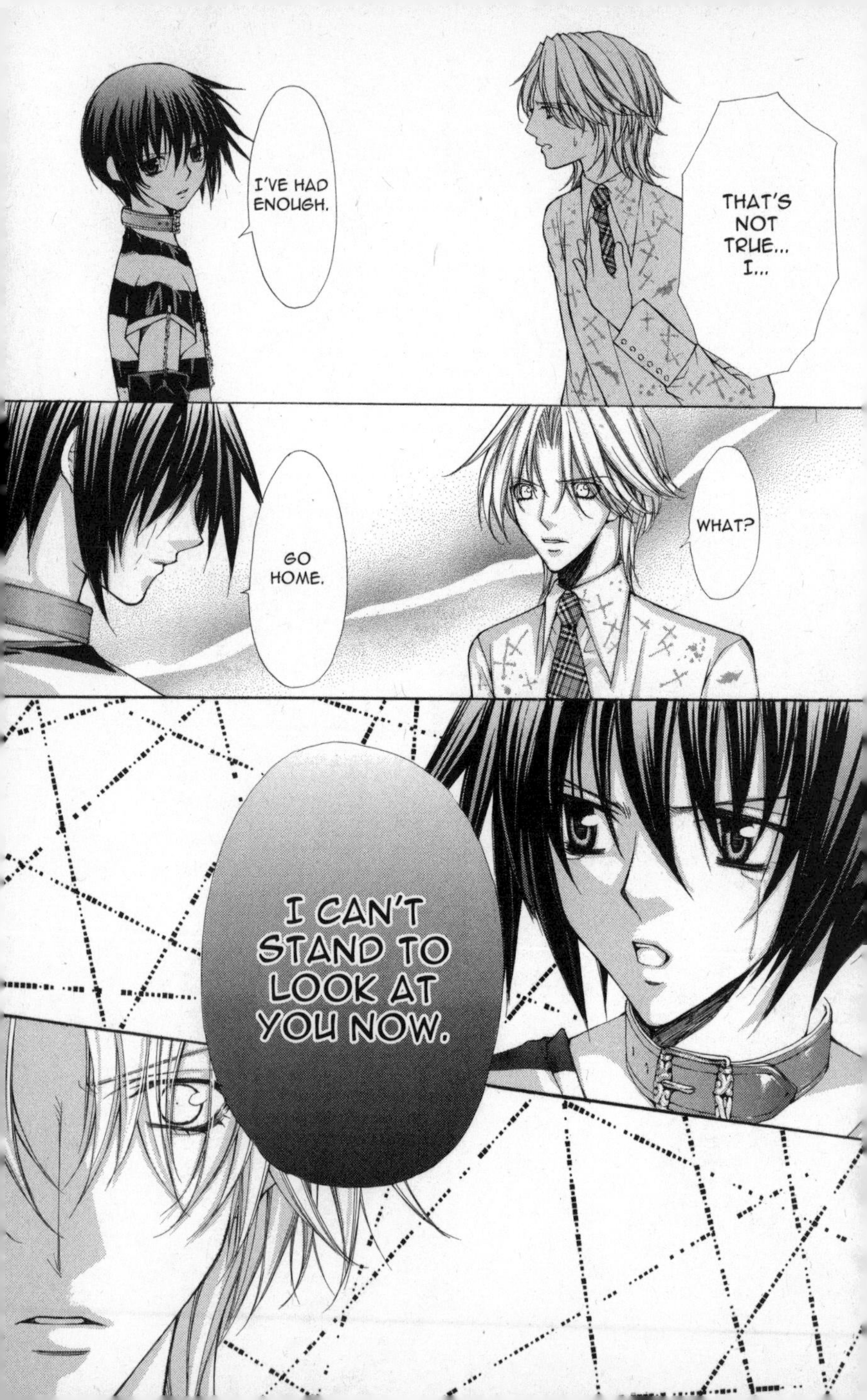
THAT'S NOT TRUE... I...
I'VE HAD ENOUGH.
WHAT?
GO HOME.
I CAN'T STAND TO LOOK AT YOU NOW.

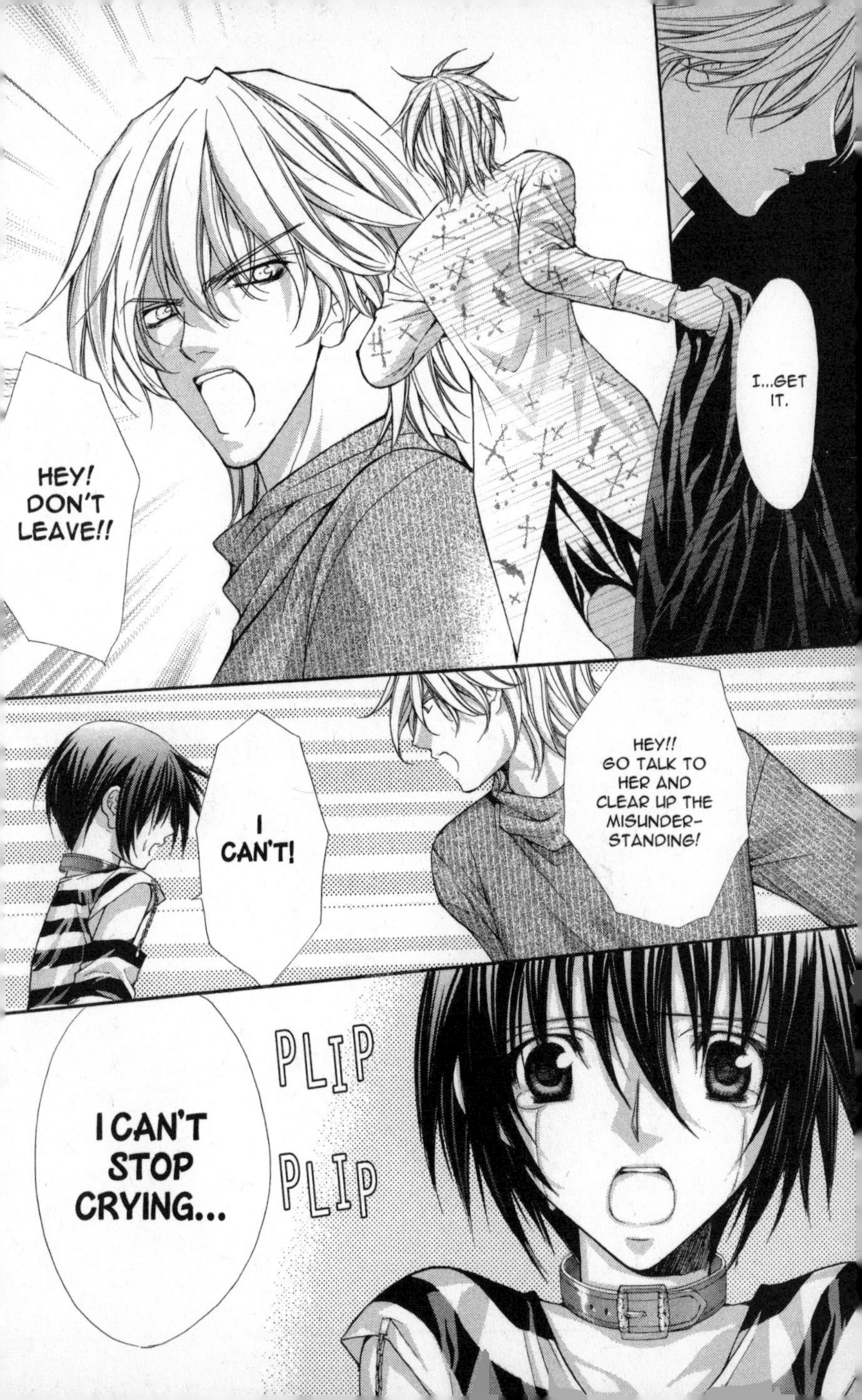
I...GET IT.
HEY! DON'T LEAVE!!
HEY!! GO TALK TO HER AND CLEAR UP THE MISUNDER-STANDING!
I CAN'T!
PLIP
PLIP
I CAN'T STOP CRYING...

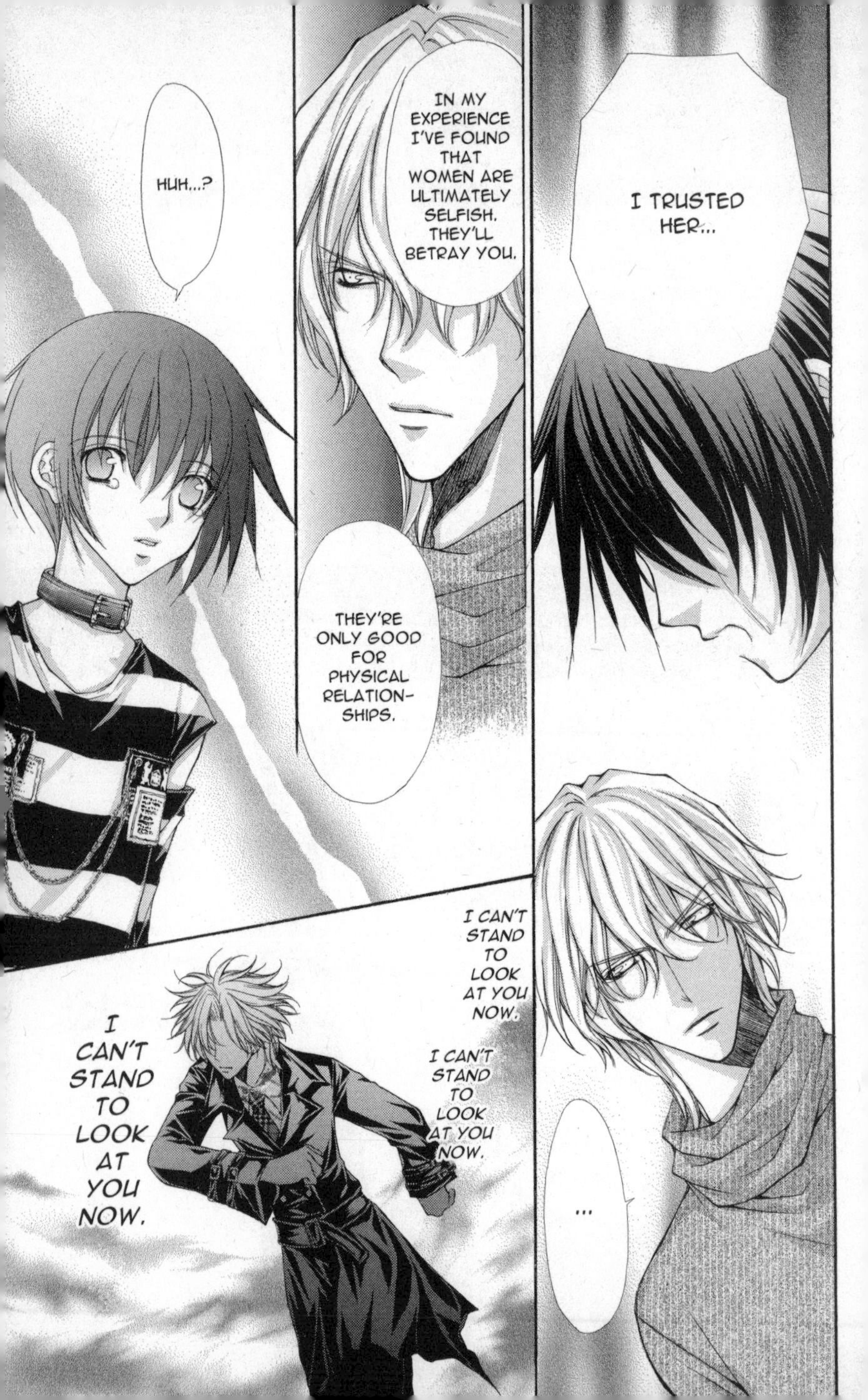
I TRUSTED HER...
IN MY EXPERIENCE I'VE FOUND THAT WOMEN ARE ULTIMATELY SELFISH. THEY'LL BETRAY YOU.
THEY'RE ONLY GOOD FOR PHYSICAL RELATION-SHIPS.
HUH...?
...
I CAN'T STAND TO LOOK AT YOU NOW.
I CAN'T STAND TO LOOK AT YOU NOW.
I CAN'T STAND TO LOOK AT YOU NOW.

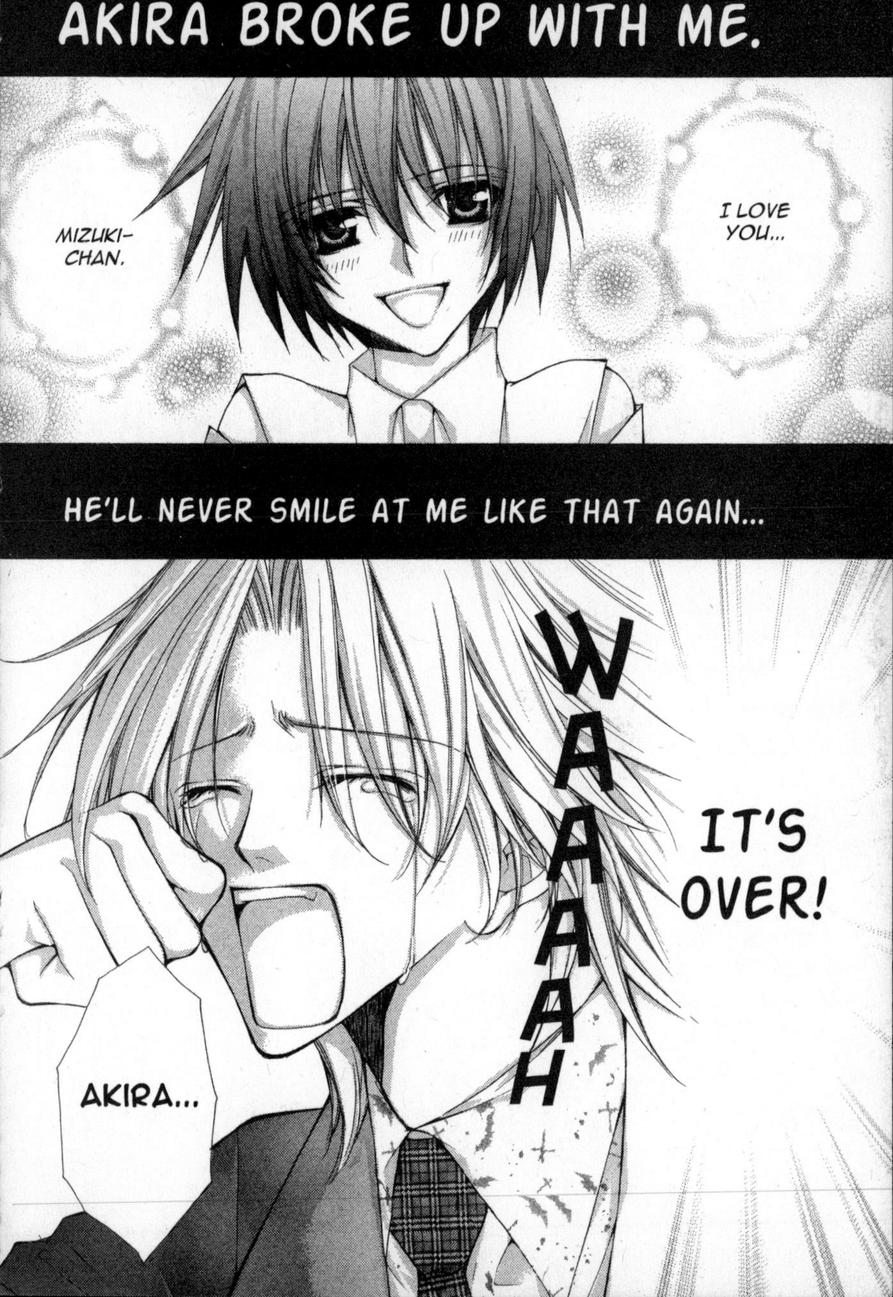
AKIRA BROKE UP WITH ME.
I LOVE YOU...
MIZUKI-CHAN.
HE'LL NEVER SMILE AT ME LIKE THAT AGAIN...
IT'S OVER!
WAAAAAH
AKIRA...

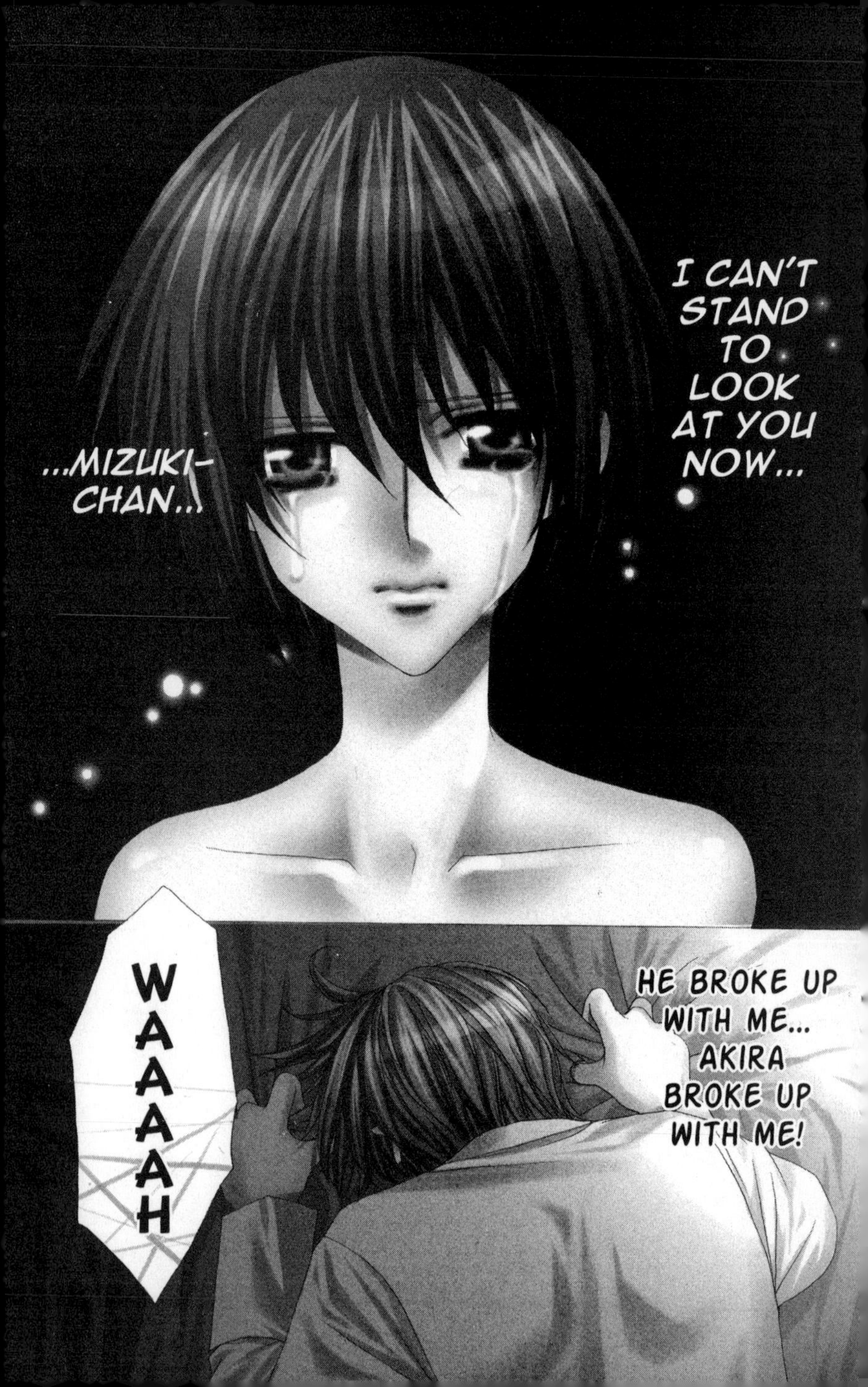
I CAN'T STAND TO LOOK AT YOU NOW...
...MIZUKI-CHAN...
HE BROKE UP WITH ME... AKIRA BROKE UP WITH ME!
WAAAAAH

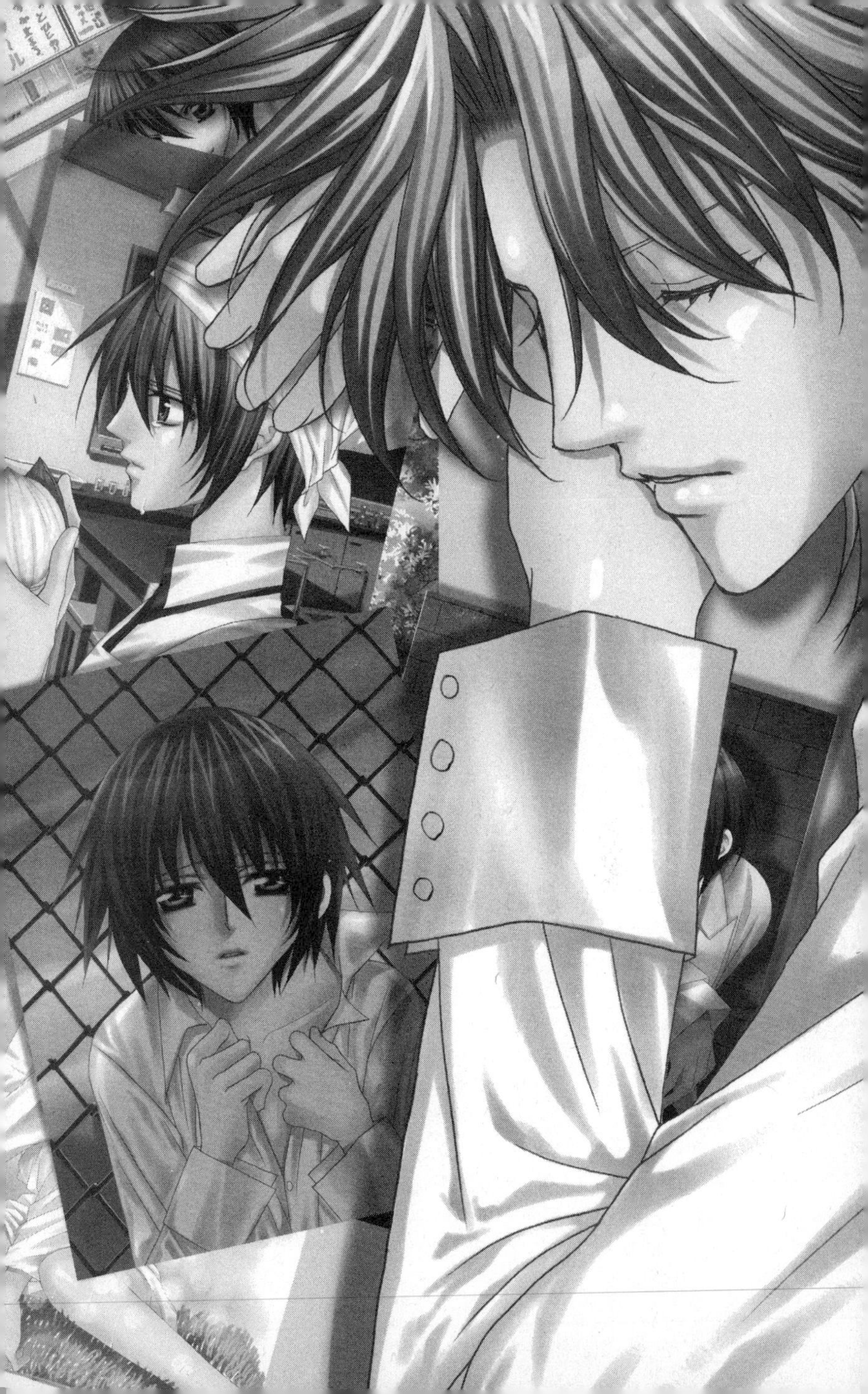

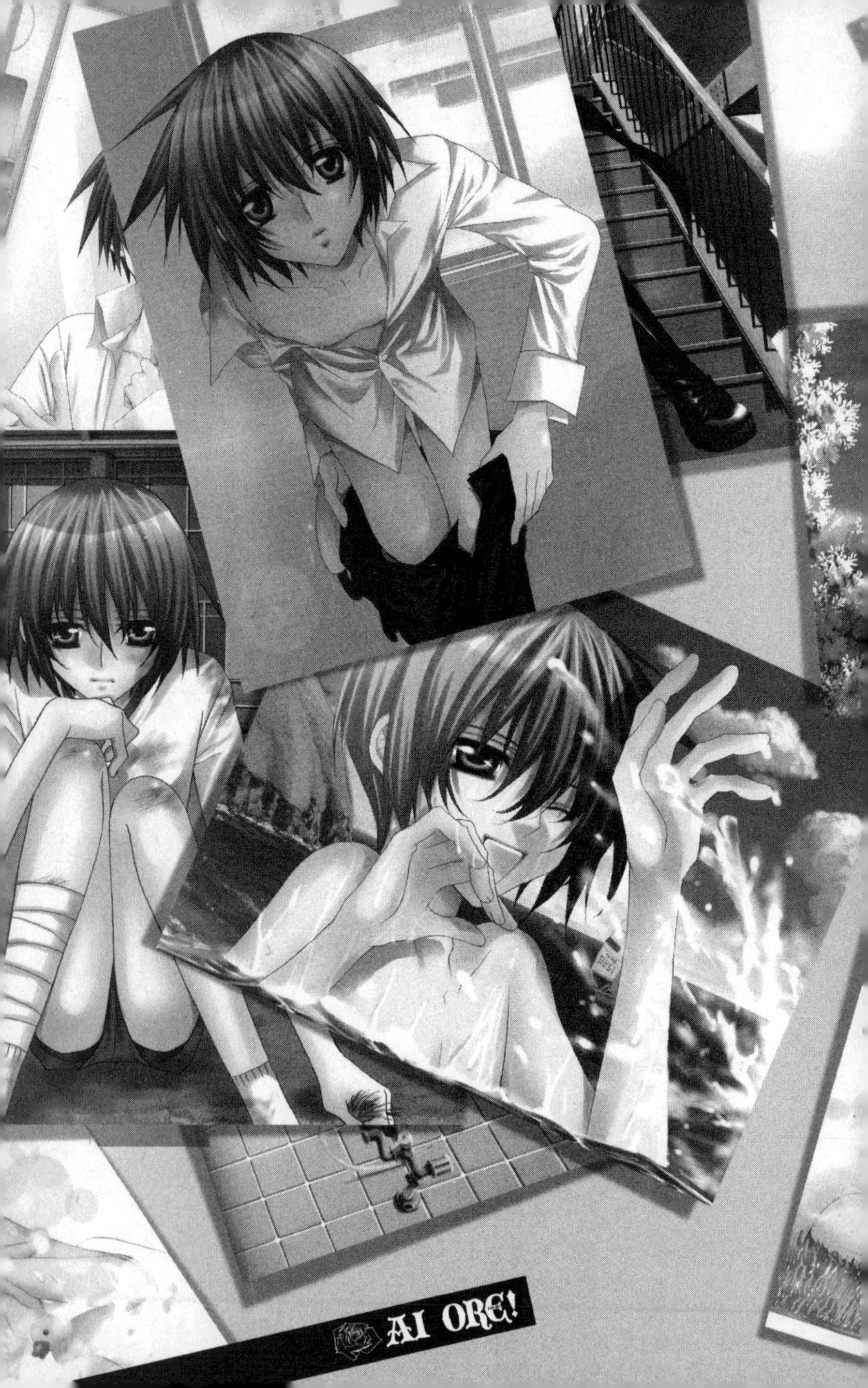
AI ORE!

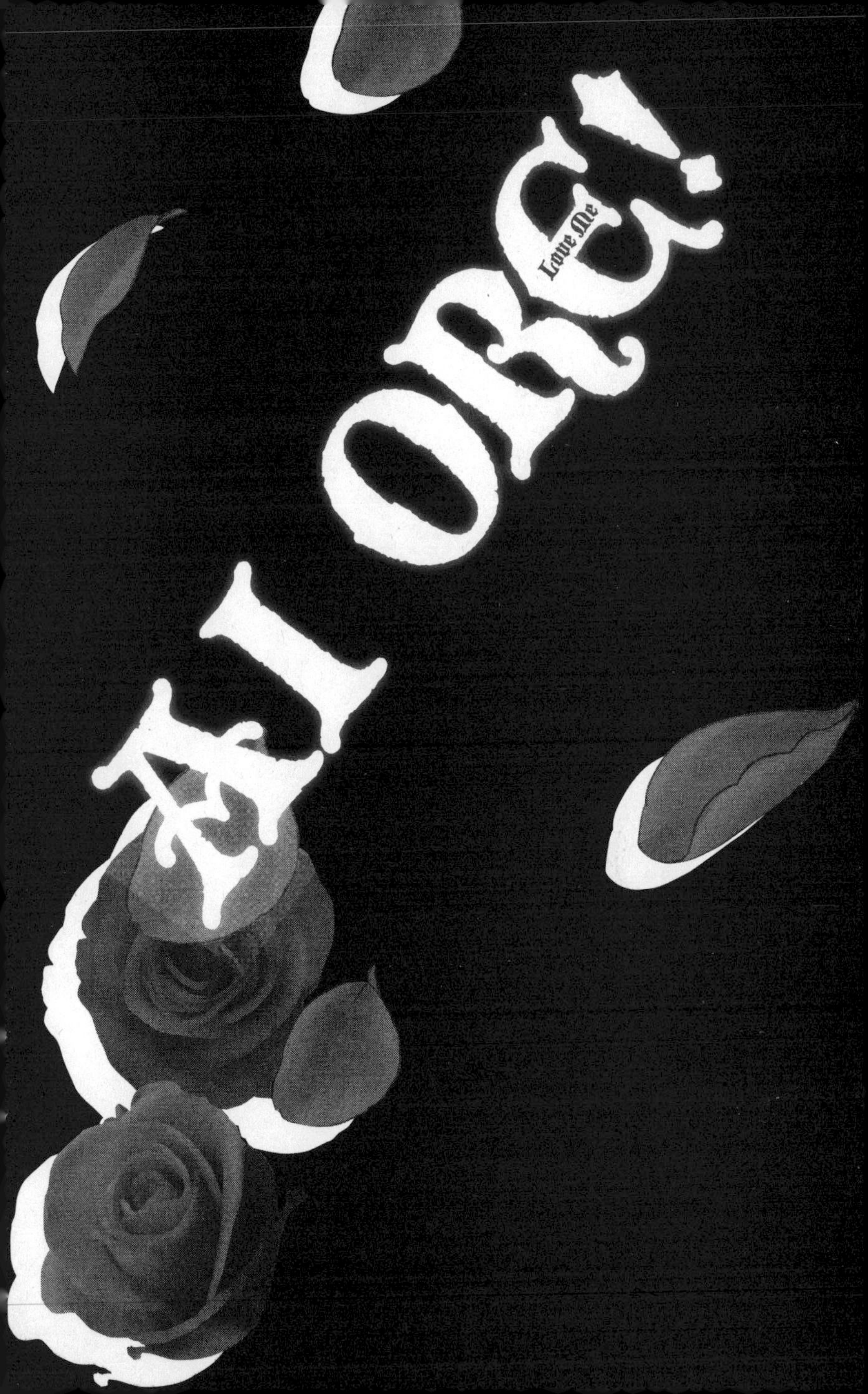
AI ORE!
Love Me

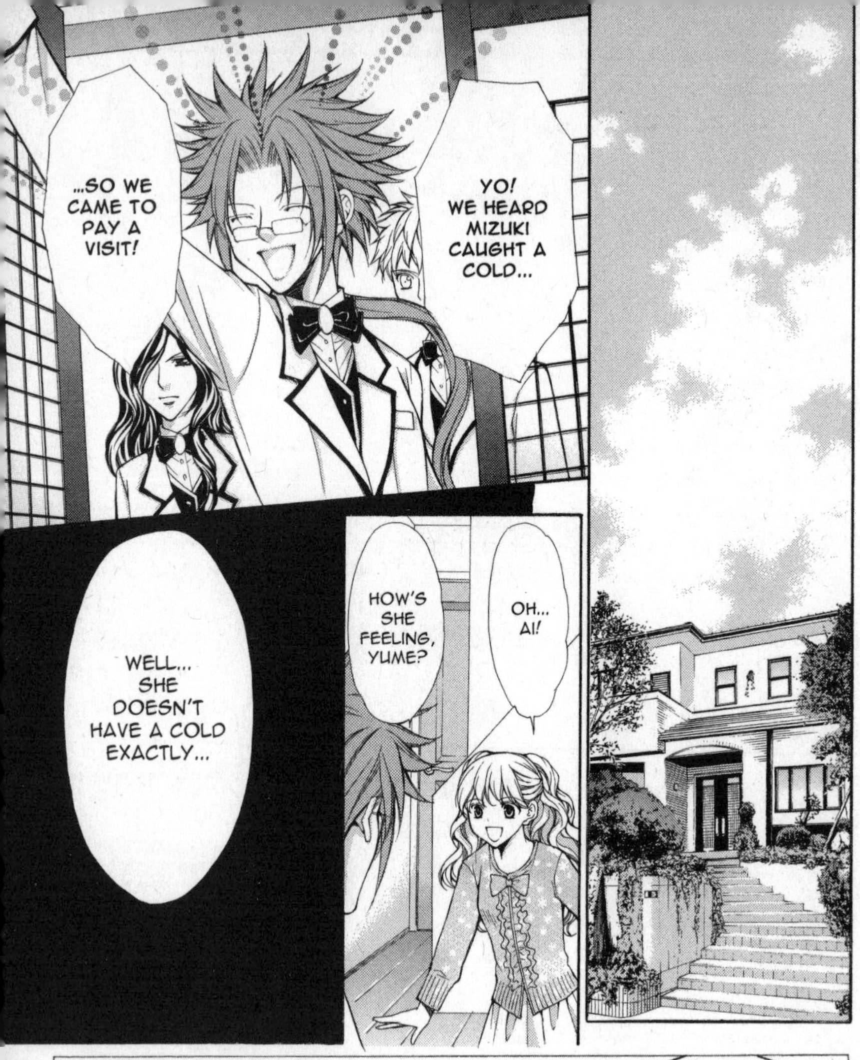
YO! WE HEARD MIZUKI CAUGHT A COLD...
...SO WE CAME TO PAY A VISIT!
OH... AI!
HOW'S SHE FEELING, YUME?
WELL... SHE DOESN'T HAVE A COLD EXACTLY...

About Sho

The porn specialist of *Ai Ore!* (laugh) I created him just because I wanted to draw a very lecherous character. He's an adult who has a very sexy aura. He's frivolous, but he also has emotional wounds of his own. I created him with readers who love characters like him in mind... I knew they would just adore him, but when I had him interact with another certain character, that character stole the scene! That character hardly appears in the story, but he has become extremely popular with many readers. Yes, that's right! I'm talking about Takumi, the new school president of St. Nobara!! I never thought he'd be so popular.

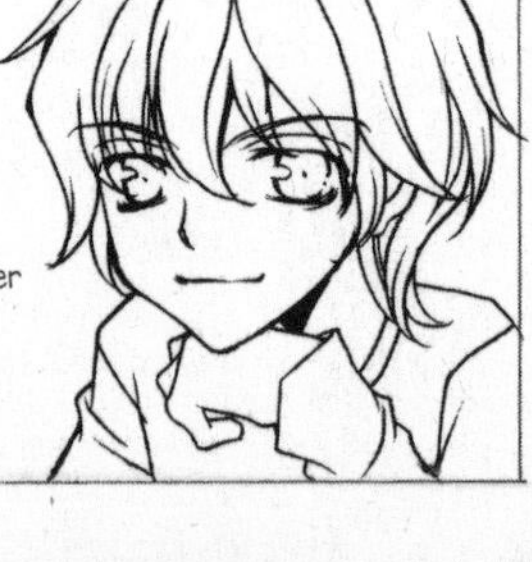

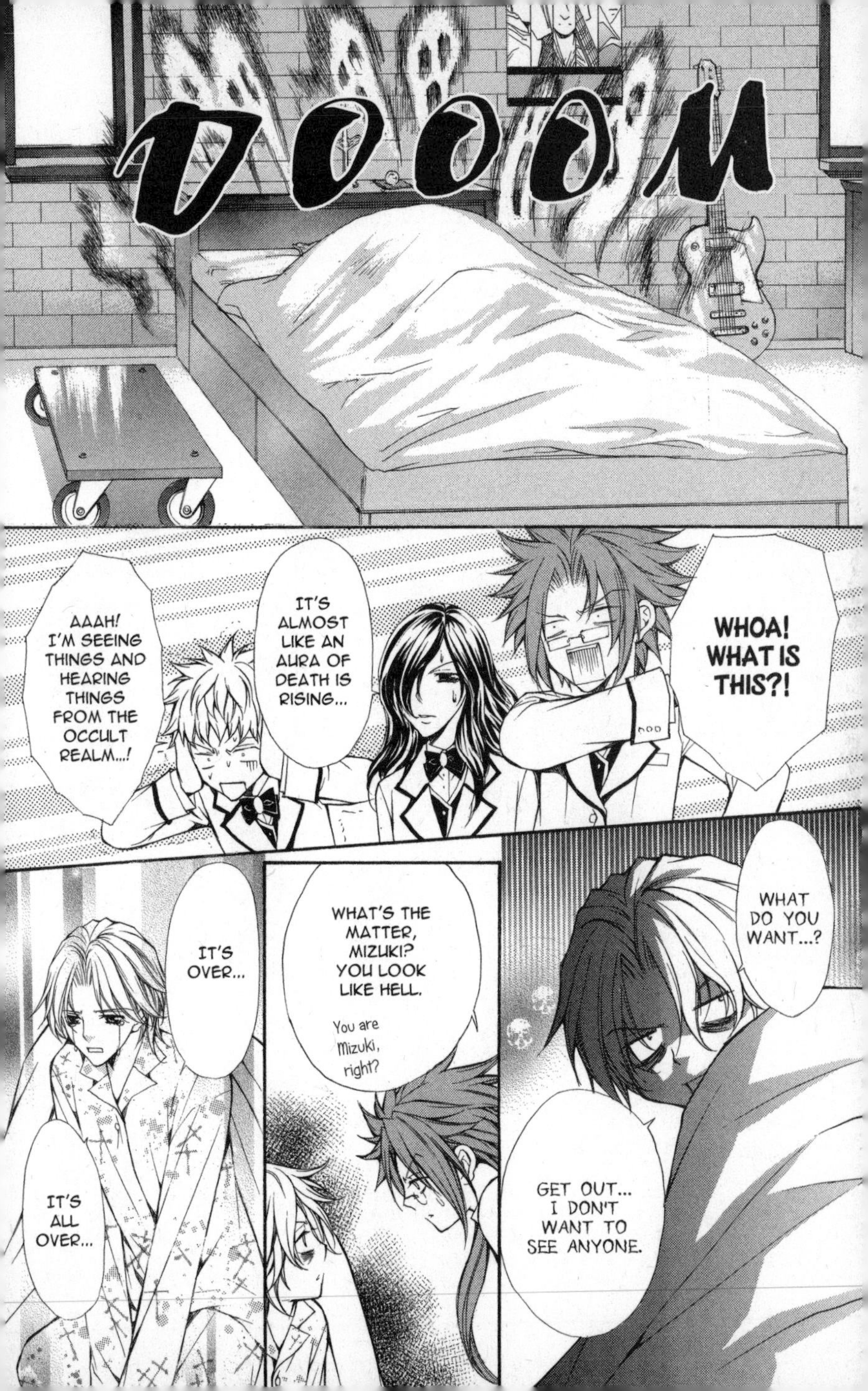
DOOOOM
WHOA! WHAT IS THIS?!
IT'S ALMOST LIKE AN AURA OF DEATH IS RISING...
AAAH! I'M SEEING THINGS AND HEARING THINGS FROM THE OCCULT REALM...!
WHAT DO YOU WANT...?
GET OUT... I DON'T WANT TO SEE ANYONE.
WHAT'S THE MATTER, MIZUKI? YOU LOOK LIKE HELL.
You are Mizuki, right?
IT'S OVER...
IT'S ALL OVER...

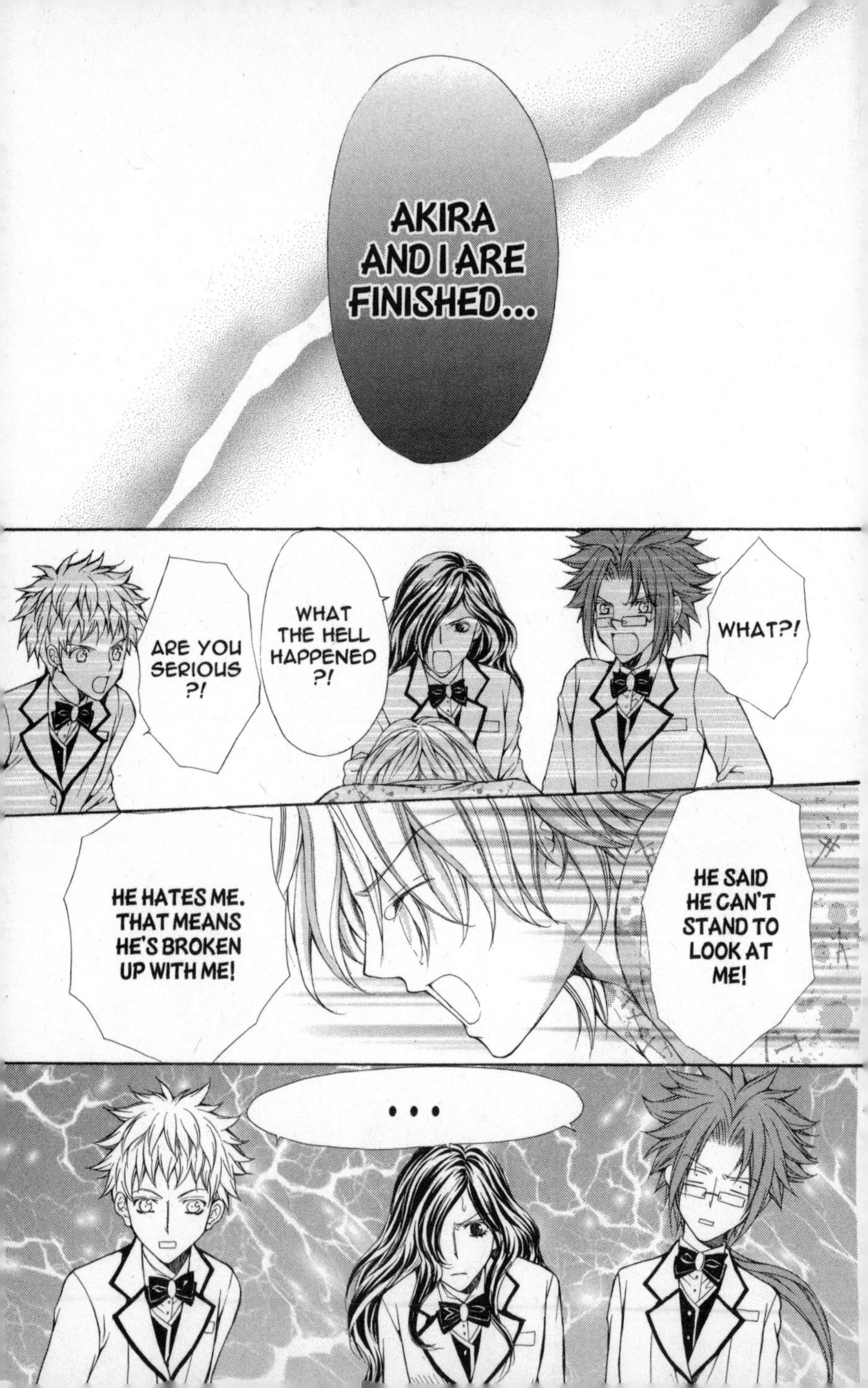
AKIRA AND I ARE FINISHED...
WHAT?!
WHAT THE HELL HAPPENED?!
ARE YOU SERIOUS?!
HE SAID HE CAN'T STAND TO LOOK AT ME!
HE HATES ME. THAT MEANS HE'S BROKEN UP WITH ME!
...

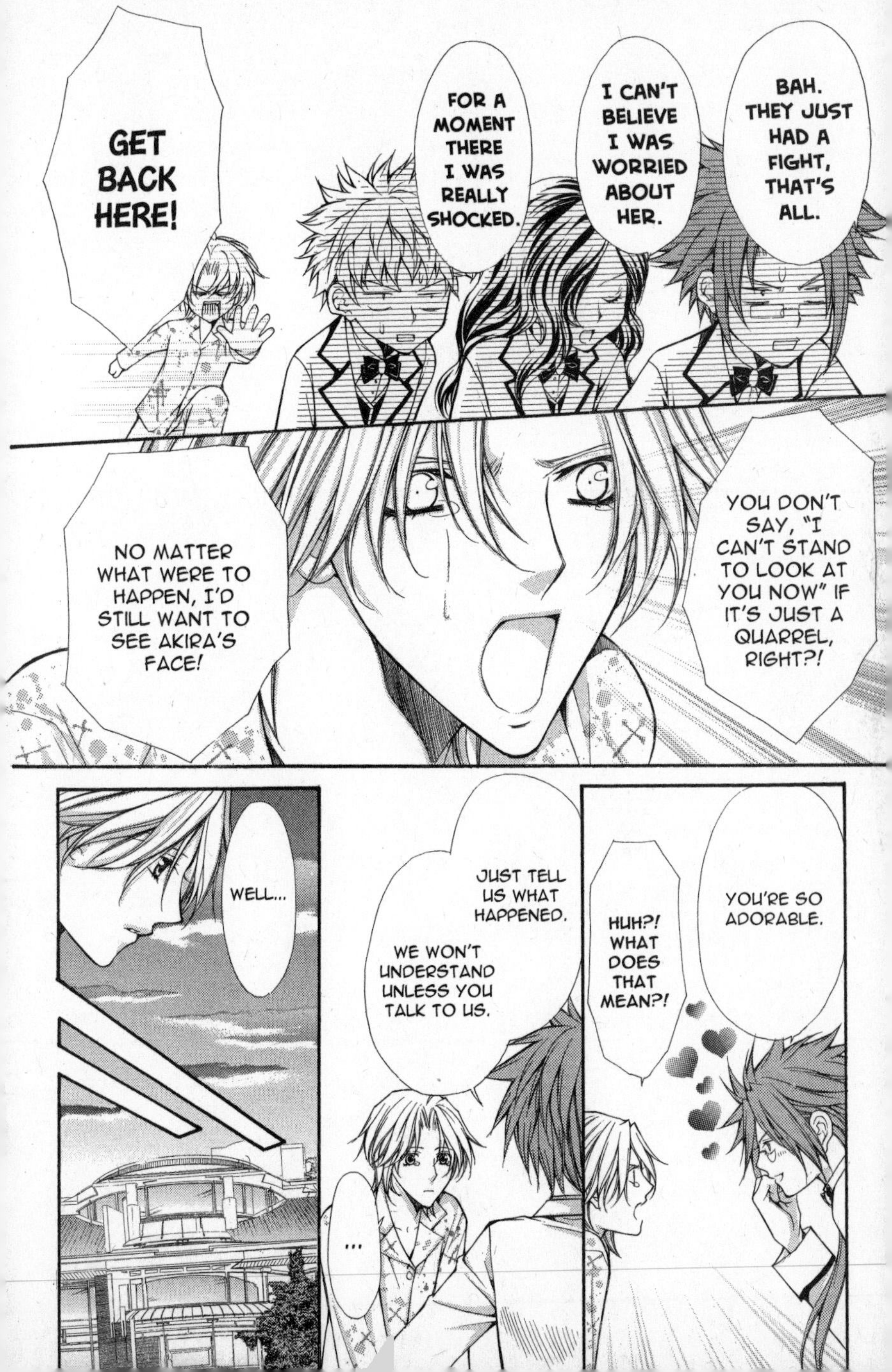
BAH. THEY JUST HAD A FIGHT, THAT'S ALL.
I CAN'T BELIEVE I WAS WORRIED ABOUT HER.
FOR A MOMENT THERE I WAS REALLY SHOCKED.
GET BACK HERE!
YOU DON'T SAY, "I CAN'T STAND TO LOOK AT YOU NOW" IF IT'S JUST A QUARREL, RIGHT?!
NO MATTER WHAT WERE TO HAPPEN, I'D STILL WANT TO SEE AKIRA'S FACE!
YOU'RE SO ADORABLE.
HUH?! WHAT DOES THAT MEAN?!
JUST TELL US WHAT HAPPENED.
WE WON'T UNDERSTAND UNLESS YOU TALK TO US.
...
WELL...

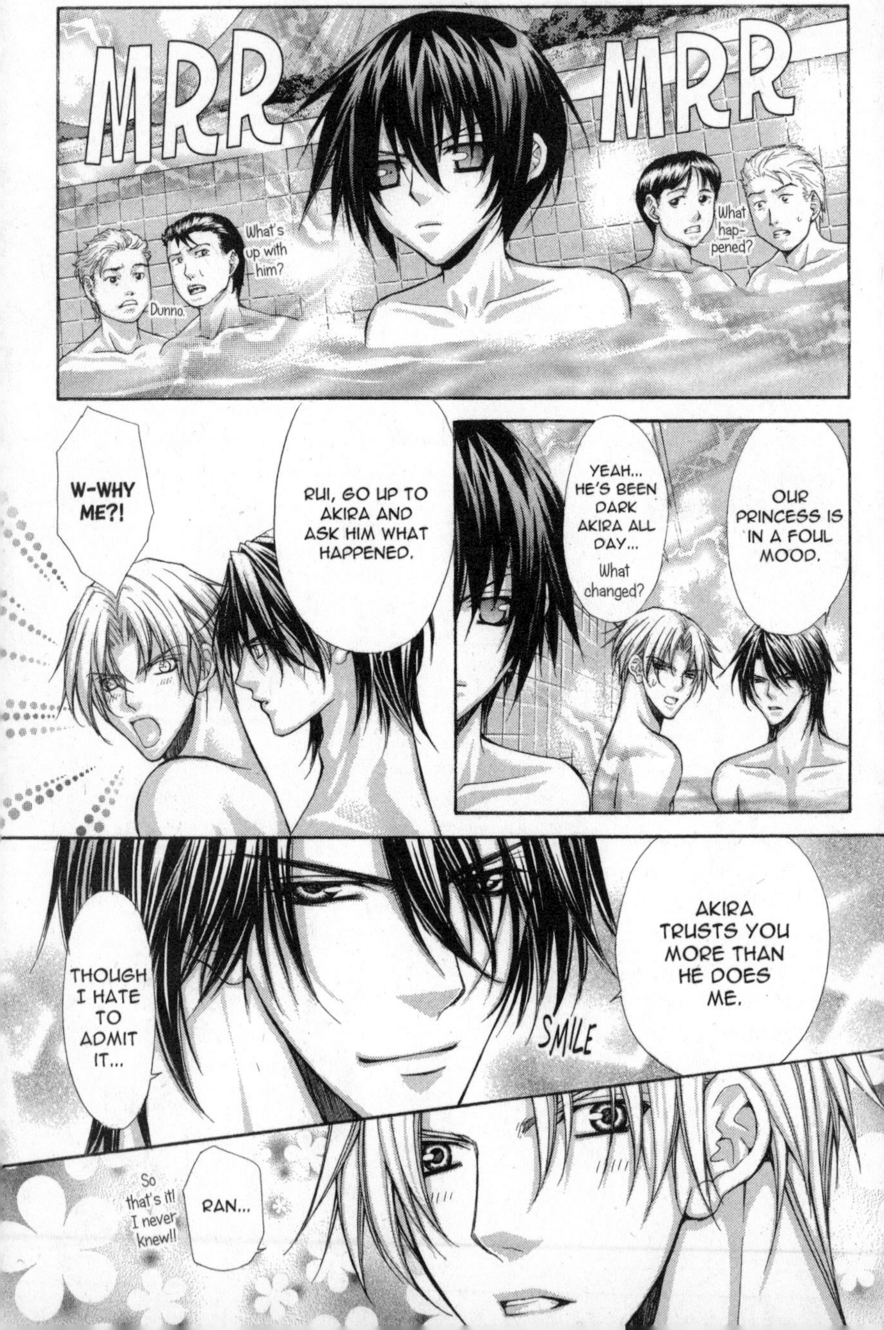
MRR
What hap-pened?
MRR
What's up with him?
Dunno.
OUR PRINCESS IS IN A FOUL MOOD.
YEAH... HE'S BEEN DARK AKIRA ALL DAY...
What changed?
RUI, GO UP TO AKIRA AND ASK HIM WHAT HAPPENED.
W-WHY ME?!
AKIRA TRUSTS YOU MORE THAN HE DOES ME.
SMILE
THOUGH I HATE TO ADMIT IT...
RAN...
So that's it! I never knew!!

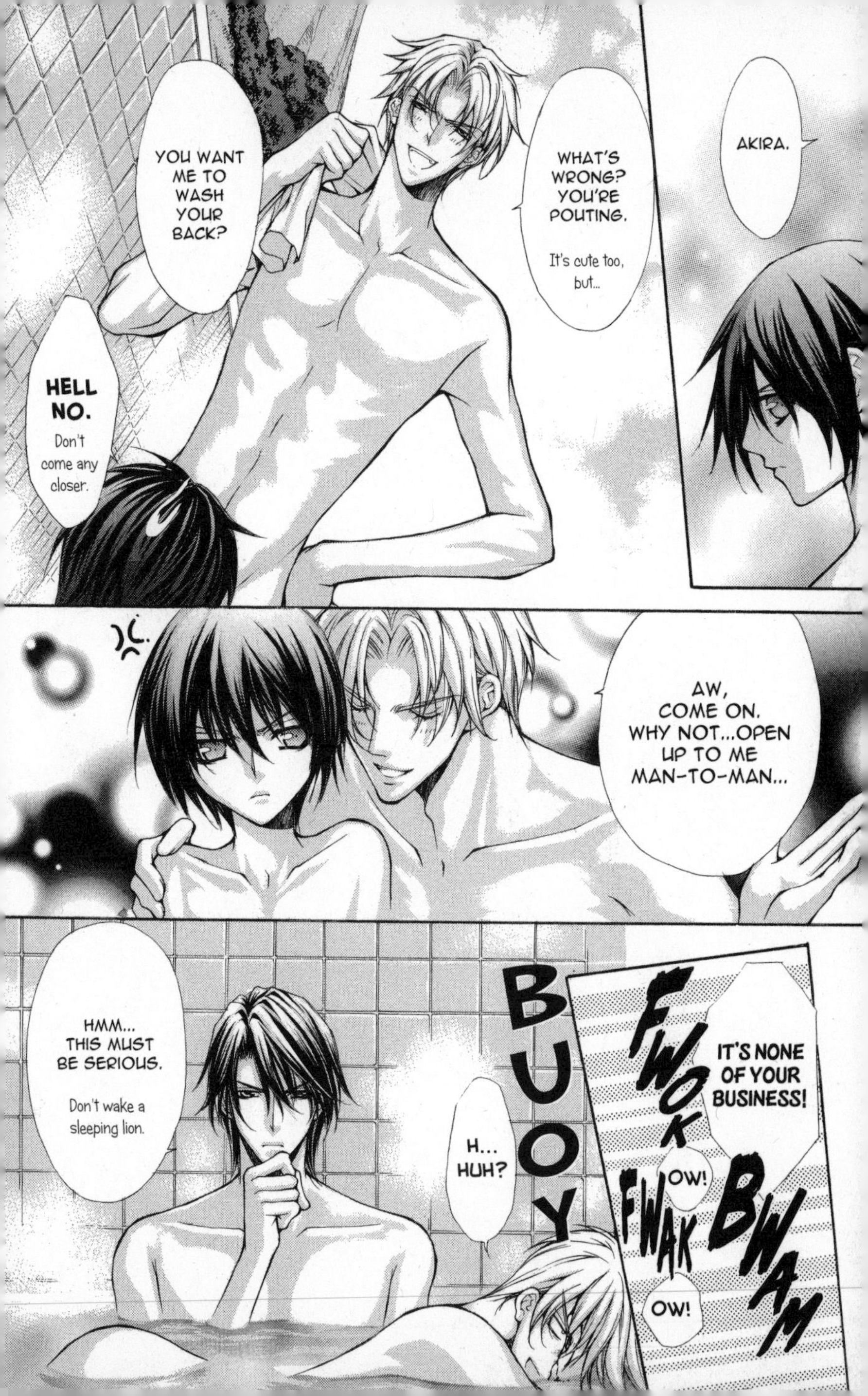
AKIRA.
WHAT'S WRONG? YOU'RE POUTING.
It's cute too, but...
YOU WANT ME TO WASH YOUR BACK?
HELL NO.
Don't come any closer.
AW, COME ON. WHY NOT...OPEN UP TO ME MAN-TO-MAN...
IT'S NONE OF YOUR BUSINESS!
FWOK
OW!
FWAK
BWAM
OW!
BUOY
H... HUH?
HMM... THIS MUST BE SERIOUS.
Don't wake a sleeping lion.

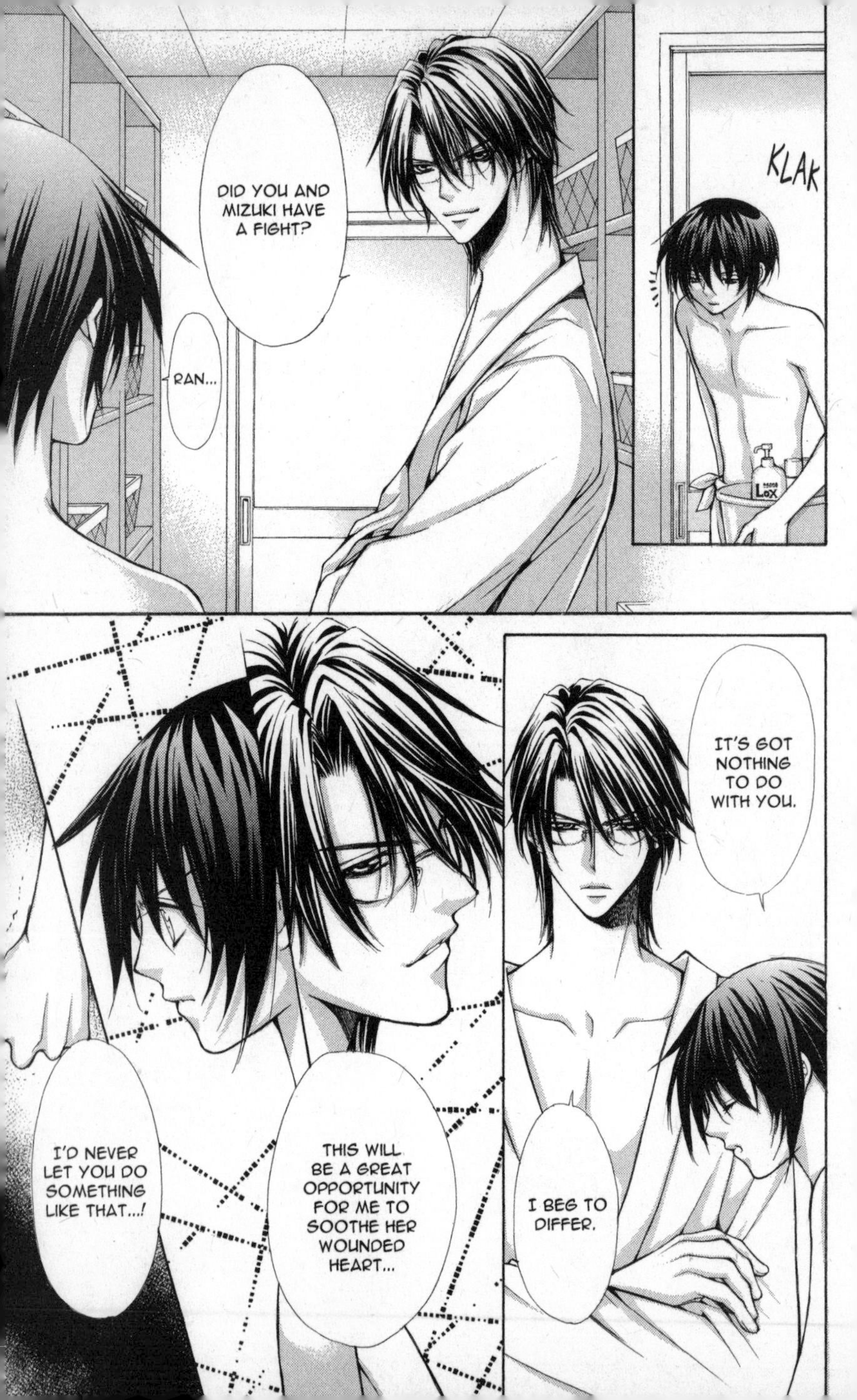
KLAK
DID YOU AND MIZUKI HAVE A FIGHT?
RAN...
IT'S GOT NOTHING TO DO WITH YOU.
I BEG TO DIFFER.
THIS WILL BE A GREAT OPPORTUNITY FOR ME TO SOOTHE HER WOUNDED HEART...
I'D NEVER LET YOU DO SOMETHING LIKE THAT...!

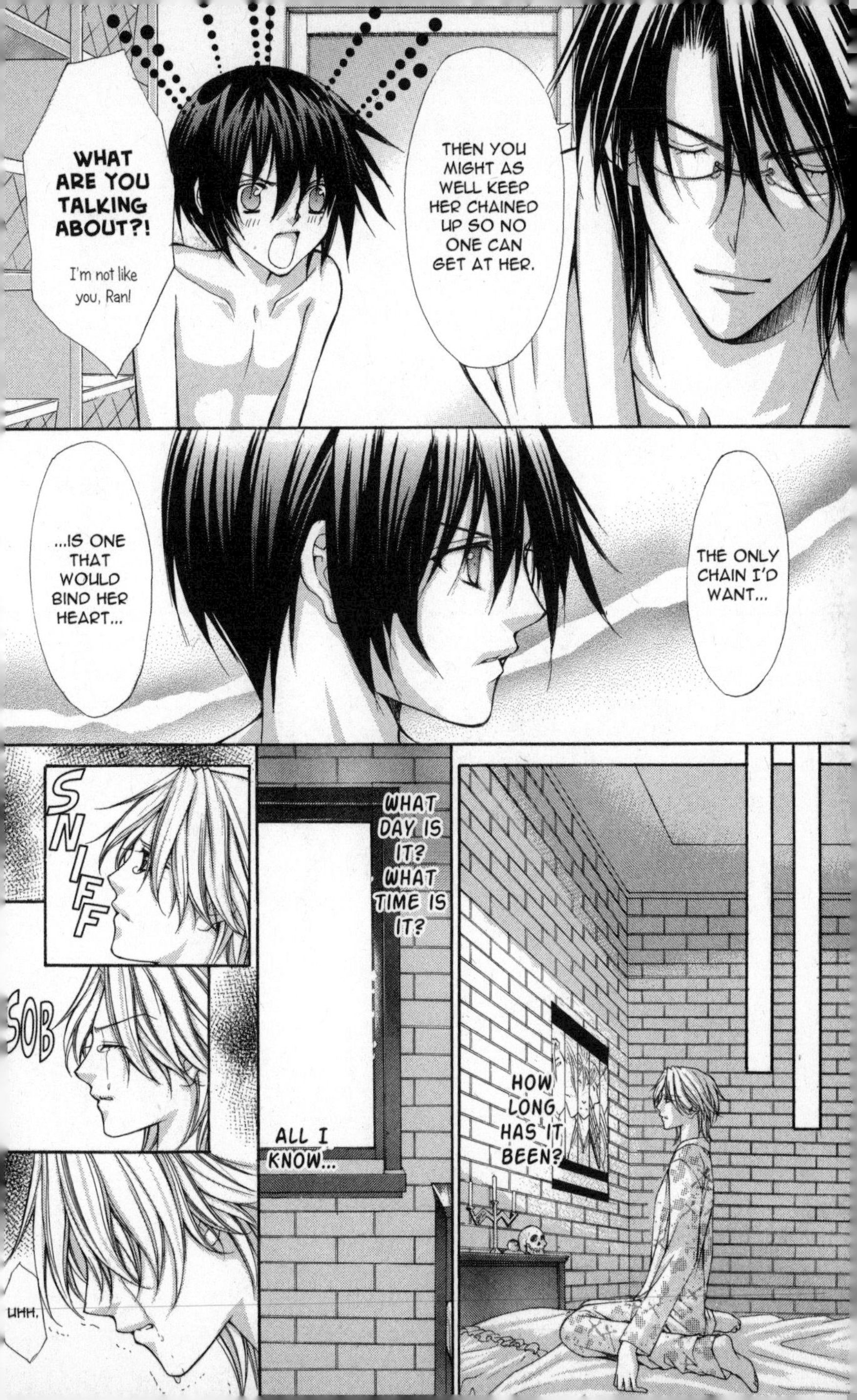
THEN YOU MIGHT AS WELL KEEP HER CHAINED UP SO NO ONE CAN GET AT HER.
WHAT ARE YOU TALKING ABOUT?!
I'm not like you, Ran!
THE ONLY CHAIN I'D WANT...
...IS ONE THAT WOULD BIND HER HEART...
HOW LONG HAS IT BEEN?
WHAT DAY IS IT? WHAT TIME IS IT?
ALL I KNOW...
SNIFF
SOB
UHH.

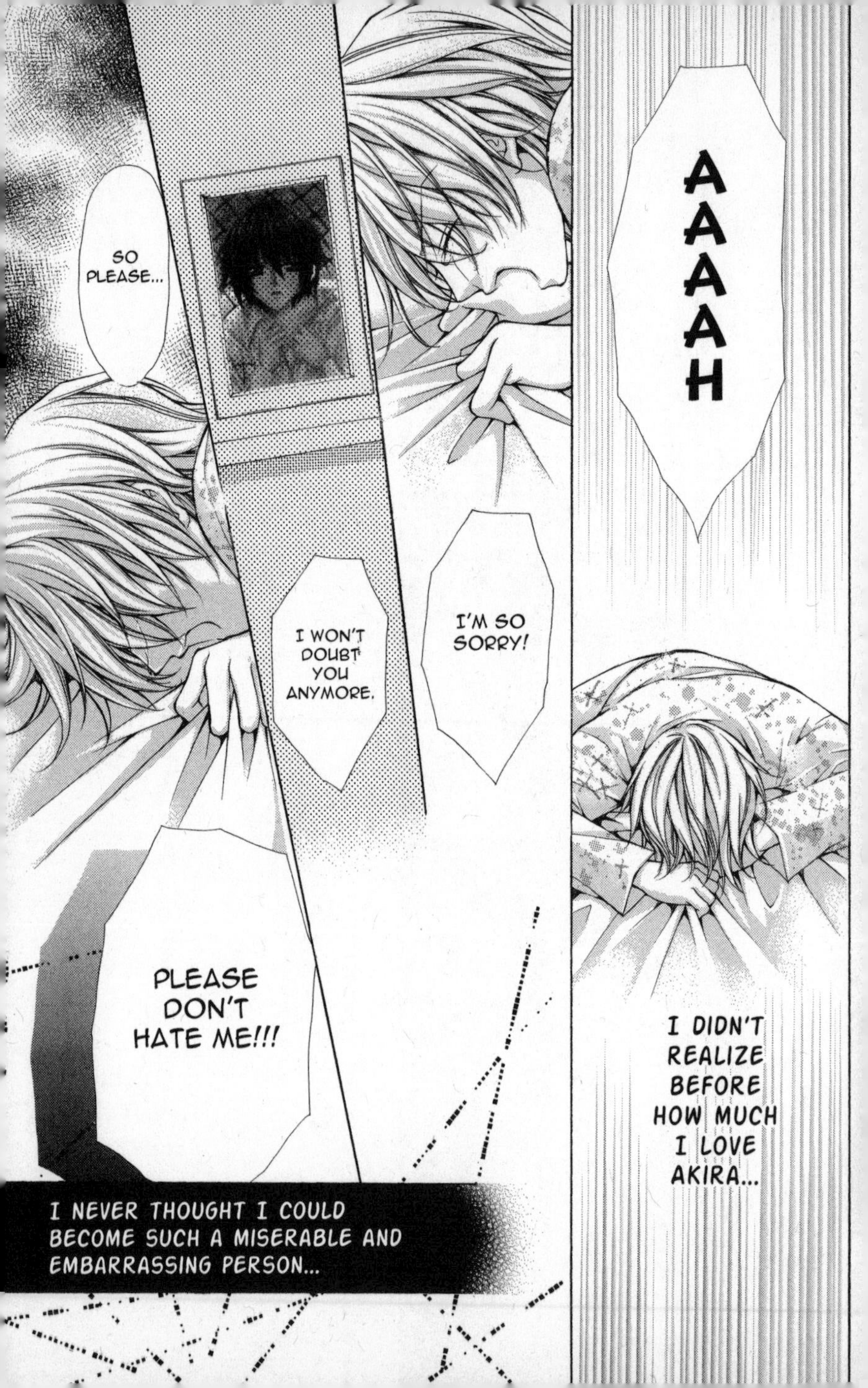
AAAAH
I DIDN'T REALIZE BEFORE HOW MUCH I LOVE AKIRA...
I'M SO SORRY!
I WON'T DOUBT YOU ANYMORE.
SO PLEASE...
PLEASE DON'T HATE ME!!!
I NEVER THOUGHT I COULD BECOME SUCH A MISERABLE AND EMBARRASSING PERSON...

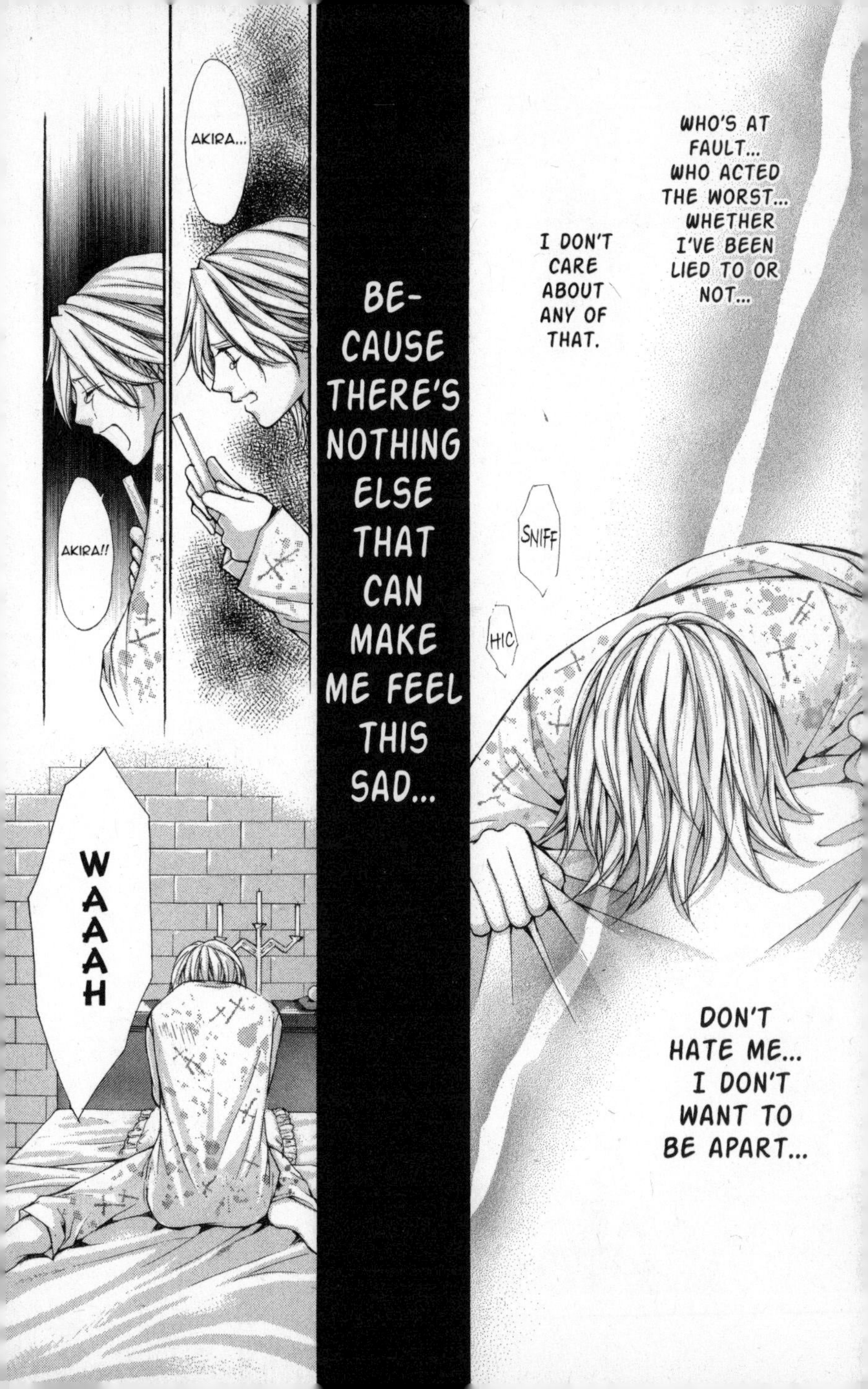
WHO'S AT FAULT... WHO ACTED THE WORST... WHETHER I'VE BEEN LIED TO OR NOT...
I DON'T CARE ABOUT ANY OF THAT.
SNIFF
HIC
DON'T HATE ME... I DON'T WANT TO BE APART...
BE-CAUSE THERE'S NOTHING ELSE THAT CAN MAKE ME FEEL THIS SAD...
AKIRA...
AKIRA!!
WAAAAH

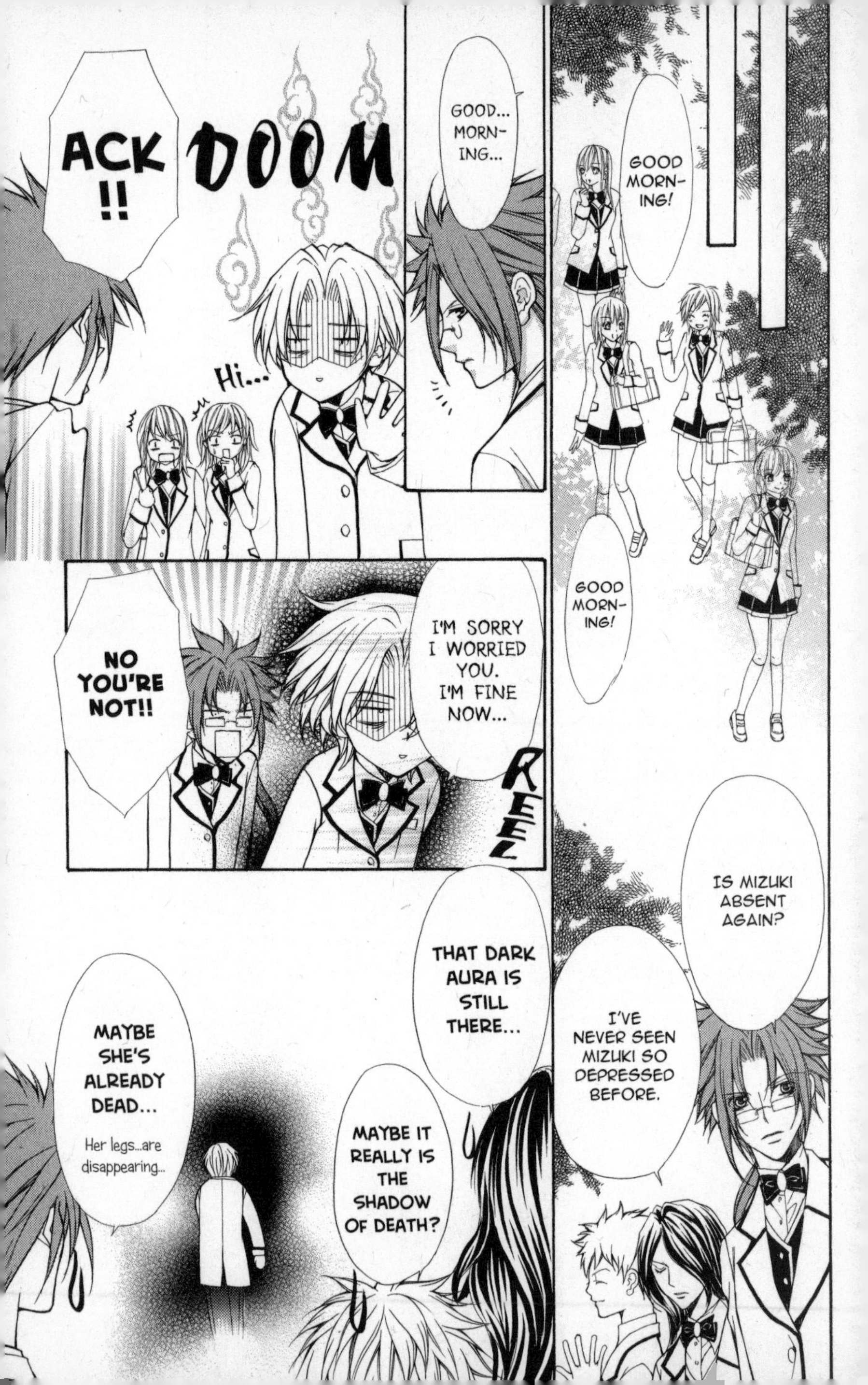
GOOD MORN-ING!
GOOD MORN-ING!
IS MIZUKI ABSENT AGAIN?
I'VE NEVER SEEN MIZUKI SO DEPRESSED BEFORE.
GOOD... MORN-ING...
ACK !!
DOOM
Hi...
I'M SORRY I WORRIED YOU. I'M FINE NOW...
REEL
NO YOU'RE NOT!!
THAT DARK AURA IS STILL THERE...
MAYBE IT REALLY IS THE SHADOW OF DEATH?
MAYBE SHE'S ALREADY DEAD...
Her legs...are disappearing...

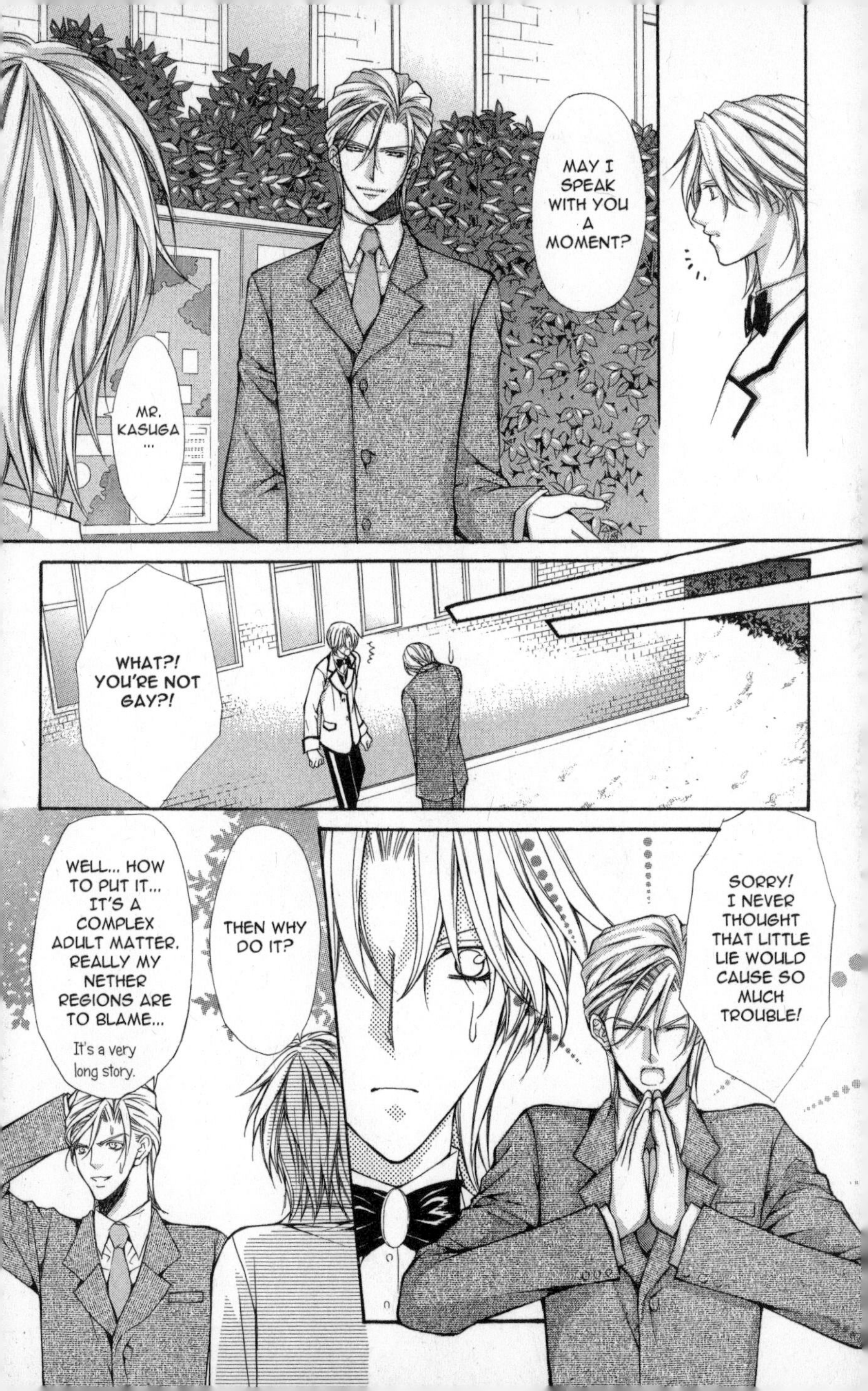
MAY I SPEAK WITH YOU A MOMENT?
MR. KASUGA ...
WHAT?! YOU'RE NOT GAY?!
SORRY! I NEVER THOUGHT THAT LITTLE LIE WOULD CAUSE SO MUCH TROUBLE!
THEN WHY DO IT?
WELL... HOW TO PUT IT... IT'S A COMPLEX ADULT MATTER. REALLY MY NETHER REGIONS ARE TO BLAME...
It's a very long story.

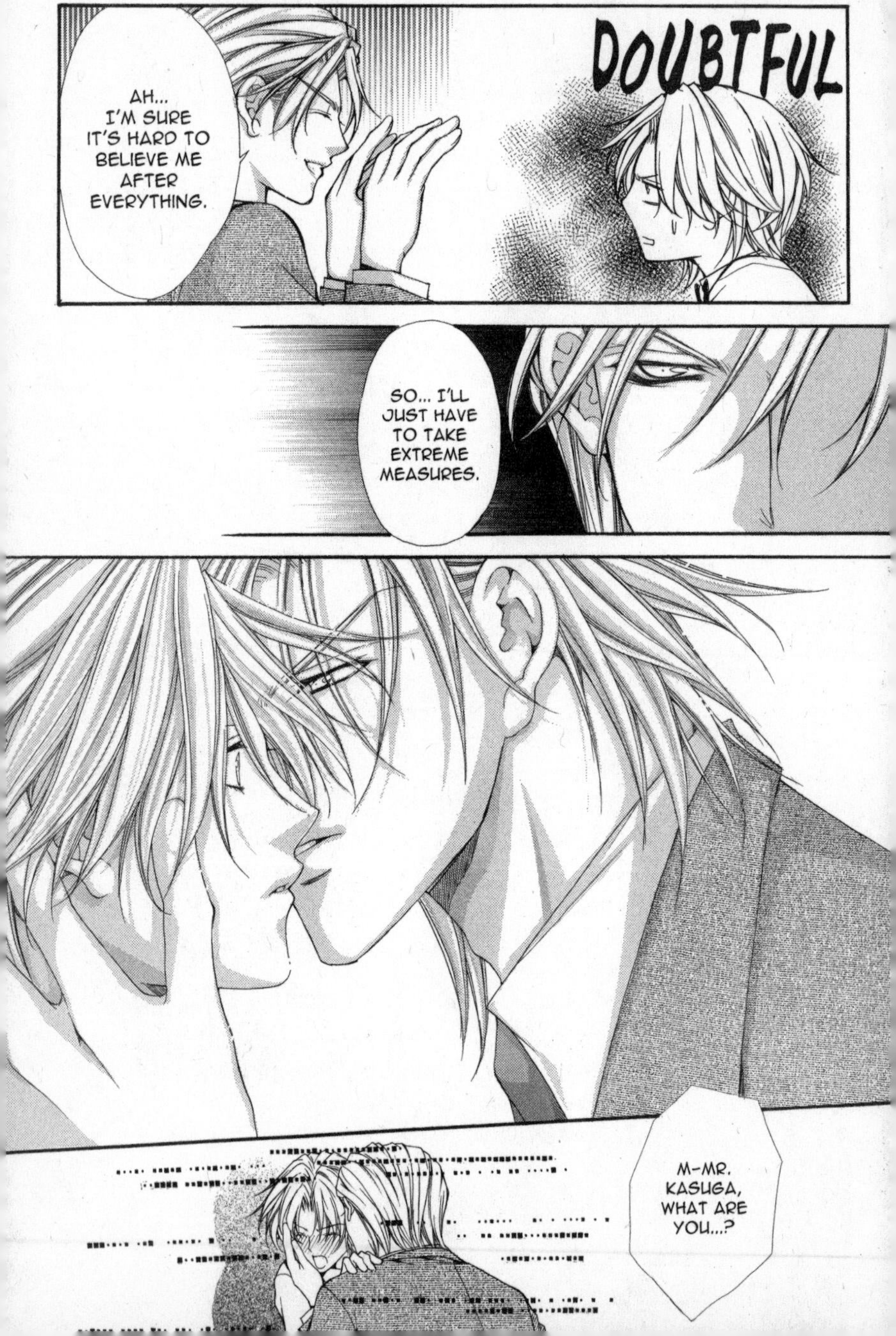
DOUBTFUL
AH... I'M SURE IT'S HARD TO BELIEVE ME AFTER EVERYTHING.
SO... I'LL JUST HAVE TO TAKE EXTREME MEASURES.
M-MR. KASUGA, WHAT ARE YOU...?

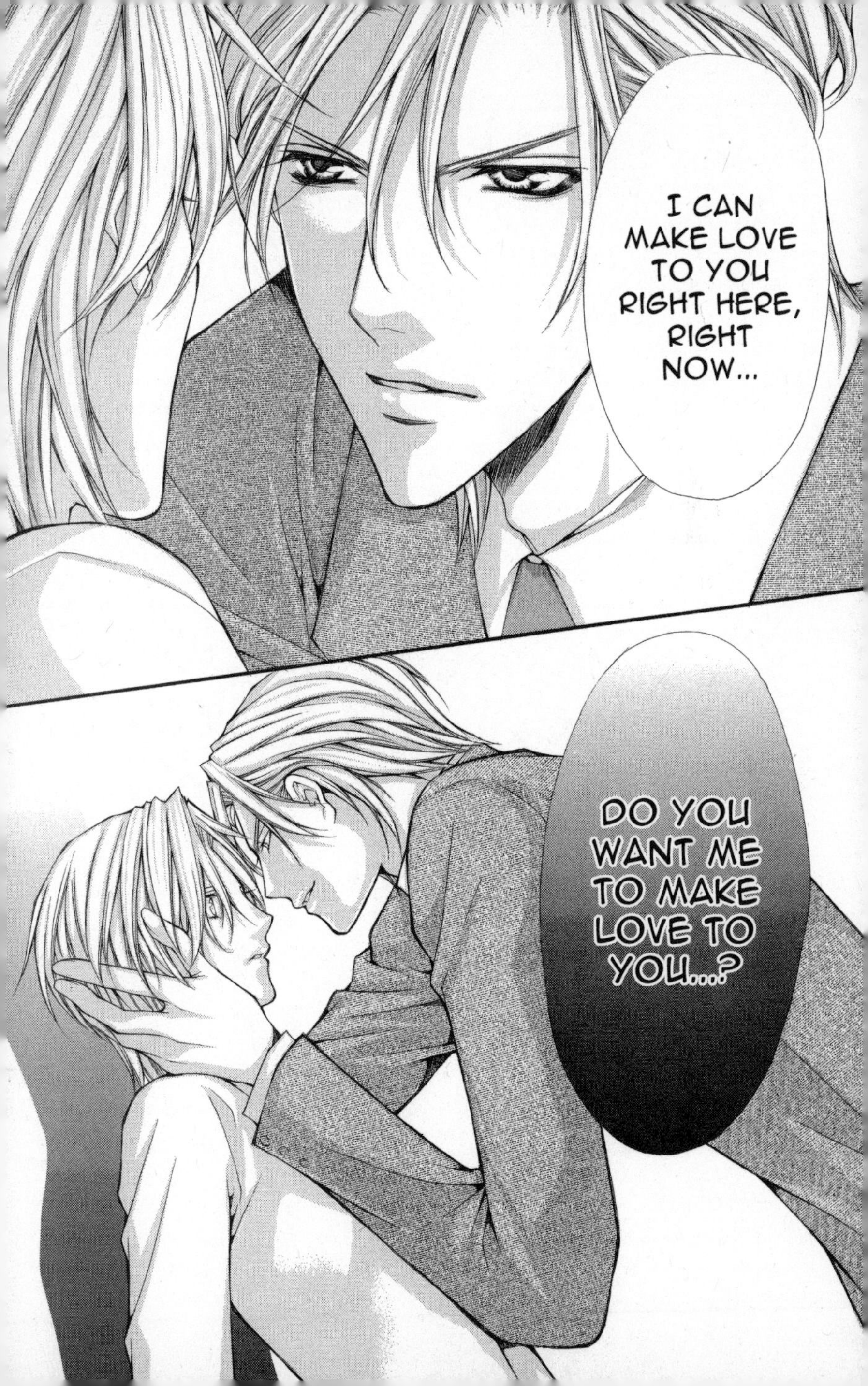
I CAN MAKE LOVE TO YOU RIGHT HERE, RIGHT NOW...
DO YOU WANT ME TO MAKE LOVE TO YOU...?

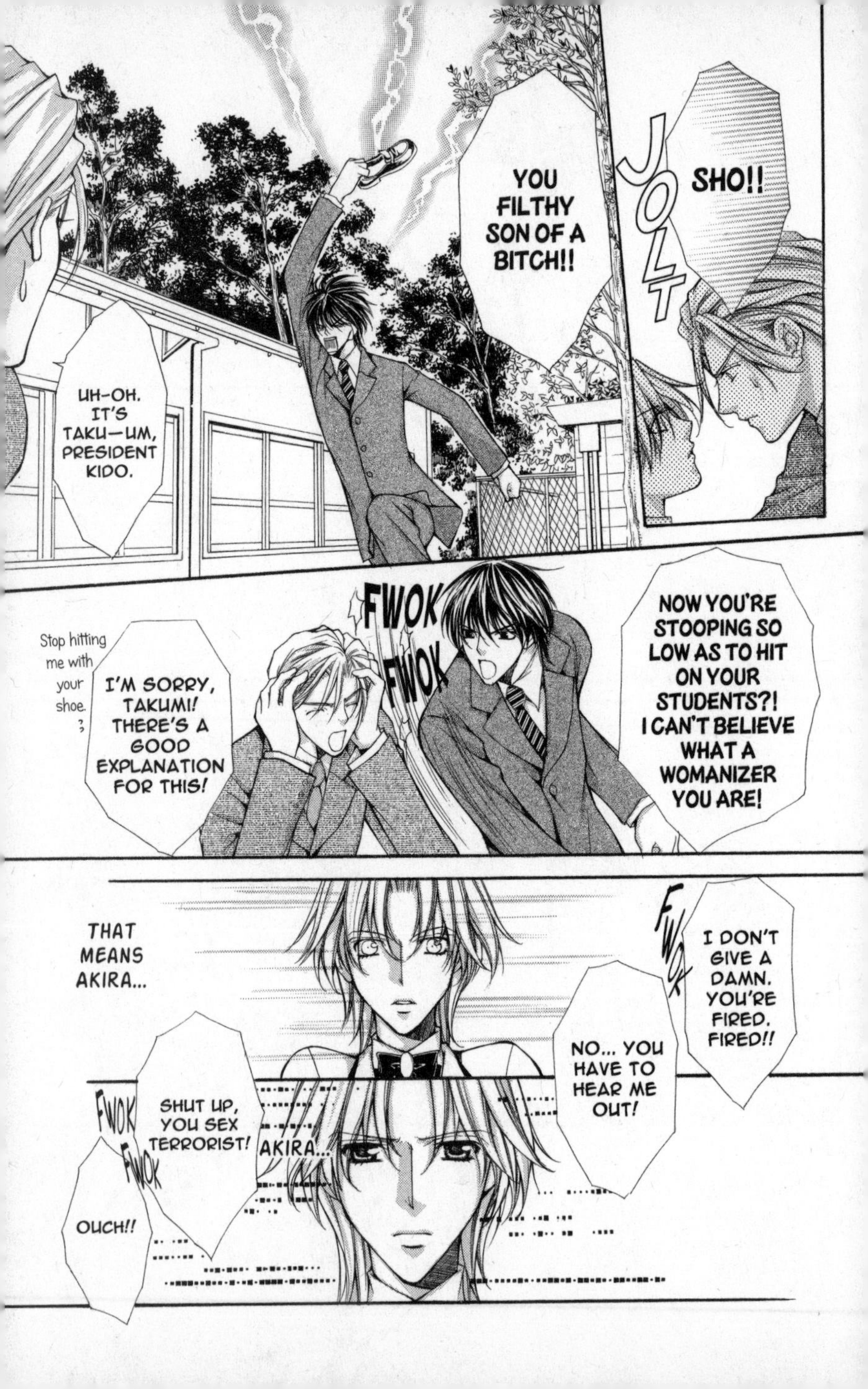
SHO!!
JOLT
YOU FILTHY SON OF A BITCH!!
UH-OH. IT'S TAKU—UM, PRESIDENT KIDO.
NOW YOU'RE STOOPING SO LOW AS TO HIT ON YOUR STUDENTS?! I CAN'T BELIEVE WHAT A WOMANIZER YOU ARE!
FWOK
FWOK
I'M SORRY, TAKUMI! THERE'S A GOOD EXPLANATION FOR THIS!
Stop hitting me with your shoe.
I DON'T GIVE A DAMN. YOU'RE FIRED. FIRED!!
FWOK
NO... YOU HAVE TO HEAR ME OUT!
THAT MEANS AKIRA...
AKIRA...
SHUT UP, YOU SEX TERRORIST!
FWOK
FWOK
OUCH!!

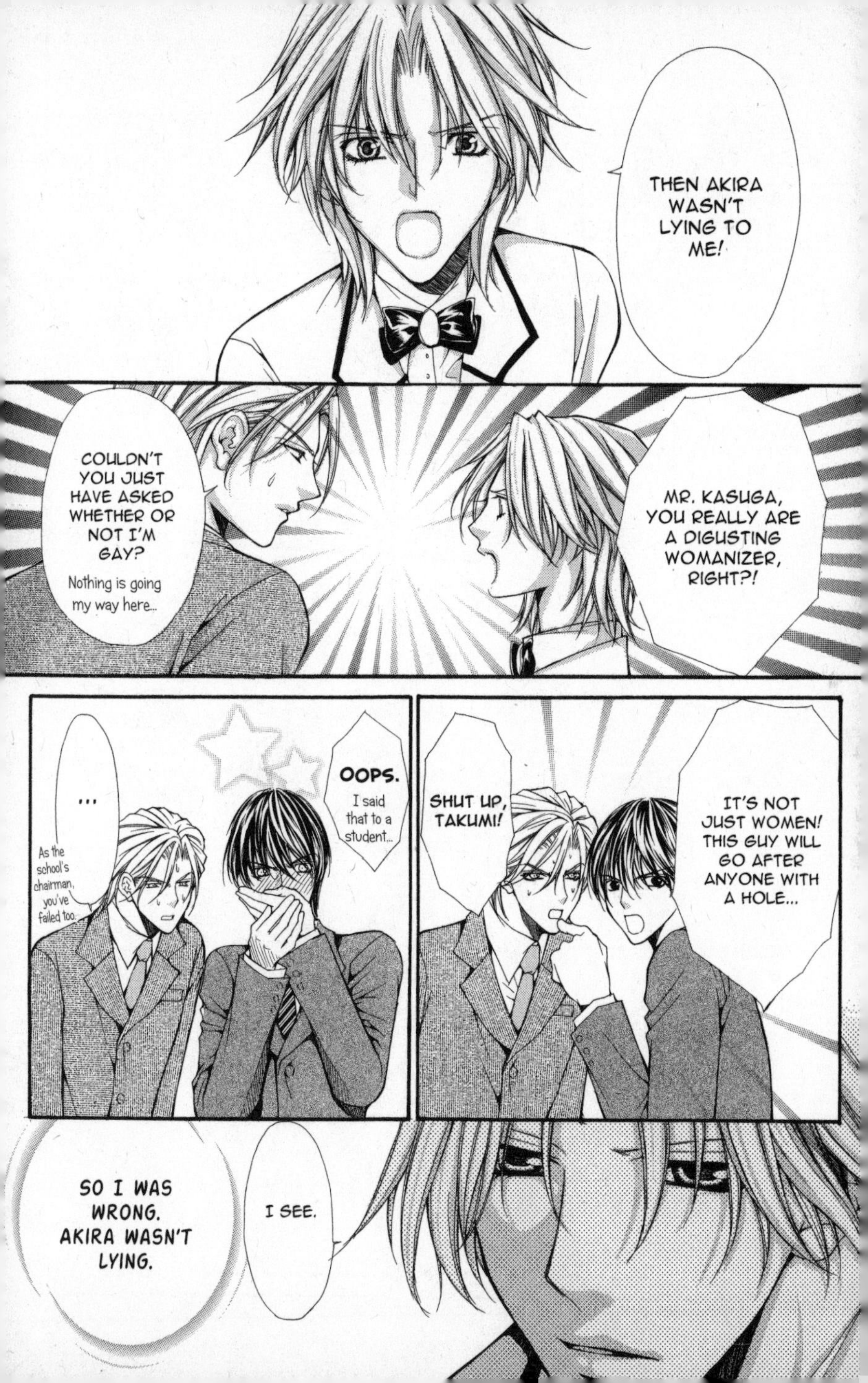
THEN AKIRA WASN'T LYING TO ME!
MR. KASUGA, YOU REALLY ARE A DIGUSTING WOMANIZER, RIGHT?!
COULDN'T YOU JUST HAVE ASKED WHETHER OR NOT I'M GAY?
Nothing is going my way here...
IT'S NOT JUST WOMEN! THIS GUY WILL GO AFTER ANYONE WITH A HOLE...
SHUT UP, TAKUMI!
OOPS.
I said that to a student...
...
As the school's chairman, you've failed too.
I SEE.
SO I WAS WRONG. AKIRA WASN'T LYING.

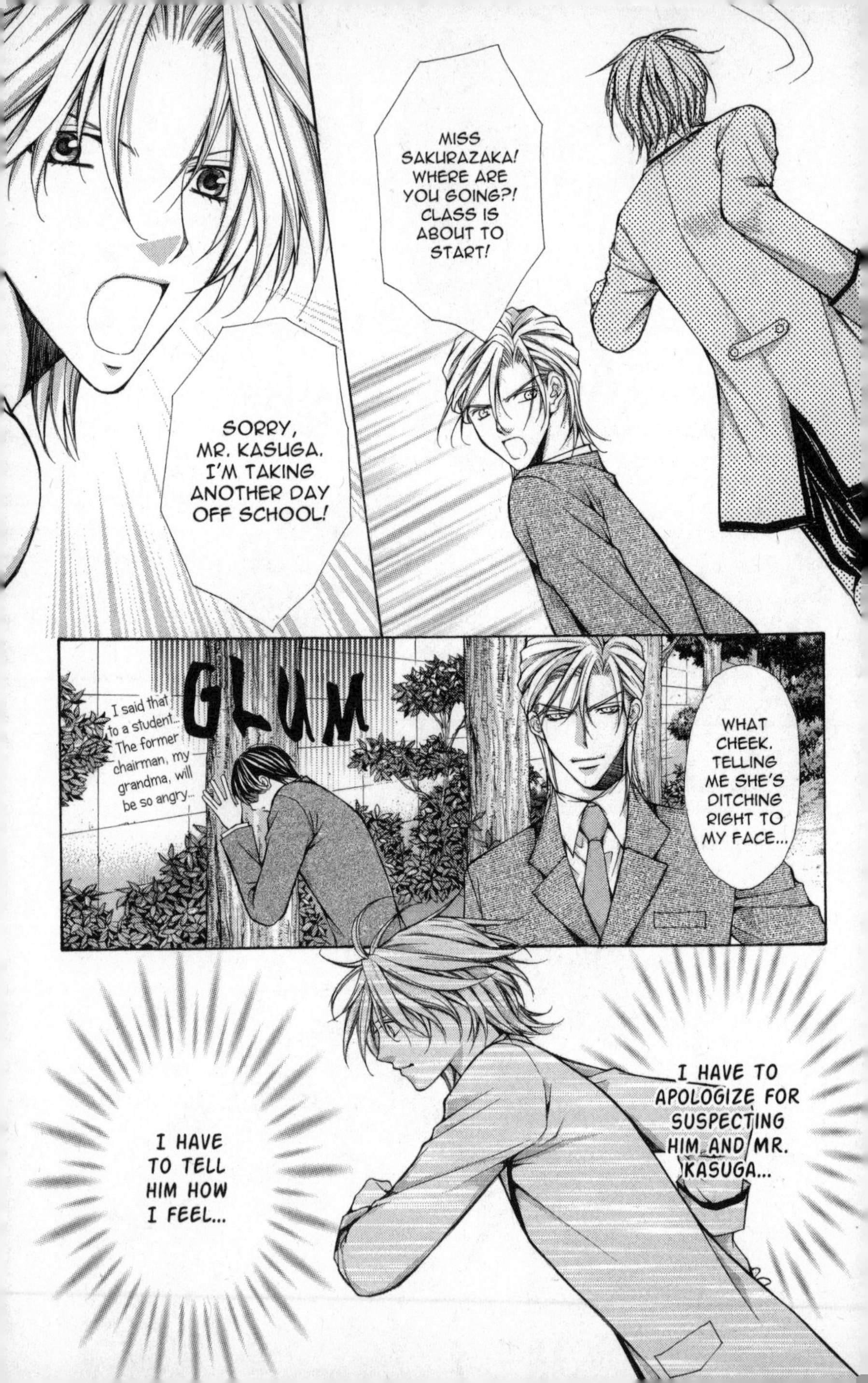
MISS SAKURAZAKA! WHERE ARE YOU GOING?! CLASS IS ABOUT TO START!
SORRY, MR. KASUGA. I'M TAKING ANOTHER DAY OFF SCHOOL!
WHAT CHEEK. TELLING ME SHE'S DITCHING RIGHT TO MY FACE...
GLUM
I said that to a student... The former chairman, my grandma, will be so angry...
I HAVE TO APOLOGIZE FOR SUSPECTING HIM AND MR. KASUGA...
I HAVE TO TELL HIM HOW I FEEL...

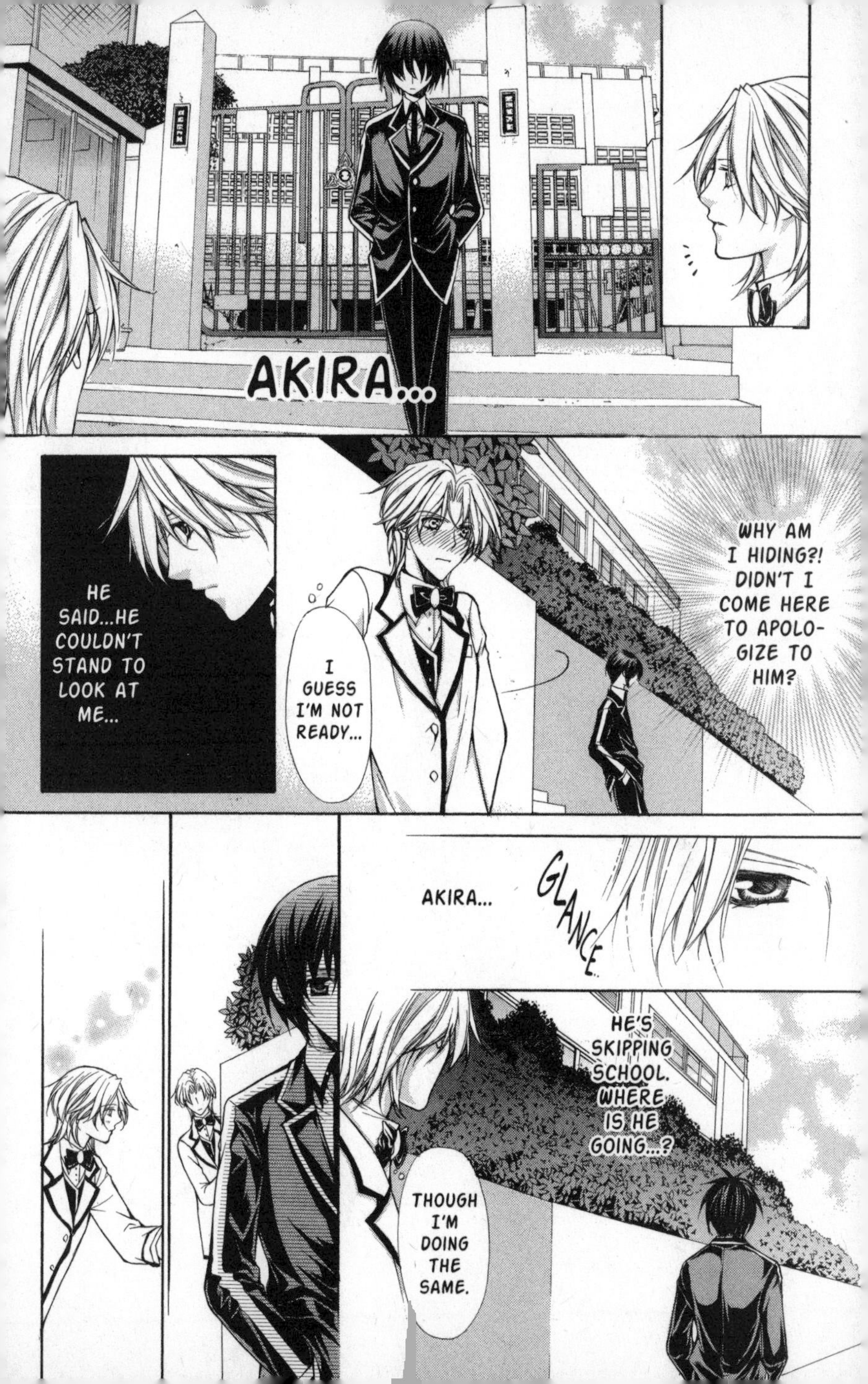
AKIRA...
WHY AM I HIDING?! DIDN'T I COME HERE TO APOLO-GIZE TO HIM?
I GUESS I'M NOT READY...
HE SAID...HE COULDN'T STAND TO LOOK AT ME...
GLANCE
AKIRA...
HE'S SKIPPING SCHOOL. WHERE IS HE GOING...?
THOUGH I'M DOING THE SAME.

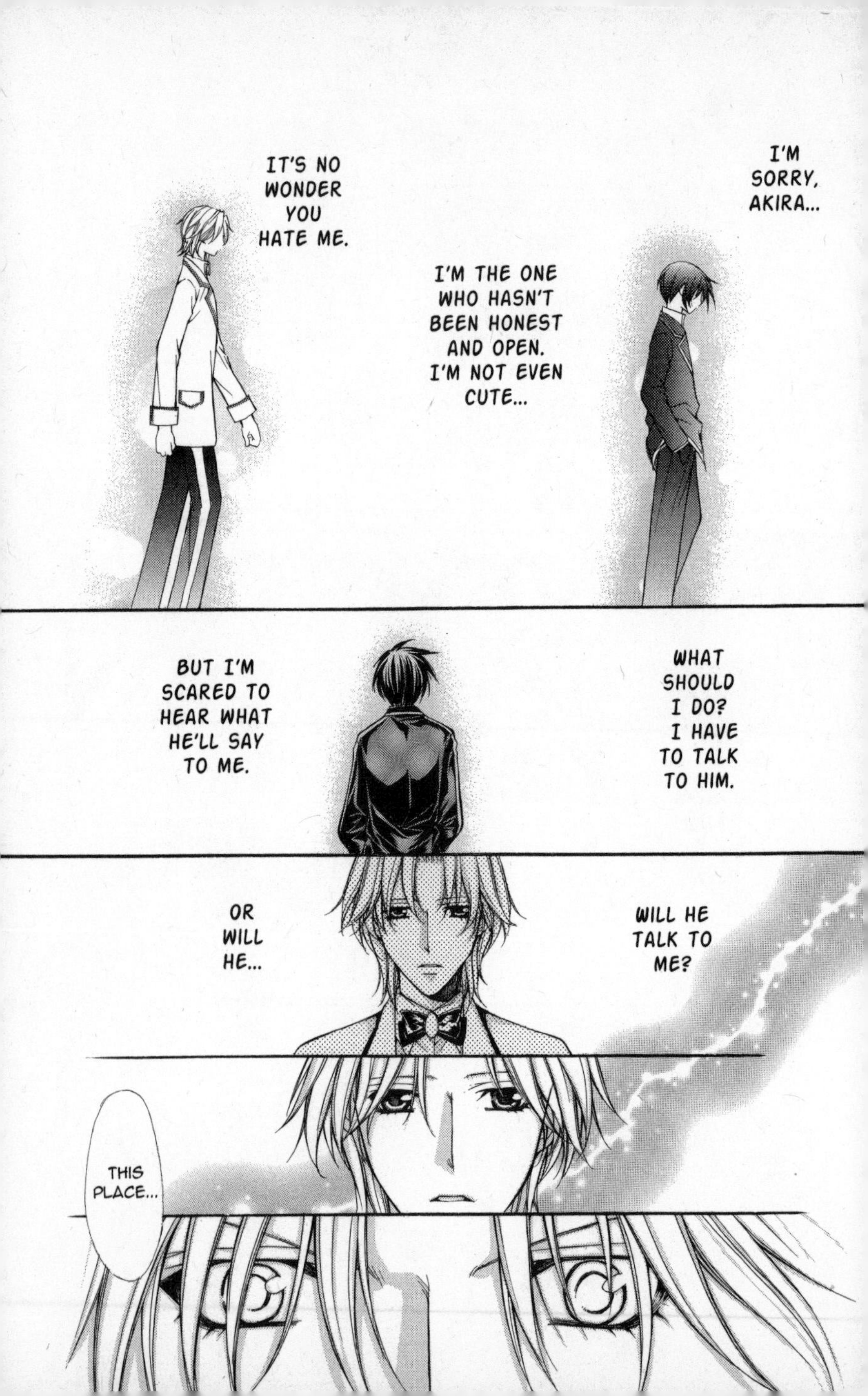
I'M SORRY, AKIRA...
I'M THE ONE WHO HASN'T BEEN HONEST AND OPEN. I'M NOT EVEN CUTE...
IT'S NO WONDER YOU HATE ME.
WHAT SHOULD I DO? I HAVE TO TALK TO HIM.
BUT I'M SCARED TO HEAR WHAT HE'LL SAY TO ME.
WILL HE TALK TO ME?
OR WILL HE...
THIS PLACE...

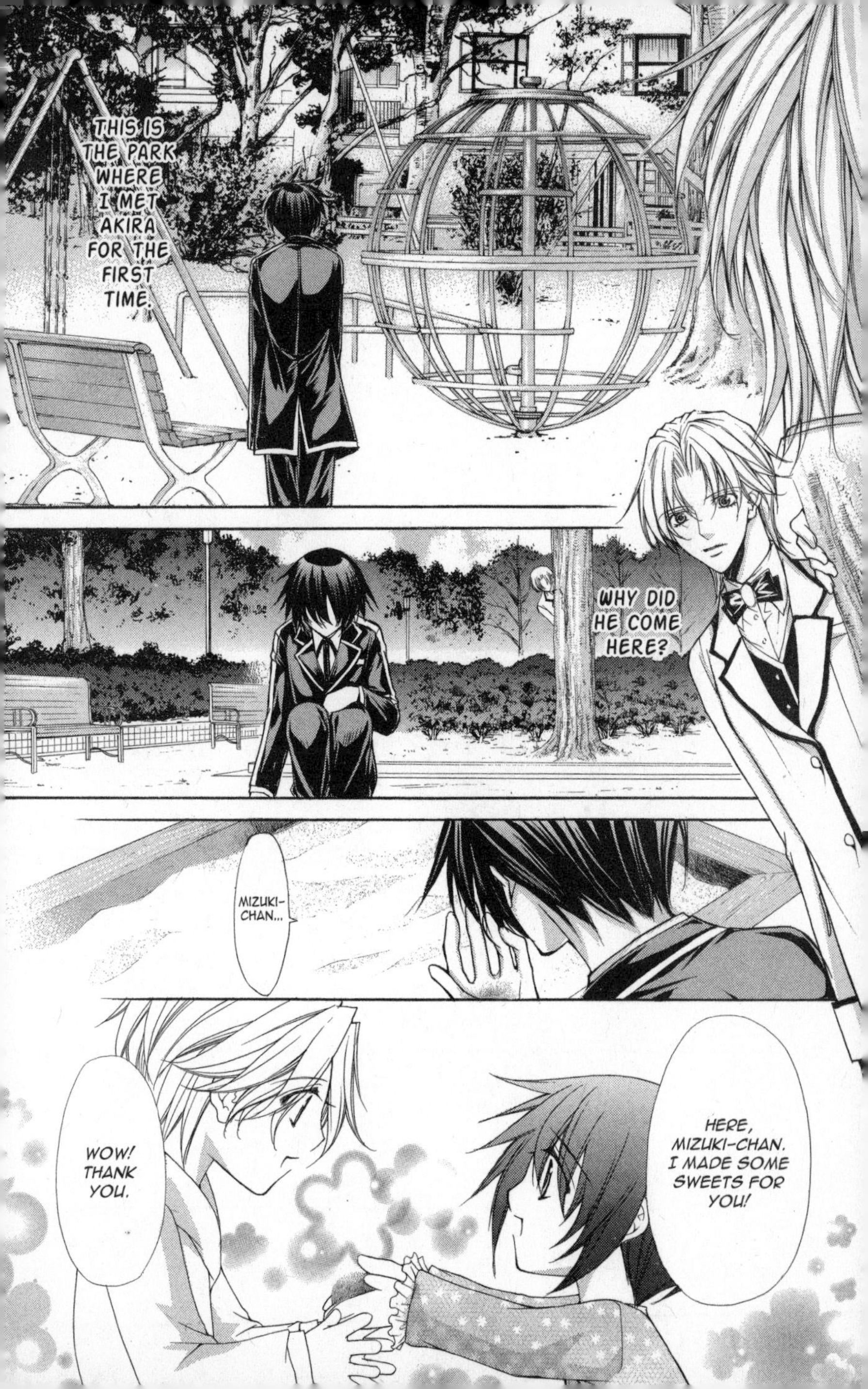
THIS IS THE PARK WHERE I MET AKIRA FOR THE FIRST TIME.
WHY DID HE COME HERE?
MIZUKI-CHAN...
HERE, MIZUKI-CHAN. I MADE SOME SWEETS FOR YOU!
WOW! THANK YOU.

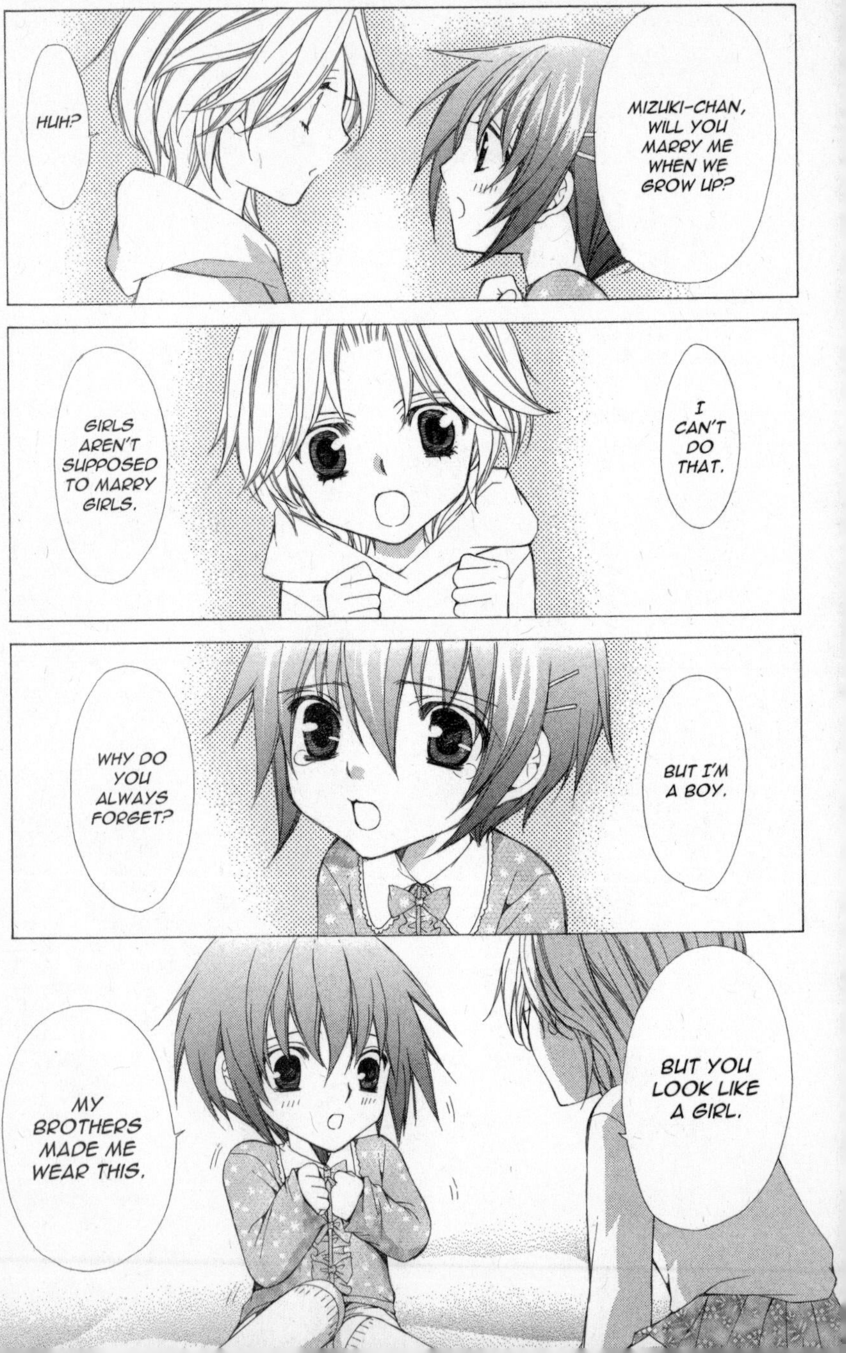
MIZUKI-CHAN, WILL YOU MARRY ME WHEN WE GROW UP?
HUH?
I CAN'T DO THAT.
GIRLS AREN'T SUPPOSED TO MARRY GIRLS.
BUT I'M A BOY.
WHY DO YOU ALWAYS FORGET?
BUT YOU LOOK LIKE A GIRL.
MY BROTHERS MADE ME WEAR THIS.

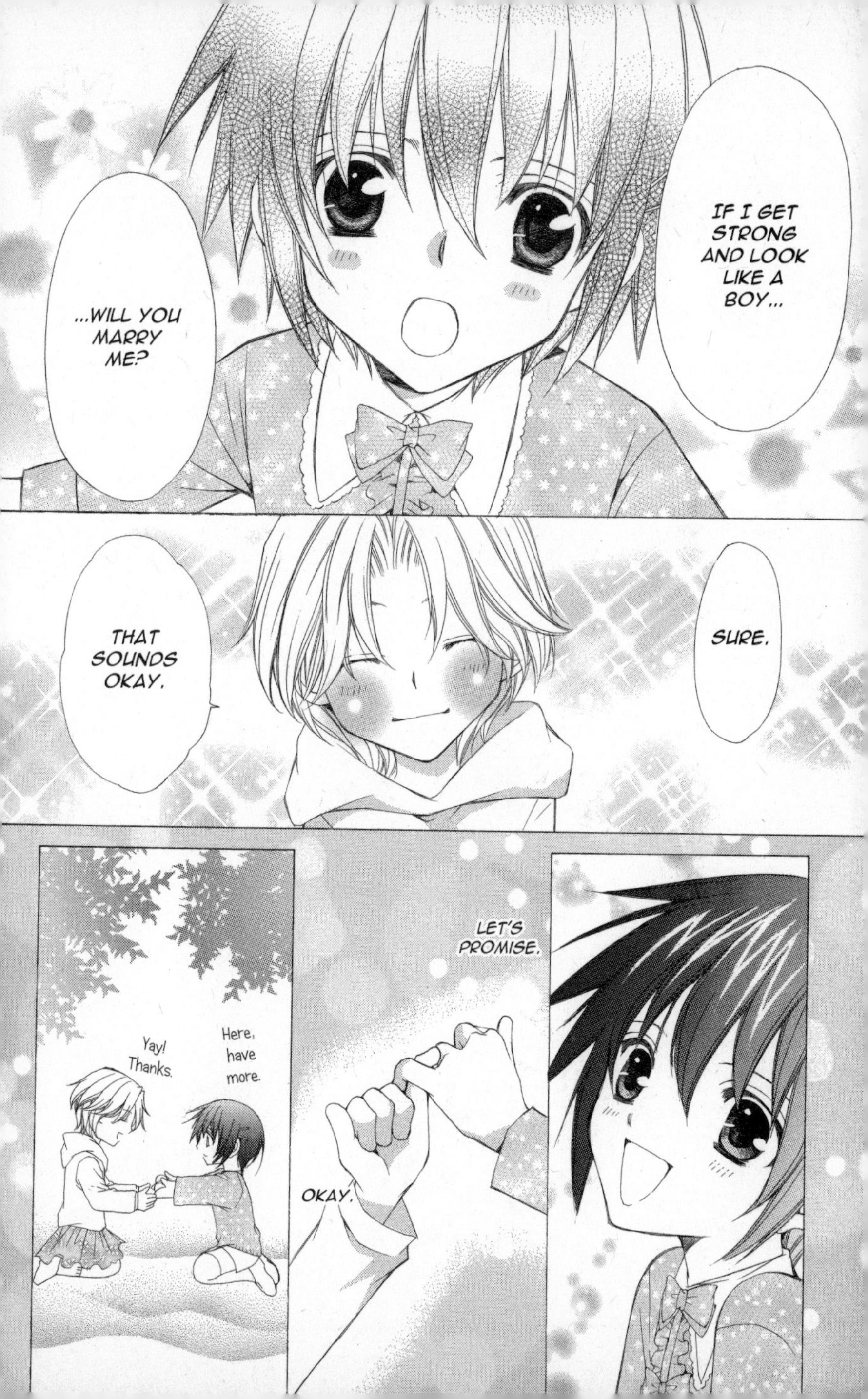
IF I GET STRONG AND LOOK LIKE A BOY...
...WILL YOU MARRY ME?
SURE.
THAT SOUNDS OKAY.
LET'S PROMISE.
OKAY.
Here, have more.
Yay! Thanks.

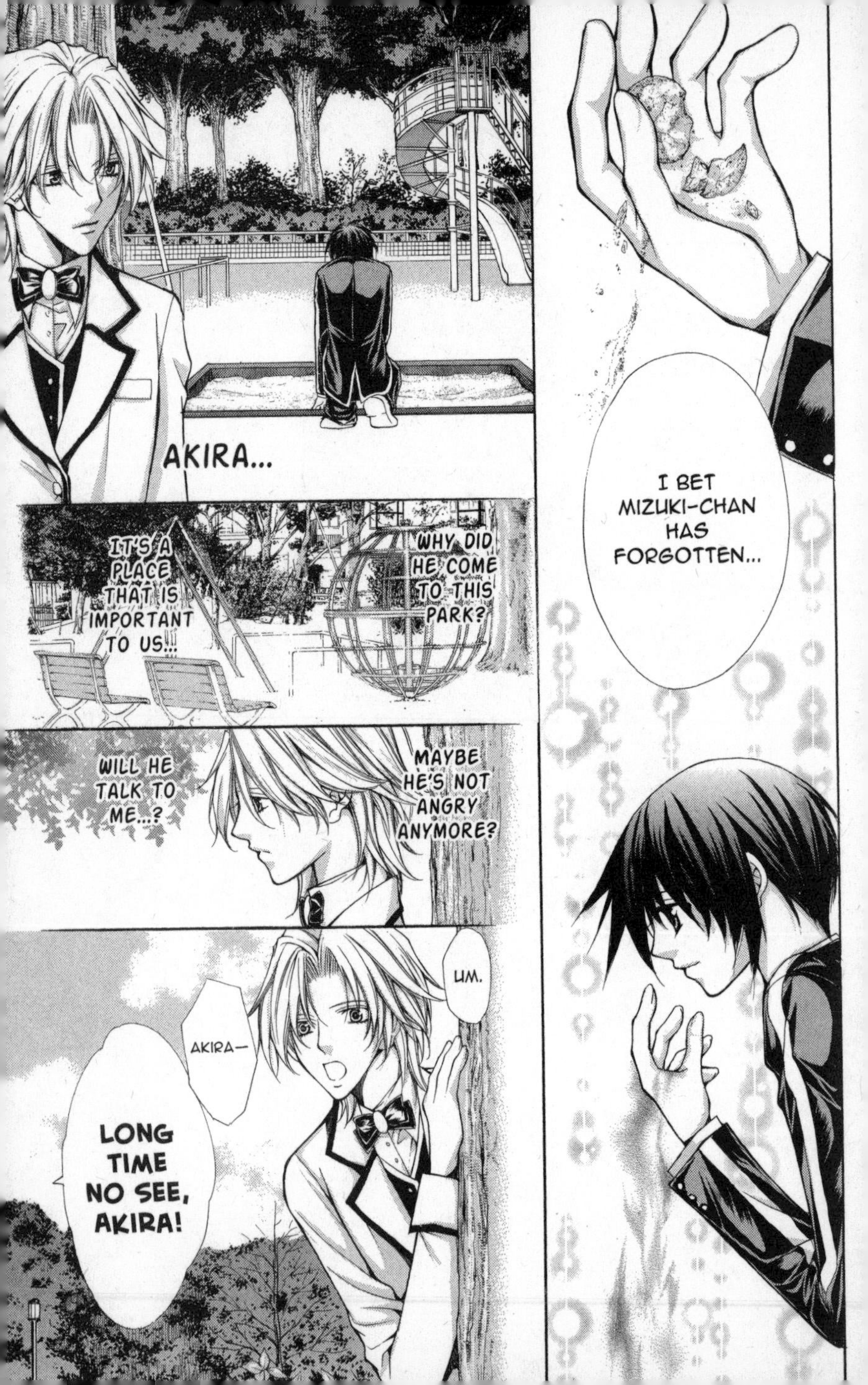

I BET MIZUKI-CHAN HAS FORGOTTEN...
AKIRA...
WHY DID HE COME TO THIS PARK?
IT'S A PLACE THAT IS IMPORTANT TO US...
MAYBE HE'S NOT ANGRY ANYMORE?
WILL HE TALK TO ME...?
UM.
AKIRA—
LONG TIME NO SEE, AKIRA!

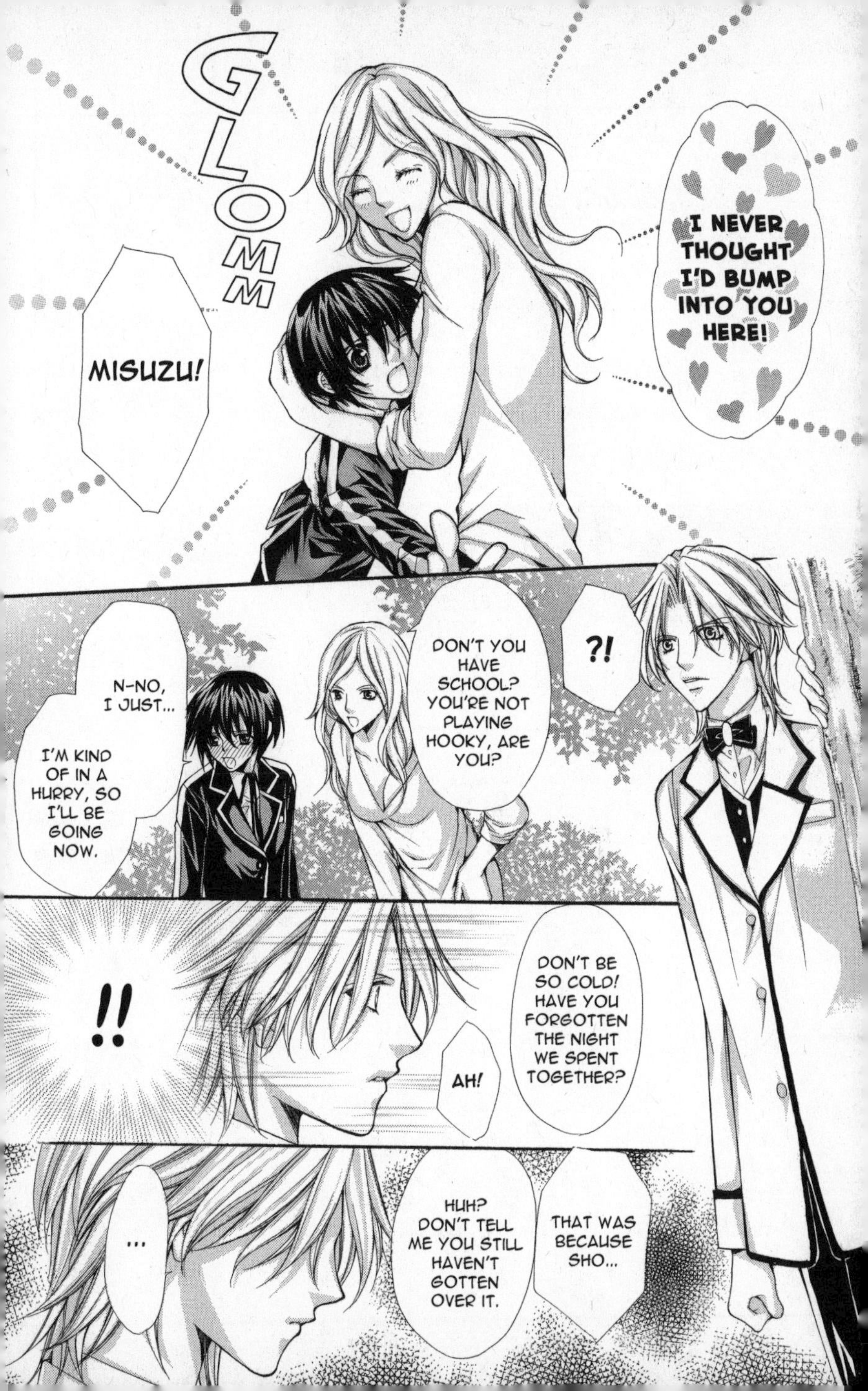
I NEVER THOUGHT I'D BUMP INTO YOU HERE!
GLOMM
MISUZU!
?!
DON'T YOU HAVE SCHOOL? YOU'RE NOT PLAYING HOOKY, ARE YOU?
N-NO, I JUST...
I'M KIND OF IN A HURRY, SO I'LL BE GOING NOW.
DON'T BE SO COLD! HAVE YOU FORGOTTEN THE NIGHT WE SPENT TOGETHER?
AH!
!!
THAT WAS BECAUSE SHO...
HUH? DON'T TELL ME YOU STILL HAVEN'T GOTTEN OVER IT.
...

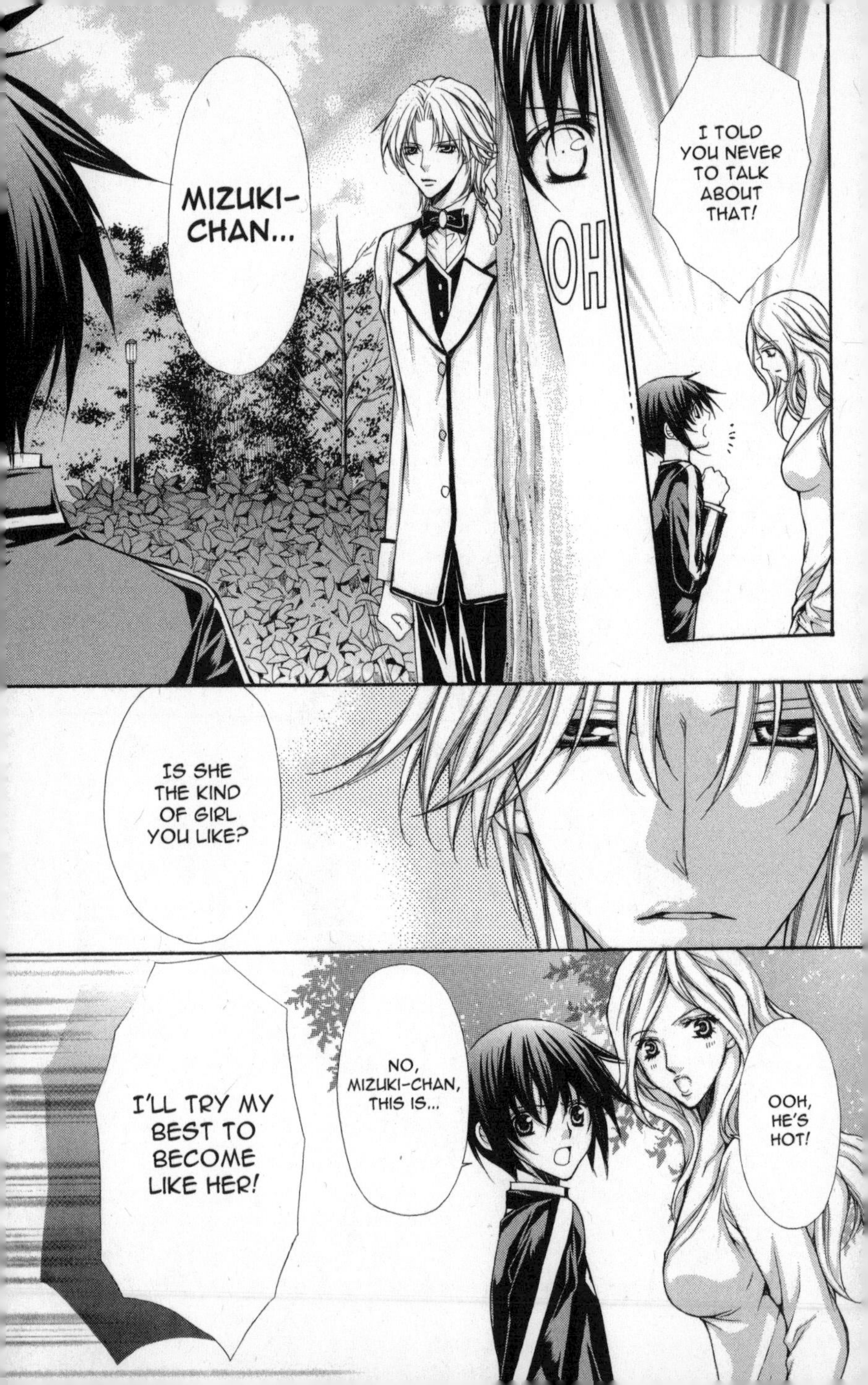
I TOLD YOU NEVER TO TALK ABOUT THAT!
OH
MIZUKI-CHAN...
IS SHE THE KIND OF GIRL YOU LIKE?
OOH, HE'S HOT!
NO, MIZUKI-CHAN, THIS IS...
I'LL TRY MY BEST TO BECOME LIKE HER!

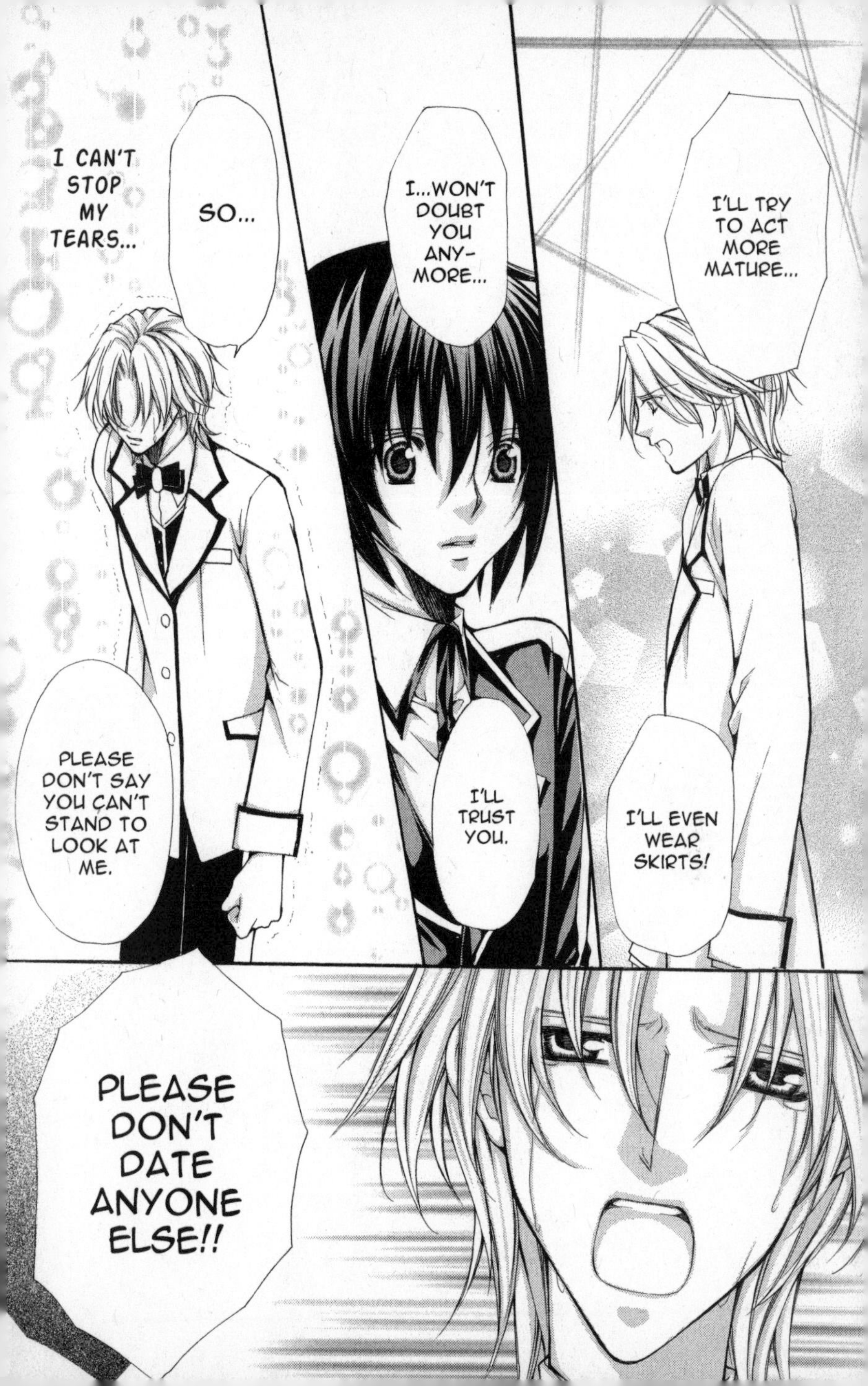
I'LL TRY TO ACT MORE MATURE...
I'LL EVEN WEAR SKIRTS!
I...WON'T DOUBT YOU ANY-MORE...
I'LL TRUST YOU.
SO...
I CAN'T STOP MY TEARS...
PLEASE DON'T SAY YOU CAN'T STAND TO LOOK AT ME.
PLEASE DON'T DATE ANYONE ELSE!!

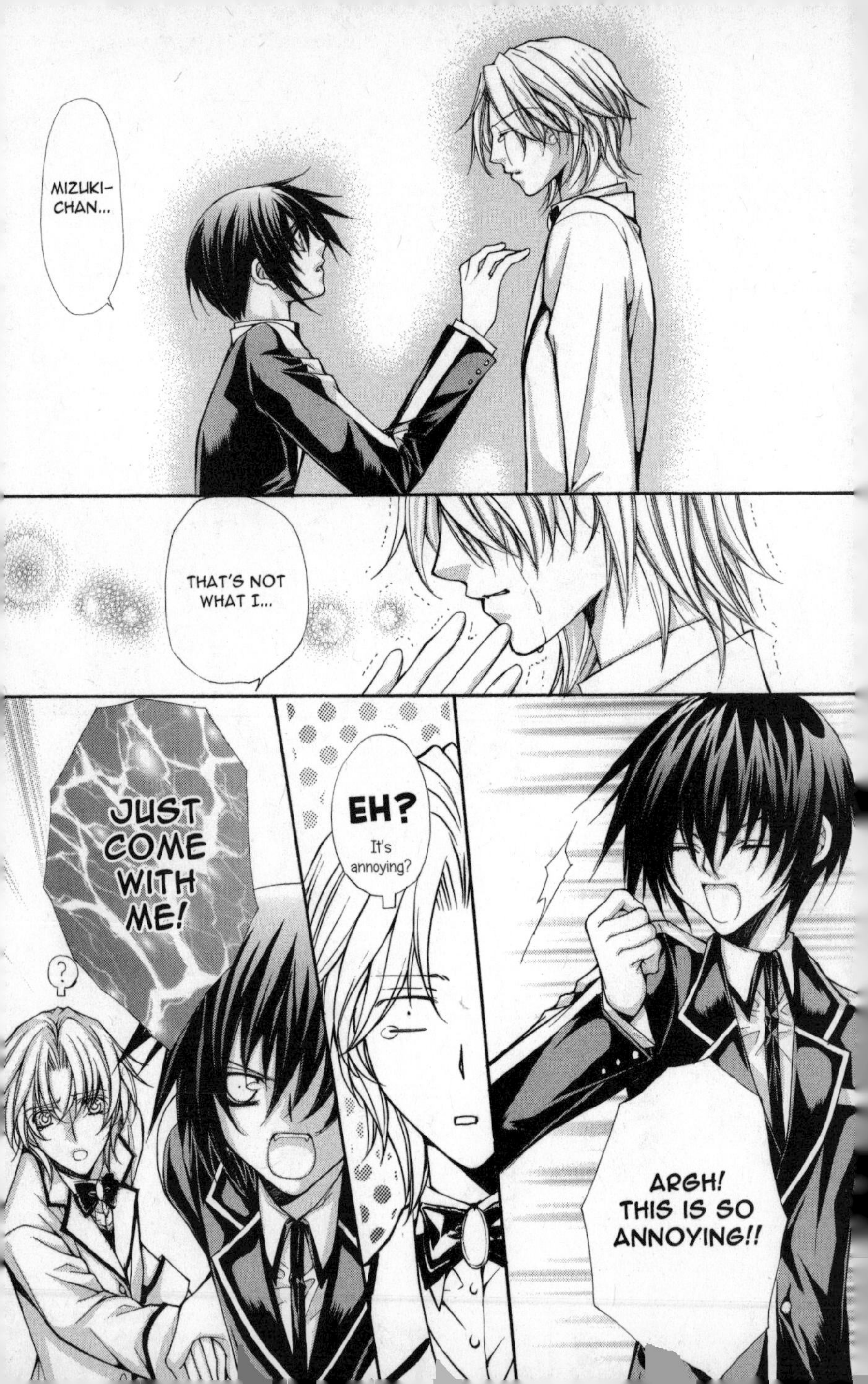
MIZUKI-CHAN...
THAT'S NOT WHAT I...
ARGH! THIS IS SO ANNOYING!!
EH?
It's annoying?
JUST COME WITH ME!
?

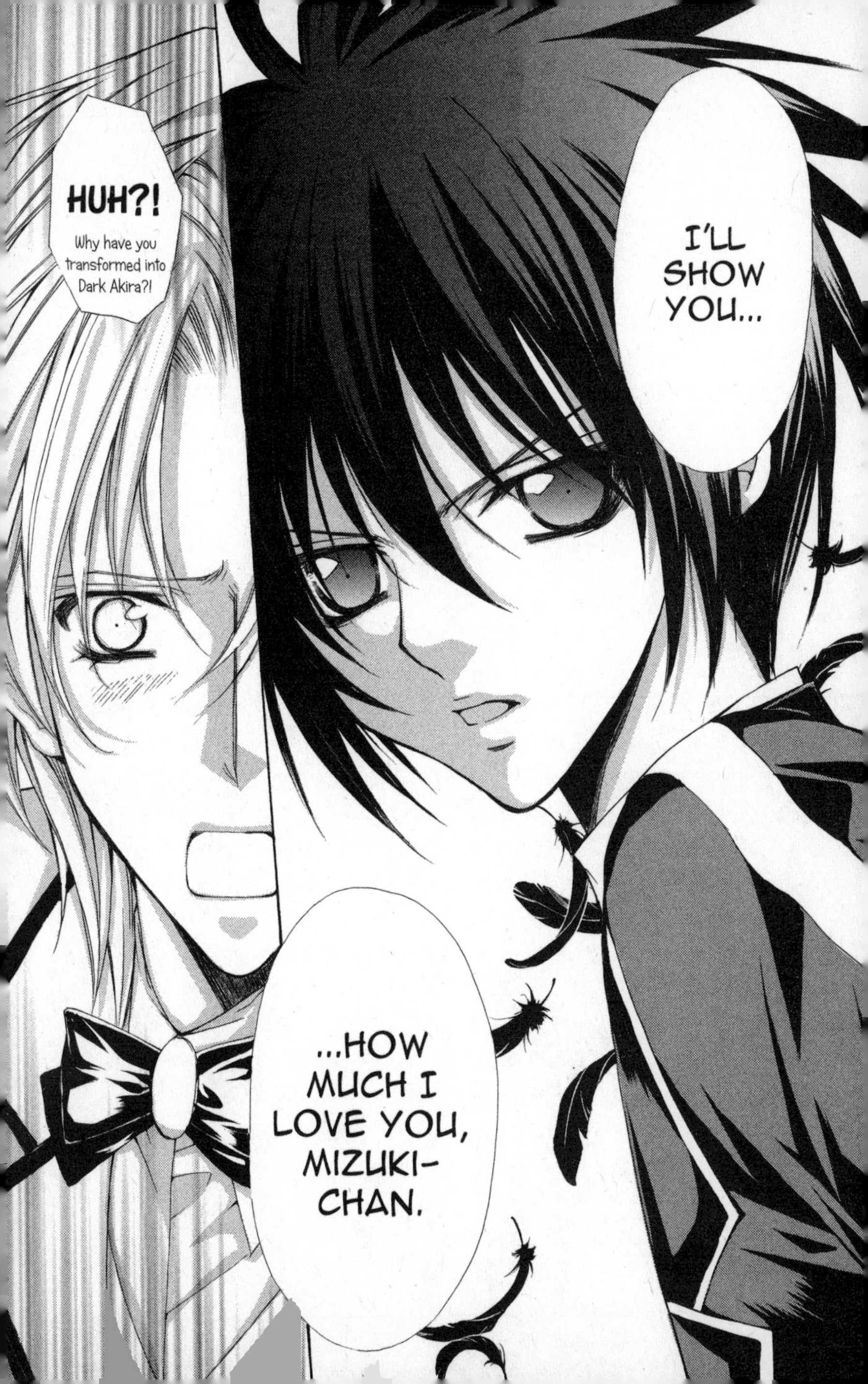
I'LL SHOW YOU...
HUH?! Why have you transformed into Dark Akira?!
...HOW MUCH I LOVE YOU, MIZUKI-CHAN.

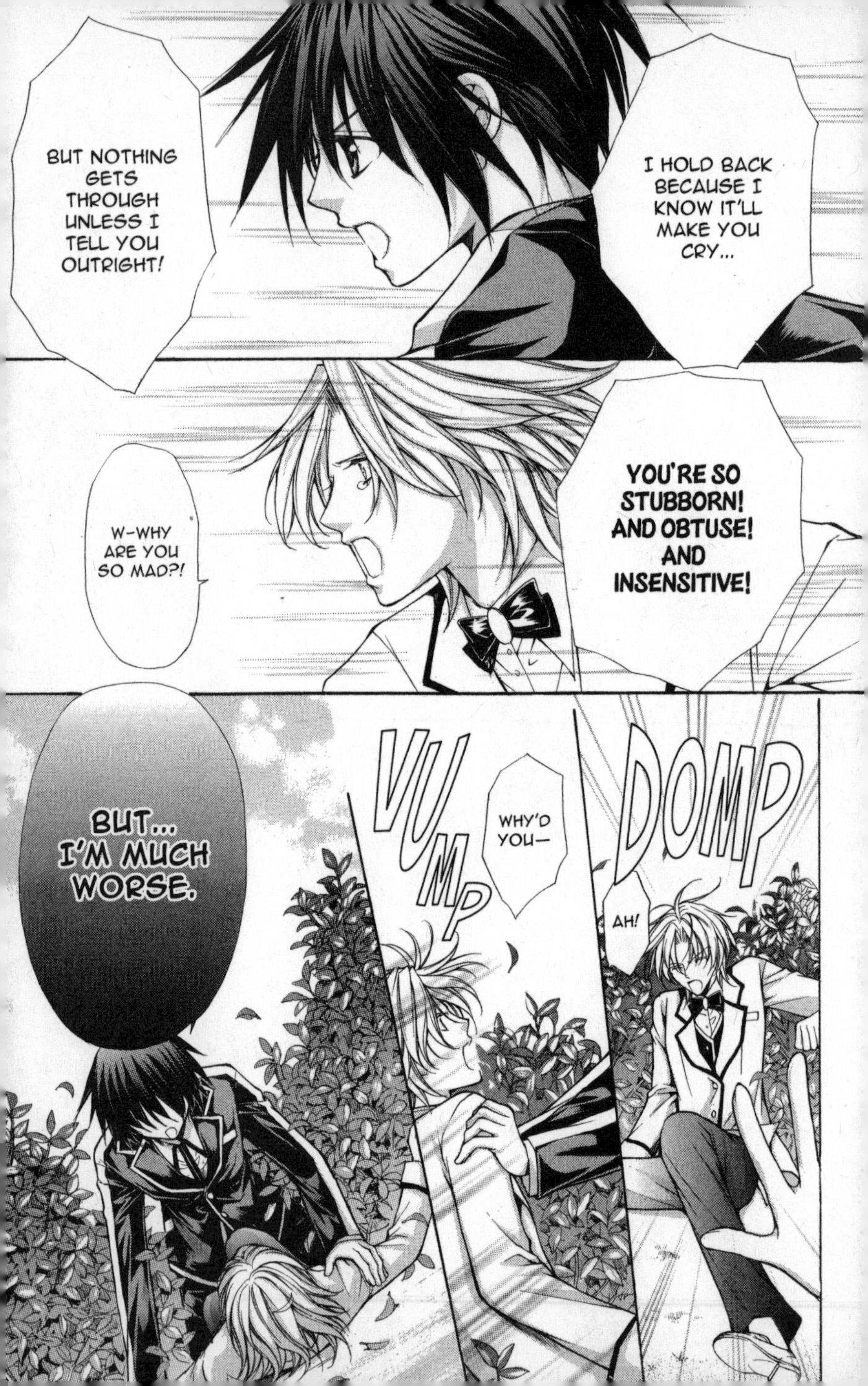
I HOLD BACK BECAUSE I KNOW IT'LL MAKE YOU CRY...
BUT NOTHING GETS THROUGH UNLESS I TELL YOU OUTRIGHT!
YOU'RE SO STUBBORN! AND OBTUSE! AND INSENSITIVE!
W-WHY ARE YOU SO MAD?!
DOMP
AH!
VUMP
WHY'D YOU—
BUT... I'M MUCH WORSE.

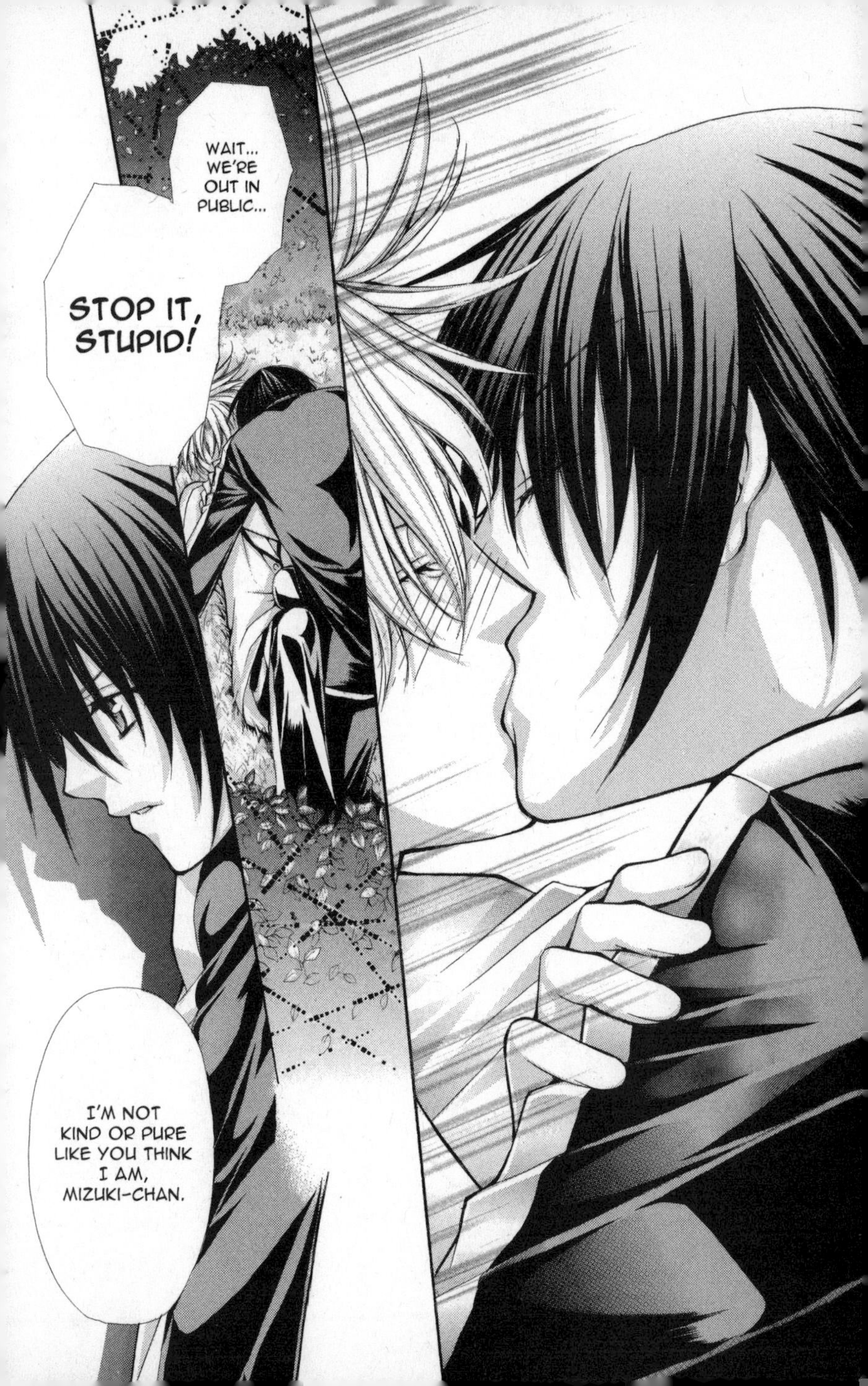
WAIT... WE'RE OUT IN PUBLIC...
STOP IT, STUPID!
I'M NOT KIND OR PURE LIKE YOU THINK I AM, MIZUKI-CHAN.

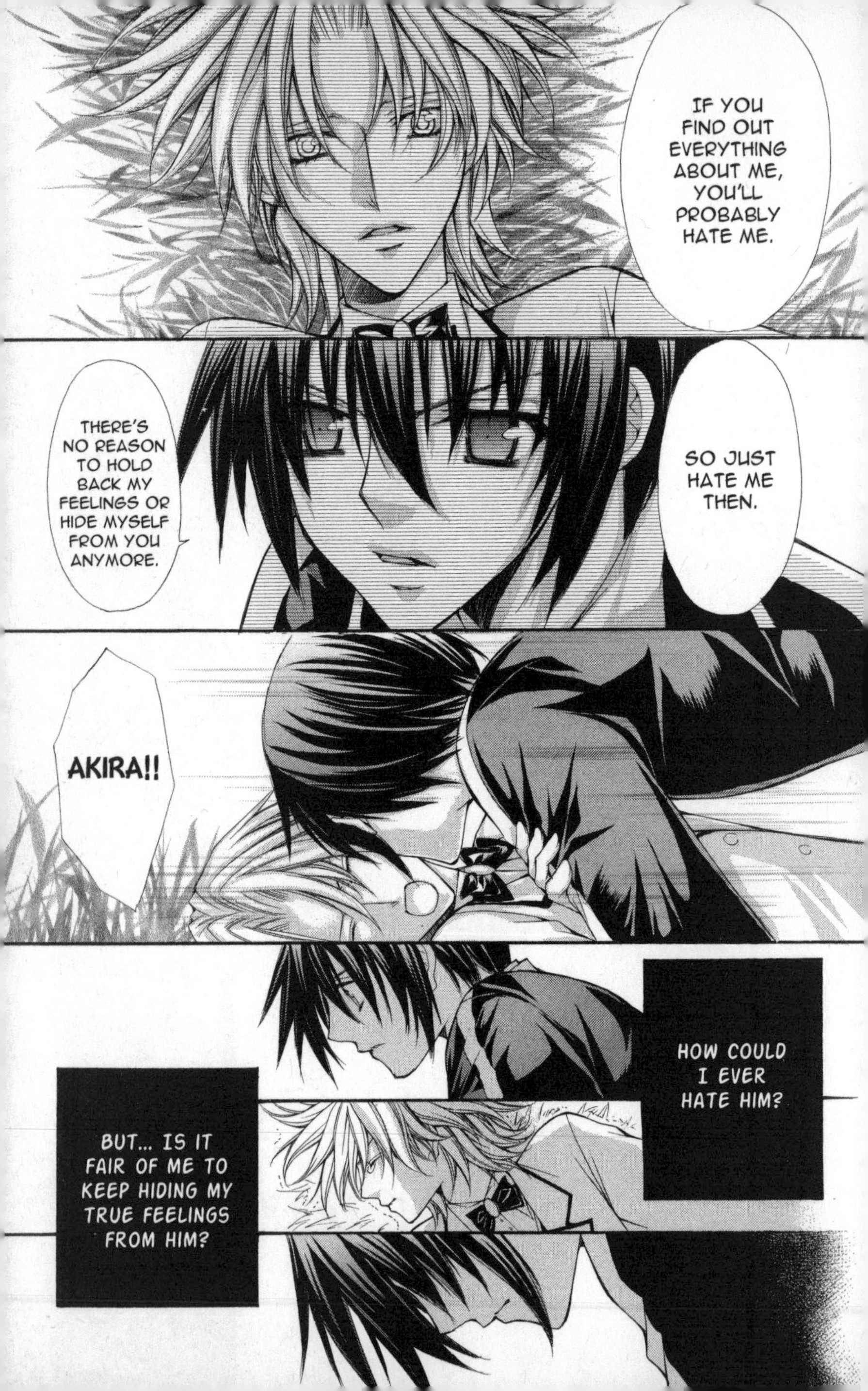
IF YOU FIND OUT EVERYTHING ABOUT ME, YOU'LL PROBABLY HATE ME.
SO JUST HATE ME THEN.
THERE'S NO REASON TO HOLD BACK MY FEELINGS OR HIDE MYSELF FROM YOU ANYMORE.
AKIRA!!
HOW COULD I EVER HATE HIM?
BUT... IS IT FAIR OF ME TO KEEP HIDING MY TRUE FEELINGS FROM HIM?

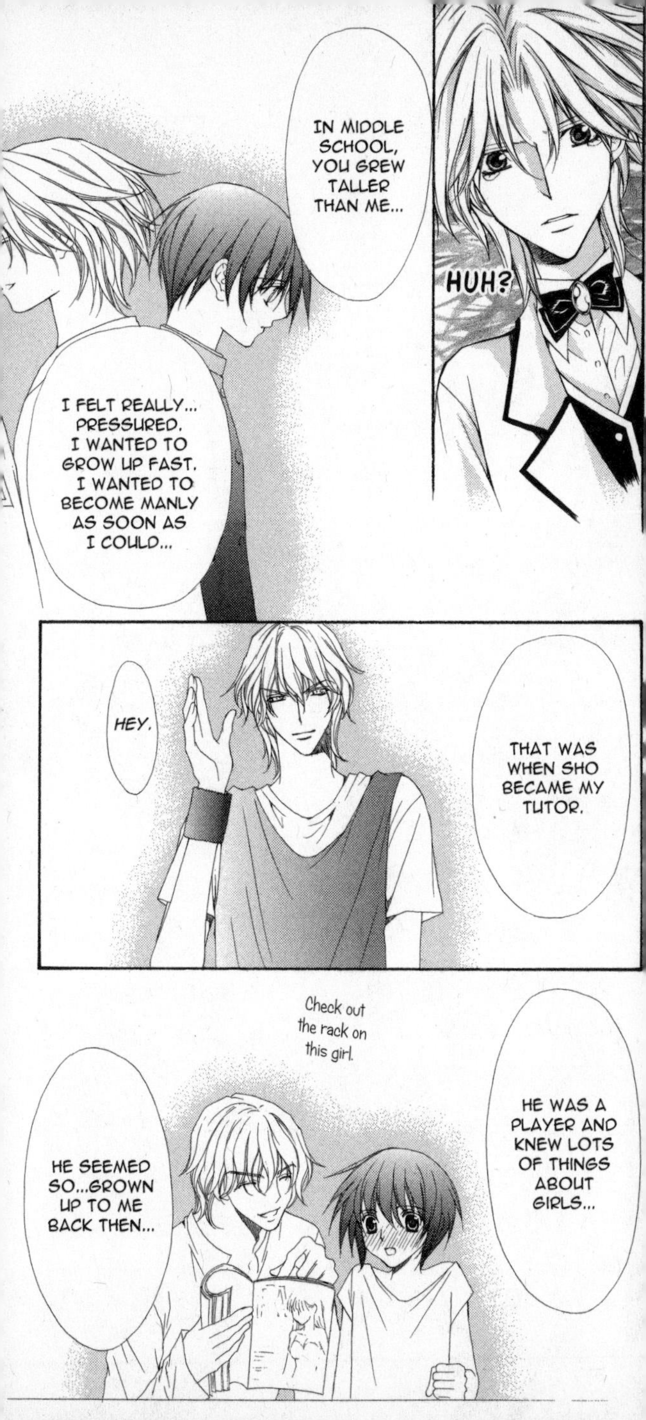
IN MIDDLE SCHOOL, YOU GREW TALLER THAN ME...
HUH?
I FELT REALLY... PRESSURED. I WANTED TO GROW UP FAST. I WANTED TO BECOME MANLY AS SOON AS I COULD...
THAT WAS WHEN SHO BECAME MY TUTOR.
HEY.
HE WAS A PLAYER AND KNEW LOTS OF THINGS ABOUT GIRLS...
Check out the rack on this girl.
HE SEEMED SO...GROWN UP TO ME BACK THEN...

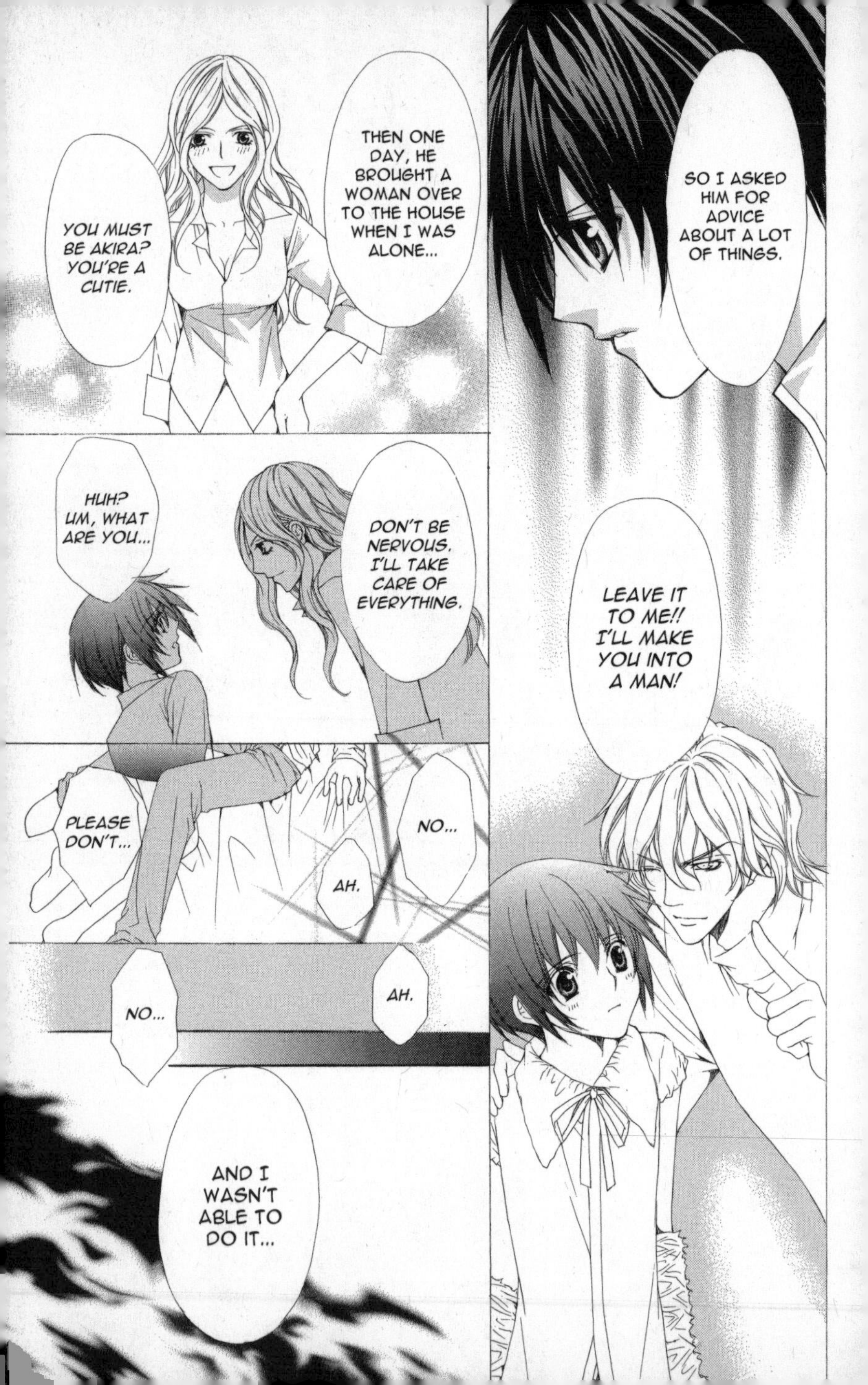
SO I ASKED HIM FOR ADVICE ABOUT A LOT OF THINGS.
LEAVE IT TO ME!! I'LL MAKE YOU INTO A MAN!
THEN ONE DAY, HE BROUGHT A WOMAN OVER TO THE HOUSE WHEN I WAS ALONE...
YOU MUST BE AKIRA? YOU'RE A CUTIE.
DON'T BE NERVOUS. I'LL TAKE CARE OF EVERYTHING.
HUH? UM, WHAT ARE YOU...
NO...
AH.
PLEASE DON'T...
AH.
NO...
AND I WASN'T ABLE TO DO IT...

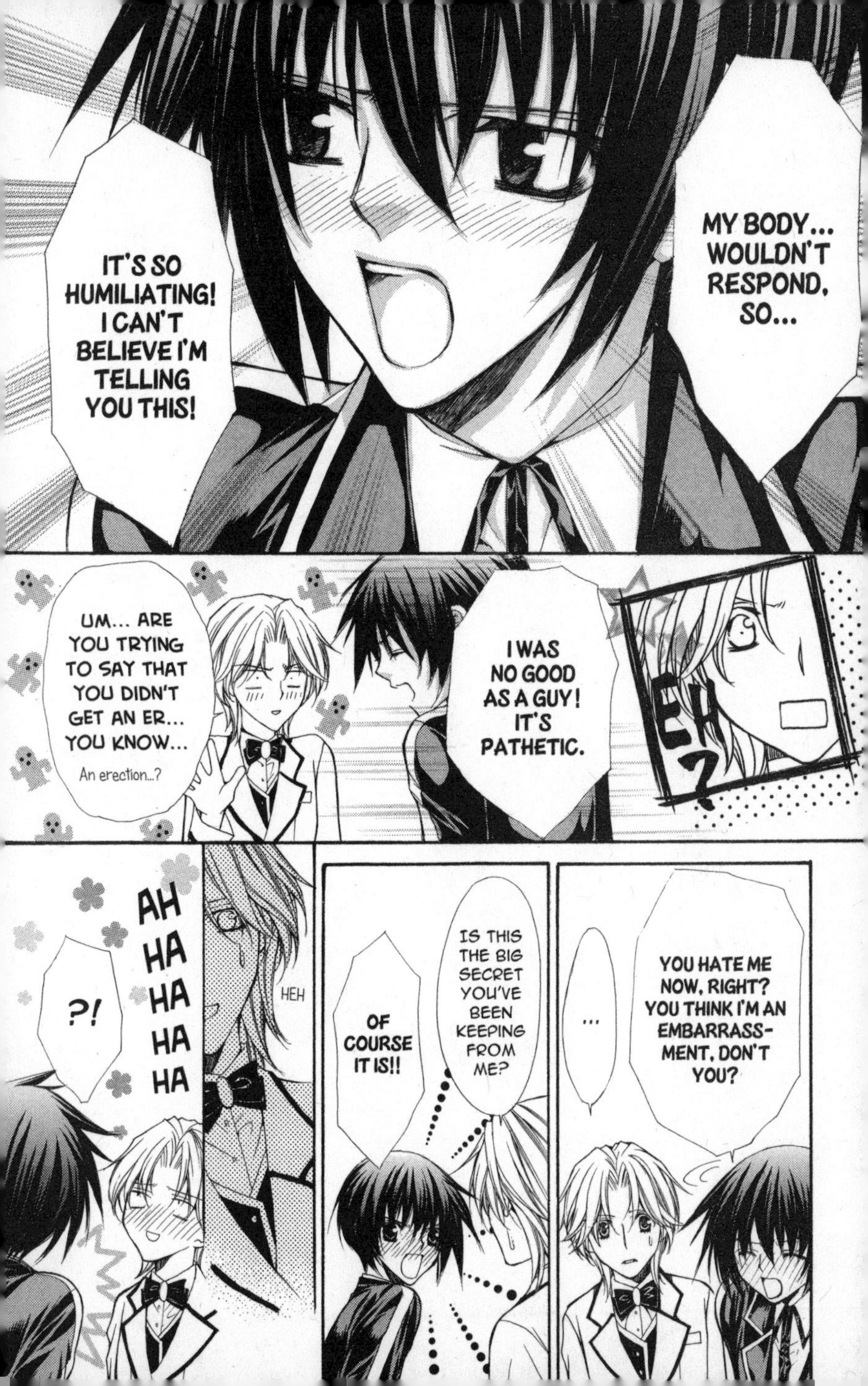
MY BODY... WOULDN'T RESPOND, SO...
IT'S SO HUMILIATING! I CAN'T BELIEVE I'M TELLING YOU THIS!
EH?
I WAS NO GOOD AS A GUY! IT'S PATHETIC.
UM... ARE YOU TRYING TO SAY THAT YOU DIDN'T GET AN ER... YOU KNOW...
An erection...?
YOU HATE ME NOW, RIGHT? YOU THINK I'M AN EMBARRASS-MENT, DON'T YOU?
...
IS THIS THE BIG SECRET YOU'VE BEEN KEEPING FROM ME?
OF COURSE IT IS!!
AH HA HA HA HA HA
HEH
?!

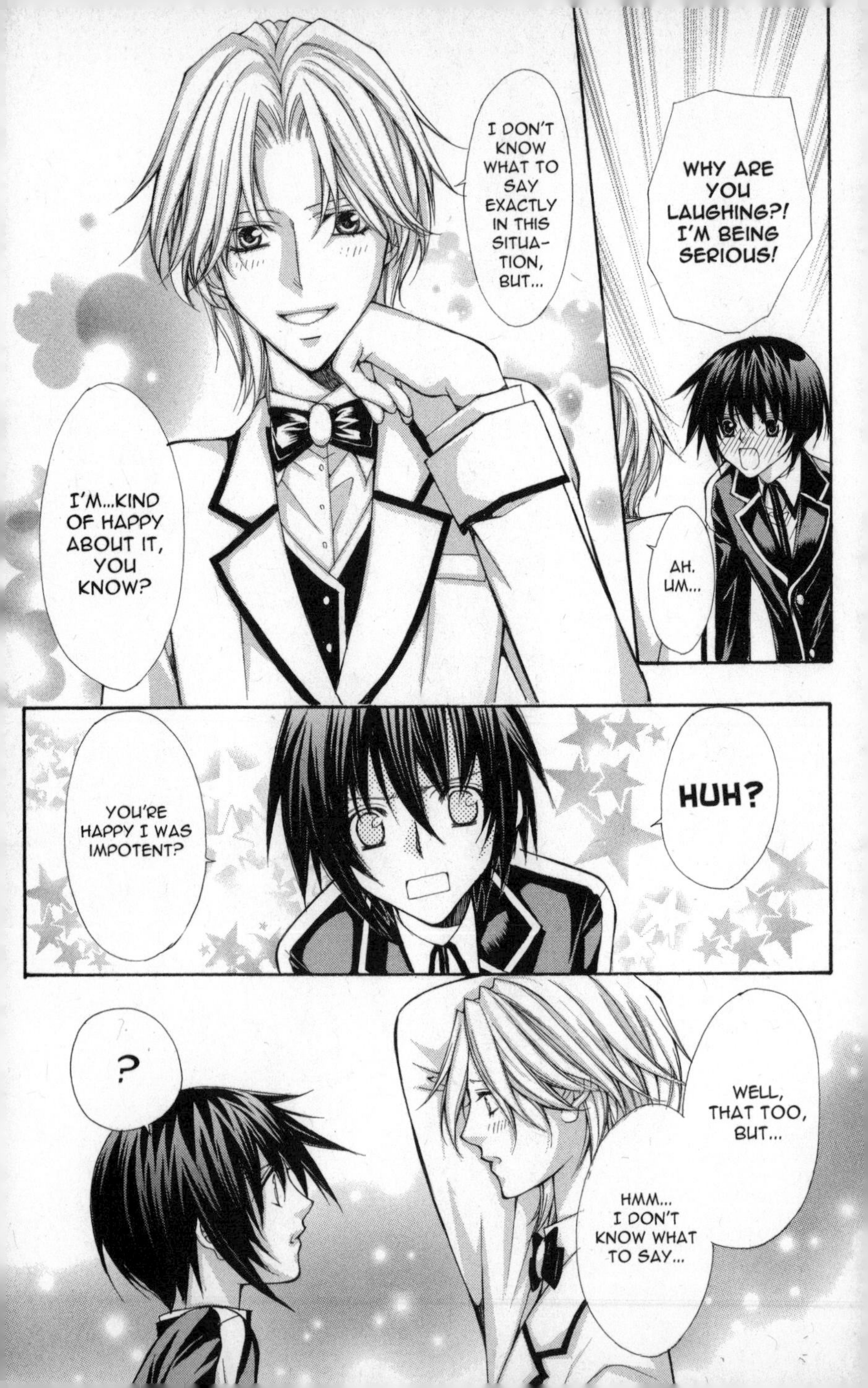
WHY ARE YOU LAUGHING?! I'M BEING SERIOUS!
AH. UM...
I DON'T KNOW WHAT TO SAY EXACTLY IN THIS SITUA-TION, BUT...
I'M...KIND OF HAPPY ABOUT IT, YOU KNOW?
HUH?
YOU'RE HAPPY I WAS IMPOTENT?
WELL, THAT TOO, BUT...
HMM... I DON'T KNOW WHAT TO SAY...
?

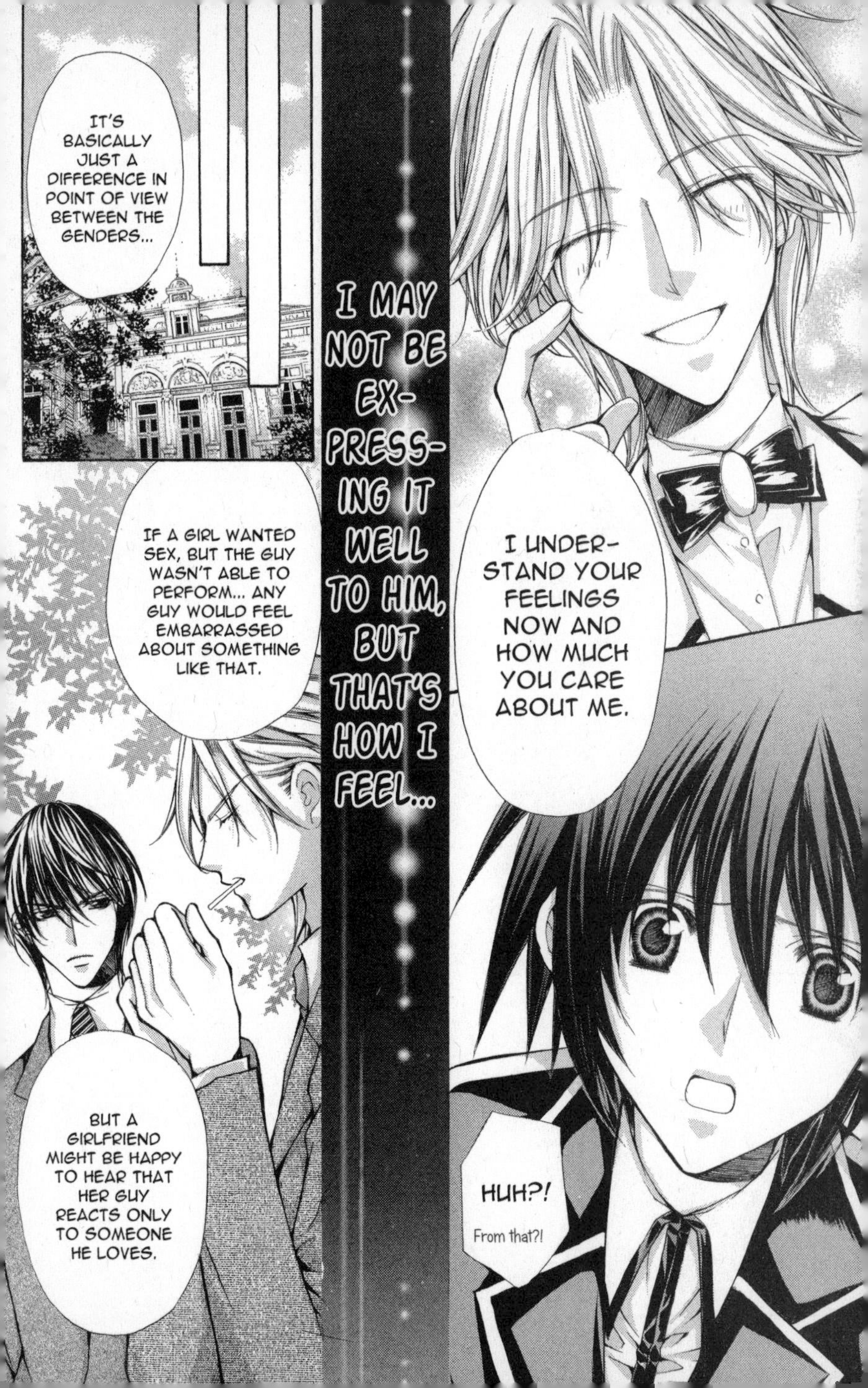
I UNDER-STAND YOUR FEELINGS NOW AND HOW MUCH YOU CARE ABOUT ME.
HUH?!
From that?!
I MAY NOT BE EX-PRESS-ING IT WELL TO HIM, BUT THAT'S HOW I FEEL...
IT'S BASICALLY JUST A DIFFERENCE IN POINT OF VIEW BETWEEN THE GENDERS...
IF A GIRL WANTED SEX, BUT THE GUY WASN'T ABLE TO PERFORM... ANY GUY WOULD FEEL EMBARRASSED ABOUT SOMETHING LIKE THAT.
BUT A GIRLFRIEND MIGHT BE HAPPY TO HEAR THAT HER GUY REACTS ONLY TO SOMEONE HE LOVES.

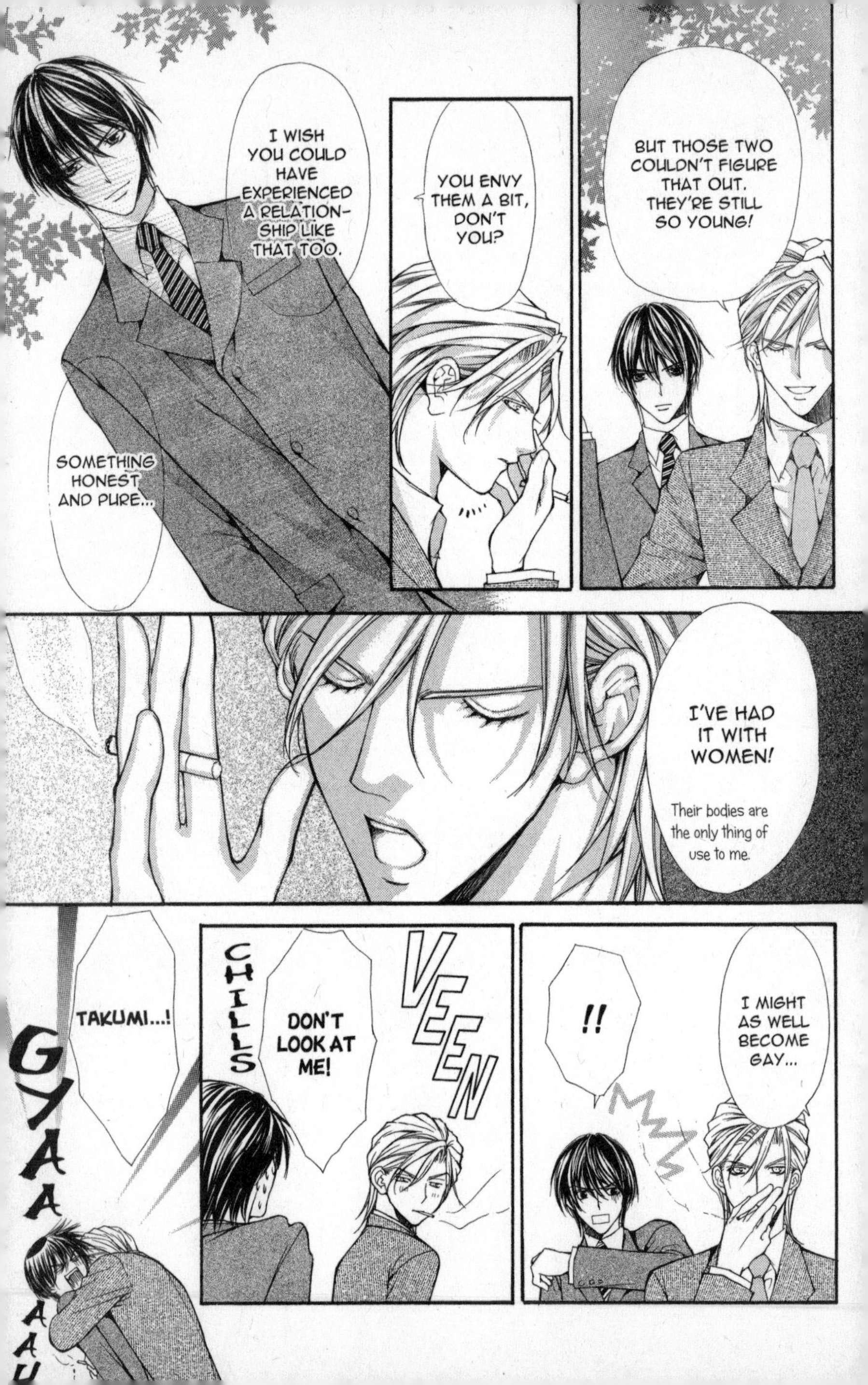
BUT THOSE TWO COULDN'T FIGURE THAT OUT. THEY'RE STILL SO YOUNG!
YOU ENVY THEM A BIT, DON'T YOU?
I WISH YOU COULD HAVE EXPERIENCED A RELATIONSHIP LIKE THAT TOO.
SOMETHING HONEST AND PURE...
I'VE HAD IT WITH WOMEN!
Their bodies are the only thing of use to me.
I MIGHT AS WELL BECOME GAY...
!!
VEEN
DON'T LOOK AT ME!
CHILLS
TAKUMI...!
GYAAAAU

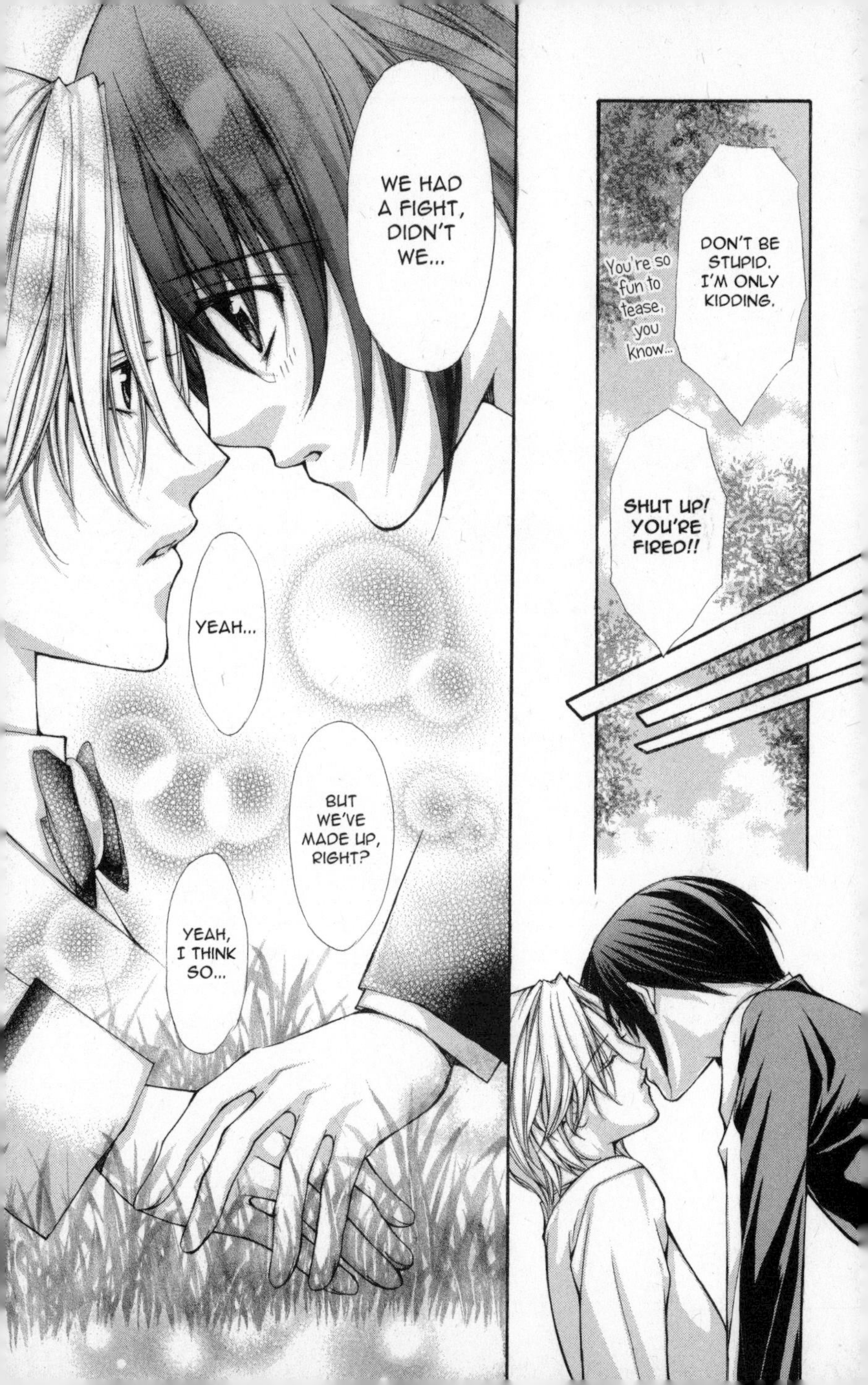
DON'T BE STUPID. I'M ONLY KIDDING.
You're so fun to tease, you know...
SHUT UP! YOU'RE FIRED!!
WE HAD A FIGHT, DIDN'T WE...
YEAH...
BUT WE'VE MADE UP, RIGHT?
YEAH, I THINK SO...

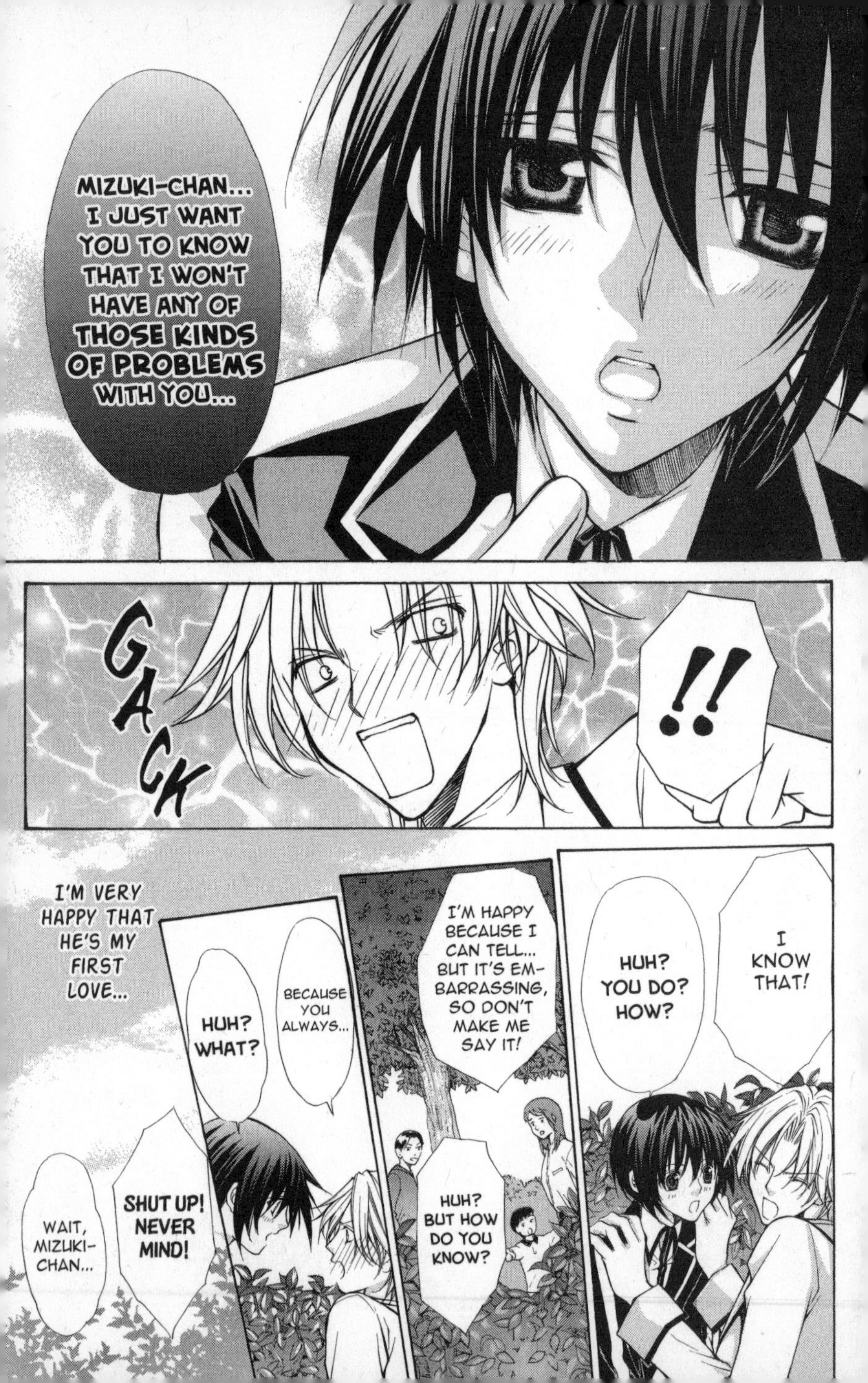
MIZUKI-CHAN... I JUST WANT YOU TO KNOW THAT I WON'T HAVE ANY OF THOSE KINDS OF PROBLEMS WITH YOU...
!!
GACK
I KNOW THAT!
HUH? YOU DO? HOW?
I'M HAPPY BECAUSE I CAN TELL... BUT IT'S EM-BARRASSING, SO DON'T MAKE ME SAY IT!
HUH? BUT HOW DO YOU KNOW?
BECAUSE YOU ALWAYS...
HUH? WHAT?
SHUT UP! NEVER MIND!
WAIT, MIZUKI-CHAN...
I'M VERY HAPPY THAT HE'S MY FIRST LOVE...

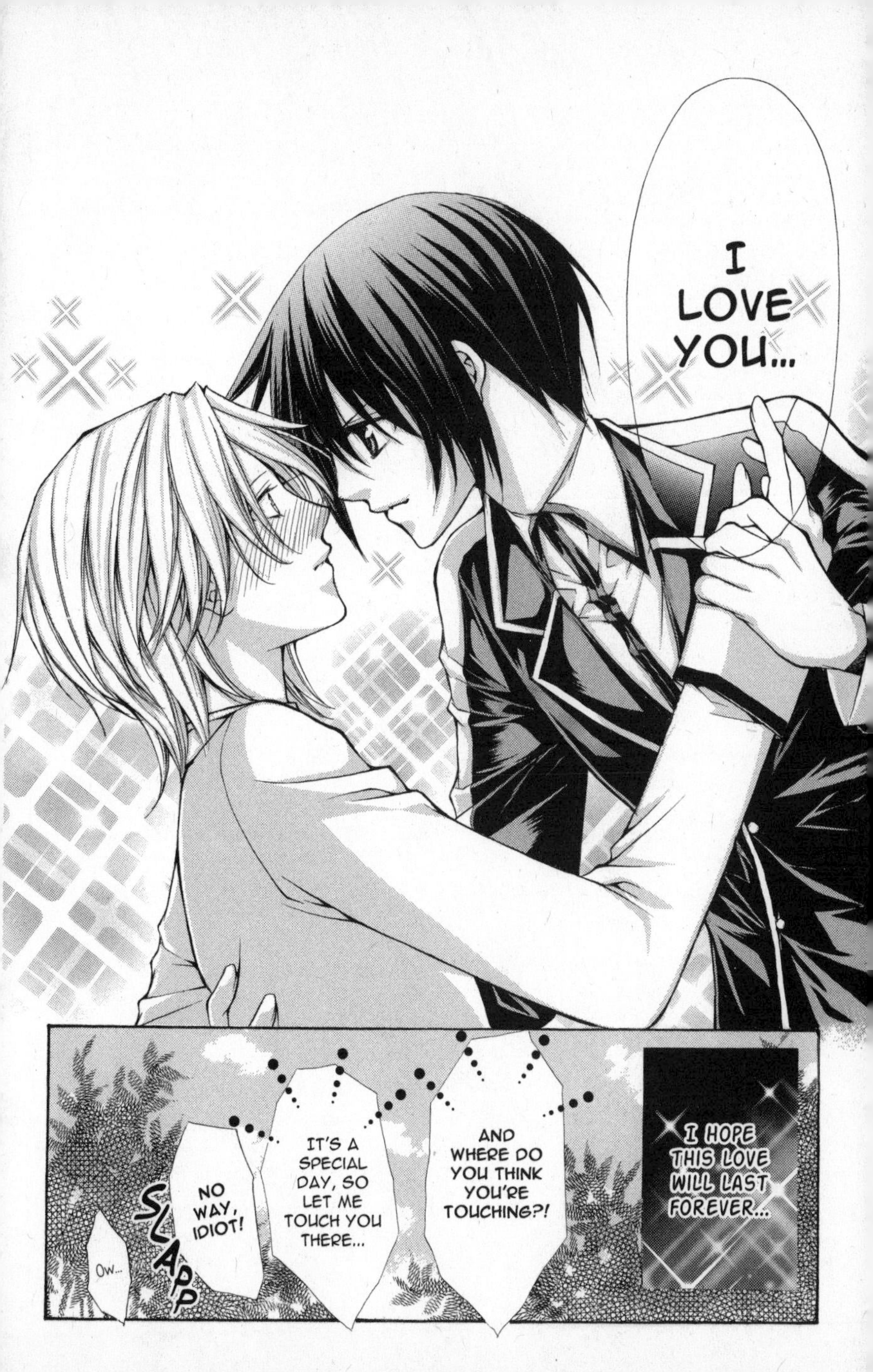
I LOVE YOU...
I HOPE THIS LOVE WILL LAST FOREVER...
AND WHERE DO YOU THINK YOU'RE TOUCHING?!
IT'S A SPECIAL DAY, SO LET ME TOUCH YOU THERE...
NO WAY, IDIOT!
SLAPP
OW...

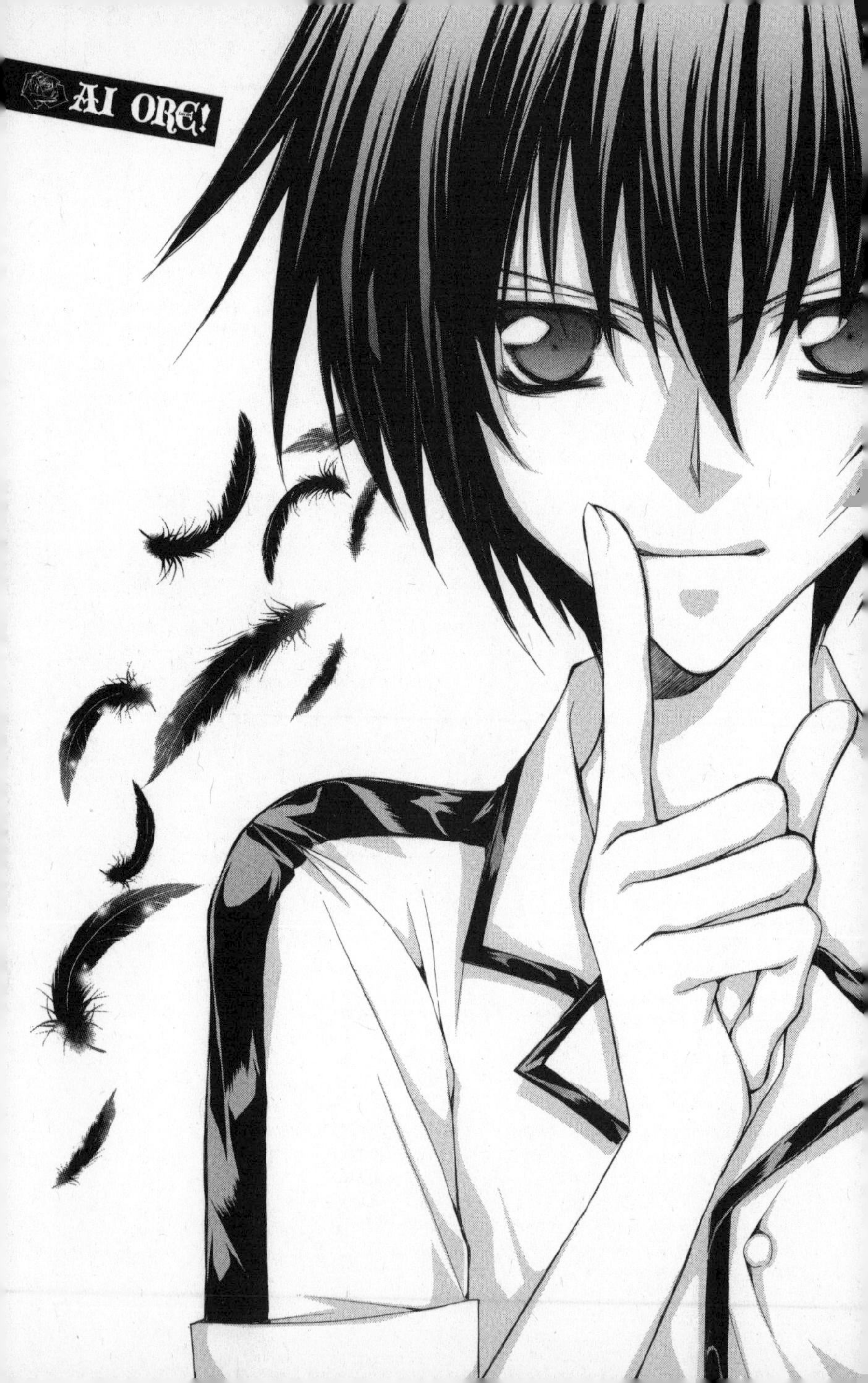
AI ORE!

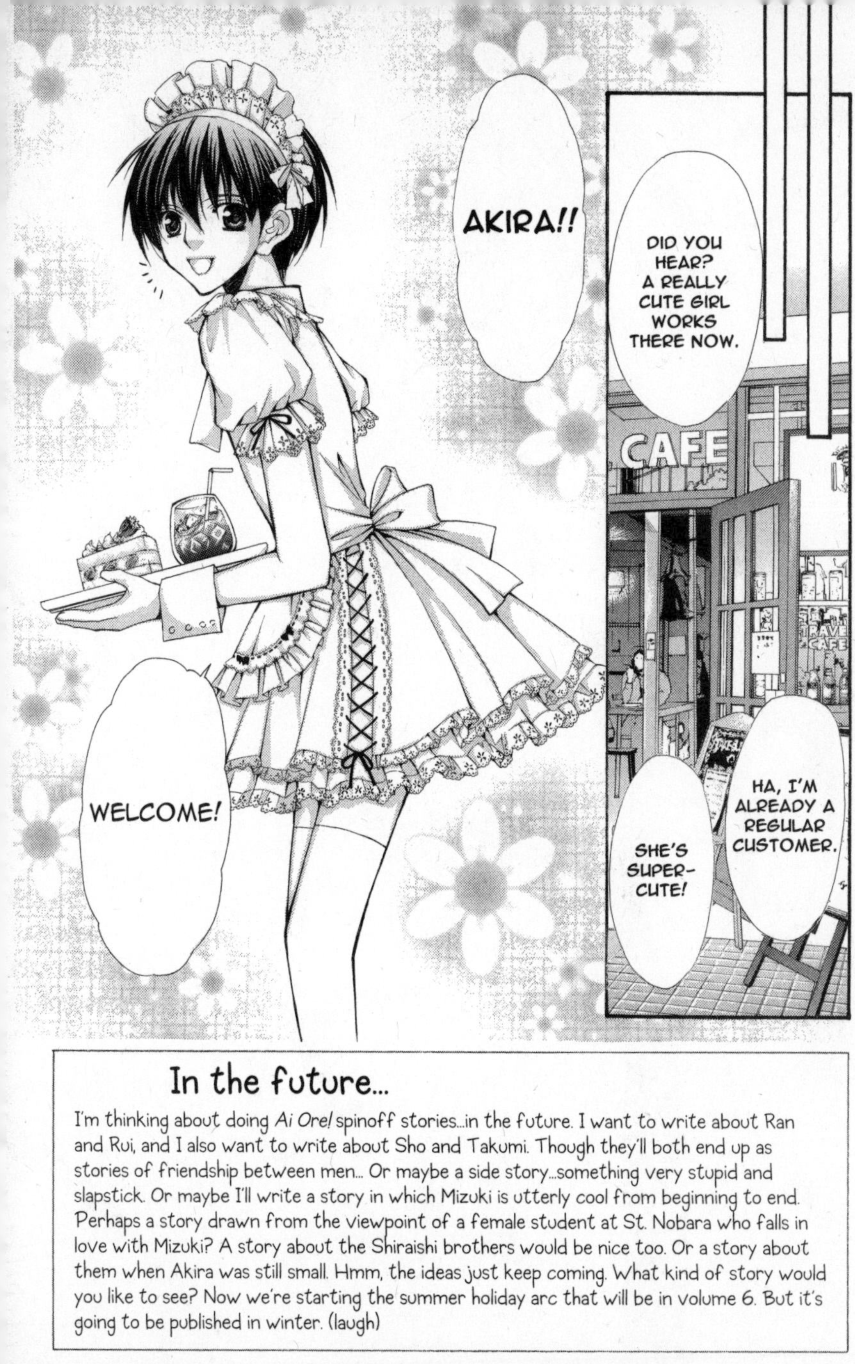
DID YOU HEAR? A REALLY CUTE GIRL WORKS THERE NOW.
CAFE
HA, I'M ALREADY A REGULAR CUSTOMER.
SHE'S SUPER-CUTE!
AKIRA!!
WELCOME!

In the future...

I'm thinking about doing *Ai Ore!* spinoff stories...in the future. I want to write about Ran and Rui, and I also want to write about Sho and Takumi. Though they'll both end up as stories of friendship between men... Or maybe a side story...something very stupid and slapstick. Or maybe I'll write a story in which Mizuki is utterly cool from beginning to end. Perhaps a story drawn from the viewpoint of a female student at St. Nobara who falls in love with Mizuki? A story about the Shiraishi brothers would be nice too. Or a story about them when Akira was still small. Hmm, the ideas just keep coming. What kind of story would you like to see? Now we're starting the summer holiday arc that will be in volume 6. But it's going to be published in winter. (laugh)

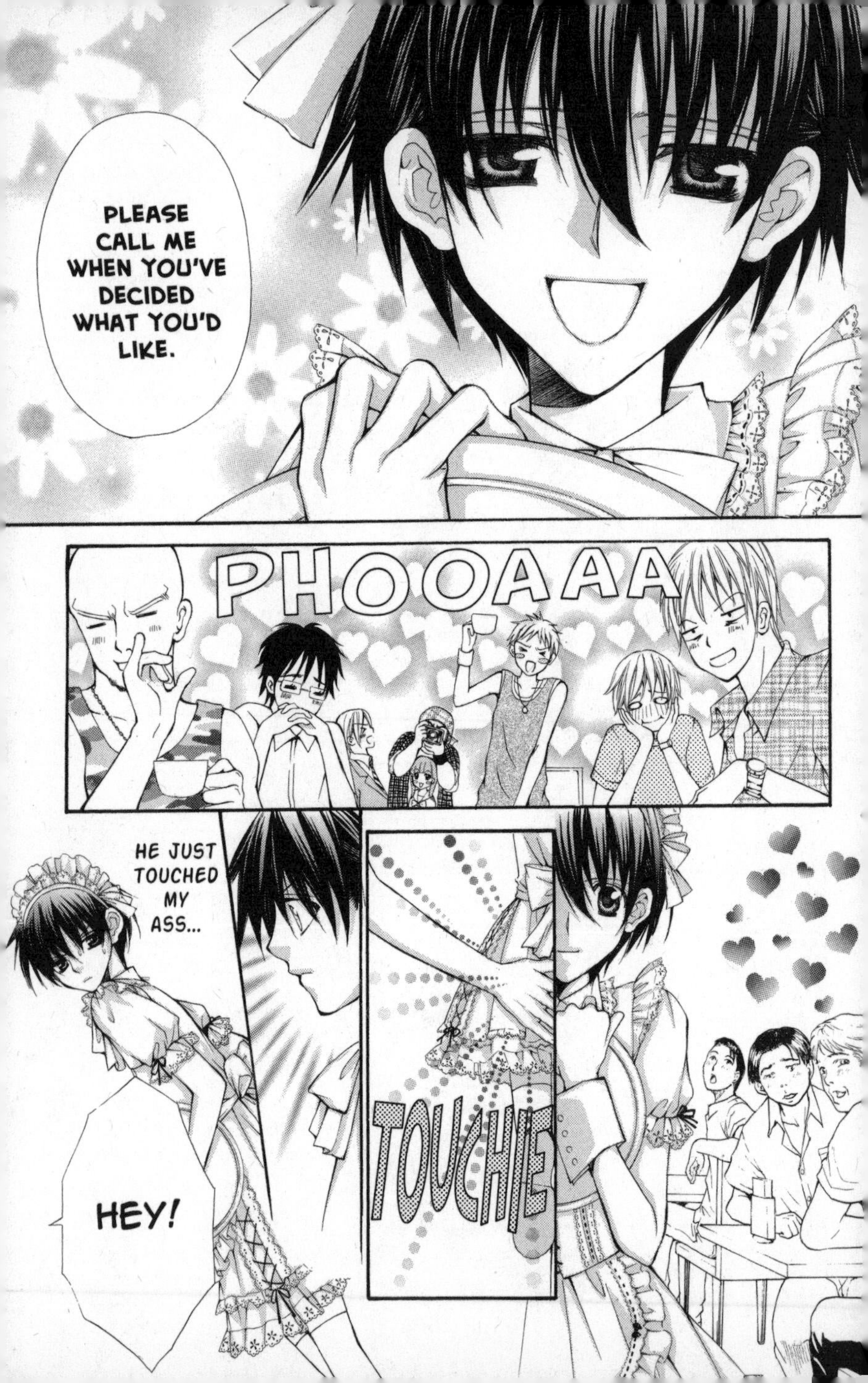
PLEASE CALL ME WHEN YOU'VE DECIDED WHAT YOU'D LIKE.
PHOOAAA
TOUCHIE
HE JUST TOUCHED MY ASS...
HEY!

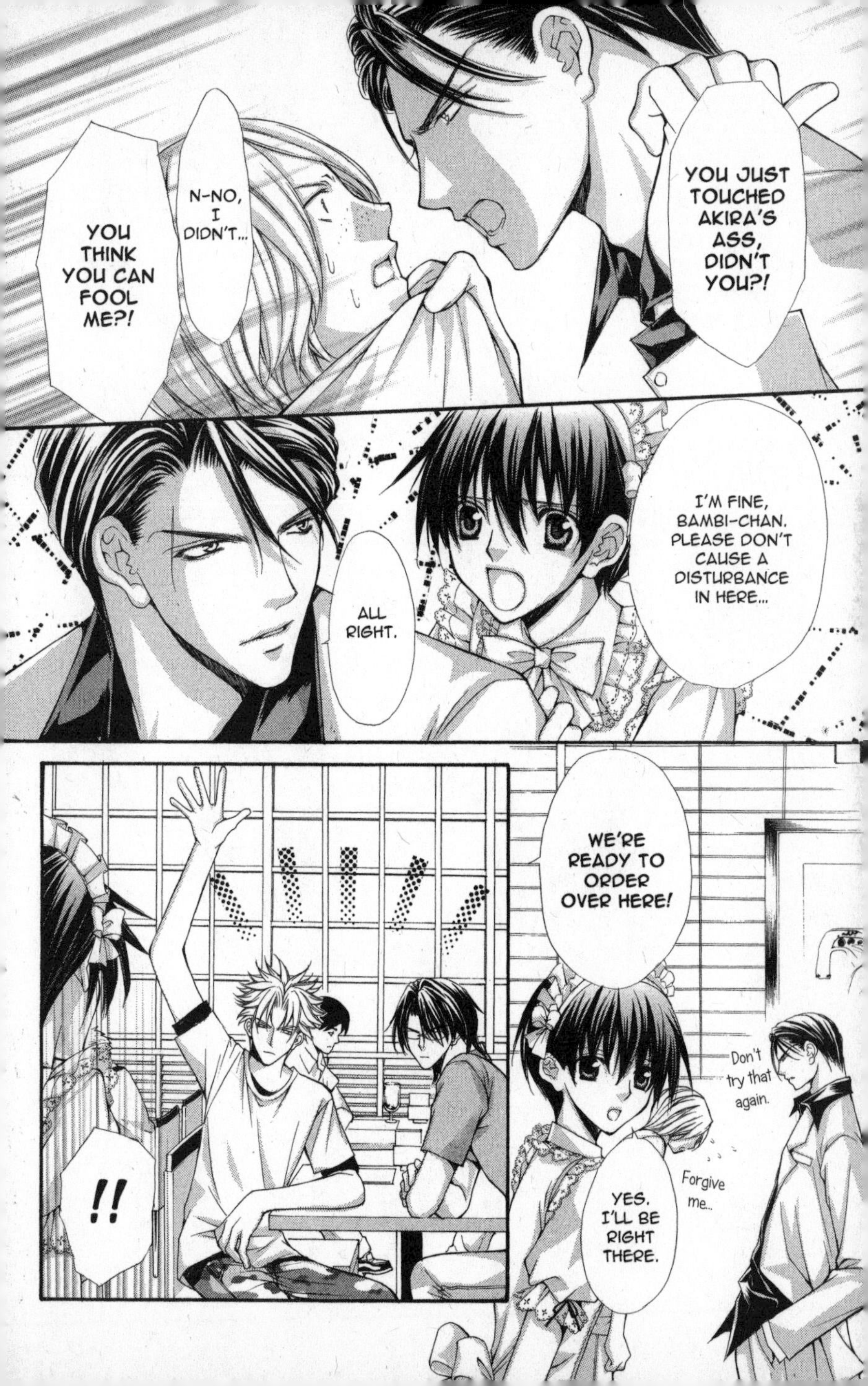
YOU JUST TOUCHED AKIRA'S ASS, DIDN'T YOU?!
N-NO, I DIDN'T...
YOU THINK YOU CAN FOOL ME?!
I'M FINE, BAMBI-CHAN. PLEASE DON'T CAUSE A DISTURBANCE IN HERE...
ALL RIGHT.
WE'RE READY TO ORDER OVER HERE!
Don't try that again.
Forgive me...
YES. I'LL BE RIGHT THERE.
!!

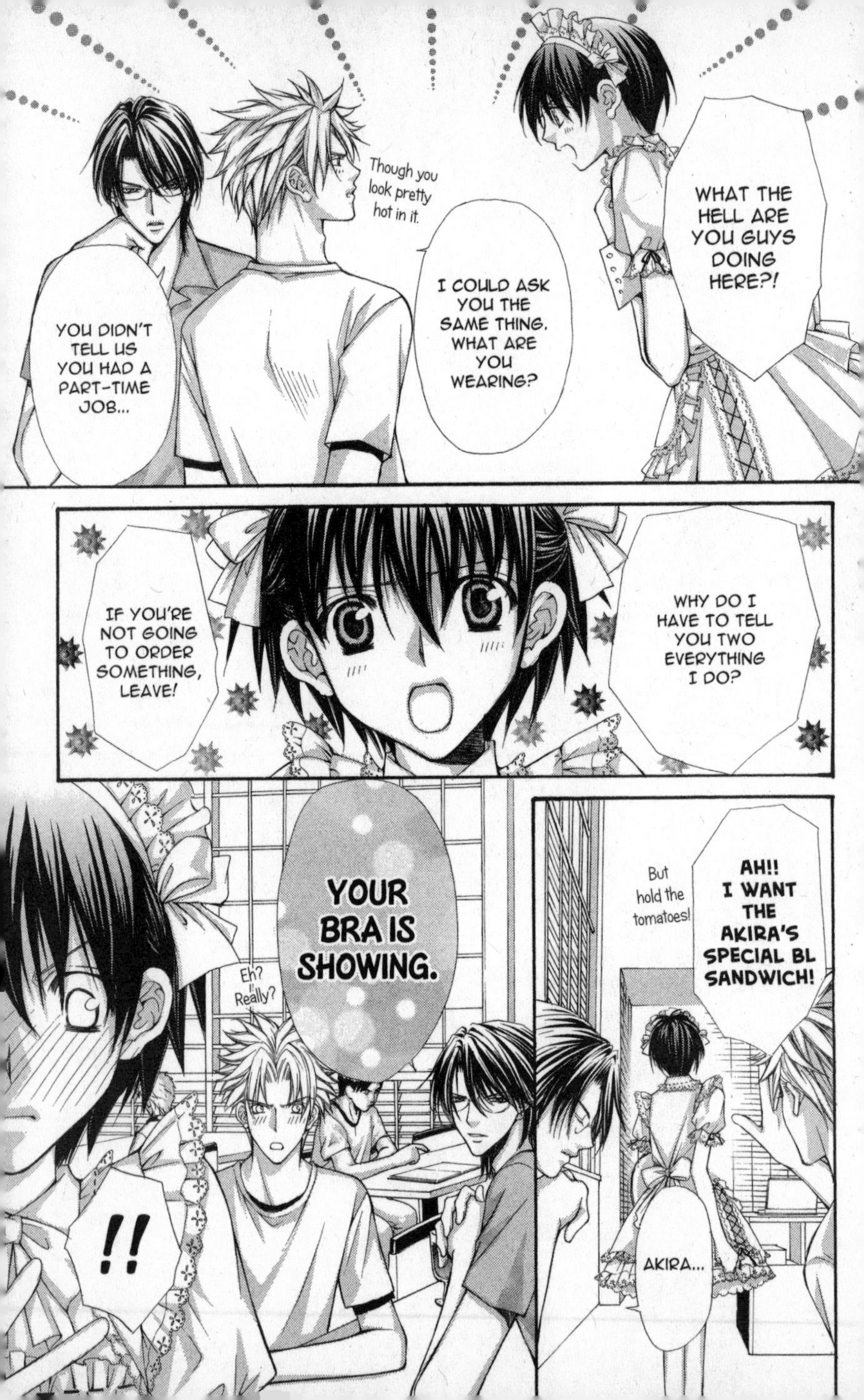
WHAT THE HELL ARE YOU GUYS DOING HERE?!
I COULD ASK YOU THE SAME THING. WHAT ARE YOU WEARING?
Though you look pretty hot in it.
YOU DIDN'T TELL US YOU HAD A PART-TIME JOB...
WHY DO I HAVE TO TELL YOU TWO EVERYTHING I DO?
IF YOU'RE NOT GOING TO ORDER SOMETHING, LEAVE!
AH!! I WANT THE AKIRA'S SPECIAL BL SANDWICH!
But hold the tomatoes!
AKIRA...
YOUR BRA IS SHOWING.
Eh? Really?
!!

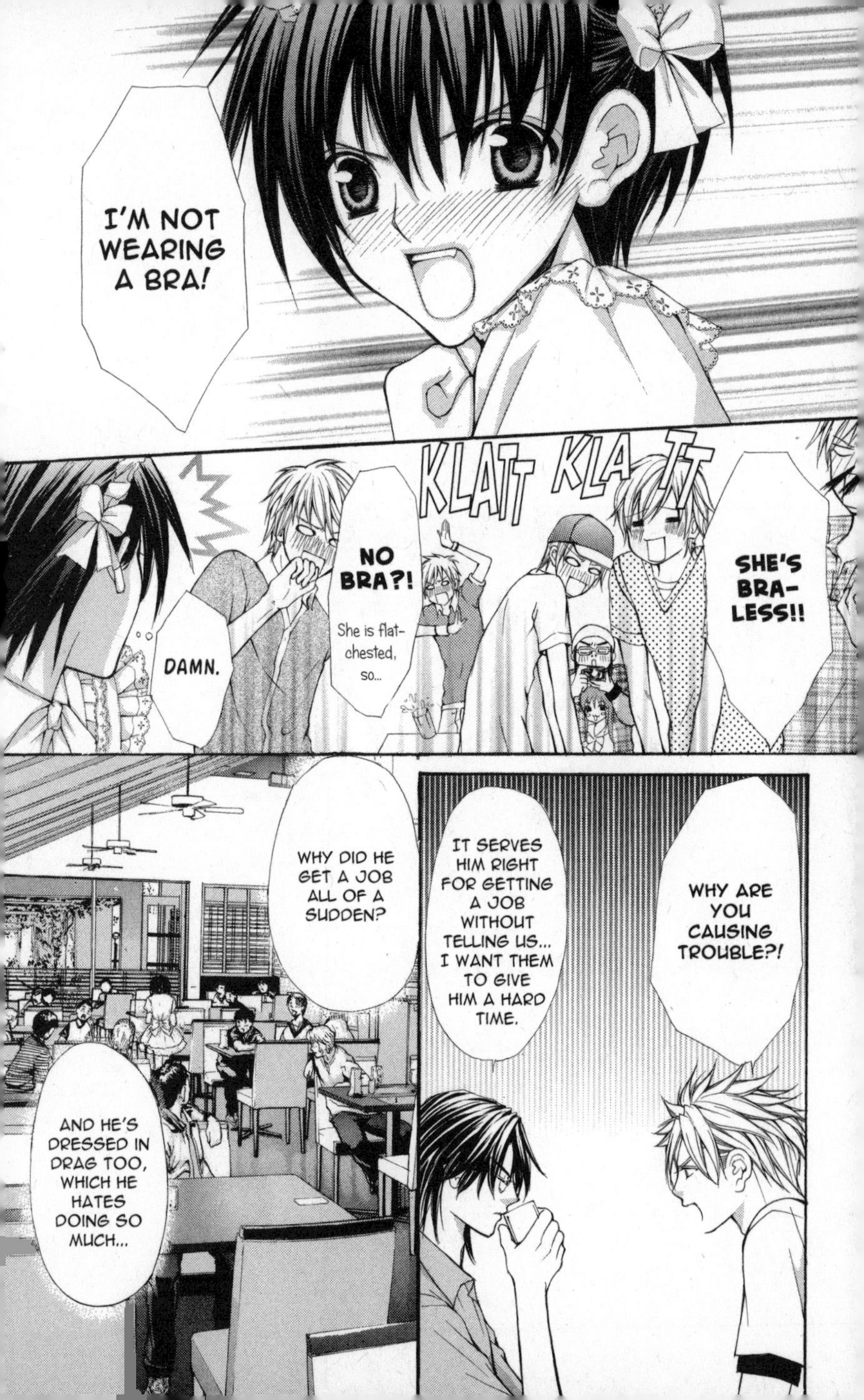
I'M NOT WEARING A BRA!
SHE'S BRA-LESS!!
KLATT KLATT
NO BRA?!
She is flat-chested, so...
DAMN.
WHY ARE YOU CAUSING TROUBLE?!
IT SERVES HIM RIGHT FOR GETTING A JOB WITHOUT TELLING US... I WANT THEM TO GIVE HIM A HARD TIME.
WHY DID HE GET A JOB ALL OF A SUDDEN?
AND HE'S DRESSED IN DRAG TOO, WHICH HE HATES DOING SO MUCH...

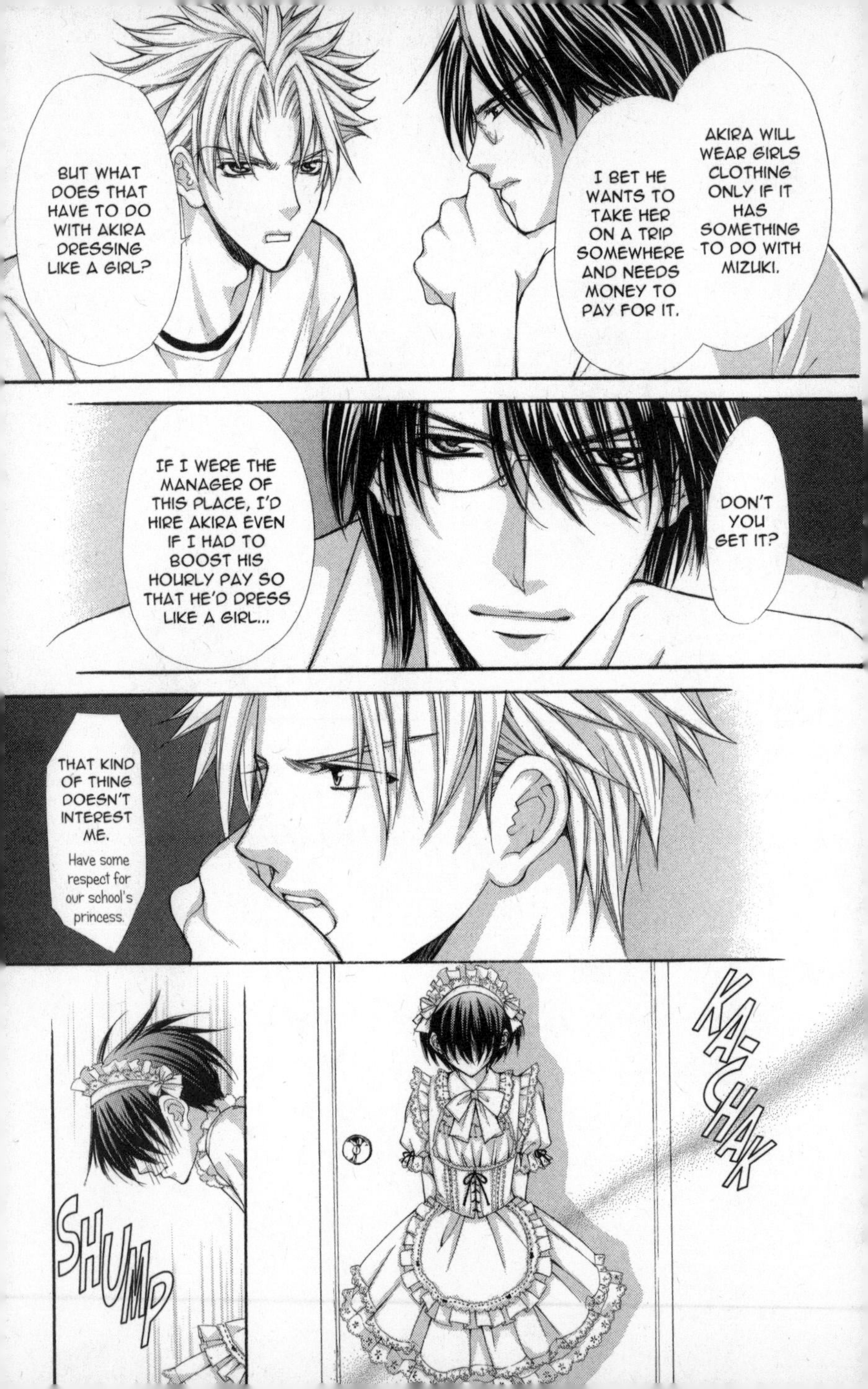
AKIRA WILL WEAR GIRLS CLOTHING ONLY IF IT HAS SOMETHING TO DO WITH MIZUKI.
I BET HE WANTS TO TAKE HER ON A TRIP SOMEWHERE AND NEEDS MONEY TO PAY FOR IT.
BUT WHAT DOES THAT HAVE TO DO WITH AKIRA DRESSING LIKE A GIRL?
DON'T YOU GET IT?
IF I WERE THE MANAGER OF THIS PLACE, I'D HIRE AKIRA EVEN IF I HAD TO BOOST HIS HOURLY PAY SO THAT HE'D DRESS LIKE A GIRL...
THAT KIND OF THING DOESN'T INTEREST ME.
Have some respect for our school's princess.
KA-CHAK
SHUMP

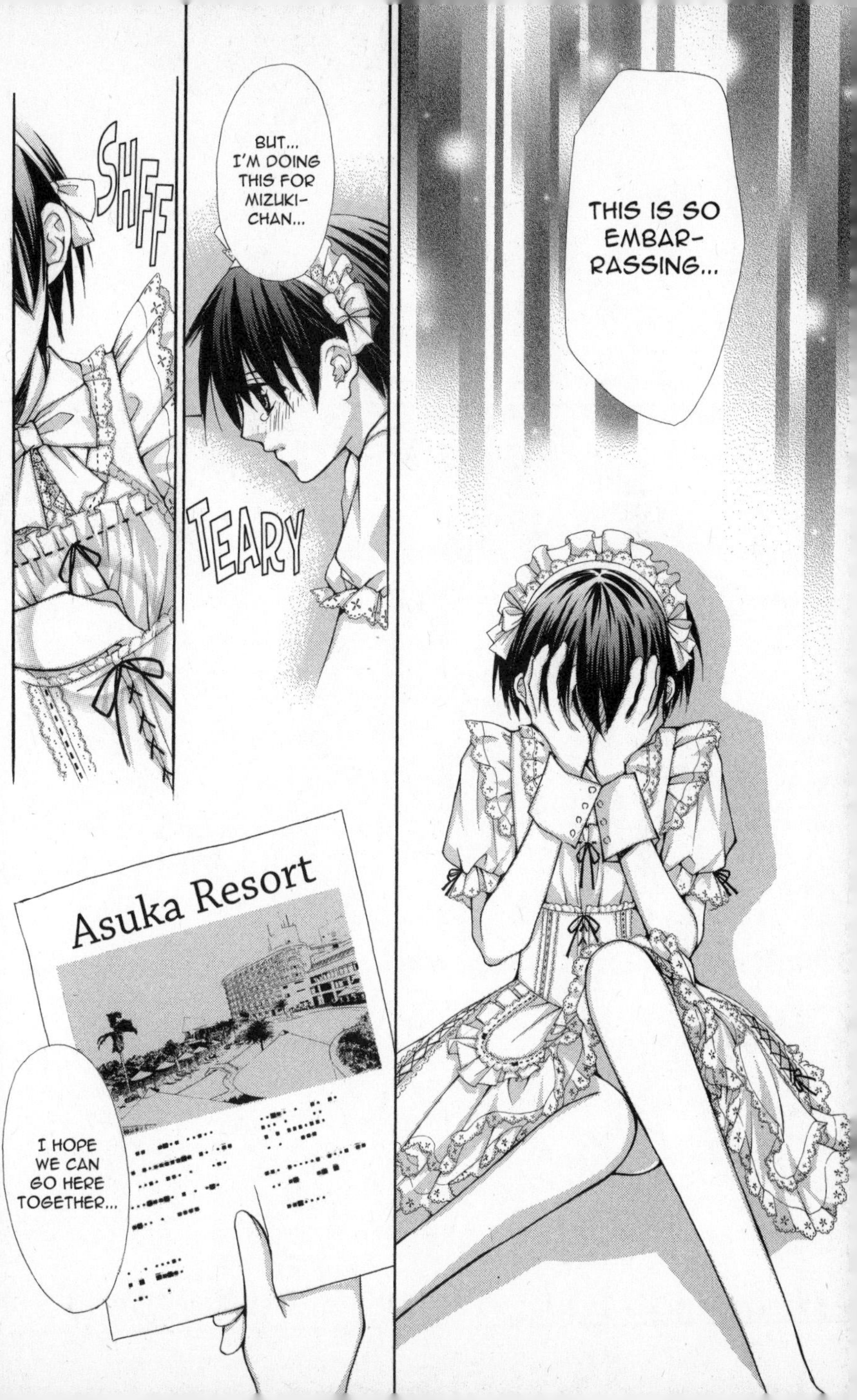
THIS IS SO EMBARRASSING...
BUT... I'M DOING THIS FOR MIZUKI-CHAN...
TEARY
SHFF
Asuka Resort
I HOPE WE CAN GO HERE TOGETHER...

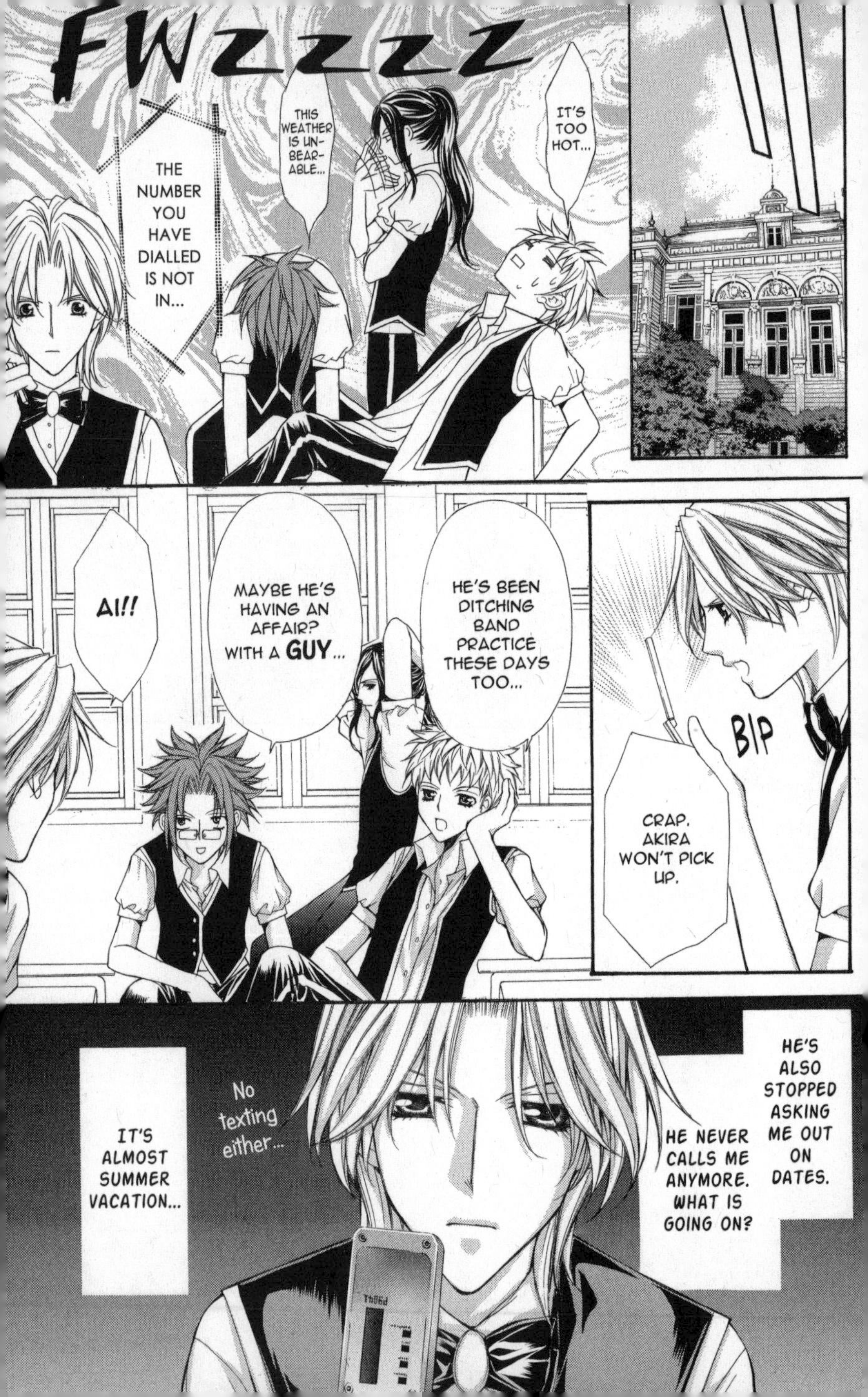
FWZZZZZ
IT'S TOO HOT...
THIS WEATHER IS UN-BEARABLE...
THE NUMBER YOU HAVE DIALLED IS NOT IN...
BIP
CRAP. AKIRA WON'T PICK UP.
HE'S BEEN DITCHING BAND PRACTICE THESE DAYS TOO...
MAYBE HE'S HAVING AN AFFAIR? WITH A GUY...
AI!!
HE'S ALSO STOPPED ASKING ME OUT ON DATES.
HE NEVER CALLS ME ANYMORE. WHAT IS GOING ON?
No texting either...
IT'S ALMOST SUMMER VACATION...

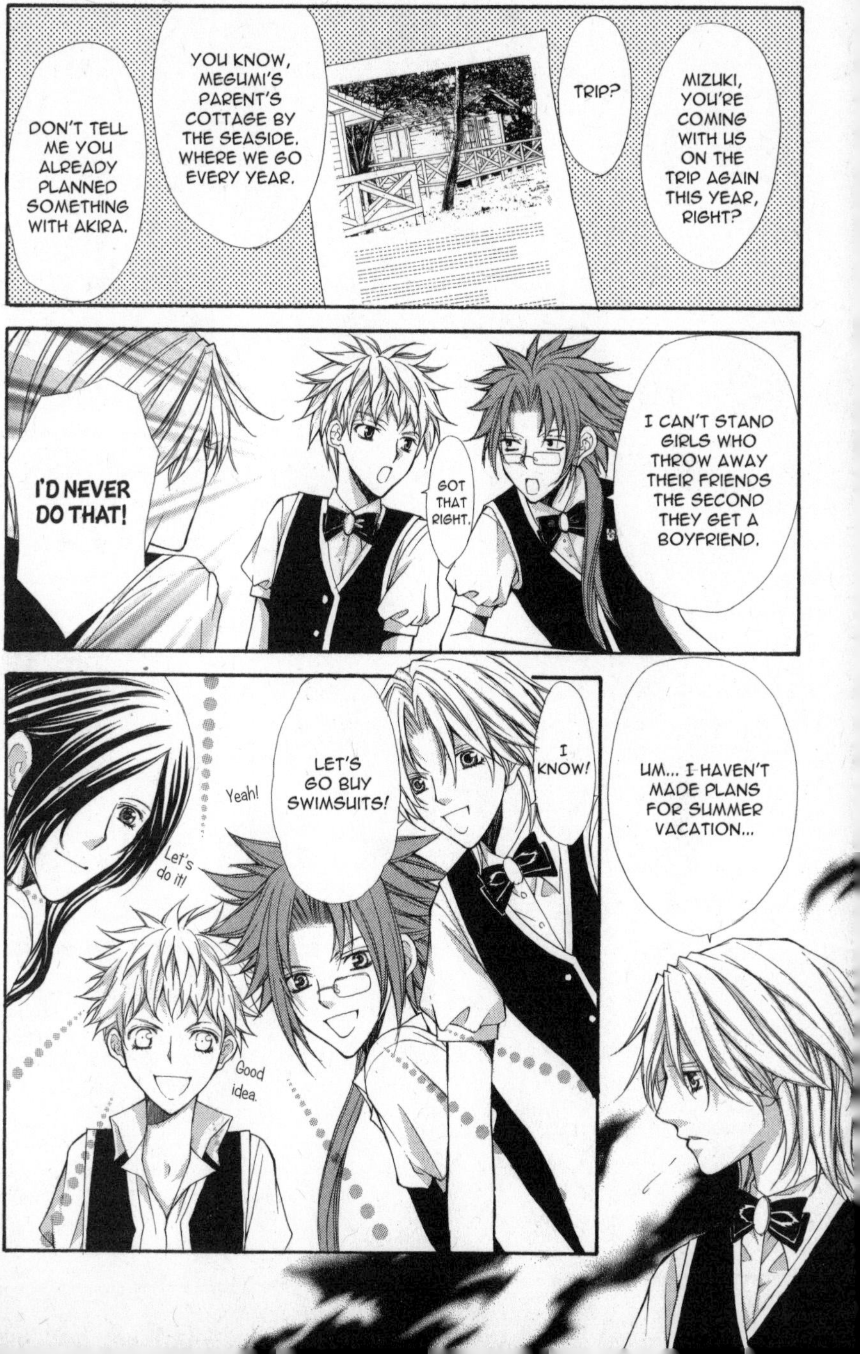
MIZUKI, YOU'RE COMING WITH US ON THE TRIP AGAIN THIS YEAR, RIGHT?
TRIP?
YOU KNOW, MEGUMI'S PARENT'S COTTAGE BY THE SEASIDE. WHERE WE GO EVERY YEAR.
DON'T TELL ME YOU ALREADY PLANNED SOMETHING WITH AKIRA.
I CAN'T STAND GIRLS WHO THROW AWAY THEIR FRIENDS THE SECOND THEY GET A BOYFRIEND.
GOT THAT RIGHT.
I'D NEVER DO THAT!
UM... I HAVEN'T MADE PLANS FOR SUMMER VACATION...
I KNOW!
LET'S GO BUY SWIMSUITS!
Yeah!
Let's do it!
Good idea.

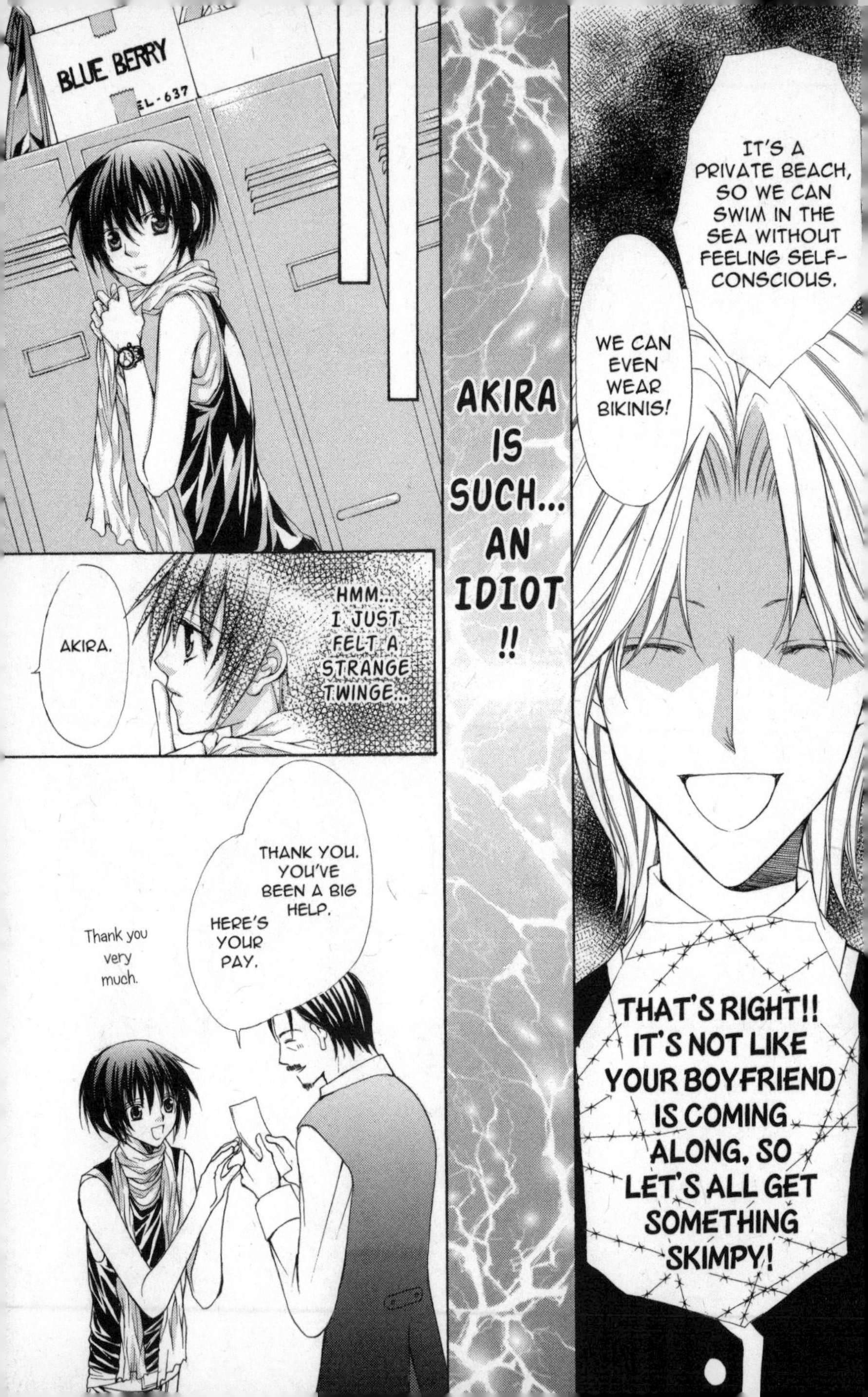
IT'S A PRIVATE BEACH, SO WE CAN SWIM IN THE SEA WITHOUT FEELING SELF-CONSCIOUS.
WE CAN EVEN WEAR BIKINIS!
THAT'S RIGHT!! IT'S NOT LIKE YOUR BOYFRIEND IS COMING ALONG, SO LET'S ALL GET SOMETHING SKIMPY!
AKIRA IS SUCH... AN IDIOT!!
BLUE BERRY
EL-637
HMM... I JUST FELT A STRANGE TWINGE...
AKIRA.
THANK YOU. YOU'VE BEEN A BIG HELP.
HERE'S YOUR PAY.
Thank you very much.

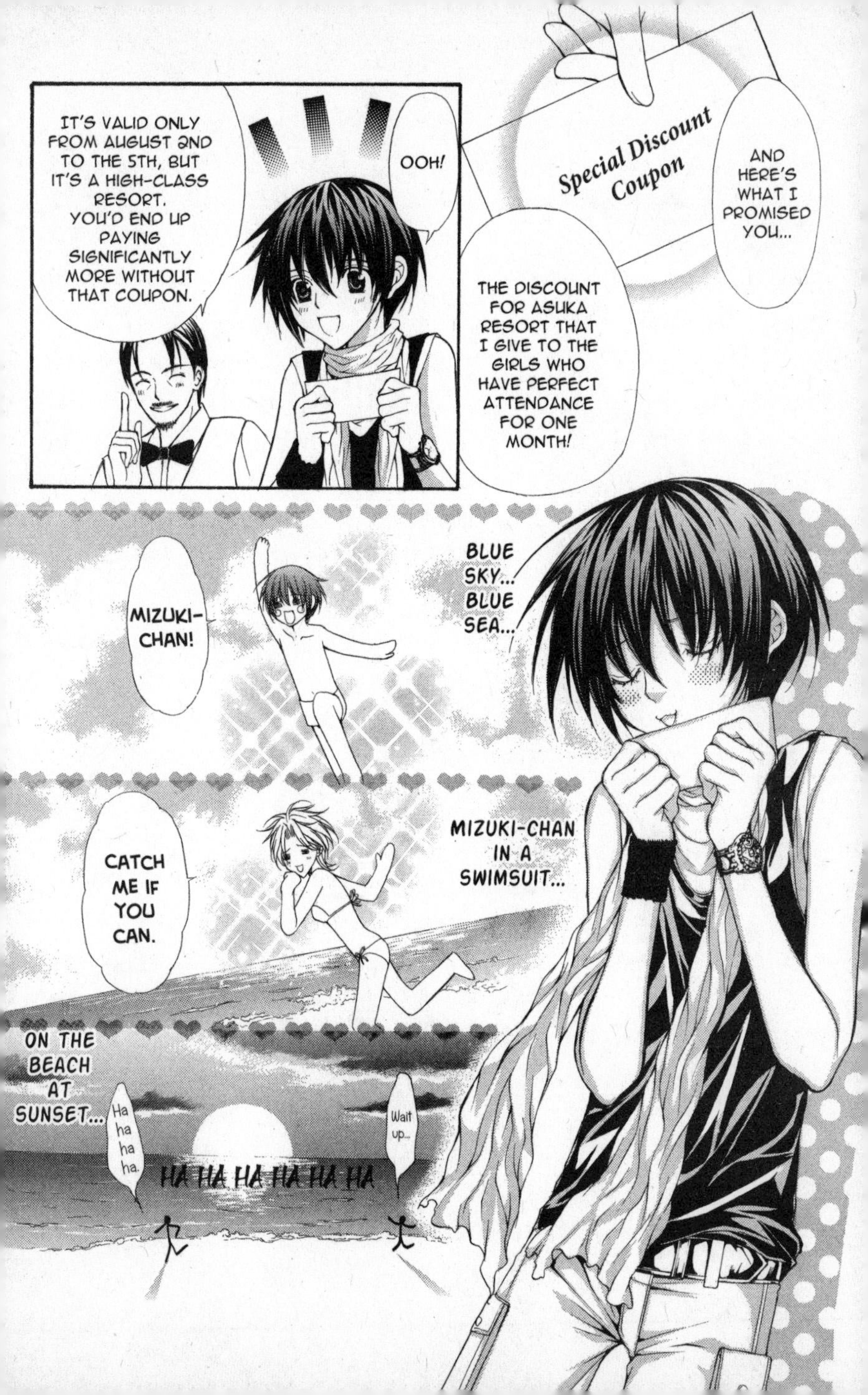
Special Discount Coupon
AND HERE'S WHAT I PROMISED YOU...
THE DISCOUNT FOR ASUKA RESORT THAT I GIVE TO THE GIRLS WHO HAVE PERFECT ATTENDANCE FOR ONE MONTH!
OOH!
IT'S VALID ONLY FROM AUGUST 2ND TO THE 5TH, BUT IT'S A HIGH-CLASS RESORT. YOU'D END UP PAYING SIGNIFICANTLY MORE WITHOUT THAT COUPON.
BLUE SKY... BLUE SEA...
MIZUKI-CHAN!
MIZUKI-CHAN IN A SWIMSUIT...
CATCH ME IF YOU CAN.
ON THE BEACH AT SUNSET...
Wait up...
Ha ha ha ha.
HA HA HA HA HA HA

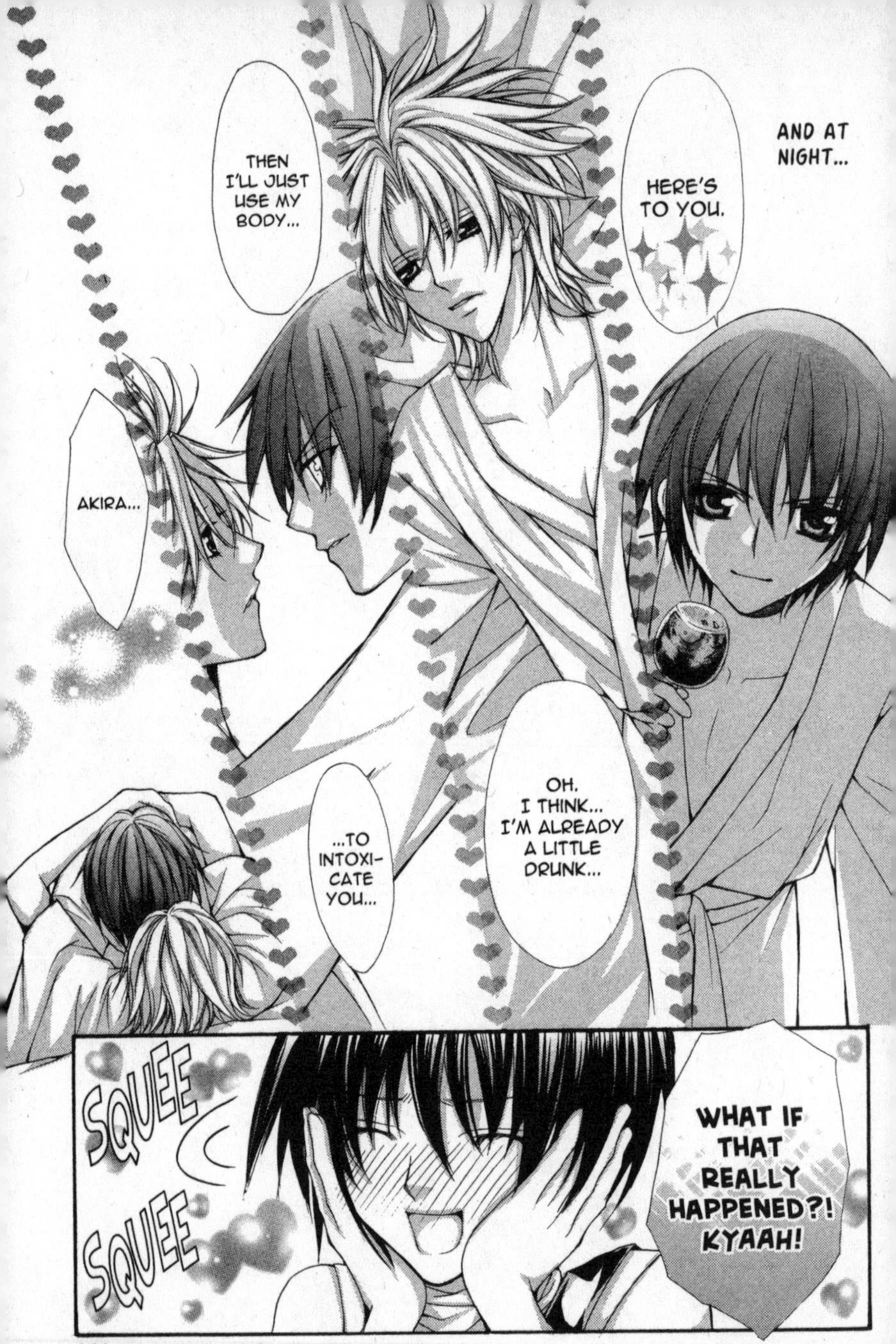
AND AT NIGHT...
HERE'S TO YOU.
OH, I THINK... I'M ALREADY A LITTLE DRUNK...
THEN I'LL JUST USE MY BODY...
...TO INTOXI-CATE YOU...
AKIRA...
WHAT IF THAT REALLY HAPPENED?! KYAAH!
SQUEE
SQUEE

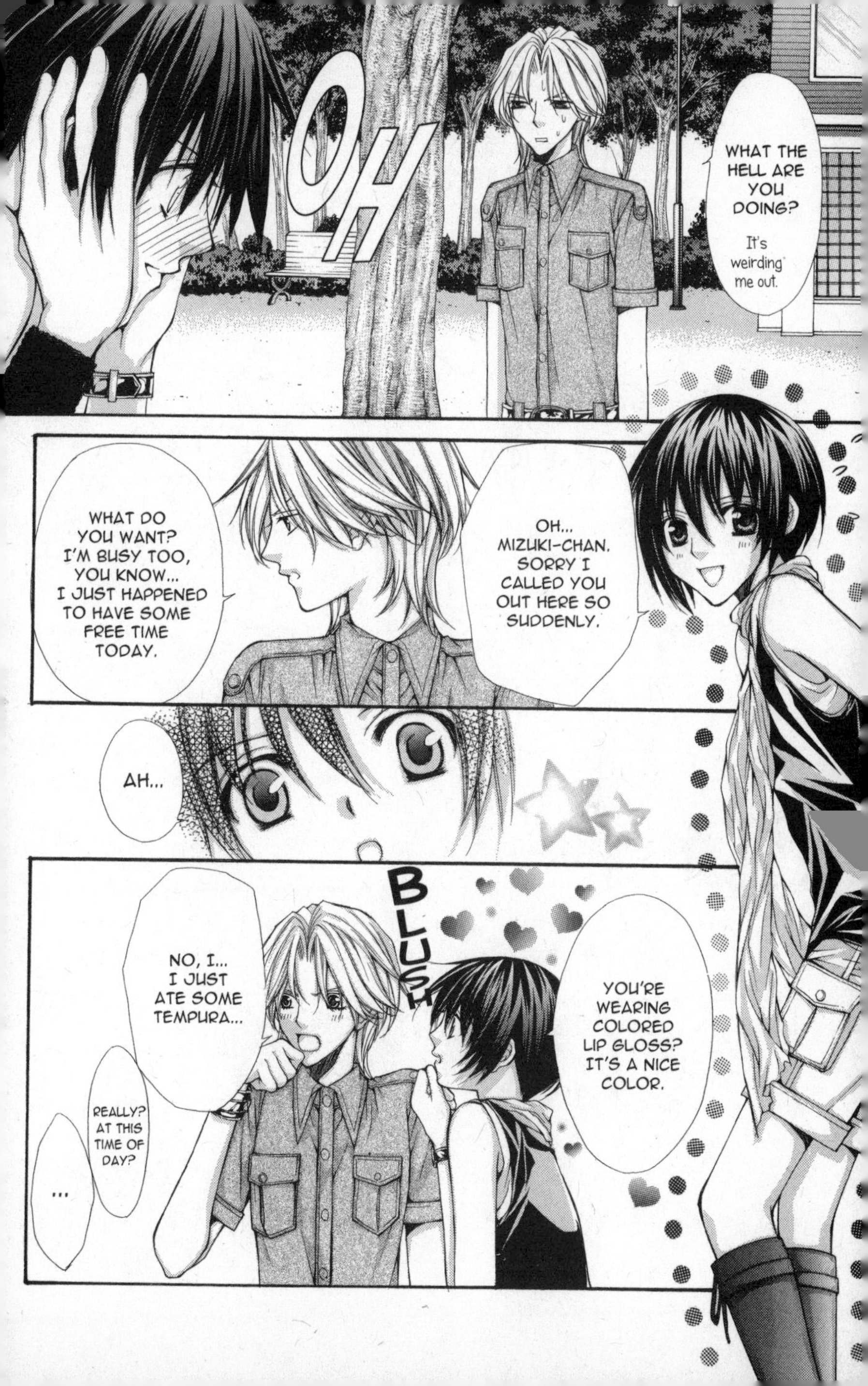
WHAT THE HELL ARE YOU DOING? It's weirding me out.
OH
OH... MIZUKI-CHAN. SORRY I CALLED YOU OUT HERE SO SUDDENLY.
WHAT DO YOU WANT? I'M BUSY TOO, YOU KNOW... I JUST HAPPENED TO HAVE SOME FREE TIME TODAY.
AH...
YOU'RE WEARING COLORED LIP GLOSS? IT'S A NICE COLOR.
BLUSH
NO, I... I JUST ATE SOME TEMPURA...
REALLY? AT THIS TIME OF DAY?
...

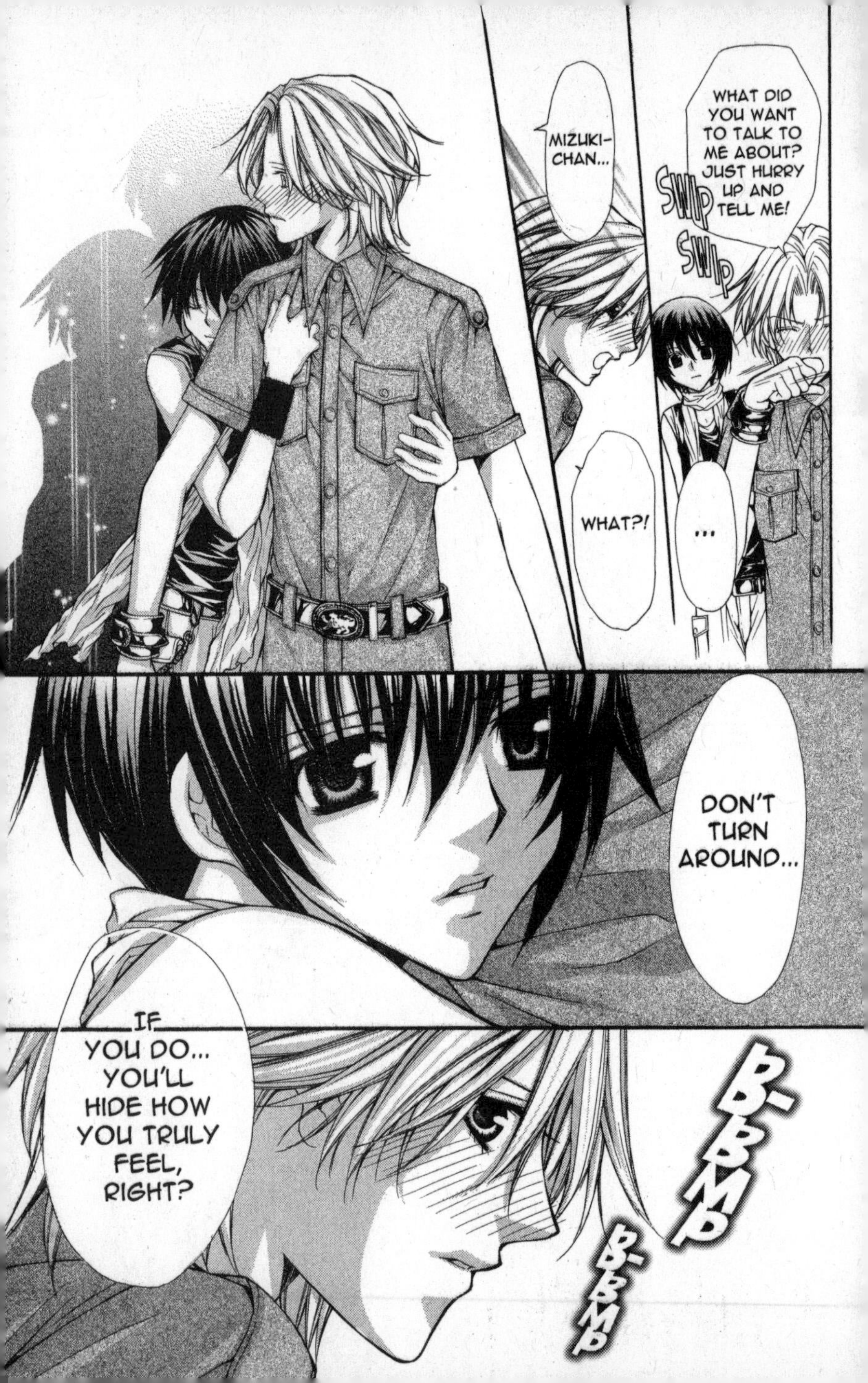
WHAT DID YOU WANT TO TALK TO ME ABOUT? JUST HURRY UP AND TELL ME!
SWIP
SWIP
...
MIZUKI-CHAN...
WHAT?!
DON'T TURN AROUND...
IF YOU DO... YOU'LL HIDE HOW YOU TRULY FEEL, RIGHT?
B-BBMP
B-BBMP

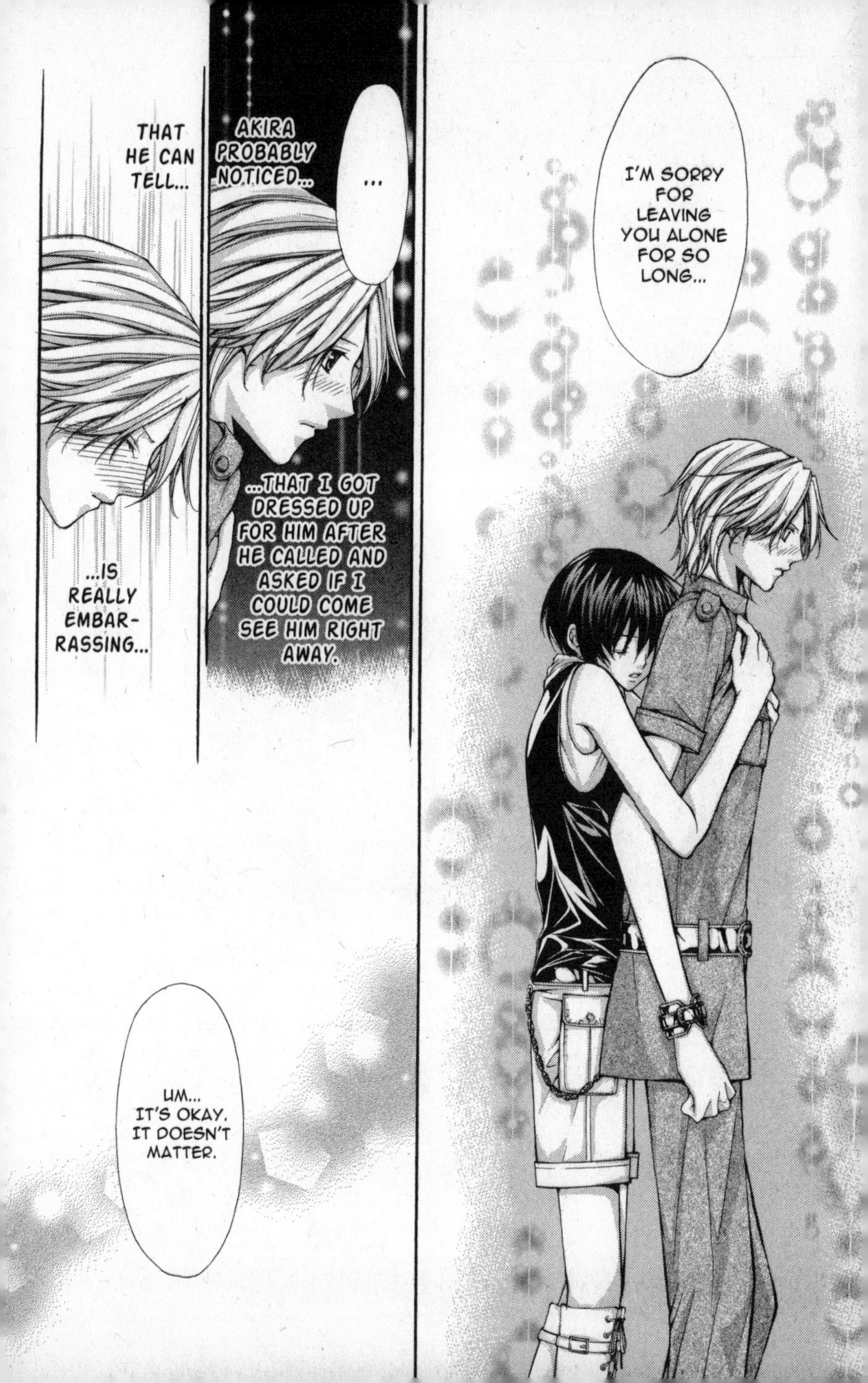
I'M SORRY FOR LEAVING YOU ALONE FOR SO LONG...
...
AKIRA PROBABLY NOTICED...
...THAT I GOT DRESSED UP FOR HIM AFTER HE CALLED AND ASKED IF I COULD COME SEE HIM RIGHT AWAY.
THAT HE CAN TELL...
...IS REALLY EMBAR-RASSING...
UM... IT'S OKAY. IT DOESN'T MATTER.

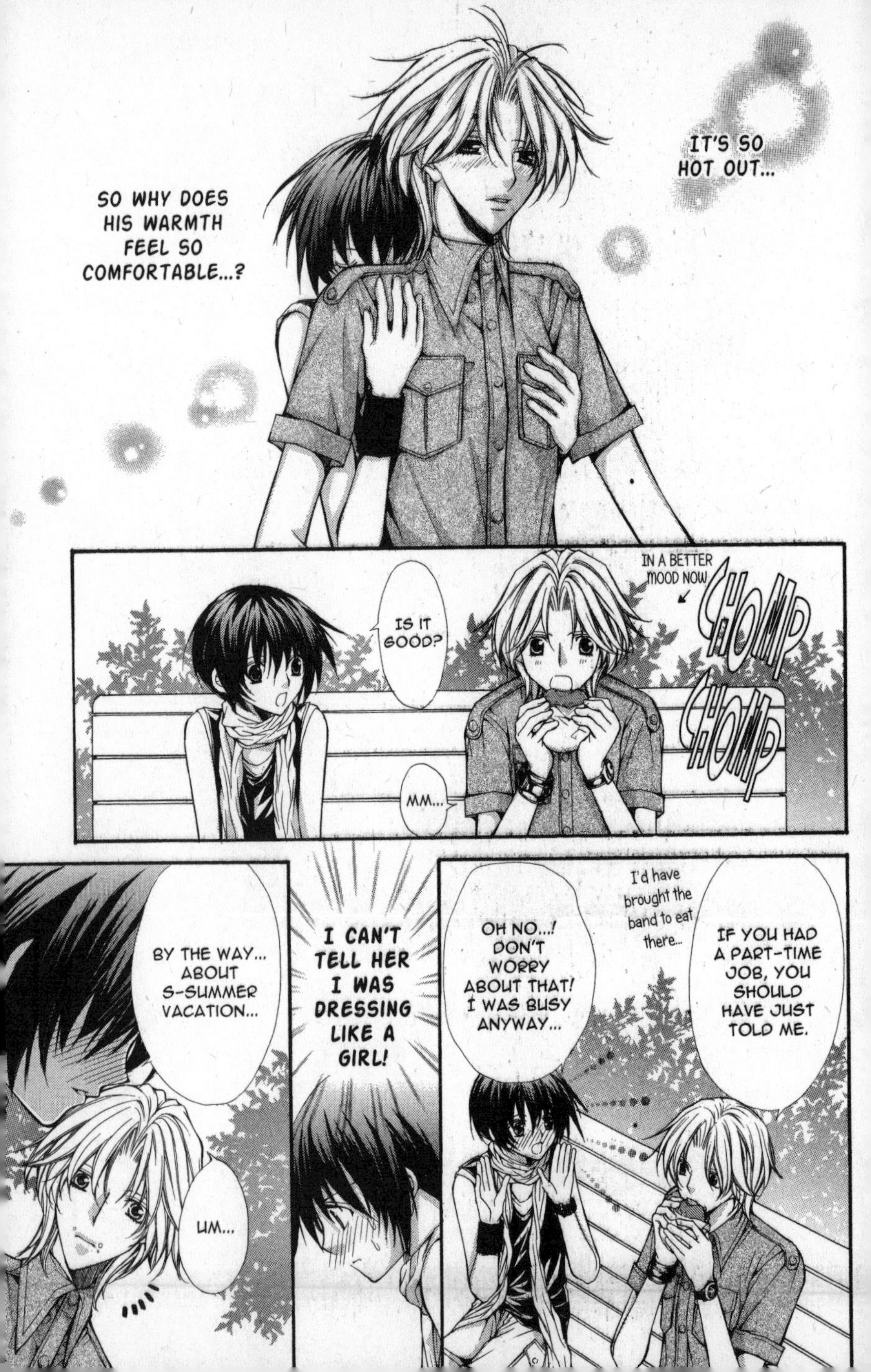
IT'S SO HOT OUT...
SO WHY DOES HIS WARMTH FEEL SO COMFORTABLE...?
IN A BETTER MOOD NOW
CHOMP CHOMP
IS IT GOOD?
MM...
IF YOU HAD A PART-TIME JOB, YOU SHOULD HAVE JUST TOLD ME.
I'd have brought the band to eat there...
OH NO...! DON'T WORRY ABOUT THAT! I WAS BUSY ANYWAY...
I CAN'T TELL HER I WAS DRESSING LIKE A GIRL!
BY THE WAY... ABOUT S-SUMMER VACATION...
UM...

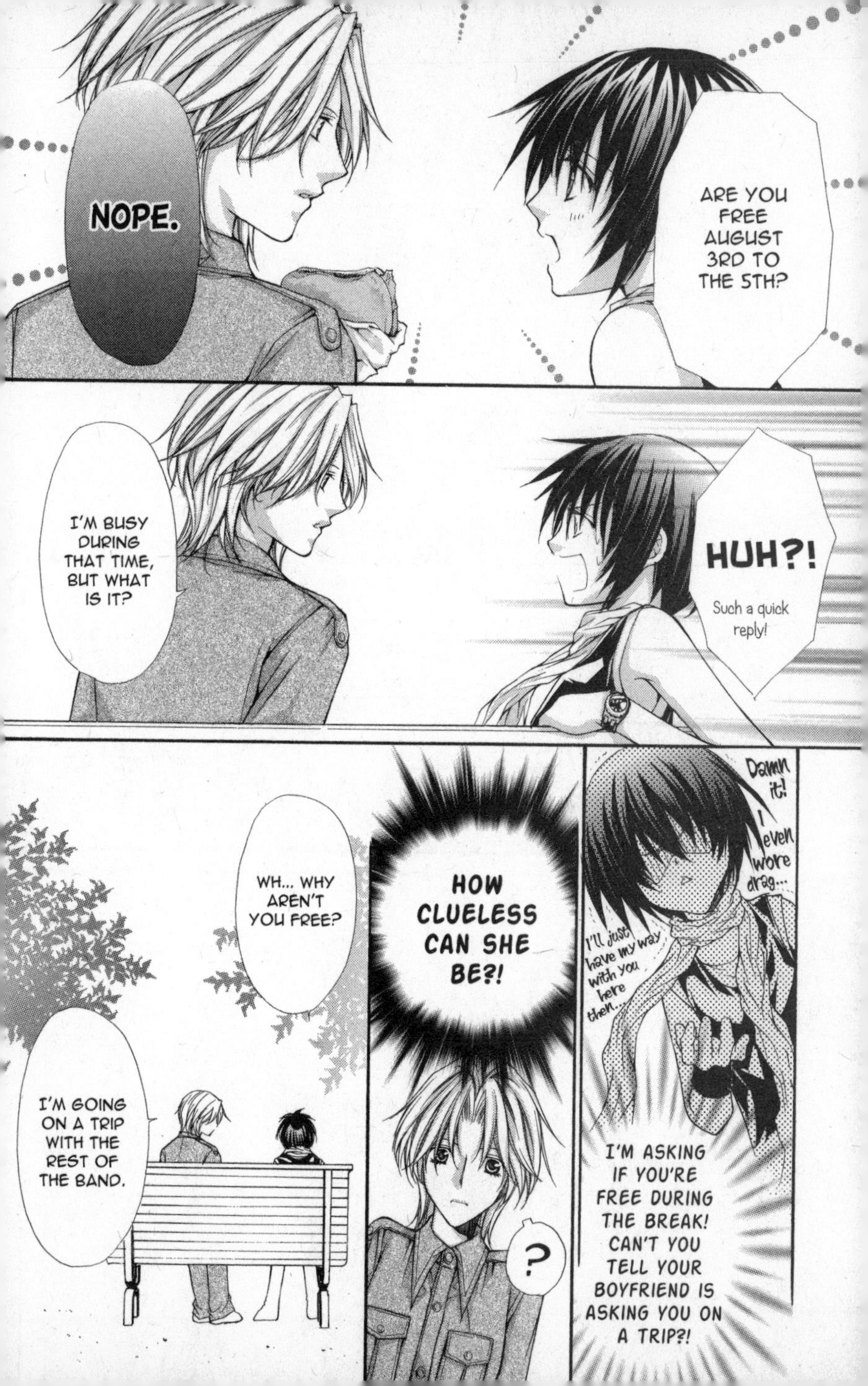
ARE YOU FREE AUGUST 3RD TO THE 5TH?
NOPE.
HUH?!
Such a quick reply!
I'M BUSY DURING THAT TIME, BUT WHAT IS IT?
Damn it! I even wore drag...
I'll just have my way with you here then...
I'M ASKING IF YOU'RE FREE DURING THE BREAK! CAN'T YOU TELL YOUR BOYFRIEND IS ASKING YOU ON A TRIP?!
HOW CLUELESS CAN SHE BE?!
?
WH... WHY AREN'T YOU FREE?
I'M GOING ON A TRIP WITH THE REST OF THE BAND.

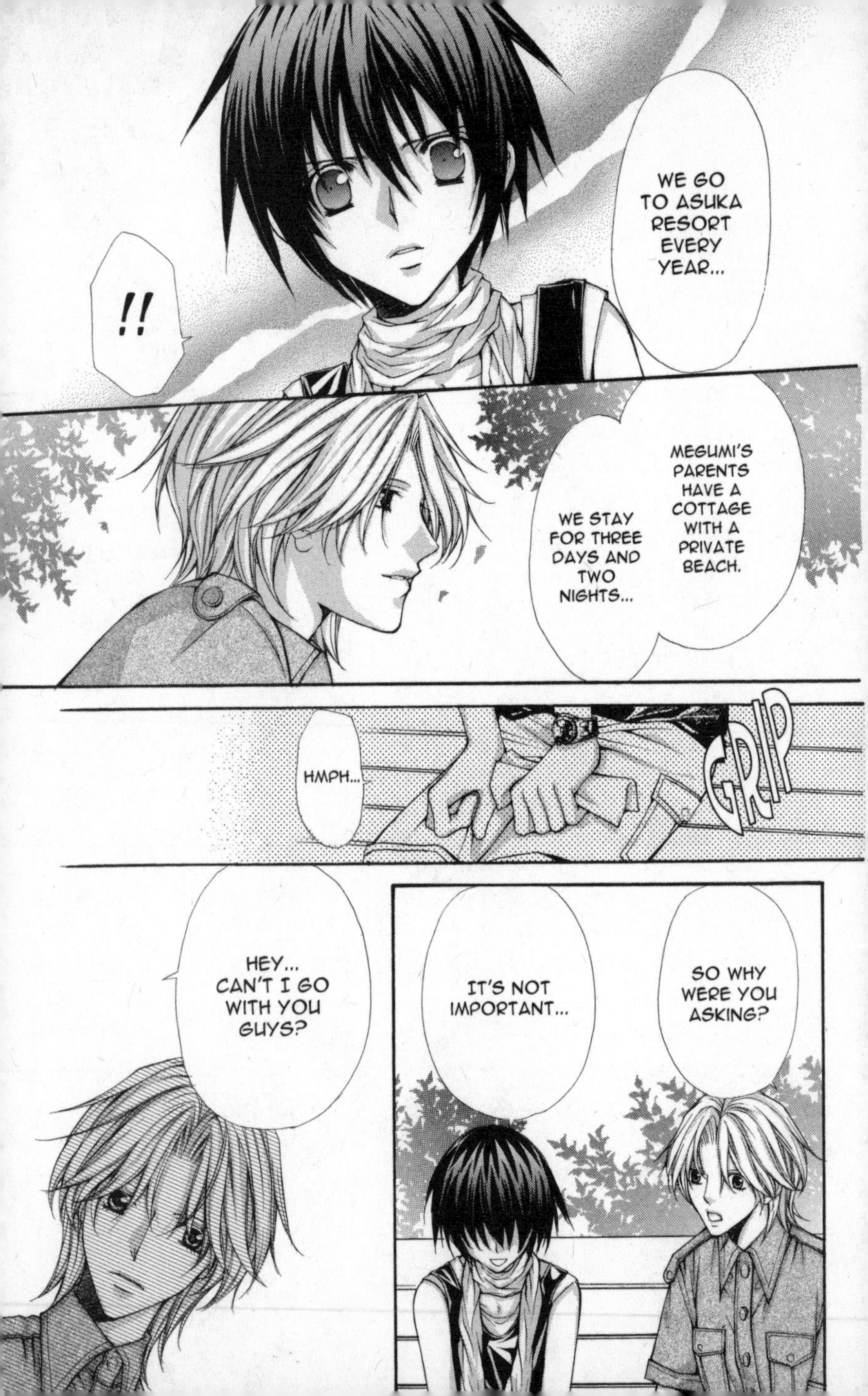
WE GO TO ASUKA RESORT EVERY YEAR...
!!
MEGUMI'S PARENTS HAVE A COTTAGE WITH A PRIVATE BEACH.
WE STAY FOR THREE DAYS AND TWO NIGHTS...
GRIP
HMPH...
SO WHY WERE YOU ASKING?
IT'S NOT IMPORTANT...
HEY... CAN'T I GO WITH YOU GUYS?

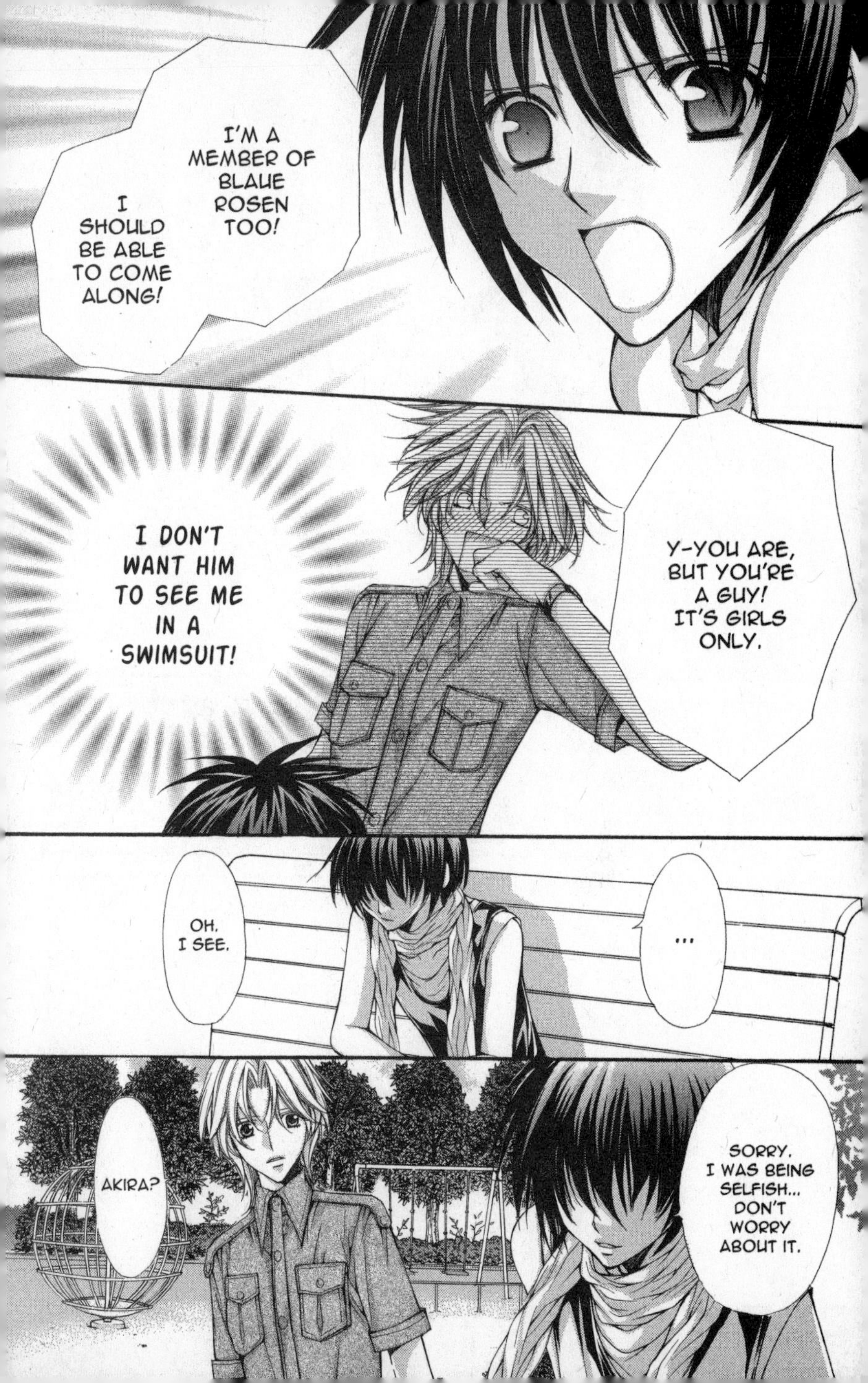
I'M A MEMBER OF BLAUE ROSEN TOO! I SHOULD BE ABLE TO COME ALONG!
Y-YOU ARE, BUT YOU'RE A GUY! IT'S GIRLS ONLY.
I DON'T WANT HIM TO SEE ME IN A SWIMSUIT!
...
OH. I SEE.
SORRY. I WAS BEING SELFISH... DON'T WORRY ABOUT IT.
AKIRA?

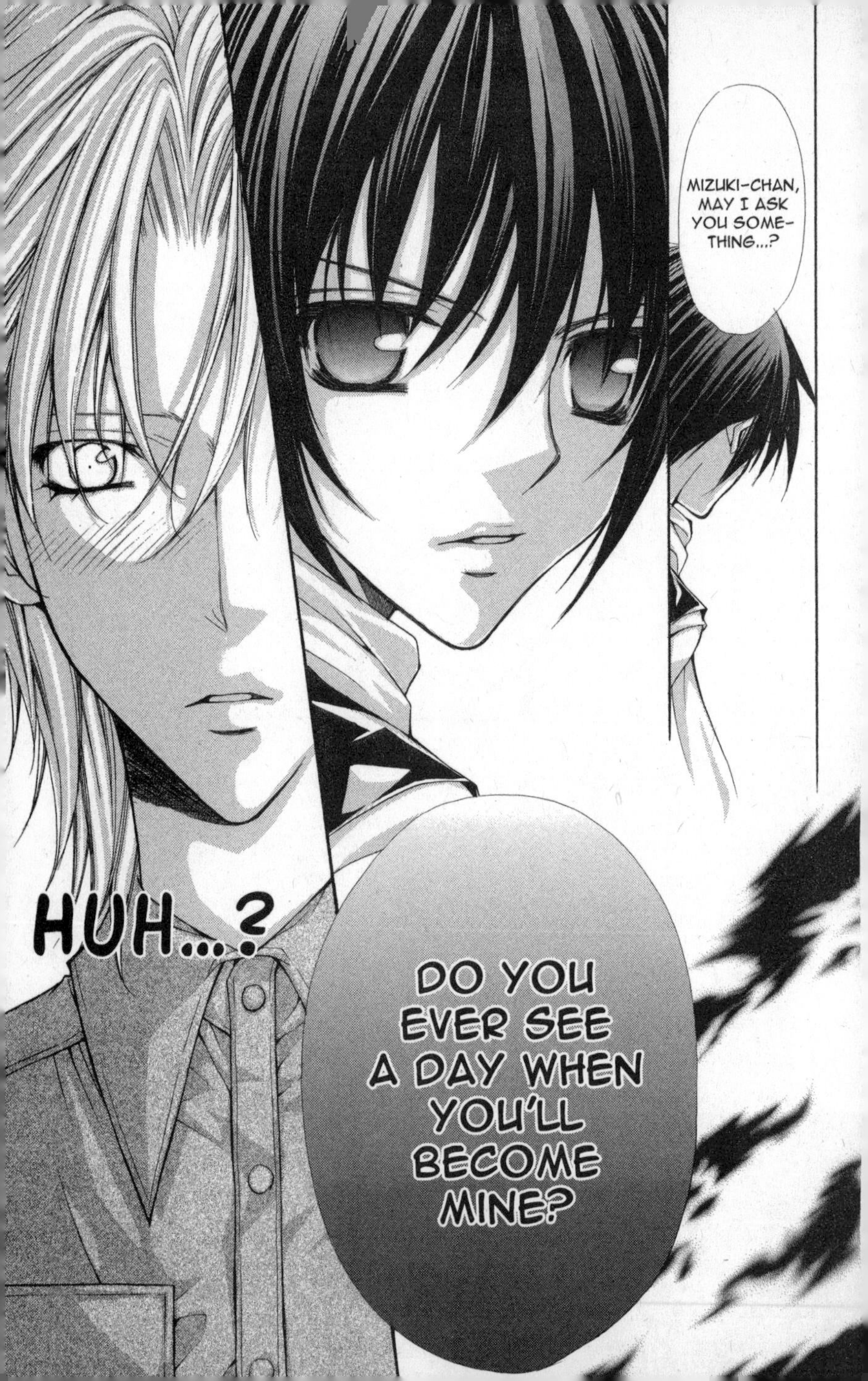
MIZUKI-CHAN, MAY I ASK YOU SOME-THING...?
DO YOU EVER SEE A DAY WHEN YOU'LL BECOME MINE?
HUH...?

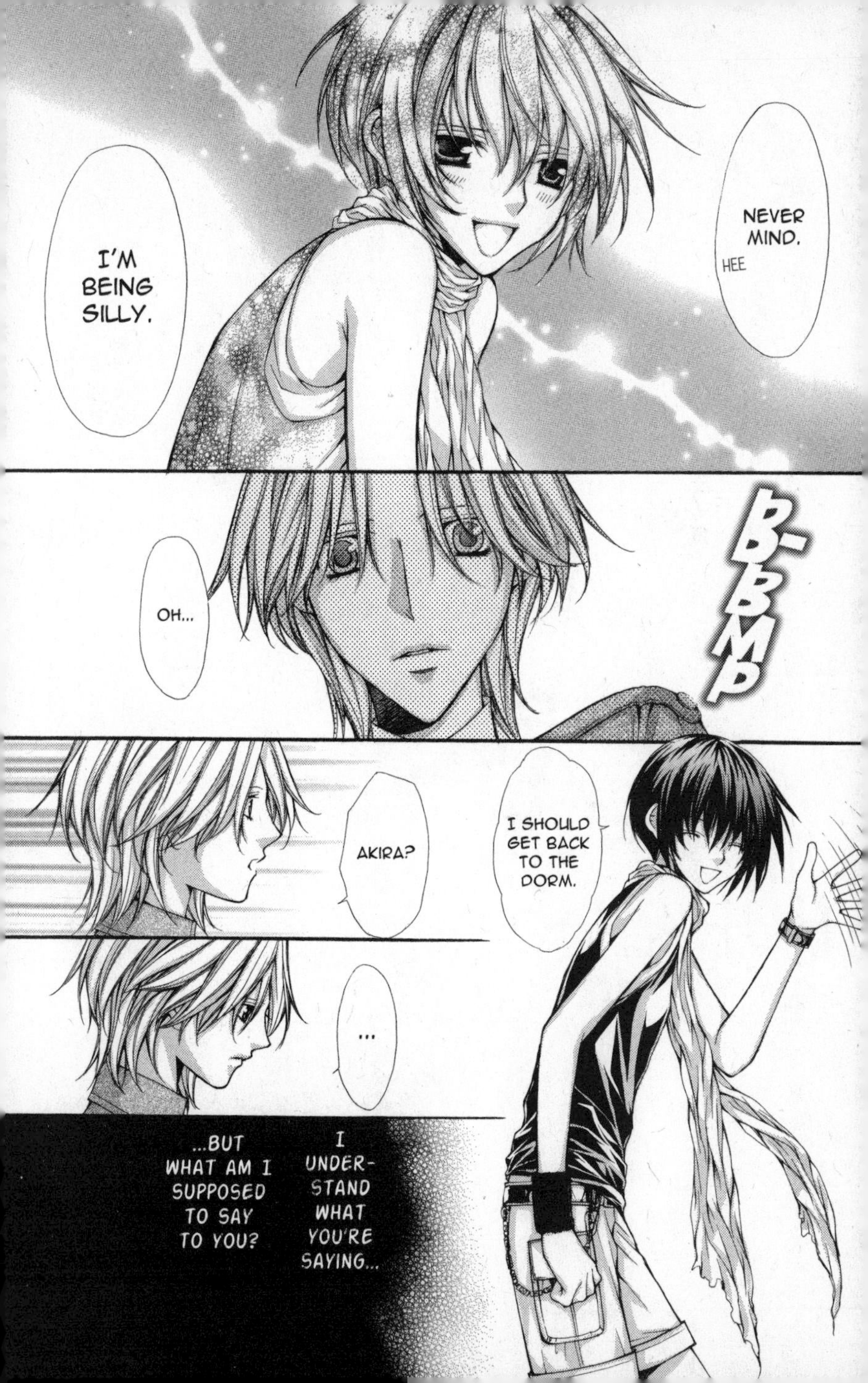
NEVER MIND.
HEE
I'M BEING SILLY.
B-BMP
OH...
I SHOULD GET BACK TO THE DORM.
AKIRA?
...
I UNDER-STAND WHAT YOU'RE SAYING...
...BUT WHAT AM I SUPPOSED TO SAY TO YOU?

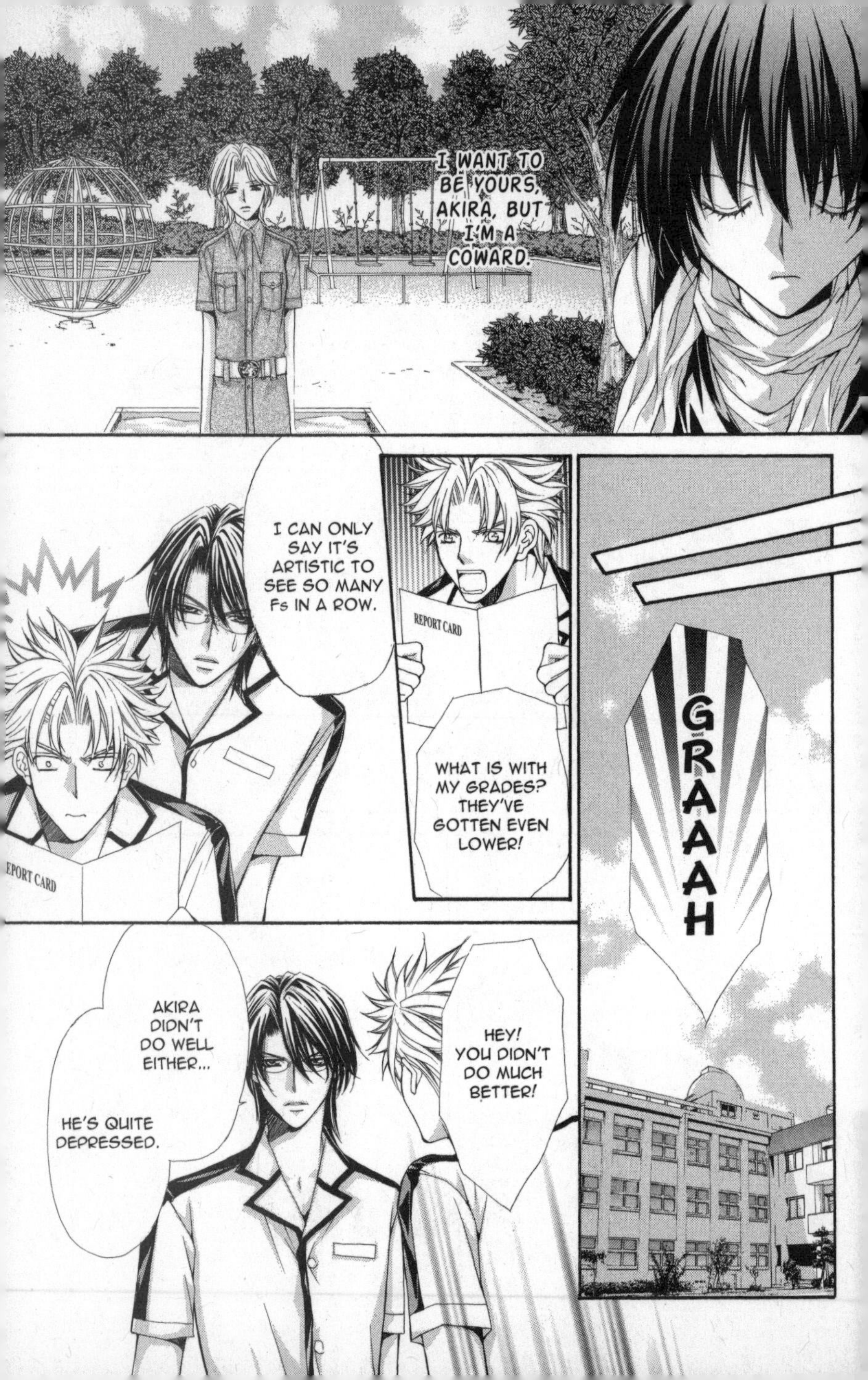
I WANT TO BE YOURS, AKIRA, BUT I'M A COWARD.
GRAAAH
REPORT CARD
WHAT IS WITH MY GRADES? THEY'VE GOTTEN EVEN LOWER!
I CAN ONLY SAY IT'S ARTISTIC TO SEE SO MANY Fs IN A ROW.
REPORT CARD
HEY! YOU DIDN'T DO MUCH BETTER!
AKIRA DIDN'T DO WELL EITHER...
HE'S QUITE DEPRESSED.

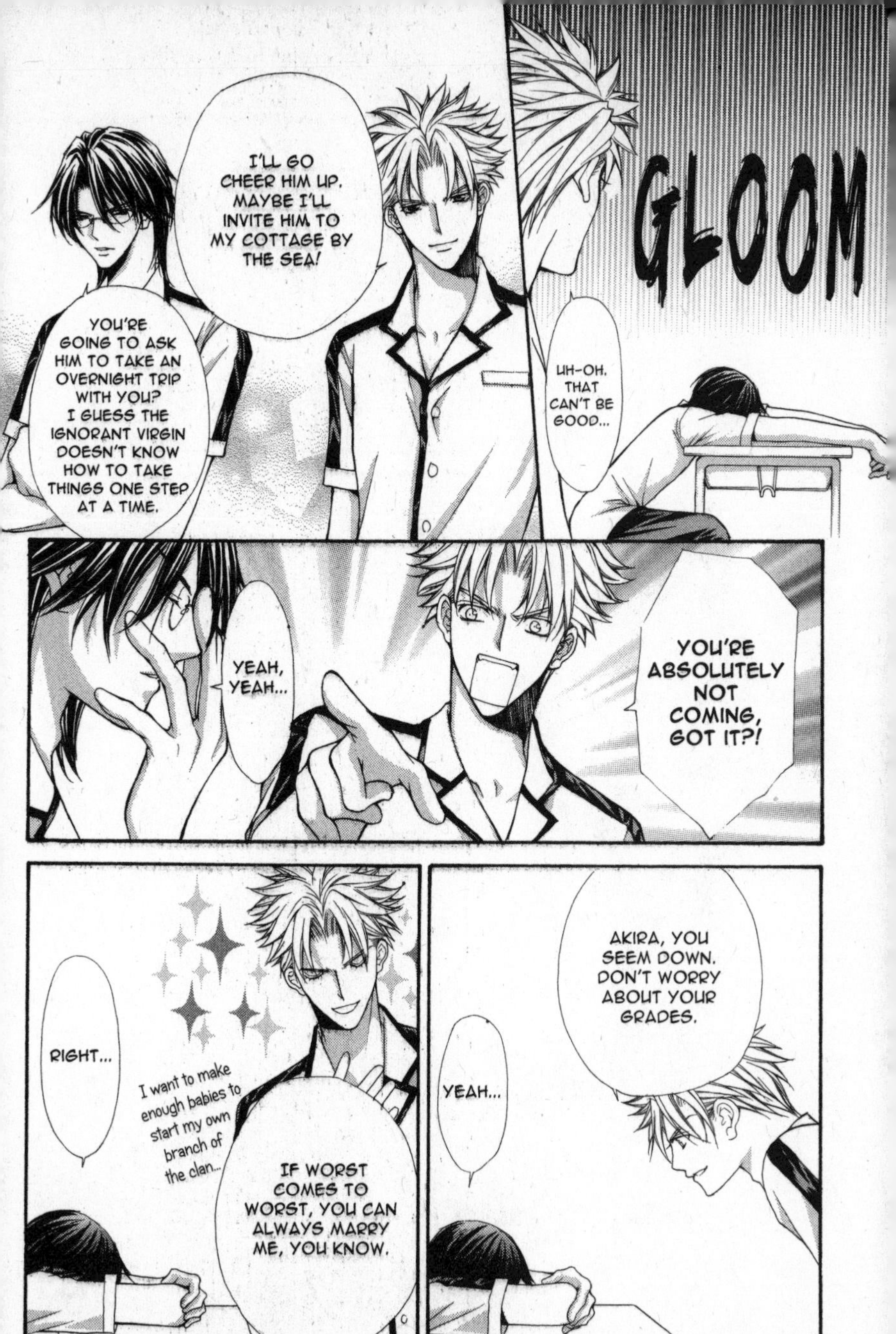
GLOOM
UH-OH. THAT CAN'T BE GOOD...
I'LL GO CHEER HIM UP. MAYBE I'LL INVITE HIM TO MY COTTAGE BY THE SEA!
YOU'RE GOING TO ASK HIM TO TAKE AN OVERNIGHT TRIP WITH YOU? I GUESS THE IGNORANT VIRGIN DOESN'T KNOW HOW TO TAKE THINGS ONE STEP AT A TIME.
YOU'RE ABSOLUTELY NOT COMING, GOT IT?!
YEAH, YEAH...
AKIRA, YOU SEEM DOWN. DON'T WORRY ABOUT YOUR GRADES.
YEAH...
IF WORST COMES TO WORST, YOU CAN ALWAYS MARRY ME, YOU KNOW.
I want to make enough babies to start my own branch of the clan...
RIGHT...

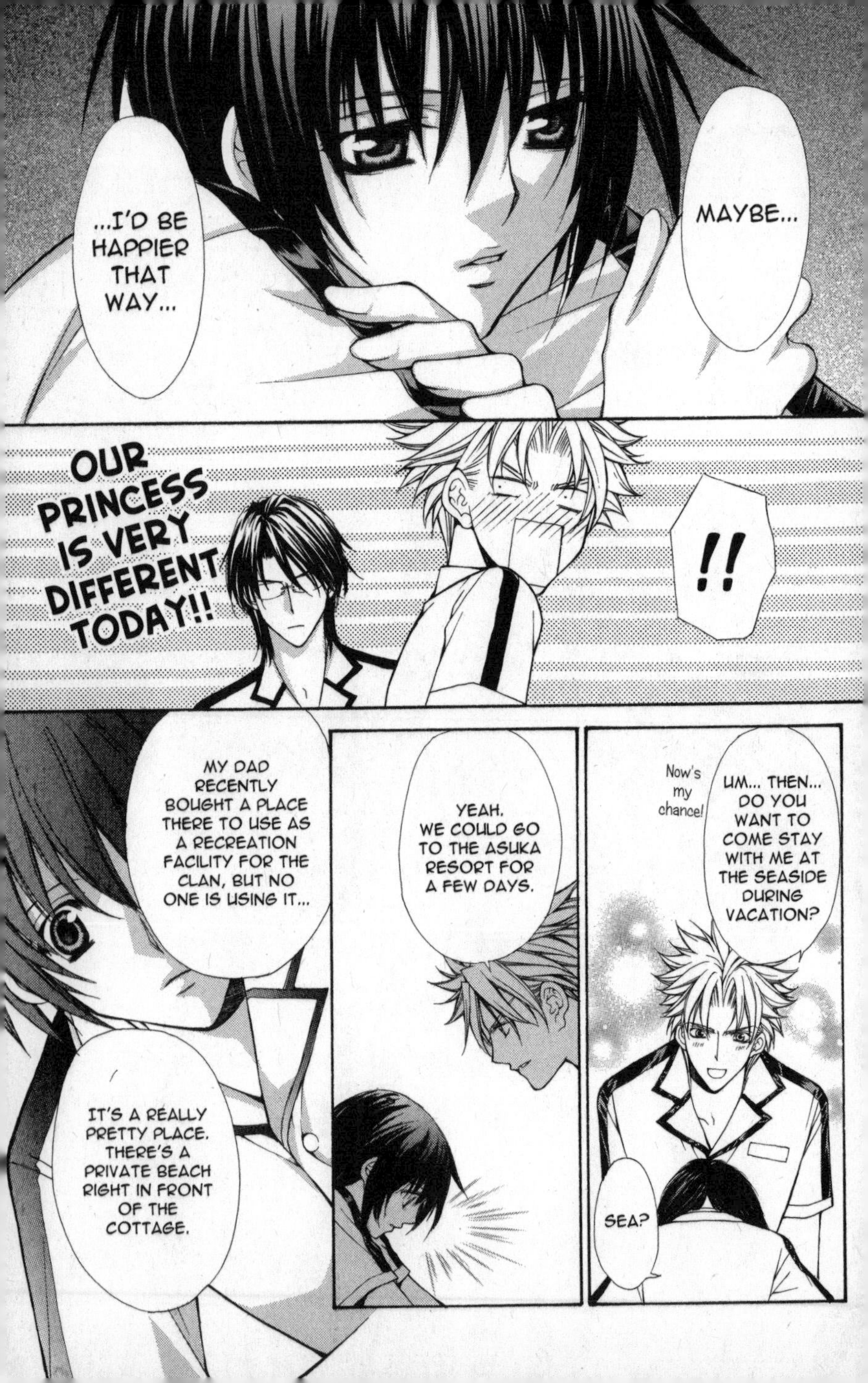
MAYBE...
...I'D BE HAPPIER THAT WAY...
!!
OUR PRINCESS IS VERY DIFFERENT TODAY!!
UM... THEN... DO YOU WANT TO COME STAY WITH ME AT THE SEASIDE DURING VACATION?
Now's my chance!
SEA?
YEAH. WE COULD GO TO THE ASUKA RESORT FOR A FEW DAYS.
MY DAD RECENTLY BOUGHT A PLACE THERE TO USE AS A RECREATION FACILITY FOR THE CLAN, BUT NO ONE IS USING IT...
IT'S A REALLY PRETTY PLACE. THERE'S A PRIVATE BEACH RIGHT IN FRONT OF THE COTTAGE.

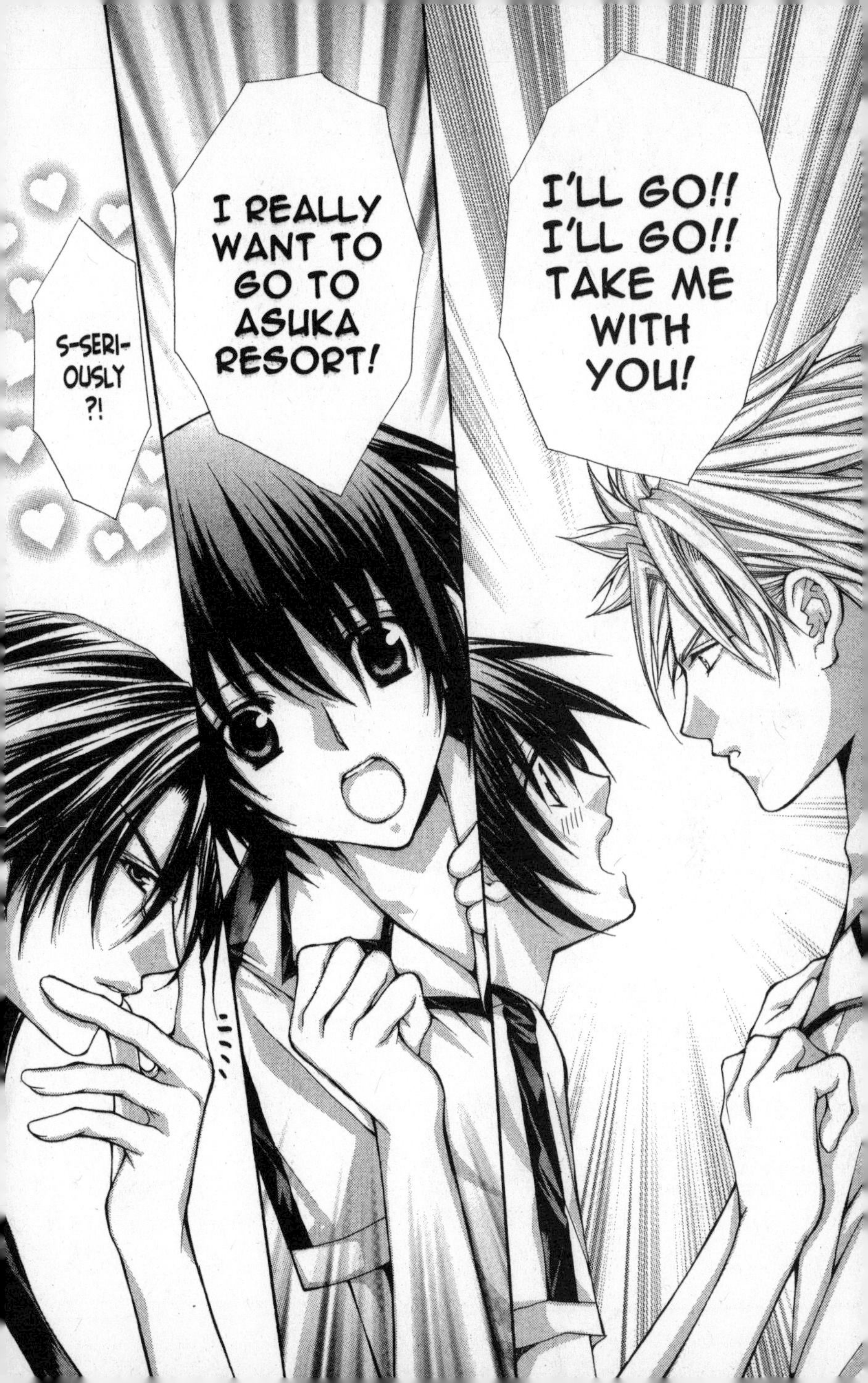
I'LL GO!! I'LL GO!! TAKE ME WITH YOU!
I REALLY WANT TO GO TO ASUKA RESORT!
S-SERI-OUSLY ?!

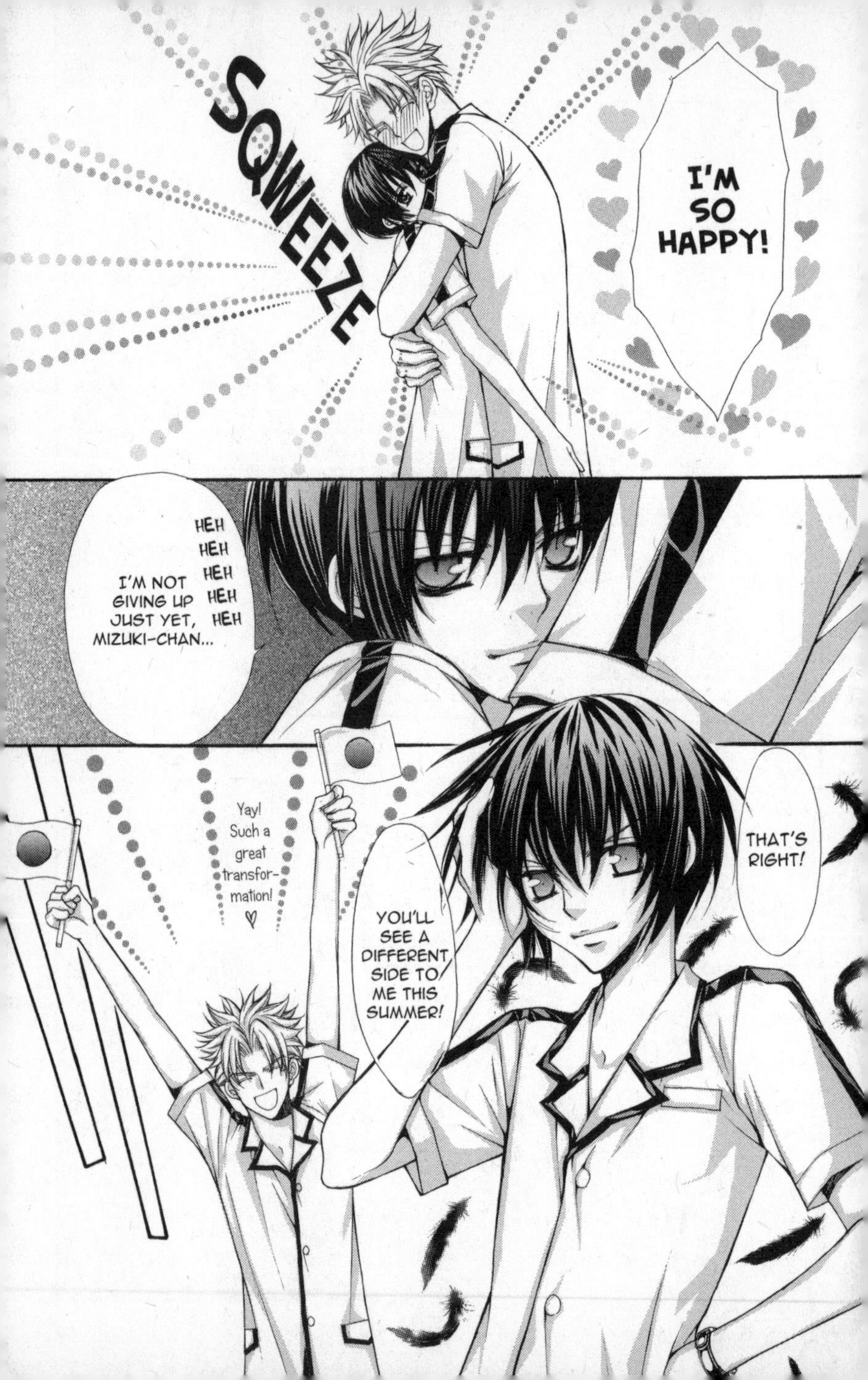
I'M SO HAPPY!
SQWEEZE
HEH HEH HEH HEH HEH
I'M NOT GIVING UP JUST YET, MIZUKI-CHAN...
THAT'S RIGHT!
YOU'LL SEE A DIFFERENT SIDE TO ME THIS SUMMER!
Yay! Such a great transfor-mation! ♡

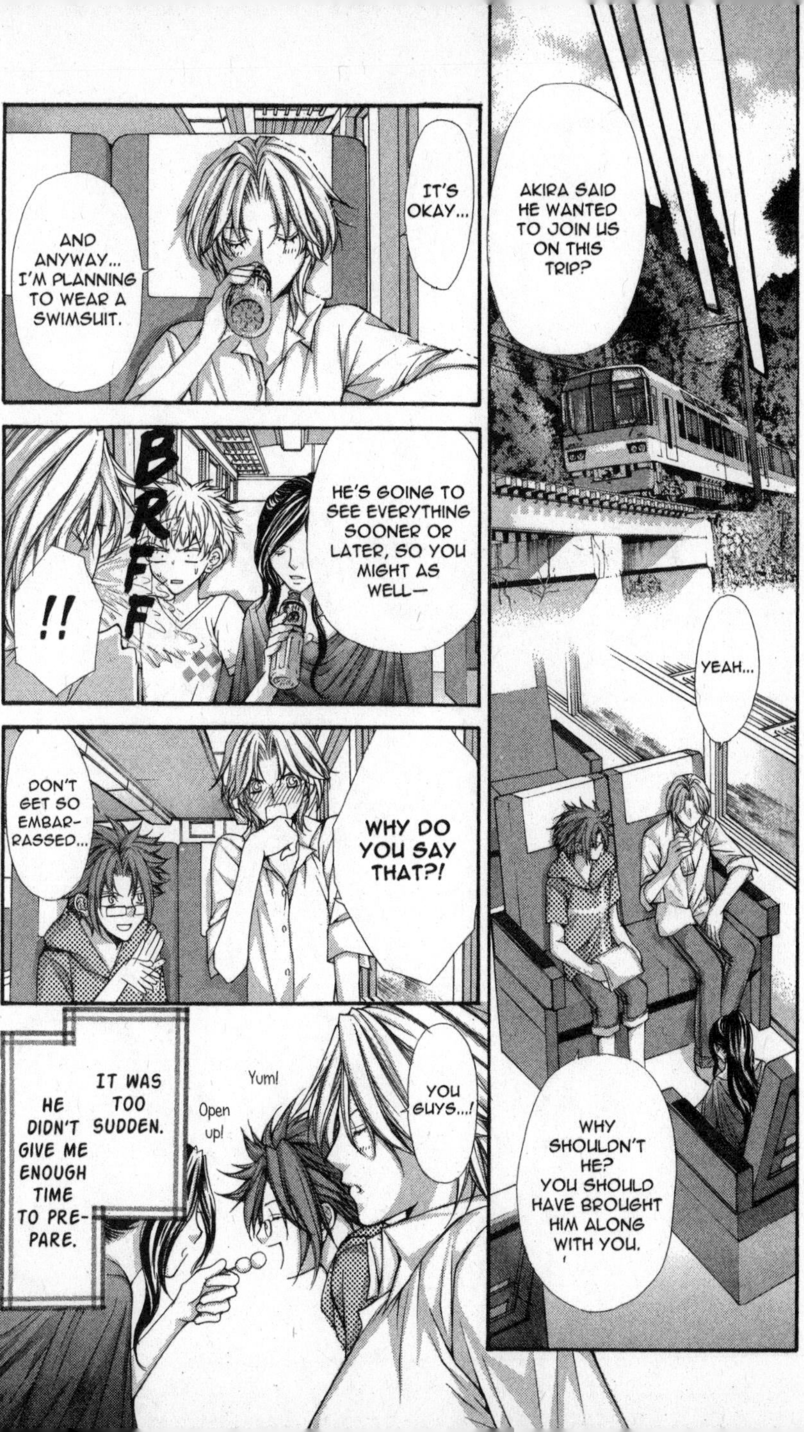
AKIRA SAID HE WANTED TO JOIN US ON THIS TRIP?
YEAH...
WHY SHOULDN'T HE? YOU SHOULD HAVE BROUGHT HIM ALONG WITH YOU.
IT'S OKAY...
AND ANYWAY... I'M PLANNING TO WEAR A SWIMSUIT.
HE'S GOING TO SEE EVERYTHING SOONER OR LATER, SO YOU MIGHT AS WELL—
BRFFF
!!
WHY DO YOU SAY THAT?!
DON'T GET SO EMBAR-RASSED...
YOU GUYS...!
Yum!
Open up!
IT WAS TOO SUDDEN.
HE DIDN'T GIVE ME ENOUGH TIME TO PRE-PARE.

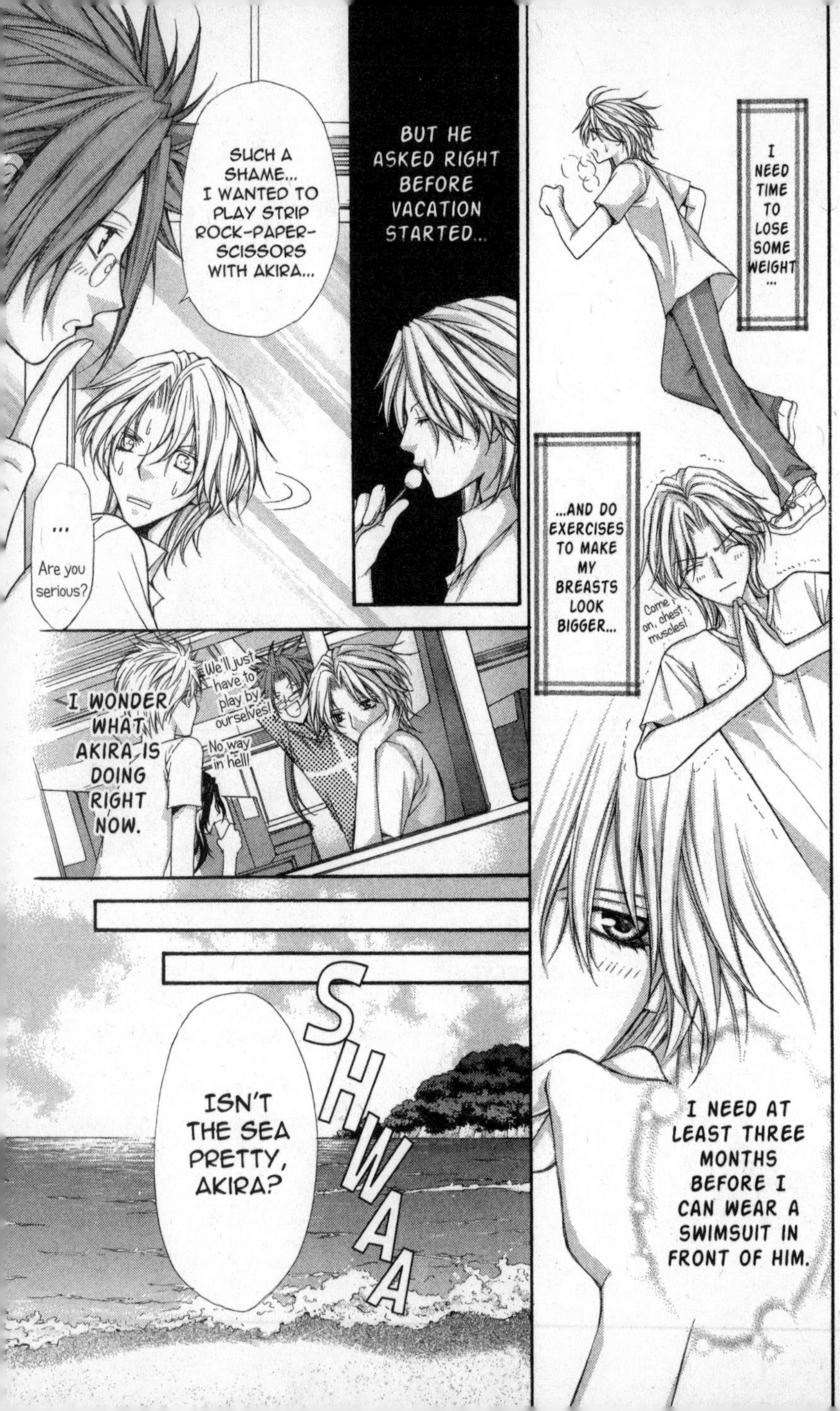
I NEED TIME TO LOSE SOME WEIGHT...
...AND DO EXERCISES TO MAKE MY BREASTS LOOK BIGGER...
Come on, chest muscles!
I NEED AT LEAST THREE MONTHS BEFORE I CAN WEAR A SWIMSUIT IN FRONT OF HIM.
BUT HE ASKED RIGHT BEFORE VACATION STARTED...
SUCH A SHAME... I WANTED TO PLAY STRIP ROCK-PAPER-SCISSORS WITH AKIRA...
... Are you serious?
We'll just have to play by ourselves!
No way in hell!
I WONDER WHAT AKIRA IS DOING RIGHT NOW.
SHWAA
ISN'T THE SEA PRETTY, AKIRA?

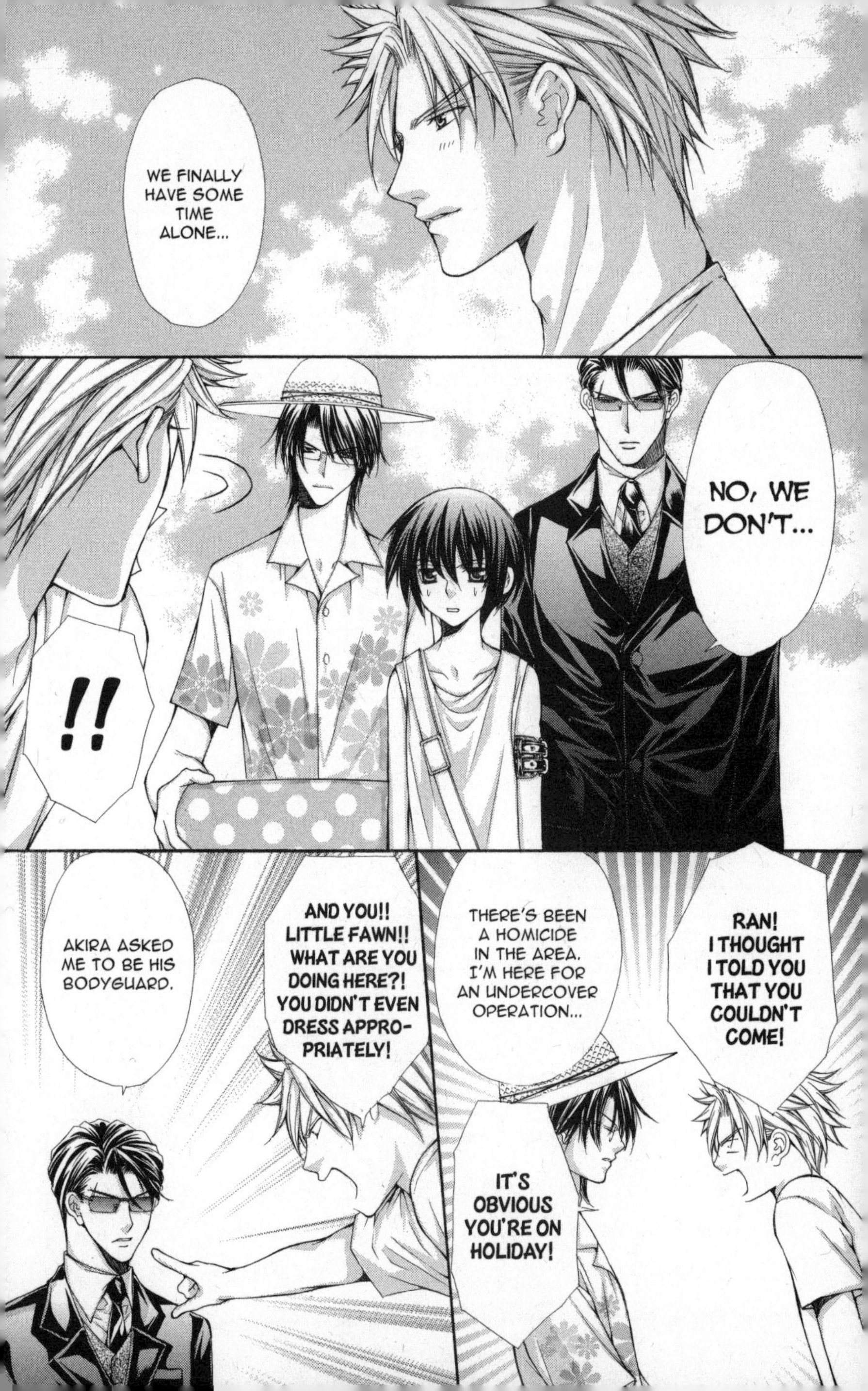
WE FINALLY HAVE SOME TIME ALONE...
NO, WE DON'T...
!!
RAN! I THOUGHT I TOLD YOU THAT YOU COULDN'T COME!
THERE'S BEEN A HOMICIDE IN THE AREA. I'M HERE FOR AN UNDERCOVER OPERATION...
IT'S OBVIOUS YOU'RE ON HOLIDAY!
AND YOU!! LITTLE FAWN!! WHAT ARE YOU DOING HERE?! YOU DIDN'T EVEN DRESS APPRO-PRIATELY!
AKIRA ASKED ME TO BE HIS BODYGUARD.

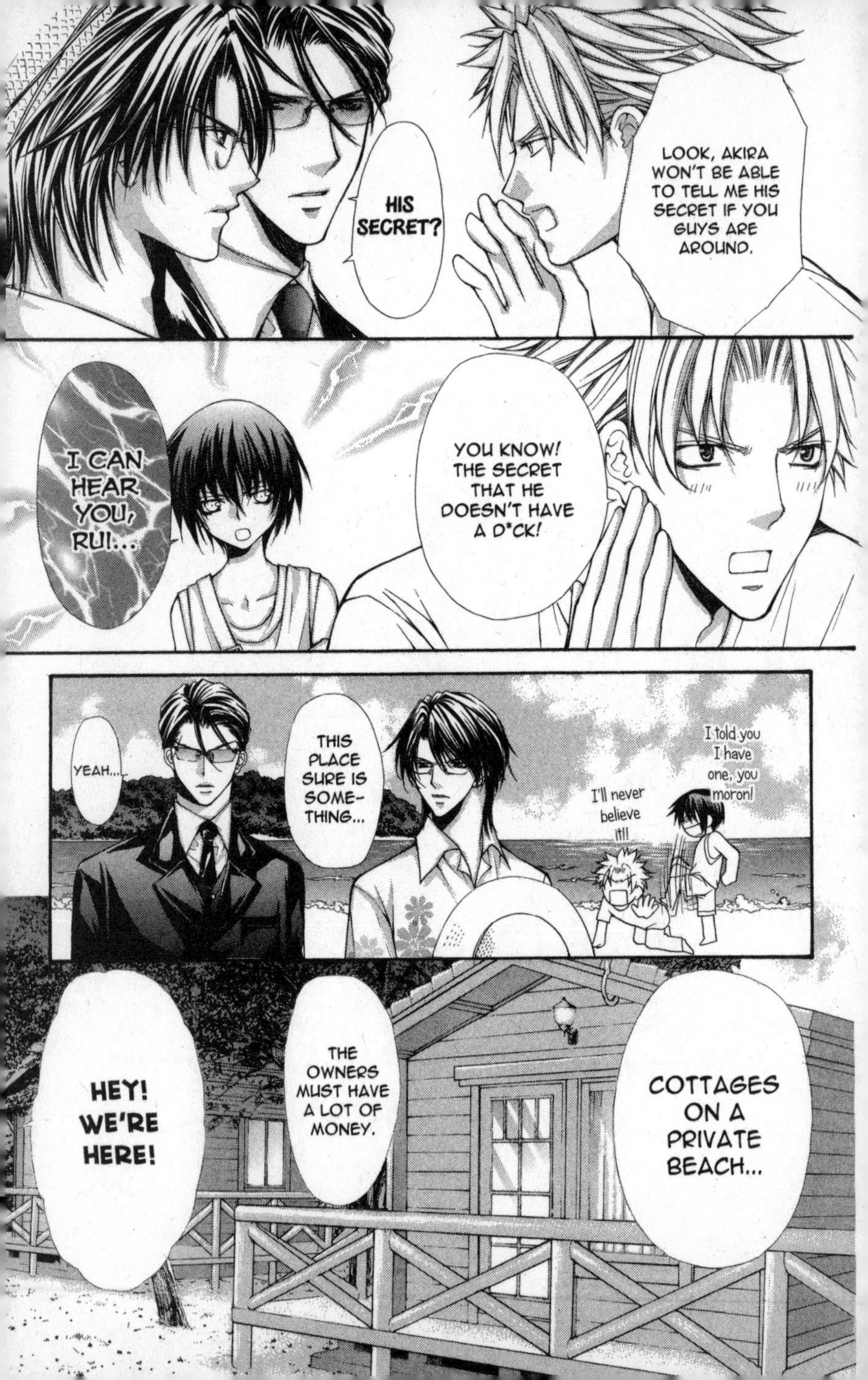
LOOK, AKIRA WON'T BE ABLE TO TELL ME HIS SECRET IF YOU GUYS ARE AROUND.
HIS SECRET?
YOU KNOW! THE SECRET THAT HE DOESN'T HAVE A D*CK!
I CAN HEAR YOU, RUI...
I told you I have one, you moron!
I'll never believe it!!
THIS PLACE SURE IS SOME-THING...
YEAH...
COTTAGES ON A PRIVATE BEACH...
THE OWNERS MUST HAVE A LOT OF MONEY.
HEY! WE'RE HERE!

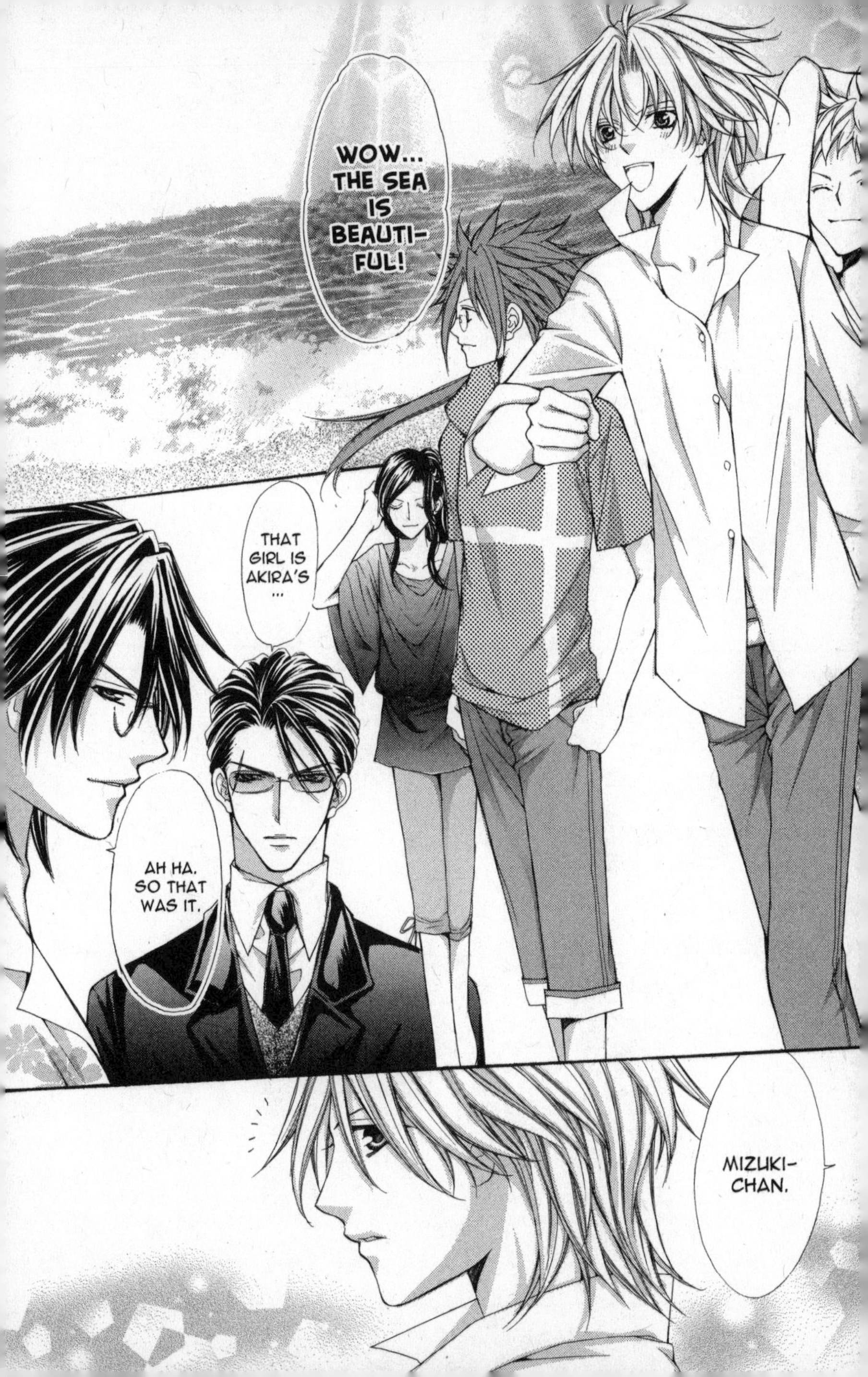
WOW... THE SEA IS BEAUTI-FUL!
THAT GIRL IS AKIRA'S ...
AH HA. SO THAT WAS IT.
MIZUKI-CHAN.

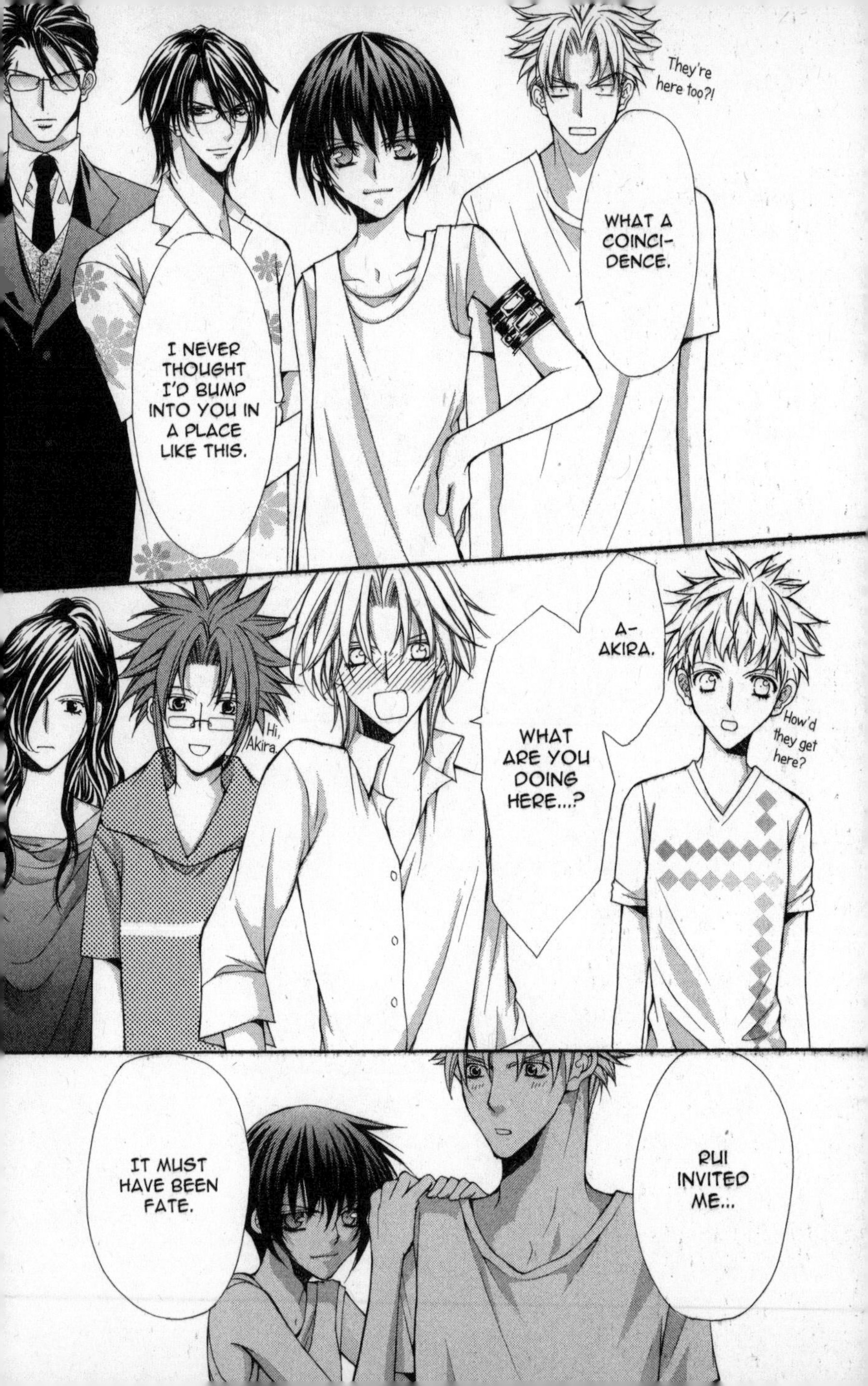
They're here too?!
WHAT A COINCIDENCE.
I NEVER THOUGHT I'D BUMP INTO YOU IN A PLACE LIKE THIS.
How'd they get here?
A- AKIRA.
WHAT ARE YOU DOING HERE...?
Hi, Akira.
RUI INVITED ME...
IT MUST HAVE BEEN FATE.

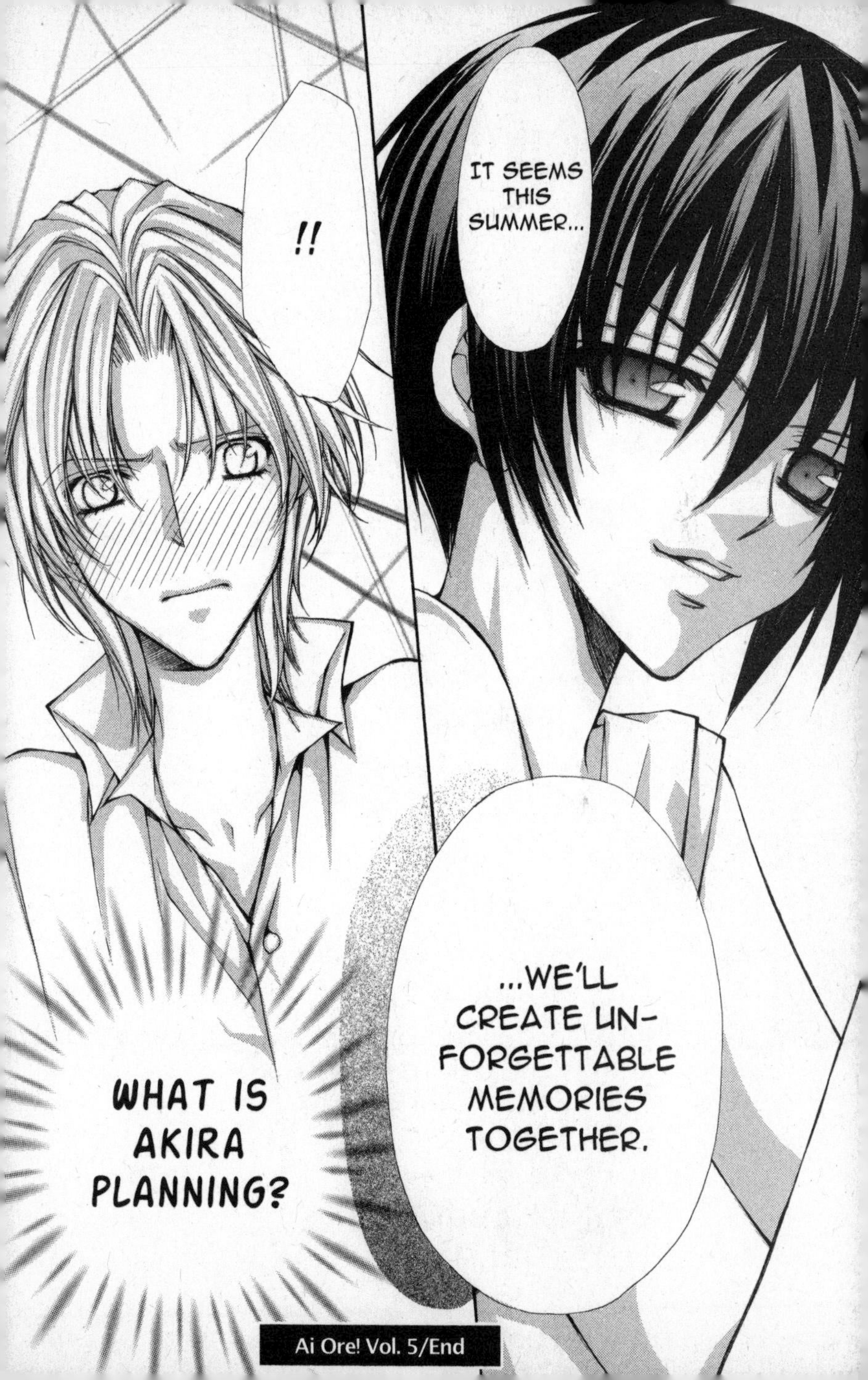
IT SEEMS THIS SUMMER...
...WE'LL CREATE UN-FORGETTABLE MEMORIES TOGETHER.
!!
WHAT IS AKIRA PLANNING?
Ai Ore! Vol. 5/End

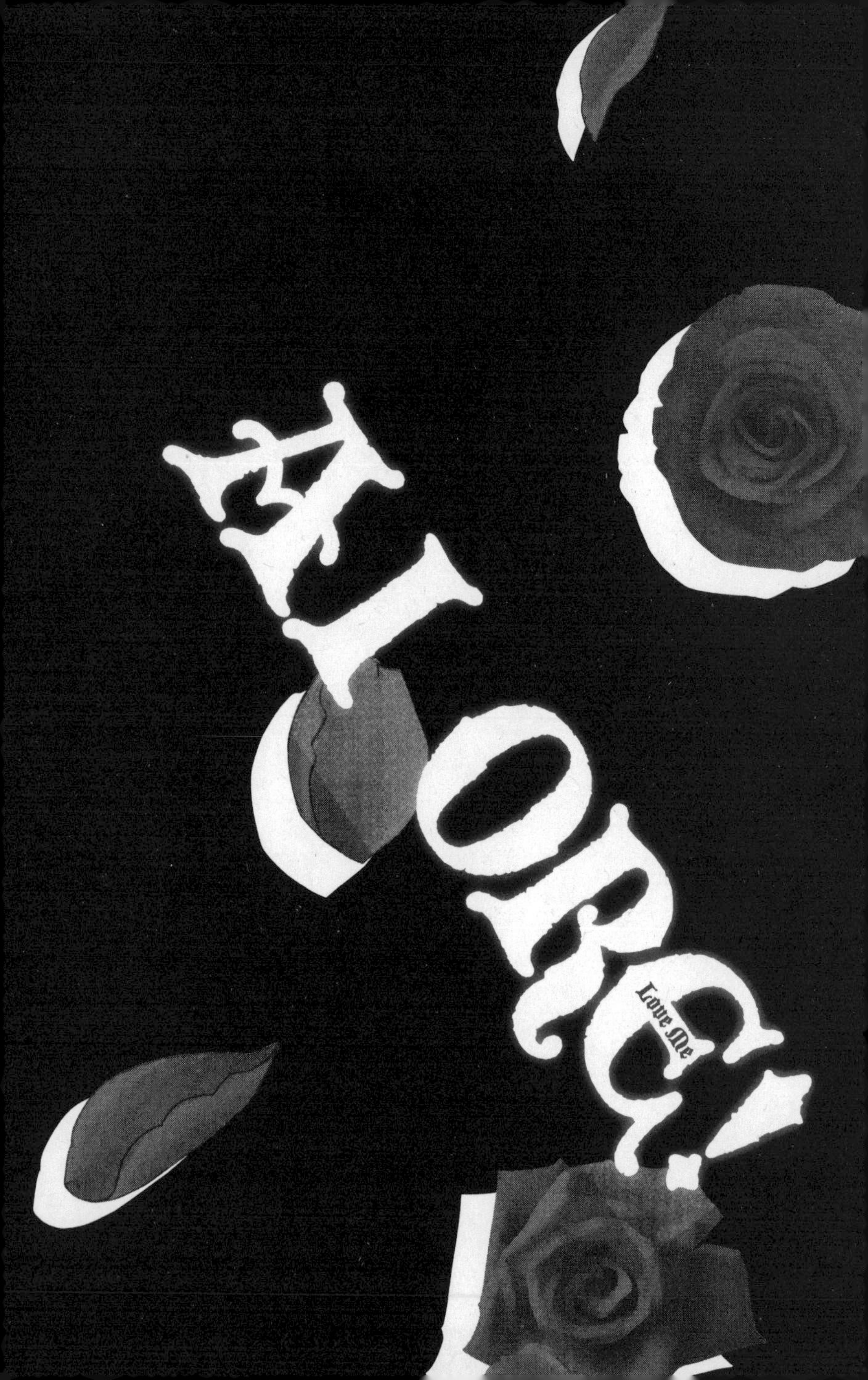
AI ORE!
Love Me

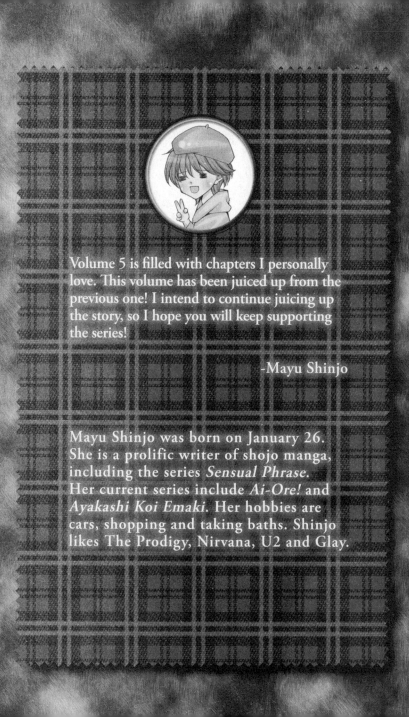

Volume 5 is filled with chapters I personally love. This volume has been juiced up from the previous one! I intend to continue juicing up the story, so I hope you will keep supporting the series!

-Mayu Shinjo

Mayu Shinjo was born on January 26. She is a prolific writer of shojo manga, including the series *Sensual Phrase*. Her current series include *Ai-Ore!* and *Ayakashi Koi Emaki*. Her hobbies are cars, shopping and taking baths. Shinjo likes The Prodigy, Nirvana, U2 and Glay.